A Passion for Piedmont

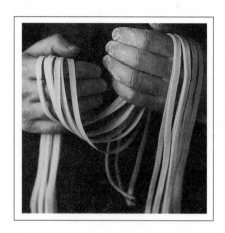

OTHER BOOKS BY MATT KRAMER

Making Sense of Wine (1989)

Making Sense of Burgundy (1990)

Making Sense of California Wine (1992)

A
Passion
for
Piedmont

Italy's Most Glorious Regional Table

Matt Kramer

William Morrow and Company, Inc.
New York

Food styling by Roscoe Betsill

Library of Congress Cataloging-in-Publication Data

Kramer, Matt.
A passion for Piedmont / Matt Kramer.
p.   cm.
Includes bibliographical references.
ISBN 0-688-11594-2
1. Cookery, Italian.   2. Cookery—Italy—Piemonte.   3. Piemonte
(Italy)—Description and travel.   I. Title.
TX723.K7 1997
641.5945'1—dc21   97–15456
                                                             CIP

Printed in the United States of America

First Edition

1 2 3 4 5 6 7 8 9 10

BOOK DESIGN BY RICHARD ORIOLO

www.williammorrow.com

For Angelo and Lucia Gaja
(who are unique in the world)

Aldo and Gemma Conterno
(who are Piedmont at its best)

Francesco and Lina Germanetti
(who are *molto Piemontese, molto Braidese, e molto generoso*)

Preface

❦

The first condition of understanding a
foreign country is to smell it.

T. S. Eliot

It is now twenty years that I have been writing full-time about food and wine. I began my career as a food writer, wine came later. In fact, I remained much more a food person than a wine sort for nearly three quarters of my writing career, first as a food editor and restaurant critic and later as a weekly food columnist.

Above all, I have always been a willing, enthusiastic cook. Note that I am not a chef. That much-overused term is (or at least should be) reserved only for professionals working in restaurant kitchens. I am not one of those. Instead, I am what you probably are: someone with an interest in good food who likes to cook. I have always done all of the cooking in our home. In the two decades that my wife, Karen, and I have been together, she has never once cooked a meal. If she knows how to cook, it is the best-kept secret of our marriage. She's happy with the arrangement and so am I.

I mention this because it is my combination of home cook and longtime food writer that informs the choice of recipes in this book. Even more, it helps explain my devotion to the particular culinary sensibility of Italy's Piedmont.

The life of every interested cook follows, I believe, a similar path. First, you want to try everything, no matter how ambitious. So you set your hand, with varying success, to such monuments as puff pastry, various (and glorious) French sauces, Peking duck, fabulously complex Indian dishes, and all sorts of other kitchen challenges. After having mastered these (or at least experimented with them), the thrill is gone. What at first seemed magical and impossible becomes formulaic.

Like great magicians, good cooks soon recognize that the dishes that look the most complicated actually are the easiest. They usually have long lists of ingredients. The hard ones are the simplest, the dishes that are so transparently simple that you don't even suspect there's any magic involved. It is the difference between artifice and artfulness. Profound home cooking is all about artfulness: the perfect pie with the impossibly good crust, the supernal beef stew, the perfectly cooked pasta.

The longer you cook, the more you become devoted to what might be called "flavor transparency." Your cooking becomes simpler. You become enthralled by ingredients—and suspicious of complication. After twenty years of thinking about food as a writer and seven-day-a-week cook, I am convinced that flavor transparency is essential to all dishes that endure, that truly deserve to be called classic. This is why I was drawn to Piedmont, as it is both a food and wine culture devoted to "transparency."

Piedmont became my "home." In fact, my wife and I moved there for a year, the better to steep ourselves in the authentic tastes of the place. Piedmont's food and wines are just so *fine*, so clear, so honest. Its flavors are vibrant, but subtle; uncomplicated yet complex. Everyone who visits Piedmont comes away convinced that he or she has eaten some of the greatest food in his or her life.

This is the food I have tried to present in this book. The glory of Piedmontese cooking lies in superb ingredients, artfully deployed. Rarely are there more than two or three flavors at work in a typical dish.

If this is your kind of cooking, then Piedmont is surely your cuisine. The recipes in this book can amplify your repertoire of daily rewarding dishes. Piedmont's deep, lasting flavors, its artfully simple perfection, can change one's life at the table.

Acknowledgments

No outsider to a place such as Piedmont insinuates himself without the frank, generous, and caring assistance of others. At first, à la Blanche Dubois, it is a reliance on the kindness of strangers. Then, over time, it becomes a reliance on friends. Either way, the need is real and, one hopes, the gratitude commensurate.

In the many years that I have been visiting Piedmont, and above all, in the one year that my wife and I lived there, much practical help has been given. Anyone who seeks to investigate Piedmontese cuisine, and the culture underlying it, must gratefully acknowledge the work of Giovanni Goria and, especially, Sandro Doglio.

But even more important than that have been the more personal insights offered by friends and colleagues. These can only be gleaned over time and are given as tokens of affection and support. I thank the people to follow for this, above all else:

Guido Alciati, Lidia Alciati, Piero Alciati, Francesco Batuello, Philip di Belardino, Chiara

Boschis, Elvio Cogno, Aldo Conterno, Gemma Conterno, Mario Cordero, Manuela Cordero, Alfredo Currado, Lucca Currado, Luciana Currado, Aldo Drago, Barbara Edelman, Maria Empson, Neil Empson, Angelo Gaja, Lucia Gaja, Lina Germanetti, Francesco Germanetti, Fiorenzo Giolito, Elio Grasso, Kathleen Hackett, Russ Parsons, Carlo Petrini, Guido Rivella, Giorgio Rocca, Nino Rocca, Rosina Rocca, Doreen Schmid, Aldo Vacca, and Carmen Wallace.

Contents

✻◈✻

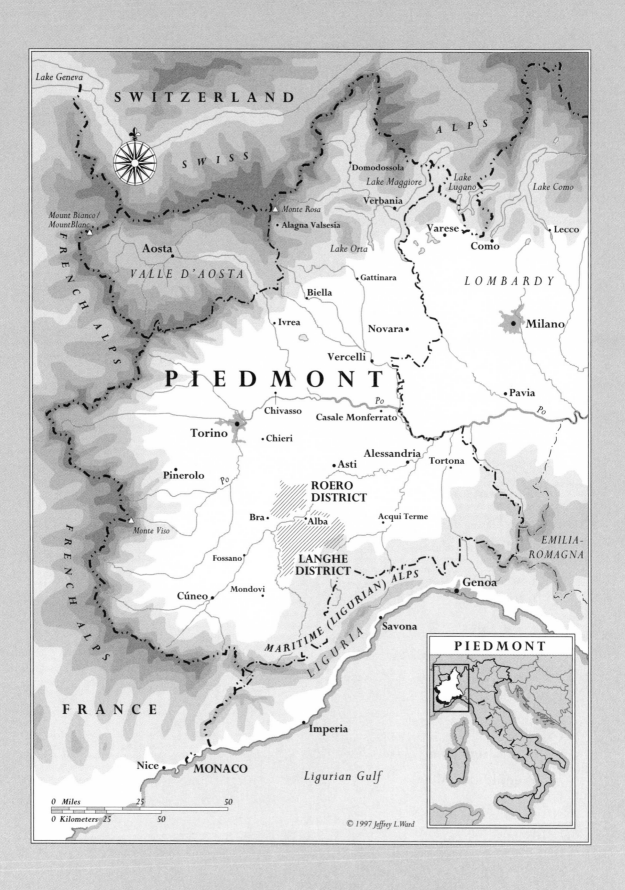

Lake Geneva

SWITZERLAND

SWISS

ALPS

Domodossola
Lake Maggiore
Lake Lugano
Lake Como

Verbania

Varese
Lecco

△ *Monte Rosa*

Como

• Alagna Valsesia

Mount Bianco /
MountBlanc △

FRENCH ALPS

Aosta

VALLE D'AOSTA

Lake Orta

LOMBARDY

• Gattinara

Biella

• Ivrea

Novara •

Milano

Vercelli

• Pavia

PIEDMONT

Po

Chivasso
Casale Monferrato

Torino

• Chieri

Pinerolo

Po

Asti

Alessandria

Tortona

**ROERO
DISTRICT**

Bra •
Alba

Acqui Terme

△ *Monte Viso*

**LANGHE
DISTRICT**

*EMILIA-
ROMAGNA*

Fossano

Mondovi

Cúneo

MARITIME (LIGURIAN) ALPS

Genoa

LIGURIA

Savona

FRENCH ALPS

FRANCE

Imperia

Nice •

MONACO

Ligurian Gulf

0 *Miles*   25   50

0 *Kilometers* 25   50

© 1997 Jeffrey L.Ward

PIEDMONT

I T A L Y

A Passion for Piedmont

Introduction

⚜

This book is the result of a longstanding food and wine affair with Piedmont. Allow me to give you a brief guided tour of this landscape that so moves me. Most travelers, even experienced Italy hands, are unfamiliar with Piedmont's geography. Partly it's because of its size. Piedmont is Italy's second largest region after Sicily, which snares the prize by having 118 more square miles of land. The Piedmontese don't care. Sicily is so far away, geographically and psychologically, that it's like saying Australia is bigger than Piedmont.

Location is also a problem. Situated in the northwest corner of Italy, Piedmont looks like a horseshoe set on its side, with the opening facing east. Piedmont's northern border is the Swiss Alps, its western border the French Alps, and to the south are the Ligurian mountains (the Italians call them *Alpi Maritime*).

So getting into (or out of) Piedmont isn't easy. The only way, without going over some pretty formidable mountains, is through the vast, flat Po Valley. That's the open end of the horseshoe.

Because Piedmont is walled on three sides by mountains—and some spectacular ones at that—visitors have long skirted Piedmont. It was—and still is—far easier to go around it than to get through it. When French tourists enter Italy, they hug the coast, following the Mediterranean shoreline all the way to Tuscany and beyond. Germans and Austrians have long penetrated Italy, but well to the east of Piedmont, typically through the Brenner Pass, which is in line with Bolzano and Verona. Only the Swiss are undaunted by the mountains (which is to be expected). They drive right on in to Piedmont. The Swiss are the greatest connoisseurs of all things Piedmontese.

Knowing this, you can imagine how isolated Piedmont was centuries ago when transport was slow and fatiguing. Unless business took you to Turin, the capital of Piedmont and seat of the ruling House of Savoy, it was a questing traveler indeed who traversed the hilly Piedmontese landscape. Even today, compared to the number who flock to Tuscany, Venice, or Umbria, few tourists visit Piedmont.

This isolation, more than anything else, is what has shaped the Piedmontese. And it has served to preserve their extraordinary cuisine to this day. The world has simply passed them by.

I have been visiting Piedmont at least once, sometimes twice, a year for ten years. I was gripped by it the moment I saw it. At first, I was baffled by it. Everyone is. The landscape is mostly hilly or mountainous (except for the Po Valley in the middle). In autumn and winter it is shrouded in fog. The summers are hot and humid. It's no surprise it's not a tourist mecca like Tuscany.

That said, few landscapes in Italy are more magical. The place is so otherworldly, especially when shrouded in fog, that you feel somehow that Piedmont is a sort of Brigadoon—not merely foreign, but transitory and secretive.

Nowhere else in Europe are there so many dishes of such depth and nuance of flavor made with so little effort as in Piedmont. The Piedmontese have a genius—there's no other word for it—for alloying simplicity with just the right amount of enhancing complication.

How and why Piedmont, alone in Italy, achieved such symbiosis is partly explained by geography: It lies next to France. More than any other neighbor, France helped shape Piedmontese tastes. French culture is a powerful force, especially in the drive toward refinement. You can see it in French food: all that straining, sieving, and reducing to essences. French manners are famously elaborate and formal, with sometimes extravagant linguistic flourishes.

Piedmontese manners, language, formality, food, wine, verbal courtesies, and its dialects—especially in the cities and large towns—all were influenced by this proximity to France. The city of Turin, for example, was entirely French-speaking until the end of the 1800s. Camillo Benso di Cavour, the architect of the Italian Risorgimento (Unification), who served the Piedmontese House of Savoy (the family who became the kings of Italy after unification in the 1860s), couldn't even speak Italian. His native languages were French and Piedmontese. In preparation for unification, he took Italian lessons.

Foodwise, the French influence lingers in a love of excess. Not for the Piedmontese is the simple austerity of Tuscan cuisine, or the robust rusticity of southern Italian cooking. Instead, Piedmont retains to this day a devotion to richness, exemplified by an unusual (for Italy) employment of mayonnaise, extensive use of béchamel sauces, and a general luxuriance reflective of the richness of their soil. As in France, almost everything grows well somewhere in Piedmont's vast territorial expanse. (Tuscan soil, in comparison, is famously meager.) So they like to pile it on in bourgeois excess.

In Turin, much of the food in earlier times simply was flat-out French. Because it was the seat of the House of Savoy—which aped the French court in everything from architecture to dress to language—it's not surprising that Turin's upper crust was so slavishly French. The lower classes were, shall we say, more "authentic."

There was one culinary benefit to Turin's French orientation: To this day, they have great pastries—rich, refined, delicate little items that only the most accomplished professional French *patissiers* could equal today. But only in Turin. Elsewhere, the indigenous Piedmontese cuisine is pretty much lacking in refined pastries or, for that matter, any desserts at all.

The French influence acknowledged, it would be a mistake to see Piedmont simply as an Italianate extension of France. The physical lay of the land prevented that. Piedmont developed its own culture, cuisine, and language that neighboring France influenced but never dictated.

Through a regional cuisine, one can extrapolate a wealth of knowledge about what grows in an area, the scope of its commerce, the limits of its imagination, and, not least, the extent and distribution of its wealth. Piedmontese cuisine, for example, actually comprises two economic realms: what the Italians call *la cucina povera* and *la cucina ricca*—the cooking of the poor and that of the rich.

As Italy's richest region for centuries, Piedmont has an elaborate historical *cucina ricca,* from which devolved the still-generous *cucina borghese,* or upper-middle-class cooking. It was in Piedmont, after all, that Italy first saw its own industrial revolution and the vast manufacturing wealth that it created. But *la cucina povera* persisted in the region's innumerable valleys and mountain slopes well past World War II.

As elsewhere in Italy, Piedmontese food remains highly localized and insistently seasonal. For example, the part of Piedmont closest to Liguria, even though separated by a mountain range, has a more elaborate vegetable cookery than the rest of the region—a Ligurian influence. Those living high in the Swiss and French Alps use much more cheese—all locally produced from high mountain pastures—than other Piedmontese.

Piedmontese cooking today is a fascinating mixture of old tastes upon which are superimposed new realities and concerns about health and modern work habits. You still find such old feast specialties as *bollito misto* and *fritto misto,* respectively mixed boiled meats and mixed fried items. Such feast meals are wealth made edible. For younger members of the middle class, they are folkloric and overly elaborate.

However, the memory of poverty remains vivid enough that even in the most modern of Piedmontese restaurants, the scale of eating is heroic. The Piedmontese table today is an explosion of food, with as many as a half-dozen *antipasti* followed by sometimes two first courses and a substantial second course, invariably consisting of meat. The old agrarian memories of poverty and hunger somehow persist: Get it in your belly while you still can. The immense wealth of the region, never greater than today, is irresistibly translated into feasts.

Today, Piedmontese food and wines are probably better than ever before. Not being a native of the area, I cannot say this definitively. It is true that the meals aren't quite as rich and long as they were even ten years ago. But they still are longer, richer, and more involved than anywhere else in Italy—anywhere else in Europe, for that matter. The wines absolutely are better: cleaner, brighter, fresher tasting.

The dishes in this book were selected with one criterion: that they taste here as they did in Piedmont. As with many other cuisines, not every Piedmontese dish travels well. Their veal, for example, is so much more flavorful than what parades under that name hereabouts as to make it a different creature altogether. So, for example, there's no recipe for *carne cruda,* an antipasto of finely chopped raw veal popular in Piedmont.

The qualities of Piedmontese dishes become apparent only upon tasting them. The recipes themselves are often so simple that merely reading them—even if one is the most imaginative cook—gives little clue as to just how good they taste.

I have deliberately chosen dishes that can easily be incorporated into one's memorized repertoire of simple dishes. I have ignored such fantasy frou-frou as fresh white truffles, which sell here for two hundred dollars an ounce, and such elaborate exotica as *finanziera* sauce, with its cockscombs and other delicacies. These and many other such dishes are legitimately part of Piedmontese cuisine, but they are special-occasion fare, sampled mostly in restaurants, and rarely, at that.

A recipe worth your time, money, and care must *taste* like the original. The author's obligation is to know what the original tastes like—and to make a decision as to whether it can reasonably be exported. That is why I spent a year in Piedmont. It was not so much to collect recipes as to collect *tastes.* Merely to offer an accurate recipe with a precise list of ingredients is not enough. Without an authenticity of taste, one has been deceived—it's like buying a bad car with a good paint job.

For the home cook, fashioning a meal along Piedmontese restaurant lines is almost unthinkable. By all means go there and feast yourself silly. Then return and eat as the Piedmontese themselves do at home: risotto, polenta, pasta, or a treasured antipasto or two. This is the real world here—and there. It is deeply rewarding and, as the recipes in this book strive to demonstrate, wonderfully appropriate and achievable on these shores.

At the Piedmontese Table

❦

The vine which adds seasoning to the ridgeline of a fine hillside, push-
ing its way into the sky, is a familiar sight, yet the curtain it creates,
simple and profound, is a magical portal.

Cesare Pavese
Feria d'Agosto (August Holiday), 1946

Some years ago, during one of my extended stays in Piedmont, my wife, Karen, came over from the States to join me in November. I picked her up at Milan's Malpensa Airport, which is way out in the countryside, only forty-five minutes from Piedmont's magical Lake Orta. Typically, flights from the States arrive in the late morning. "Hungry?" I inquired. "Always," she said with a smile.

Malpensa Airport is in the Po Valley. The landscape is flat and uninteresting. The day was gray, but not too murky. We headed off, rushing along the flat expanses of the valley, crossing barren rice fields, punching through occasional patches of fog, and then, as we drew close to Alessandria, the hills began to reveal themselves. We were en route to the Langhe, which is Piedmont's gastronomic heartland—the home of its greatest cooks, finest wines, and the world's best white truffles.

The Langhe is its own world, secretive, almost Appalachian in its remove, enfolded in Piedmont's most involuted hills. As with a jungle, you don't just wander into the Langhe by chance. We headed to the hilltop village of La Morra, smack in the heart of the Barolo wine zone. There is one of Piedmont's classic traditional restaurants, Il Belvedere. But "the beautiful view" was nowhere to be seen on this gray day, shrouded as it was in clouds and mist.

We had no reservation for lunch. In Piedmont, except for a few restaurants in Turin, no one bothers with that nicety at lunchtime. What's more, we were late, arriving at nearly two P.M. In France, you'd be turned away. In Piedmont (and elsewhere in Italy), the *cuoco* (cook) only despairs that, had you not had the good sense to come to his or her restaurant, well, you might have missed lunch! And for a Piedmontese restaurant to allow that to happen is bad manners. In deep-country Piedmont, hospitality has real and personal meaning.

Il Belvedere is a simple country restaurant with an unusually large dining room, but this was a Saturday in November, which meant that Piedmont's most devoted and abundant tourists—Germans and Swiss—were down for the weekend to savor Langhe's famous fresh white truffles. The place was packed. No matter. As if pulling a rabbit out of a hat, Gianfranco Bovio, the owner, simply created a table where none had existed before.

As in so many of Piedmont's best restaurants, there is no menu. Gianfranco's sister, Maria Vittoria, is the chef, and you get what she cooks that day. Unlike France, where it's usually men in the kitchen and women at the reception, in Piedmont many of the best restaurants see the reverse: Nearly all of Piedmont's best cooks are women.

Gianfranco arrived at our makeshift table, rubbing his hands in anticipation of our expected pleasure. "How would you like to begin?" he inquired. "Maybe some *antipasti?*" There is no way you can eat in Piedmont without antipasti; you see, *antipasti* in Piedmont are a rite, a frenzy even. Restaurants think nothing of serving six or eight separate *antipasti* plates, served sequentially. Then comes the *primo,* the first course—and later the *secondo,* or second course.

We braced ourselves for the onslaught. Naturally, we would begin with *antipasti*. "But have pity on us, Gianfranco." I pleaded. "My wife only just arrived from the States a couple of hours ago." He smiled and said, "Of course, of course." We briefly discussed wine (we began with a Dolcetto from his own vineyard) and sat back, secure in the knowledge that we had no other concern than pleasure—and endurance.

The first antipasto was a classic: *carne cruda,* or finely chopped raw veal. Sometimes it's served in paper-thin slices instead of finely chopped. Raw meat is not to everybody's taste, but it must be said that until you've tasted Piedmont's veal, you might want to reserve judgment. Piedmont has its own breed of cattle, an ancient race, that is raised in a prescribed and closely inspected fashion. There's no other veal like it. The waiter brought two small plates of *carne cruda,* along with an armful of two-foot-long *grissini,* or breadsticks, which he strewed on the tablecloth like pick-up sticks.

Gianfranco popped up from nowhere, bearing a bowl of fresh white truffles and a truffle slicer. White truffles are always served raw and are shaved over the food at table. The delight of fresh white truffles is derived not only from their incomparable smell, but from the never-to-be-forgotten sound of their being shaved—*phfft, phfft, phfft*—as the delicately thin slices drift down onto your plate like snowflakes. Fresh white truffles transform *carne cruda* into another dish altogether.

The second antipasto was another classic: *sformato di cardo con fonduta,* a baked then unmolded custard infused with the flavor of cardoons. Cardoons are an autumnal Piedmontese favorite, a vegetable that tastes much like artichoke. In fact, cardoons are related to artichokes, but look different, more resembling long, curved, tough-looking stalks of blanched white celery. This being Piedmont, where they are obsessive about their ingredients, they distinguish between two types of cardoon: *lunghi* and *gobbi.* The *lunghi,* or long ones, are the regular stalks, conventionally grown. The *gobbi* (literally, humped) are bent over when very young and partially buried to make them more tender. They are more expensive.

Our *sformato di cardo* was cloaked with delectably rich *fonduta,* a melted cheese sauce composed of two Piedmontese cheeses, Fontal and Fontina. "Some truffles on the *sformato?*" inquired Gianfranco, as if he really needed to ask.

Just when the last of the scrumptious *sformato* was disappearing, Gianfranco arrived at the table with a suggestion for another antipasto. "That's great," I responded. "But really, three *antipasti* will be enough." He hid his disappointment with professional aplomb. "Yes, you are right," he agreed. "But I'm sure that you'll want this last one."

A few minutes later, a waiter arrived carrying two plates of what looked, at first glance, to be a steak. Each plate was almost completely covered to the rim. But the fragrance was something else again. I suddenly realized that we each had an enormous porcini mushroom. They abound in Piedmont and can grow to stupefying dimensions.

This dish was the essence of Piedmontese simplicity. Maria Vittoria obtained picked-that-morning porcini with caps as thick as a book. The tough stem was removed (and no doubt added to a stock), and the cap scored diagonally on top in two directions, creating an incised diamond-shaped pattern. A bit of chopped fresh garlic was sprinkled on and the mushroom caps were grilled on each side, like steaks. Just before serving, delicate Ligurian olive oil was drizzled on top, and the grilled porcini were brought sizzling to the table to be eaten with knife and fork.

After a kindly interval, Gianfranco returned to the table to inquire about the *primo*. In Langhe, it's always pasta, either handmade *tajarìn* (tagliatelle) or *agnolotti* (ravioli). Because the Langhe is in southern Piedmont, you almost never are offered risotto. Only north of the Po River—really, only in the Po Valley itself—is risotto the habitual *primo,* with pasta as a subsidiary alternative.

Tajarìn is a cult in the Langhe, and Maria Vittoria participates in Langhe's passionate *tajarìn* competition, serving a magnificently rich, made-that-morning rendition. Typically, you get it with either a meat sauce or melted butter and sage. Since this was truffle season, that automatically meant the more appropriate butter and sage, as the Langaroli see *tajarìn* as one of the classic vehicles for savoring fresh white truffles. Sure enough, Gianfranco arrived, truffles in hand, to shower the tangle of golden *tajarìn* with a near-eclipse of shavings.

By now, we were full. (We also were slightly tipsy, as we had ordered a bottle of Barolo to accompany the grilled porcini and the *tajarìn*.) Once again, Gianfranco materialized, to tempt us with the *secondo*. "You can have either a *brasato* or a *stinco,*" he suggested. Both are traditional classics, the *brasato,* or "braised," referring to veal or beef braised in local red wine. *Stinco* means shin, in this case, a roasted veal shank.

When I first started eating in Piedmont, I always felt obliged to order a *secondo*. I thought it was rude not to. Only later was I mercifully told that one could forgo the *secondo* without giving offense. So we spurned the offerings, which Gianfranco took with characteristic good grace. "I understand completely," he said. "But of course, you will want dessert."

He was right about that. Maria Vittoria makes one of the Langhe's finest versions of *panna cotta,* the local version of crème caramel. Hers is stunningly dense yet delicate. She uses no gelatin, a trick that I have never been able to pull off at home. But then, Piedmontese cream is so thick that you literally have to squeeze it out of the carton like toothpaste. Her *panna cotta* is irresistible. We said so, and Gianfranco beamed.

By now, the restaurant was clearing out. For the Bovio family, that meant little, as the dinner hour was soon to arrive. A bottle of grappa and two small glasses were put on our table. The grappa was made from grapes from Gianfranco's nearby vineyard. I had a small glass (my wife can't abide the stuff). I left the table to settle up, as you don't pay the bill at the table in most Italian restaurants. I returned to retrieve my wife. She had that distant sated-with-pleasure look. I promised to get her to the hotel for a nap. She smiled and murmured, "Wonderful, wonderful."

But what I didn't tell her was that we were expected for dinner with friends in a few hours.

The Particularity
of Piedmont

※❦※

Everyone who visits Italy—or lives there, for that matter—finds a place that calls to them. Sometimes the appeal is evident, even obvious: Venice, Rome, the sculptured landscape of Tuscany, sun-washed Capri, or sea-drenched Sicily.

My place is Piedmont. I like the people. The Piedmontese are not, truth to tell, the "sunny Italians" celebrated in song and film. If anything, they are famous among other Italians for being *chiuso*, or closed. They are, however, wonderful, steadfast friends and—even by Italian standards—generous souls. But there is a stylish reserve about them. Sometimes you also get a whiff of sadness. It's probably from the autumn fogs, but my Piedmontese friends say that's not it.

More than in most places in Italy, everything about Piedmont—the character of its people, its wines, foods, fashions, architecture, and manners—is a function of landscape. It's a gorgeous landscape, without question Italy's most varied, as it traverses alpine extremes, the flat Po Valley, and Italy's richest, most truffle-filled soil. It is Italy's most agriculturally potent land, growing ingredients and wines of stunning intensity and character. In fact, one Piedmontese province, Cúneo, has the second-highest agricultural production (measured in value) of any province in Italy. That same province also produces what are universally recognized as Italy's greatest red wines, Barolo and Barbaresco.

Piedmont is virtually encased, surrounded on three sides by mountains. To this day, it is unusually difficult to either enter or leave Piedmont. For centuries, the locals didn't bother to try, as the still-active Piedmontese dialect so vocally reveals. Piedmont is on the way to nowhere. Many travelers heading from Italy to France skirt it, by following the coast road along the Riviera through Liguria. Others cut diagonally across northern Piedmont to take the Mont Blanc tunnel into Switzerland. But mostly, the only people who find themselves in Piedmont are there because they really want what only Piedmont can offer: Europe's greatest food. There's also business to be done: Fiat cars in Turin, Olivetti computers in Ivrea, and thousands of small manufacturing firms. But it's the food that makes everyone stay.

What makes Piedmont's cuisine the more striking is how close southern Piedmont is to the Mediterranean. Yet the cooking is dramatically different from Mediterranean cuisine, although a few tastes—such as a love of pesto—have filtered through. Piedmont is cut off from the Mediterranean by a wall of mountains, the *Alpi Maritime*, the Ligurian mountains. On the other side of them is Liguria, a sliver of land with tastes and traditions utterly different from those of Piedmont. Nowhere else in Europe can you drive, as we frequently did, from a freezing-in-winter/sweltering-in-summer Continental climate to a Mediterranean seashore adorned with olive and palm trees in little more than an hour.

But where Liguria looks forever out to the sea, Piedmont is landlocked and introspective. Liguria's cuisine is all about vegetables, which are celebrated, as they are so hard won from the terraced patches of garden wrested from steep, rocky hillsides. In comparison, Piedmont leans against Liguria on a map like an elephant against a snake. Historically, Piedmont took from culinary Liguria what it had to offer: olives and olive oil, a liking for that exaltation of basil called *pesto,* imported Spanish anchovies via Genoa, imported salted stockfish or *baccalà,* and various spices and salt. These were transported over the mountains by mules, working on regular schedules. The same mules returned to Liguria loaded with Piedmont's marvelous red wines, as well as with hard currency.

A confluence of forces shaped Piedmontese cooking—and attitudes—in a way different even from neighboring Lombardy, east of Piedmont. More than any other province, Lombardy bears the closest resemblances to Piedmont. Each is entirely inland. Their cuisines are more similar than not, except that Lombardy, which shelters most of Northern Italy's big mountain lakes, has a much greater repertory of fish dishes.

The effect of landscape on ease of travel offers some insight into how these two otherwise similar provinces could evolve somewhat differently. Lombardy is a creature of the flat Po River valley. Even though all of northern Lombardy is Alpine foothills, that landscape was not the determining influence of Lombardian culture and cooking as it was for Piedmont. This is because mountains only form one (the northern) border of Lombardy, where in Piedmont they wall off three borders: north, south, and west.

It was the Po River valley that exerted the great influence on Lombardy. Like choice bits of meat on a skewer, Lombardy's sophisticated, wealthy cities—Milan, Crema, Brescia, Pavia, and Mantova—are threaded through the Po Valley. Lombardy never was as "closed" as Piedmont, as the flat, easily traveled Po River valley created a landscape of openness and receptivity to outside influences from nearly all sides. French fashions came via Piedmont on the west and the intoxicating cosmopolitanism of the Venetian Republic arrived from the east. Unlike Piedmont, there's no air of brooding about Lombardy.

Because of its string of cities, Lombardy is even wealthier than Piedmont—and showier about it. Traditional Piedmontese sensibility would never countenance a dish such as *risotto alla Milanese,* in which the rice is given a flamboyant golden hue by a generous infusion of expensive saffron threads. Milan's classic risotto was created during the Renaissance, when gold was thought to have health-giving properties and the fashion was to shower gilt, or paper-thin beaten gold, over various dishes. Saffron gave rice a golden color and demonstrated a family's wealth at the same time, as the imported spice was as expensive then as now. To this day, Milanese and other Lombardese dote on the dish. You never see it in Piedmont, which has its own risotto creations.

Although rich in its own right, Piedmont has always been more reserved—Boston to Lombardy's New York. Piedmont's cooks and winegrowers are famously—and unapologetically—among Italy's most conservative. This has been a blessing for modern-day eaters and drinkers, as what a wealth of goodness they have to conserve!

Springtime Arrival

✤❧✤

For years, getting to Piedmont was easy enough. These were short-term visits, a few weeks at a time at most. You bought your round-trip airline tickets, carved out some time on your calendar, rented a car at a preposterous price, and off you went.

But moving to Piedmont for a year, well, that's something different altogether. You just can't *move* to Piedmont, not easily anyway. Unlike Tuscany, which has a vast trade in tourist villas, Piedmont sees almost no resident foreigners. So finding a house to lease isn't easy. My wife and I were (so we were told) the first Americans in anybody's memory to actually live full-time in our section of Piedmont. And our section, an area divided into two neighboring districts called Langhe and Roero, sees more visitors than any other.

But, with the help of friends, we found a house. Our Piedmontese friends declared it *un sogno,* a dream. So it was. Our landlords, the Germanettis, lived only four kilometers (two and a half miles) away in Bra, a largish town. But such is Piedmont's *campanilismo*—the strongly held Italian notion about localism, that you don't go beyond the sound of your church bell tower, the *campanile*—that ours was their summer house.

It was an old farmhouse, replete with an impossibly deep cistern, located at the end of a long, steep private drive. The house had been beautifully restored, but because it was so isolated, the Germanettis' sixteen-year-old daughter had decreed that she wasn't going to spend the summer away from the "scene" in Bra. So for the first time ever, the house was discreetly made available for lease. Our friends heard about it and helped us make the arrangements.

We were in the countryside, in a little hamlet (a collection of houses, really) improbably named *località* America dei Boschi—the American woods. Naturally, we were curious about the name. Everyone admitted that America dei Boschi was pretty odd, but nobody knew for sure its origins. That said, Italians use the word *America* unusually. The name is synonymous with riches and, to a lesser extent, with something huge. When somebody in Italy has had good fortune, he is said to have "found America." You still hear this expression in Italy today, never mind that Northern Italy now is richer than the United States.

Angelo Pellegrini, in his memorable book *The Unprejudiced Palate* (1948), recalls just this phrase as an immigrant peasant child in the early part of this century. "When I arrived in America," he wrote, "I recalled and immediately understood a saying I had frequently heard in Italy. When one had met with a bit of good fortune, such as an unusual yield from the vine or perhaps a meager inheritance, his friends would say to him, *'Eh, l'hai trovata l'America!'* (Ha, you have found your America!)."

In America dei Boschi, the local woods were so unusually large for such an otherwise densely populated area that the scale was "like America." Alternatively, the abundance of mushrooms and truffles in these woods, their very richness, could be conveyed only by the magic invocation of "America."

Having found a house, we then faced the problem of buying a car. This shouldn't have been difficult, but keep in mind that in Italy, even for the Italians, any time you intersect with the government is sure to be a tribulation. And when it comes to the unbelievably complicated paperwork of car buying, even Italians throw up their hands and turn the problem over to their local *Auto Practica*, the universal name for the private local agencies everywhere in Italy that handle all of the paperwork for a fee. It's kind of a protection racket, only in this case they are protecting you from the Italian bureaucracy. For about three hundred dollars they'll get your documents through the system. Nearly everybody agrees it's worth the money.

But we had worse problems: We didn't have a permanent visa. Good, law-abiding Americans, we certainly wanted one. In fact, we pleaded for it. I had even tried to pull a few strings with well-connected Italian government types in New York, to no avail. The waiting list for a permanent visa was six years. The reason for the implausible delay, we were told, was Albanian refugees.

Obviously this snag wasn't going to keep us from moving to Italy. But it did pose problems with getting a car. Buying a car is no problem. They'll sell to anyone. But getting it insured—which all cars must be in Italy—is something else again. You can't get automobile insurance as a nonresident unless you have a *permesso di soggiorno,* a legal document permitting you to stay. How do you get a *permesso di soggiorno?* Why, with a permanent visa, of course. Our visa was the standard three-month tourist visa, which entitles you to nothing.

Despite this, we managed to obtain car insurance (840,000 *lire*). But how? *Semplice.* As fate would have it, our landlord Germanetti was—still is—a lawyer (in Italian, an *avvocato*)—so he became known affectionately as the germinating avocado. Moreover, he specializes in insurance suits.

We explained our dilemma. He marched us from his office, down three flights of stairs and over twelve steps to an adjoining office building. We labored up two flights of stairs and found ourselves in one of the six or so insurance agencies skulking in said building. Germanetti commanded them to give us insurance. *"Certo, avvocato!"* replied the complaisant insurance lady. And that was that.

But what about the *Certificato di Residenza* you need to take title of the car? The germinating avocado thought he had this problem solved, courtesy of a well-placed sister in the local city hall. She, however, failed us in our minute of need.

"A *Certificato di Residenza* is no problem," she decreed in Piedmontese dialect. The city hall *sorella* then went on to say that getting these *innocenti Americani* a *Certificato di Residenza* would be no problem, but they not only must be *residenza* for at least fifteen days before it could be issued, even by a sister of mercy in city hall, they also must have a permanent visa. Or a document other than a mere tourist visa. We already had insurance in our name—the hard part—for a car that we couldn't technically own.

Undeterred, our landlord sprouted anew with yet another *bella idea*. "*Perché, no?*" he said largely to himself, and then stopped to savor the thought. Privately, he was congratulating himself on his ability in the Italian national pastime called *"fare furbo."*

To be *furbo* is to be cunning, foxy, and in general to have screwed someone royally. It can be exercised on a grand scale (the state tax system); a slightly smaller scale (the local bureaucrats); and, most commonly, on a daily basis against your fellow *furbisti* by jockeying for position in a supermarket checkout line or getting one car ahead in an apparently endless traffic jam.

Anyway, after savoring the delicious furbosity of his idea, the germinating avocado let us in on the deviousness. No question, it was *furbo* to the *massimo*. "Why not get an Italian Automobile Club thirty-day residence permit?" he inquired.

"Why not?" we agreed. "But who could get us such a permit?" "No problem," he replied. "The automobile dealer can issue one himself. He has the forms in his desk drawer."

That was how we bought our 1982 Lancia with forty-three thousand miles on it. It died the next day. The problem was electrical: A coil collapsed, taking with it a hundred and seventy thousand *lire*. Naturally, it was a Sunday. We did the only reasonable thing: We went to lunch.

Antipasti

The glory of the Piedmontese table is, indisputably, its *antipasti*. The name itself
means "before the meal," but given the Piedmontese penchant for piling on as
many as eight *antipasti* at a sitting, one can be forgiven for thinking that it *is* the
meal.

Even in other regions of Italy, where locals jealously insist that theirs is the best
food, the *antipasti* of Piedmont are famous. Partly, it's the sheer quantity. Compared
with, say, Tuscany, where their idea of an antipasto is either the delicious *bruschetta*
(grilled bread with olive oil, salt, and garlic) or *crostini di fegato* (toasted bread with

chopped chicken livers), the Piedmontese believe that fewer than three *antipasti* is shameful. In fairness, that standard applies only to Sunday lunches, meals with friends, and above all, dining out.

But the greatness of Piedmontese *antipasti* is not quantity. Rather, it is the stunning clarity and melding of flavors of such a variety of dishes. The Piedmontese like their food declarative yet refined. Rarely are Piedmontese *antipasti* complicated dishes. They rely upon what the Italians call the *materia prima*, the foundation ingredients. These ingredients are subjected to amazingly little manipulation. But the insight of the Piedmontese cook is such that what results is a revelation of taste. It is difficult to credit so much distinctive flavor from so little "cooking." Yet it's so. You can't ask for more—or better—than that.

For the Piedmontese cook, the decision about which *antipasti* to serve is based on three elements: the season, the style and scale of the meal, and, not least, which *antipasti* can be prepared entirely ahead of time and which must be attended to just before serving.

This last point is, for the home cook, critical. The most unappealing meals I've attended have been those where the host is constantly on the move, cooking too many dishes that require his or her attention at the last minute. In Piedmont, where several *antipasti* might begin the meal, all good home cooks offer, say, two *antipasti* that are prepared well in advance and perhaps one, such as a *frittata* or a *sformato*, that needs attention before being served. Much, of course, depends upon the guests. With family and close friends, everyone might sit in the kitchen and then *mamma* feels free to cook, all the while participating in the conversation.

With this in mind, I have arranged most of the *antipasti* recipes into two groups: antipasti made entirely ahead of time and those cooked just before serving. This approach, I believe, makes it much easier to choose from the array.

Antipasti That Can Be Prepared Ahead

Anchovies in Red Sauce

Acciughe in Salsa Rossa

Acciughe in salsa rossa is a great favorite among Piedmontese traditionalists. It is terrifically simple to put together but, it must be admitted, it doesn't look like much. However, the taste is memorable.

Serve this dish at room temperature, accompanied by a rustic, country-style bread, or with hot polenta alongside. Traditionally, it is presented garnished with chopped hard-cooked egg, thin slices of lemon, and—in the summer— freshly torn basil leaves.

makes 6 servings

20 whole salted anchovies, rinsed, filleted, soaked in cold water briefly, drained, and very finely chopped

1 tablespoon salt-packed capers, rinsed and crushed

One 3½-ounce can solid white tuna, drained and finely crumbled

2 garlic cloves, very finely chopped

1 small red bell pepper, peeled with a vegetable peeler, cored, seeded, and finely chopped

6 tablespoons prepared tomato sauce

3 tablespoons red wine vinegar

Small handful of fresh basil leaves, finely chopped

1 teaspoon fresh thyme or oregano leaves, finely chopped, or ½ teaspoon dried

1 teaspoon dry mustard

1 teaspoon sugar

Salt

Freshly ground black pepper

Combine all of the ingredients in a large mixing bowl. Taste for seasonings. Let sit at room temperature for several hours or, better yet, refrigerate overnight. Serve at room temperature.

Anchovies in Green Sauce

Acciughe al Verde

This is the dish to serve anchovy-haters. I have tested this on several such sorts and the result, every time, was astonishment: "I never knew anchovies could be like this!" They are right. No one whose experience with anchovies has been limited to the scrawny little fillets embalmed in acrid olive oil could possibly suspect such goodness. The secret to *acciughe al verde* lies in getting the sort of anchovies that the Italians themselves use. This takes a little looking in neighborhood specialty stores—or, even easier, ordering the anchovies by mail (about which more farther on).

In Piedmontese homes, *acciughe al verde* are served in their terrine, which is passed around the table, everyone forking out as much as they dare. Typically, the anchovies are eaten with a knife and fork, the delectable *verde* part being sopped up with bread.

Such is the Piedmontese love of anchovies that I was surprised at how rarely this dish ever found its way into other, obvious, vehicles, such as a sauce for polenta or pasta, or as a topping for pizza. I have used it with all three items. When I've asked my Piedmontese friends about whether they do the same, they grin sheepishly and say there's never enough left for such a purpose. But of course they must—it's simply too good on polenta, especially, not to be so employed.

WORTH NOTING

Preparing ahead of time *Acciughe al verde* are much better if allowed to "marry" for 4 to 6 hours or, better yet, overnight. What's more, they hold their flavor, refrigerated, for several weeks if tightly sealed.

Italian parsley After the anchovies, the next most critical ingredient is flat-leaf Italian parsley. Resist the temptation to substitute curly-leaved parsley. Its flavor is not at all the same. Cilantro can be mistaken for Italian parsley in appearance because it, too, is flat-leaved. But compared side by side, the differences in leaf shape and, especially, scent become immediately apparent. Cilantro has a very strong, metallic smell and flavor, whereas Italian parsley smells sweet and herbaceous, almost like a newly mowed lawn.

makes 4 servings

8 whole salted anchovies

Leaves from 1 small bunch fresh Italian parsley

2 medium-size garlic cloves, peeled

About 6 tablespoons extra virgin olive oil

2 tablespoons red wine vinegar

Large pinch of cayenne or other ground hot red pepper (essential)

To clean the anchovies (figure this will take about 20 seconds per anchovy): A newly opened can will have a thick layer of moist salt on top. Gently poke a finger underneath the salt and you'll hit the first layer of anchovies. Lift the anchovies carefully from the can. Under lukewarm running water, gently rub the salt from the sides of the anchovy until it feels fairly smooth. Turn it belly side up. Let the running water (not too forceful) open up the already gutted anchovy. Run your thumbnail from the end of the opened belly to the tail to free each fillet from the spine. Pull off one fillet, exposing the spine. Then pluck off the spine, which will free the second fillet. Discard the spine and tail, and place the anchovies in a bowl of cold water to freshen.

To make the *acciughe al verde*, process the parsley and garlic together in a food processor until finely chopped. Do not puree the parsley. Stop the processor, add the 6 tablespoons olive oil, the vinegar, and cayenne, and process briefly to combine.

Drain the anchovies and place in a small bowl or a presentation terrine. Mix the sauce thoroughly with the anchovies. The consistency should be that of a thick liquid; add more olive oil if you like. Cover tightly and let sit at room temperature for at least 4 hours or, better yet, overnight.

Acciughe al verde should always be served at room temperature. Barbera is the ideal red wine to accompany this dish, along with bread or *grissini*.

Green Cabbage with Anchovy Sauce
Cavolo con Salsa Acciugha

One of the benefits of living in the hamlet of America dei Boschi was that it is just two and a half miles from Bra, which happens to be the national headquarters of Italy's extraordinary food organization, Arcigola (see Arcigola Slow Food—The World's Most Extraordinary Food Club, page 285).

Arcigola has its own public restaurant next to its offices. The name says it all: Boccondivino, the divine mouth. It surely is the world's finest executive dining room. Boccondivino's chef, Maria Pagliasso, looks like everybody's fantasized (or real) Italian grandmother.

One of her dishes, which Piedmontese food authority Sandro Doglio says is peculiar to Bra, is this captivatingly simple antipasto, which combines fresh cabbage with a sauce of vinegar-brightened pureed anchovies. At Boccondivino, it is served alongside a portion of *Peperoni Ripieni con Tonno* (see page 34).

This dish can be made days in advance if desired, but do not add the anchovy sauce to the cabbage shreds until just before serving, or the cabbage will become soggy.

makes 4 servings

4 whole salted anchovies, rinsed, filleted, soaked briefly in cold water, and drained

2 tablespoons extra virgin olive oil

1 tablespoon white wine vinegar

1/4 head green cabbage, core removed and very thinly shredded

To make the dressing, put the anchovies, oil, and vinegar in a food processor or blender and process until very smooth. Place a small handful of the thinly shredded cabbage on each plate and spoon about 1 tablespoon of the dressing in a band across the midsection of the cabbage shreds. Serve cool but not cold.

Anchovies Worth Their Salt

When the Piedmontese make *acciughe al verde* or any other dish where anchovies are featured, such as their presentation of roasted red peppers garnished with whole anchovy fillets, their first order of business is to head to the local market. The anchovies preferred in Piedmont, and elsewhere in Italy, are packed not in oil, but in salt. Improbable as it sounds, these salt-packed anchovies are *less* salty than the standard fillets packed in olive oil. Why, or how, that is, I don't know, but it's true. At the market, Italians can find several sizes of anchovies, the largest being the most expensive. Invariably these are from Spain. (See The Cult of *Bagna Caôda*—page 131—for more on the Spain/Piedmont anchovy connection.) Although a fresh anchovy is white-fleshed, salt-cured anchovies are reddish in color, the result of the six-month-long brine-curing process. They are not cheap.

Such anchovies can be found in the States, although not without some looking. As in Italy, they are packed in cans. The best brand that I've come across so far is, ironically, Sicilian rather than Spanish. The label of the snappy, colorful can, with 1 pound, 5 ounces of anchovies huddled inside, reads "Acciughe Salate" (salted anchovies), from the shipper Agostino-Recca in Sciacca, Sicily. These sell for $18 a can and can be bought by mail order from Corti Brothers, 5810 Folsom Boulevard, Sacramento, California 95819 (telephone: 916-736-3800).

Unopened, anchovies preserved in salt can be kept indefinitely in the cupboard. Once opened, the can should be sealed with aluminum foil or plastic wrap and stored in the refrigerator, where it will keep almost forever. So there's no need to be concerned about buying such a seemingly large quantity. Besides, once you taste *acciughe al verde*, the supply will quickly disappear.

Tornavento Restaurant's Shredded Carrot Salad with Tongue

Insalata di Carotte e Lingue Tornavento

Tornavento (meaning weathervane) is one of Piedmont's best restaurants, located in the small hilltop town of Treiso, smack in the middle of the Barbaresco wine zone in the southern part of Piedmont. It is an unusually beautiful restaurant, with a gorgeous view of the vineyards off its open-air terrace.

Unusually for Piedmont, Tornavento is owned and run by a woman, Luisella ("Leila") Gobbino. Marco Serra is the chef, as well as a partner. Marco is young and wonderfully talented, a protégé of one of Piedmont's most applauded older chefs, Cesare Giaccone of Dei Cacciatori da Cesare in Albaretto della Torre, high in the above-the-vines hills of the Alta Langhe.

Marco Serra's cooking is respectful of tradition but has a modern, light touch. This "salad" of shredded carrots, slices of soft cheese, and thin slices of tongue simply sauced in a mixture of olive oil, wine and balsamic vinegars, and fresh basil is unmistakably Piedmontese.

I have served this dish frequently to guests, always to raves. Marco Serra uses very thinly sliced veal tongue, but I have often substituted thin slices of prosciutto to equally good effect. This salad can be made entirely in advance, but add the oil and vinegar dressing only just before serving. Serve just barely cool.

makes 6 servings

To poach the tongue:

1 medium-size onion, quartered

1 large carrot, sliced into chunks

2 bay leaves

1 teaspoon salt

1 teaspoon cracked black pepper

*Small handful of fresh Italian parsley
    leaves*

1 veal tongue

For the salad:

3 to 4 large carrots, coarsely shredded

*2 small semifirm creamy textured cheeses,
    such as goat's cheese (chèvre), sliced
    ⅛ inch thick*

¾ cup extra virgin olive oil

*¼ cup white wine vinegar, or more
    to taste*

2 tablespoons balsamic vinegar

*Small handful of fresh basil leaves,
    very finely chopped*

Salt

Freshly ground black pepper

To cook the tongue, combine all of the poaching seasonings in a large pot of water. Bring to a boil. Add the tongue, reduce to a gentle boil, cover, and let cook until fork-tender, about 2 hours. Remove the tongue from the water, let cool slightly, and peel off the skin. When the tongue is completely cool, slice lengthwise as thin as possible. Strain the poaching liquid and reserve for use as a soup base or for stock.

To assemble the salad, place a handful of carrots in the center of each individual serving plate to form a small mound. Place the cheese slices on top of the carrots, then top with about 4 slices of tongue.

Whisk together the olive oil, vinegars, basil and salt and pepper to taste. Taste for pungency and adjust with more white wine vinegar if necessary. Spoon the dressing evenly over each arranged salad and serve.

Mixed Salad of Vegetables in Mayonnaise

Composta di Verdure in Maionese

❧❧❧

The French influence on Piedmontese cooking is never so apparent as it is in this summer salad. It used to be a favorite here in America, better known to us by its French name, *salade Russe* (Russian salad). The French themselves, who once doted on it, seem to have forsaken this old glory. The Piedmontese, however, still clamor for it. You can find it in almost every Piedmontese *salumeria*, or delicatessen.

All the vegetables are cut into bite-size cubes and cooked only briefly so that they still retain a slight crunch. The selection of vegetables can—and should—vary with what's freshest and most seasonal. The object is a variety of bright colors and fresh tastes. This is an ideal summer lunch, to be served outdoors with a carafe of rosé and chunks of crusty bread.

makes 6 servings

4 carrots

4 waxy-type potatoes, peeled

1/2 head cauliflower

2 zucchini

1 red bell pepper, cored and seeded

1 large onion

6 green onions (scallions), white and green parts

1/2 cup green peas

Two 3 1/2-ounce cans solid white tuna, drained

1/2 cup white wine vinegar

1/2 cup olive oil

Juice of 1/2 lemon

1 1/4 cups mayonnaise, preferably homemade

Cut all the vegetables (except the peas, of course) into small bite-size cubes or pieces. Steam or boil separately until each is just barely cooked; the vegetables should retain a slight crunchiness. Let cool completely.

Toss the vegetables with the tuna, vinegar, olive oil, and lemon juice in a large bowl. Combine with the mayonnaise. Transfer to a large oval platter or serving bowl and refrigerate for several hours. Serve cool but not cold.

Salad of Chicken Breasts and Prosciutto

Insalata Capricciosa

You commonly see salads in Piedmont that are rarely seen elsewhere in Italy, such as *insalata capricciosa*. It employs mayonnaise as a dressing, a French influence.

Insalata capricciosa is an interplay of chicken and prosciutto paired with the crunch and licorice tang of raw sweet fennel. The hearty Piedmontese appetite likes something more substantial than just a few lettuce leaves. Because sweet fennel is an autumn and winter vegetable, that's when this salad is most often served. But untraditional substitutions, such as crunchy jícama root, fresh water chestnuts, pencil-thin asparagus spears, or thinly sliced raw cabbage, work wonderfully.

makes 6 servings

2 tablespoons olive oil

3 boneless, skinless chicken breast halves, pounded thin

Salt

Freshly ground black pepper

4 thin slices prosciutto di Parma (about $1/4$ pound), fat removed and sliced into strips $1/2$ inch wide and 4 inches long

1 medium-size fennel bulb, stem trimmed, bulb thinly sliced crosswise and cut into strips $1/4$ inch wide

About 6 tablespoons mayonnaise, preferably homemade

1 large head lettuce, rinsed, dried, and torn into small pieces

Put the oil in a large sauté pan over medium heat. When the oil is hot, cook the chicken breasts on both sides until cooked through but still tender, about 3 minutes. Set aside to cool.

When the chicken is cool, slice into $1/4$-inch-wide strips. Transfer to a large mixing bowl and season with salt and pepper. Toss to combine. Add the prosciutto and fennel and toss gently to mix. Add the mayonnaise a tablespoon at a time, tossing until the mixture is just lightly coated. Add the lettuce and toss again. Adjust the dressing with additional spoonfuls of mayonnaise to taste. Taste for seasoning and adjust accordingly. Serve slightly chilled or at room temperature.

Stuffed Zucchini Flowers

Caponét

One of Piedmont's summer food passions is the dish locals call *caponét*, a dialect word. Restaurants take pity on the rest of us, identifying the dish in plain Italian as *fiori di zucchine farciti,* stuffed zucchini flowers. It's always served as a summertime antipasto.

Although stuffed zucchini flowers sounds exotic, it's really one of the easiest dishes to make. And if you've got a home garden (or even just a local farmer's market nearby), the supply of zucchini flowers from very young zukes is readily accessible. The only challenge to this dish is making it within a few hours—a day at most—of plucking the yellow flower from the growing zucchini, as they are extremely perishable. The size of the flower is unimportant, though larger is better, if only because a large flower holds more stuffing.

This antipasto can be served either hot from the pan or at room temperature. Once cooled, though, it does not reheat well. But it does taste as good cool as hot, so it is ideal if made ahead of time—say, during the morning when the flowers are freshly picked—and then served for dinner.

makes 6 servings

2 tablespoons extra virgin olive oil

1/4 pound ground veal

1/4 pound ground pork

1/3 pound salami, finely chopped

1 garlic clove, very finely chopped

Small handful of fresh Italian parsley
    leaves, finely chopped

2 large eggs

1 ounce Parmigiano-Reggiano cheese,
    grated (1/4 cup)

Salt

Freshly ground black pepper

12 good-size zucchini flowers

2 tablespoons olive oil

2 tablespoons unsalted butter

Place the extra virgin olive oil in a large sauté pan over medium heat. When the oil is hot, add the veal, pork, salami, garlic, and parsley and stir briskly to blend. When the meats are fully cooked, about 5 minutes, transfer to a large mixing bowl and let cool completely.

When the meats are cool, add the eggs and cheese and season with salt and pepper. Mix to combine.

Gently stuff each zucchini flower with the meat mixture, closing the opening by pressing the tips of the petals together. Do not worry if the flowers don't stay closed. During cooking, the flowers will wilt, and the petals can be easily wrapped around the filling before serving.

To cook, place the 2 tablespoons olive oil and butter in a large sauté pan over very low heat. When the butter is melted, set the stuffed zucchini flowers in the pan and roll in the butter/oil mixture to coat on all sides. Cover and let cook for 15 to 20 minutes. Midway through the cooking, turn over the flowers. Remove from the pan and serve either hot or at room temperature.

Mushrooms in Parsley and Garlic
Funghi Trifolati

Trifolati refers to almost anything—fish, vegetables, meats—that is cooked with chopped garlic and parsley, which are the yin and yang of Italian cookery. Surely the most famous such dish is porcini mushrooms so treated. The Italian reverence for allowing their raw ingredients to shine is never so apparent as in a dish like this.

For this dish, only fresh mushrooms can be used. If you see fresh porcini, this is your recipe. An excellent alternative would be portobello mushrooms, which now are commonly available.

makes 6 servings

1 pound fresh porcini or portobello mushrooms, stems removed (and reserved for stock)
2 tablespoons olive oil
1 thick slice bacon, cut into small dice

2 garlic cloves, very finely chopped
Salt
Freshly ground black pepper
1/4 cup finely chopped fresh Italian parsley leaves

Rinse the mushrooms caps, pat dry, and slice into 1/4- to 1/3-inch-thick slices. If any of the caps are very large, first cut them in half, then slice. Set aside.

Add the olive oil and bacon to a large sauté pan over medium heat. When the bacon is getting crisp, drain nearly all of the oil and fat from the pan.

Place the pan over low heat, add the garlic, and cook for 2 minutes, stirring, taking care that the garlic does not burn. Add the mushrooms, tossing them vigorously to mix with the garlic. Sprinkle with salt and pepper, stirring to combine. Cover and let the mushrooms stew over very low heat for 15 minutes. Sprinkle with the parsley, stirring to combine. Serve immediately on warm plates.

Stuffed Onions

Cipolle Ripiene

❦

Stuffed onions are a Piedmontese favorite, with numerous variations found throughout the region. This version came from the monumental New Year's Eve dinner mentioned in the preface to the *Pate di Tonno* recipe (see page 33). When I asked what made this version of stuffed onions so different, the cook smiled and confessed to the addition of ground hazelnuts, one of Piedmont's best products and a speciality of the Langhe zone, where the dinner took place. Other nuts, such as walnuts, almonds, chestnuts, or pecans, work equally well.

This is an ideal dish to make ahead of time, as it reheats well. I like to serve it as part of a Thanksgiving feast for just this reason, as well as for its golden, autumnal look.

makes 6 servings

6 large onions, peeled but root left attached

1 ½ cups fresh bread crumbs, soaked in ½ cup plus 2 tablespoons milk

3 large eggs

3 ounces Parmigiano-Reggiano cheese, grated (¾ cup)

12 blanched almonds or hazelnuts (see page 283), finely ground

Large pinch of ground cloves

Pinch of sugar

Salt

Freshly ground black pepper

1 large egg yolk, beaten with 2 tablespoons milk for egg glaze

¼ cup (½ stick) butter

Preheat the oven to 400°F.

Cook the onions in boiling water to cover for about 5 minutes. Remove from the water and when cool enough to handle, slice off 1 inch of the top of each onion. Scoop out the interior, leaving a thin shell. Finely chop the onion tops and scooped-out interiors. Combine the chopped onions with the soaked bread crumbs, eggs, cheese, ground nuts, and seasonings, stirring thoroughly to blend. Stuff the cavity of each onion with the filling. Place in a buttered terrine or baking dish.

Brush the exterior of each onion with the egg glaze and top each one with a nugget of butter. Cover the onions loosely with aluminum foil and bake for 1½ hours. Serve hot, warm, or at room temperature.

"Electric" Cheese

Tomini Elettrici

✦✦✦

It's not fair to call this a recipe, as it is so simple. Yet it frequently appears on Piedmontese tables and it is so good. A *tomini* is a small, disk-shaped soft cheese that looks very similar to a small fresh goat cheese. The taste is creamier and richer, though, as it's made from a blend of goat's and cow's milk. But fresh goat cheese is an ideal substitute.

To make *tomini elettrici*, simply sprinkle a generous pinch or two of mild chili powder over each cheese. Then drizzle a generous dollop of extra virgin olive oil over the peppered cheese. Serve with *grissini* (breadsticks) or rustic bread alongside.

Spicy Cheese

Sancarlin

✦✦✦

Sancarlin (Piedmontese dialect for Saint Charles) is an alpine specialty, one of those mountain dishes that can bring you back to life after a morning on the slopes or a brisk walk in the cold air. It is a variation on *tomini elettrici* that makes use of a softer cheese, such as mascarpone or ricotta. A very soft, spreadable goat cheese is also ideal. The dish is best if refrigerated for forty-eight hours before serving, which lets the flavors marry.

Sancarlin is traditionally served with plain boiled potatoes. Alternatively, it is spread on toasted bread or focaccia, or scooped up with *grissini*.

There is a near-addictive quality to this dish. Once, in a restaurant in Turin, I witnessed a diner who was rigorously pursuing a serious diet fall to pieces upon being served *Sancarlin*. She concluded, rightly, that if you have to lapse, *Sancarlin* is the way to go.

makes 6 servings

8 ounces mascarpone, fresh ricotta, or soft goat cheese (chèvre)	*2 small dried hot red peppers, stems and seeds removed and very finely chopped*
2 garlic cloves, very finely chopped	*Salt*
2 tablespoons extra virgin olive oil	*Freshly ground black pepper*

Combine all the ingredients in a mixing bowl and mix well to blend. Cover tightly and let sit in the refrigerator for at least 48 hours, or longer. Bring to room temperature before serving.

Chicken Pâté with Black Olive Paste
Pâté di Pollo con Pasta di Oliva Nera

✿❀✿

Piedmont's ancient trade with Liguria is evident in this dish, as Piedmont is too cold in the winter for olive trees to survive. All sorts of olive products were carried over the mountains separating Mediterranean Liguria from continental Piedmont.

Black olive paste is available in many specialty shops. I have found no significant differences among the various brands I've tried. It keeps indefinitely if refrigerated. However, because making olive paste is so easy—and cheaper than buying the prepared version—I've included a recipe for it here.

This pâté is served in slices, on lettuce leaves, garnished with slices of green and black olives.

makes 12 servings

To poach the chicken:

1 fryer chicken (about 4 pounds)

1 medium-size onion, quartered

1 leek, green and white parts, thickly
    sliced and thoroughly rinsed

1 large carrot, thickly sliced

For the pâté:

1 teaspoon salt

½ cup (1 stick) unsalted butter, cut
    into pieces

2 tablespoons black olive paste, homemade
    (recipe follows) or store-bought

Grated zest of 2 lemons

1 tablespoon freshly ground black pepper,
    or more to taste

Freshly grated nutmeg

Place the chicken in an 8-quart pot with the onion, leek, and carrot. Add cold water to cover. Bring to a boil, then reduce the heat and let simmer until the meat is tender, about 1 hour. Remove the chicken and drain, reserving the poaching liquid for a stock or soup base.

When the chicken is cool enough to handle, remove and discard the skin. Remove all of the meat from the bones and place in a food processor. Process the chicken until it is a smooth puree, about 3 minutes. Add the salt and process to combine.

With the processor running, add the butter. Then add the olive paste and process briefly to blend. Finally, add the lemon zest, black pepper, and nutmeg to taste. Process briefly to blend. Taste for seasonings and adjust accordingly. (You will have about 3¹/₂ cups of pâté.)

Transfer the pâté to a buttered 1-quart terrine. Cover tightly with plastic wrap and refrigerate for several hours or, preferably, overnight.

To unmold, run a thin knife around the perimeter of the pâté. Then lower the mold into hot water for 30 seconds. Invert onto a serving plate and slice.

Homemade Black Olive Paste

Pasta di Oliva

makes 1 cup

1 pound oil-cured black olives, pits
    removed
¹/₂ cup extra virgin olive oil

Grated zest of 1 lemon
1 tablespoon freshly ground black
    pepper

Combine all of the ingredients in a food processor. Process to a fine puree. Refrigerate until needed. The paste will keep indefinitely if stored in a tightly sealed jar in the refrigerator.

Liver Pâté

Pâté di Fegato

❧❦❧

Liver pâté is a classic in France and it slipped easily across the border into Piedmont, where it has long been a favorite. The Piedmontese twist is something you don't find in the French versions: sage and rosemary. Fresh herbs are desirable but not essential. Either fresh or dried, the herbs make a pleasing, invigorating difference.

makes 6 servings

2 tablespoons unsalted butter

½ pound calf's liver, trimmed of
    membranes and thinly sliced

½ pound chicken livers, trimmed of
    membranes and coarsely chopped

Leaves from 2 large sprigs fresh rosemary,
    very finely chopped, or
    1½ tablespoons dried, finely ground
    in a mortar or a blender

20 fresh sage leaves, very finely chopped,
    or 1½ tablespoons dried, finely
    crumbled

¼ cup dry red wine

1½ cups (3 sticks) unsalted butter,
    cut into small pieces

1 teaspoon salt

Freshly ground black pepper

¼ cup brandy

Melt the 2 tablespoons butter in a large sauté pan over medium-low heat. Add the calf's and chicken livers and rosemary. Cook briefly, turning to brown the pieces on all sides. Add the sage and wine and stir to blend. Partially cover the pan and cook over low heat, stirring occasionally, until the livers are cooked and firm, about 10 minutes. Remove from the heat and let cool completely.

When the liver is cool, puree in a food processor until absolutely smooth, several minutes. With the processor running, add the butter pieces, salt, and pepper to taste. Continue processing until all of the butter is incorporated. Pour in the brandy and process to combine.

Transfer the puree to a buttered 1-quart terrine. Cover tightly with plastic wrap and refrigerate for several hours or, preferably, overnight.

Serve directly from the mold in thin slices. Or unmold by running a thin knife around the perimeter of the pâté, then dipping the mold into hot water for 30 seconds and inverting onto a serving plate.

Tuna Pâté

Pâté di Tonno

꧁꧂

Pâté di tonno is a Piedmontese classic that I've had many times, but it was never more memorably served than during a heroic New Year's Eve dinner party. Piedmont abounds in great home cooks and this dinner party, an expansive family affair, funneled some of the best home-cooking talent I know under one roof. Dinner lasted—I do not exaggerate— from 6 P.M. to 1 A.M., and only afterward did the cognac and grappa start to flow. I'd be less than honest if I said that I could recall every dish in the flood of food that evening.

But I do recall the *pâté di tonno*. Not only is it one of my favorite Piedmontese antipasti, but it was served early in the meal, when I still had the presence of mind to jot down a few tips from the cook. What follows is my own reconstruction, which comes pretty close to what I so vividly remember. Unless you're really concentrating, one has to be *told* what this pâté is made from, as it is so utterly different in taste and texture from what we usually think of as tuna. Best of all, it is quick to assemble.

Traditionally, *pâté di tonno* is molded in a simple rectangular form. Molds with patterns are not advised, simply because the patterns do not show well. In Piedmont, a fancy presentation of *pâté di tonno* has it finished in aspic, but in homes, aspic is ignored and a homemade mayonnaise is served alongside. Frequently the *pâté* is garnished with coarsely chopped Italian parsley, or served simply with bread or *grissini*.

WORTH NOTING

Type of tuna   I've made this dish using several different kinds of tuna and found that the kind to use is "solid white," packed either in water or oil. "Chunk light" delivers a coarser texture and darker color, as well as less flavor.

Temperature   Although *pâté di tonno* needs to be refrigerated to firm it (the butter is essential as it adds texture, flavor, and binding), it should not be served straight from the fridge. It is best served cool, but not refrigerator cold.

Storage   Serve within two days of its making, when the flavors are still bright and fresh.

makes one 1½- to 2-cup mold; 4 servings

One 6-ounce can solid white tuna,
    drained
1 whole salted anchovy, fillets rinsed,
    filleted, soaked briefly in cold water,
    and drained

¼ cup (½ stick) unsalted butter (cold
    from the refrigerator is fine)

continued

Place the tuna and anchovies in a food processor and process to create an extremely fine, smooth puree, 1 to 2 minutes. Add the butter and process again until thoroughly pureed. Transfer the pâté to a mold, cover tightly with plastic wrap, and refrigerate for several hours or overnight.

To serve, run a thin knife around the sides of the pâté and unmold onto a plate. Serve cool.

Peppers Stuffed with Tuna
Peperoni Ripieni con Tonno

The Piedmontese love of tuna finds its way into yet another antipasto. Although similar to the tuna sauce employed for *vitello tonnato*, the tuna filling here is stiffened with just enough butter to give it some body. *Peperoni ripieni* is one of Piedmont's all-time favorites, the better for being sauced with something so simple that it hardly calls for a recipe: extra virgin olive oil mixed with chopped fresh basil. The combination of sweet pepper, enriched tuna, and this basil-infused sauce results in a kaleidescope of tastes greater than the sum of its simple parts.

WORTH NOTING

Removing pepper skins Composed of cellulose, pepper skins are difficult for many people to digest. It is important to remove them for greater edibility and refinement. Several methods are suitable, such as peeling the skin with a vegetable peeler or either baking for 30 to 45 minutes at 375°F or charring the pepper over a gas flame until completely blackened, then placing in a plastic bag for a few minutes so the steam will help further loosen the skins.

For this recipe, I recommend baking the peppers, as they must be cooked and baking lets the juices escape, while charring leaves a smoky taste that conflicts with the bright, pure tastes of the tuna and basil.

Hothouse versus field-grown peppers Peppers grown in hothouses (the supply source during the winter and spring) typically are smaller and more evenly formed than those grown in the field, as well as softer and more tender. Therefore, they take less time to bake than field-grown peppers. Sometimes hothouse-grown peppers come with a sticker attached that reveals the source. If not, ask your produce person where his come from.

The olive oil The Piedmontese use the light, delicate olive oil from nearby Liguria, which lies over the mountains that separate Piedmont from the Mediterranean. Ligurian olive oil is Italy's most subtle. That from the Chianti Classico zone, farther south, is slightly more pronounced in flavor but equally fine. Both are expensive, but worth it for use in sauces, as in this dish, where the quality of the oil is so much on display.

makes 4 servings

2 large red or yellow bell peppers, stems removed	*1 tablespoon olive oil*
	1 tablespoon unsalted butter
One 3½-ounce can solid white tuna, drained	*Finely chopped fresh basil leaves*
	Extra virgin olive oil

Preheat the oven to 375°F. Place the peppers stem side down on a baking sheet and bake about 30 minutes if the peppers are hothouse grown, 45 to 60 minutes if field grown. The skins of the peppers will balloon and juices will ooze from the base. Remove from the oven and let cool.

Slice off the top and bottom of each pepper and remove the seeds. Slice each pepper lengthwise in half to create two equal flat pieces. Set aside.

To make the stuffing, place the tuna in a food processor or blender. With the processor running, add the olive oil and butter and process until the stuffing is satiny smooth, about 1 minute.

To assemble, spread the stuffing in an even layer over the side of the flat peppers and roll up. Place on a serving plate and refrigerate until the tuna filling is firm.

Just before serving, mix the basil with enough extra virgin olive oil to create a liquid sauce that easily runs off a spoon. Spoon a generous dollop of the mixture over the top of each serving. Serve barely cool.

Veal with Tuna Sauce

Vitello Tonnato

❧

Tuna figures in a great many Italian dishes and nowhere more inventively—even wittily—than in Piedmont. The genius of Piedmontese cooking lies in its ability to transform just a few fine ingredients, with just a few simple techniques, into dishes of a taste and texture never previously imagined. The distinctiveness of Piedmontese cooking is nowhere more evident than in this famous dish.

Whether credit for creating *vitello tonnato* should go to the Piedmontese or the Milanese is open to discussion, but the Piedmontese version is, in my opinion, the better of the two. A traditional Milanese tuna sauce uses cream; the French-influenced Piedmontese version uses mayonnaise.

That said, the employment of mayonnaise as we know it today is relatively new, appearing only in the last century. Originally, the *tonnato* was less solid, with the tuna, anchovies, and capers being whisked together with semi-hard-cooked egg yolks and a cup or so of olive oil. This resulted in something semiliquid. Clearly, this is a mayonnaise of sorts. One thing is certain: *vitello tonnato* (*vitel tonné* in Piedmontese dialect) is loved more in Piedmont than anywhere else.

Vitello tonnato tastes best if prepared at least a day in advance, as the veal should be cooled and the sauce takes on an added depth of tuna flavor if left to "marry" overnight. Traditionally, and most commonly, the veal is carved into thick slices from a braised roast. These slices are overlapped on a large platter and liberally slathered with the tuna sauce, completely covering the slices, like frosting a cake. The platter is served family-style and passed around accordingly.

Alternatively, individual plates of *vitello tonnato* may be prepared. Here, the tuna sauce is served in a dollop on each serving, the better to see the veal. This more elegant presentation is also more useful for smaller dinners, where purchasing individual slices of thinly pounded veal scaloppine makes more sense than forking over for an expensive veal roast.

Although I've never seen it done in Piedmont, experiment reveals that the tuna sauce works wonderfully well with chicken and turkey breasts. They should be boned and pounded as thin as possible, then sautéed. Given the cost difference between veal and poultry, I urge you to try these variations, as well as the traditional veal.

Use "solid white" tuna only. Chunk light or chunk white produces a coarser texture and lesser flavor. It doesn't matter whether the tuna is water- or oil-packed.

Homemade mayonnaise This is essential, as store-bought mayonnaise is too sweet and bland. Also, the mayonnaise is lemon-infused, as lemon juice is used instead of vinegar. It is best to use only a light, flavorful olive oil, such as one from Liguria.

Type of veal Different cuts of veal can be used for roasting: rump, shoulder, leg, or loin. The finest, silkiest texture comes from the leg and loin.

Serving temperature Serving *vitello tonnato* at an appropriate temperature is important, as the flavors are subtle, and are blunted if the dish is served refrigerator-cold.

makes 4 servings

For the sauce:

Two 6-ounce cans solid white tuna, drained

8 anchovy fillets, preferably salt-packed

2 teaspoons salt-packed small capers, rinsed

2 tablespoons white wine vinegar

½ cup mayonnaise, preferably homemade

To make the veal with slices from a braised roast:

One 3-pound boned and tied veal roast, from leg or loin

2 carrots, sliced into chunks

1 large onion

¼ cup white wine vinegar

1 large sprig fresh rosemary

2 bay leaves

8 black peppercorns

½ bottle dry white wine

To make the sauce, place everything except the mayonnaise in the bowl of a food processor or blender and process, scraping the bowl occasionally, to a really smooth texture, about 2 minutes. Add the mayonnaise and process to blend thoroughly. Refrigerate in a tightly sealed container until needed. The sauce improves in flavor if refrigerated overnight.

To cook the veal, place all of the ingredients in a large casserole with cold water to barely cover and bring to a boil. Cover the casserole tightly, lower the heat to medium-low, and let simmer for about 1½ hours. Using an instant-read meat thermometer, start checking the veal after 1 hour of braising, removing it from the heat when the thermometer reads between 145° and 150°F for meat on the rosy side or medium-rare; medium is 160°F, well done 170°F. Remove the veal and let it cool completely at room temperature, then wrap tightly and refrigerate overnight. Reserve the braising liquid for use as a soup base or for risotto.

continued

Traditionally, *vitello tonnato* is served cut into slices between ¹/₃ inch and ¹/₂ inch thick. Personally, I prefer much thinner slices, especially for medium-rare meat. Slice the roast as thin as possible. Layer these very thin slices either on individual plates (two per plate) or in overlapping slices on a large platter. Slather the tuna sauce over the slices or, alternatively, place generous dollops in an attractive pattern in the middle of the slices, the better to reveal the color of the veal.

To make with individual scaloppine slices: If you are making *vitello tonnato* for just a few people, it makes sense to purchase individual slices of veal scaloppine. These are simply slices from the leg, which is also what a veal roast is. In some neighborhoods, what the Italians call a *scaloppine* is identical to what Germans know as a *schnitzel*.

To make individual portions of *vitello tonnato*, purchase one veal *scaloppino* per person. Have the butcher pound each slice as thin as possible. Sauté the scallops for little more than 30 seconds on each side, as the veal is already tender and so thinly sliced. Let cool completely.

Season very lightly with salt and pepper. Serve on individual plates, placing a generous dollop of tuna sauce in the center of each slice.

A "Tuna" of Rabbit
Tonno di Coniglio

Just why the Piedmontese decided to call this dish *tonno* I can't say. Tuna has nothing to do with it, nor does it resemble any tuna dish of my acquaintance. Sandro Doglio, in his authoritative *Gran Dizionario della Gastronomia del Piemonte*, suggests that the delicacy and texture of the dish give it a refinement echoing the once-precious tuna. Whatever the reason, this is a classic, traditional dish that deserves the best extra virgin olive oil (Ligurian or Chianti Classico), as the oil is so fundamental to the finished dish. Chicken (especially a flavorful capon) or turkey substitutes perfectly for rabbit.

This dish tastes best if made ahead, covered, and refrigerated for at least forty-eight hours, or, preferably, three or four days. Serve it accompanied by a good rustic bread and a red wine such as Barbera. Alternatively, serve on a bed of lettuce leaves, adding a drizzle of vinegar.

1 large carrot, sliced into chunks

1 celery stalk, thickly sliced

1 medium-size onion, quartered

2 bay leaves

Small handful of fresh Italian parsley leaves

1 rabbit, cut into pieces, or 4 individual rabbit hindquarters

15 to 20 fresh sage leaves

1 head garlic, separated into cloves, peeled, and very thinly sliced

Salt

Freshly ground black pepper

Extra virgin olive oil

Red or white wine vinegar

Place the carrot, celery, onion, bay leaves, and parsley in a casserole with a tight-fitting cover. Cover generously with cold water and bring to a simmer. (Alternatively, a mixture of dry white wine and water can be used for additional flavor.) Add the rabbit and let simmer, covered, until tender, about 1 1/2 hours.

Remove the rabbit from the casserole. Strain the stock and reserve it, and vegetables, if desired, to use as a soup or sauce base. When the meat is cool enough to handle, strip the meat from the bones, discarding all the bones. Shred into bite-sized chunks.

To assemble, line a small terrine with a layer of the sage leaves. Several times, place a layer of rabbit strips over the sage leaves, followed by a layer of garlic slices. Season with salt and pepper, then drizzle with a thin layer of olive oil. Repeat the layering. Cover the final layer generously with olive oil so that no part is exposed to air. Refrigerate until needed. The flavor will improve over several days.

To serve, bring to room temperature and lightly sprinkle each serving with vinegar to taste.

Vinegar-Marinated Eggs and Zucchini

Carpione di Uova e Zucchiné

✻❀✻

The Piedmontese like things tart, as their native wine grapes Nebbiolo and Barbera so well demonstrate. *Carpione* is yet another example of this predilection for the acidic "cut." The term refers not to a particular dish but instead to a manner of preparation. The closest equivalent in English would be "pickled," but the acidity for the typical *carpione* preparation falls short of the preserving powers of true pickling. Traditionally, *in carpione* was a technique for preserving, at least for a short time, various fish, specifically carp, hence the name. The Piedmontese found it to be an invigorating, cooling dish during their hot, humid summers and soon applied the preparation to other items.

Today, the most familiar *carpione* dish is one using poached or fried eggs and zucchini. The clarity of the three flavors—egg, vinegar, and zucchini—is magnified by the technique. The ingredients can be multiplied as needed. (If making more than one serving, you will probably need to use less oil proportionately.)

For each serving:

¼ pound small zucchini, sliced lengthwise into ¼ to ⅜-inch-thick strips

3 tablespoons olive oil

1 large egg

1 large garlic clove, very finely chopped

For the marinade:

3 large fresh sage leaves, immersed for 30 seconds in boiling water (this brightens the color)

2 tablespoons white wine vinegar

1 tablespoon extra virgin olive oil

Salt to taste

Freshly ground black or white pepper to taste

Dry both sides of the zucchini slices with paper towels. Heat 1 tablespoon of the olive oil in a non-stick skillet over medium-low heat. When the oil is hot—it should swirl in the pan like water—fry the egg sunny-side up. (The Italians descriptively call this *uova all'occhio di bue:* a bull's-eye egg.) When the white is firm but the yolk still liquid, slide it from the pan onto a plate and set aside to cool.

Return the skillet to medium heat and add to it another tablespoon of olive oil. When the oil is hot, add the zucchini strips. Fry lightly on both sides until cooked through. Remove from the pan and set aside to cool completely.

In a very small pan, gently cook the garlic in the remaining tablespoon olive oil over very low heat to relieve its raw bite, about 3 minutes. Do not let the garlic turn brown, as that will make it bitter. Remove from the heat to cool completely, leaving the garlic in the oil.

Meanwhile, whisk together the marinade ingredients. In a shallow bowl, place the zucchini strips and fried egg in layers, splashing some of the marinade and the garlic-infused olive oil on top of each as you go. When all of the ingredients are layered, pour over any remaining marinade and the garlic in olive oil. Seal tightly with plastic wrap and refrigerate for several hours, or overnight. Serve cool but not cold.

Vinegar-Marinated Chicken Breasts

Petti di Pollo in Carpione

✺

The taste for food *in carpione* quickly extended beyond the original fish to various vegetables (onions as well as zucchini are favorites) and eventually to chicken and turkey. This is the dish I always make when preparing a batch of chicken stock. I buy several whole chickens and cut them up, reserving the breasts for *petti di pollo in carpione*. Like many Piedmontese *antipasti*, a larger portion serves perfectly as a first course.

Fresh sage and rosemary are essential, as they bring a bright dimension to this dish. Similarly, a good wine vinegar—imported from either Italy or France—is called for.

This is a favorite dish of everyone who has ever tasted it, as the combination of finely chopped herbs allied with a slightly bracing hint of vinegar is striking yet subtle.

makes 4 antipasto servings; 2 first-course servings

3 tablespoons olive oil

2 large whole boneless, skinless chicken breasts, pounded thin, sliced lengthwise into 1/4-inch-wide strips, and strips cut in half

Salt

For the marinade:

1/4 cup extra virgin olive oil, or more to taste

1 medium-size onion, very finely chopped

2 large garlic cloves, very finely chopped

15 to 20 fresh sage leaves, very finely chopped

Leaves from 1 large sprig fresh rosemary, very finely chopped

1/4 cup red or white wine vinegar, or more to taste

Salt

Add the oil to a large sauté pan over medium heat. When the oil is hot, cook the chicken strips on both sides until cooked through but still tender, about 3 minutes. Remove from the heat, lightly salt, and let cool.

To make the marinade, add the extra virgin oil to a nonstick skillet over medium-low heat. When the oil is hot, add the onion, garlic, sage, and rosemary, reduce the heat to low, and cook gently. When the onion is soft and translucent, remove the pan from the heat and let cool.

Combine the chicken strips with the marinade. Add the vinegar and salt to taste, blending thoroughly. Taste and add more vinegar, oil, and/or salt as desired. Cover tightly with plastic wrap and refrigerate for several hours, or overnight, to blend the flavors. Serve cool or at room temperature.

Piedmontese Garlic Bread

Soma d'Aj

🐜🐚🐜

The world's most famous garlic bread is surely Tuscany's *bruschetta*. Indeed, because Tuscany grows its own glorious olive oil, pride of authorship must go to it. But Piedmont has its *soma d'aj* (pronounced soo-mah die), its *bruschetta*. (In the region of Latium, or Lazio, south of Rome, it's called *fettunta*.)

Anyway, the idea of this dish was independently arrived at everywhere if only because it's so basic: a slice of bread (toasted or not) lightly strewn with finely chopped garlic, liberally doused with olive oil, and lightly dusted with salt. In Piedmont in the old days, the oil would have been strictly Ligurian.

Soma d'aj was workers' food, especially the vine tenders. During the harvest, when they stopped for a break, they would nibble on fresh Dolcetto or Barbera grapes. Neither grape variety has especially tannic skin, and they are a delicious counterpoint to the pungency of garlic—which probably was eaten raw.

At home *soma d'aj* was once a common accompaniment to wine at the between-meals snack called a *merenda*. It was something to help the wine go down. But you will never find *soma d'aj* in a Piedmontese restaurant, as you commonly find *bruschetta* in Tuscan restaurants, for the abundant Piedmontese table finds this dish too plain and simple.

One other variation of *soma d'aj*, apart from serving it with grapes, sets it apart: the addition of either a strong, well-aged Gorgonzola cheese or the pungent, grappa-soaked (and powerful smelling) spreadable cheese called *brus*. This latter cheese was surely the "people's choice," if only because it keeps for months and it has a potent flavor. To understand its appeal—which is mostly lost on nonagricultural sensibilities—you'd have to be picking grapes in a muddy vineyard in foggy Piedmont in mid-October. Then *brus*, like a shot of whiskey in the morning, suddenly makes perfect sense.

For each serving:

1 slice rustic, country white bread	*Extra virgin olive oil*
1 garlic clove, very finely chopped	*Salt*

Lightly toast the slice of bread. Sauté the garlic in a little olive oil over low heat, taking care not to let it color. Strew the garlic evenly over the toasted bread. Drizzle a little extra virgin olive oil over the bread and garlic. Sprinkle a large pinch of salt evenly over the bread. Serve.

Focaccia

ﾟ✿ﾟ

Focaccia has now become well known in America. Of all the breads one can make, few are faster to put together and bake than focaccia. And few lend themselves to more variations.

In Piedmont, you see focaccia all the time, especially in areas close the Ligurian border, where it is almost a way of life. Focaccia is worth adopting in our own lives, if only because it's so tasty and speedily created, as it needs only one rising before baking.

makes 1 large focaccia

3 cubes fresh compressed yeast or
   3 tablespoons dry yeast
3 cups lukewarm water
9 cups (2 pounds) unbleached all-purpose
   flour or more if needed

½ teaspoon salt
Olive oil as needed
Semolina flour to dust baking sheet
1 teaspoon coarse salt

In a large mixing bowl, whisk the yeast together with the warm water to blend thoroughly. Let it sit until the mixture begins to foam. In another large bowl, combine the flour with the ½ teaspoon salt and mix to blend. Gradually add the flour to the yeast mixture and stir to create a soft but firm dough. Add more warm water or flour if necessary, a little at a time, to achieve this.

Turn out the dough onto a floured work surface and knead until it is smooth and elastic, about 5 minutes. Coat the inside of a large mixing bowl lightly with olive oil and place the dough in the bowl, turning it over to ensure that it is coated with the oil. Cover with a clean cloth and let rise at room temperature until it has almost doubled in size, about 1 hour.

Preheat the oven to 400°F. Strew some semolina flour on a heavy baking sheet.

Remove the risen dough from the bowl and place it on the sheet. Pat it into a square, rectangle, or circle of approximately ½-inch thickness. Focaccia should be a bready, chewy item, so it is best to leave the dough thicker rather than thinner. Sprinkle with the coarse salt. With the end of a wooden spoon or a finger, dimple the dough all over. Drizzle olive oil over the surface, then add any desired toppings (see below).

Place the baking sheet in the lower third of the oven and bake until the focaccia is golden brown, about 25 minutes. Serve warm, or allow to cool and reheat as needed. Focaccia keeps well if tightly wrapped after being completely cooled.

Variations

With onions: A classic Ligurian treatment. Thinly slice half a large onion and spread the rings evenly over the top of the dough. Add a touch more olive oil and a goodly sprinkling of coarse salt, then bake.

With cheese: An Italian favorite is mascarpone softened slightly with a bit of cream and mixed with blue cheese. For best results, add this topping midway through the baking to prevent overcooking of the cheese.

With bacon: Crisply fry or broil ½ to 1 pound of thin-sliced bacon. Let cool and crumble. Either mix the completely cooled crumbled bacon into the dough itself or shower the bits on top, along with some finely chopped green onion (scallion) tops.

With herbs: When fresh herbs, such as rosemary, basil, oregano, or sage, are available, mix in 3 to 4 tablespoons of one finely chopped fresh herb with the dough while kneading. The focaccia then only needs a topping of good olive oil and coarse salt.

Breadsticks

Grissini

Although breadsticks are found nearly everywhere in Italy, for once there's no dispute about who's entitled to claim them as their own. It's the Piedmontese. *Grissini* are as Piedmontese as, well, chocolate-covered hazelnuts.

The traditional story about how *grissini* were invented involves the Piedmontese royal family, whose family physician suggested the thin, crispy breadsticks as a palliative. Maybe it's true, maybe not. It seems more likely that home cooks had long been fashioning left-over bread dough into thin strips to use up every scrap of dough (and precious space in wood-fueled brick baking ovens).

Today, *grissini* are almost literally part of the Piedmontese table, as they never are placed on a plate or platter. Rather, the breadsticks are simply laid on the tablecloth. This practice evolved no doubt out of practicality. The sheer length of grissini, at least as classically fashioned, pretty much precludes any kind of platter, as it would take up too much table space (as well as be difficult to store).

This bring us to the question of length. Not to put too Freudian a point on it, the Piedmontese have a fixation about *grissini* length. Longer is better, with the longest *grissini* stretching to nearly three feet. The taste doesn't change, though.

continued

Then there's the discussion about the ideal thickness of *grissini*. The thinner the *grissini*, the crunchier and crisper. But some like them chewy. When *grissini* are fashioned into a short, stubby length the size and diameter of a fat frankfurter, they are no longer termed *grissini*. Instead, they are called *rubate*. And *rubate*, say Piedmontese culinary classicists, are the *real*, authentic breadsticks: the ones served to the king.

You can make *grissini* as you like. Want them chewy? Just make 'em fatter. Crispy? Long and skinny. *Grissini* keep well if tightly wrapped and are easily reheated just before serving. The yield for this recipe is dependent on the size of the *grissini* you make.

3½ cups (12¼ ounces) all-purpose flour

Large pinch of salt

1 cube compressed fresh yeast or

   1 tablespoon dry yeast

½ cup lukewarm water

¼ cup olive oil

Combine the flour and the salt in a small bowl and set aside. Add the yeast to the warm water in a large bowl and whisk to blend. Set aside until it begins to foam. Add the flour to the yeast and stir to create a soft but firm dough. Add the olive oil and add more water if necessary, at little at a time, if the dough is too firm.

Turn out the dough onto a floured work surface and knead until it is smooth and elastic, about 5 minutes. Lightly coat the inside of a large mixing bowl with olive oil and place the dough in it, turning it over to ensure that the ball of dough is coated with oil. Cover with a clean cloth and let rise at room temperature until the dough has nearly doubled in size, about 1 hour.

Preheat the oven to 400°F. Lightly brush one or two heavy baking sheets with olive oil.

Remove the risen dough from the bowl and divide into small pieces. Using the palms of your hands, roll each piece into a thin stick the length of your baking sheet. Place the strips on the oiled baking sheet, leaving 1 inch between them. Bake until the breadsticks are crisp and browned, 10 to 15 minutes. Let cool and serve.

Antipasti That Are Cooked Just Before Serving

※※※

Il Sformato (Flan)

When the Italians put an s in front of a noun, the odds are good that something is being unrolled, unraveled, undone, or—in the case of *sformato*—unformed. In France, this same dish goes by the name *timbale*, or flan.

Who first invented the genre is open to question. Probably it was the Italians, as the foundation of a classic *sformato* is what the Italians call *besciamella* and the French call *béchamel*. We Americans know it as white sauce.

The French say that *sauce béchamel* was invented (not surprisingly) by a Frenchman, the Marquis Louis de Béchameil, who was the maître d'hôtel, or lord steward, for Louis XIV, which puts matters in the late 1600s. That he himself created the sauce is absurd on the face of it, as no nobleman ever put his hand to making a dish in those days.

The Italians retort that this is arriviste posturing. They were cranking out *besciamella* centuries before that, they assert, pointing to a sauce called *balsamella* popular in the Romagna region since the 1300s.

Anyway, for centuries all *sformati* were made with *besciamella*. Nowadays, the trend is to substitute cream, which its proponents submit is more modern. It's also more insipid, as it dilutes the intensity of flavor of whatever ingredient is added. Given their love of intense, pure flavors, it's not surprising to discover that the Piedmontese make their *sformati* in the traditional manner.

In the past, a *sformato* was a classic bourgeois dish, made at home in a large ring mold, not only to help it cook faster and more thoroughly, but so that a rich sauce such as *fonduta* or *finanziera* could be poured into the center well for serving.

Because of this extreme Edwardian richness, *sformati* went out of style and were only resurrected in the 1980s. Restaurateurs across Northern Italy made them extremely chic, serving them as *antipasti*, unmolded from four-ounce ramekins. The popularity of these little *sformati* (variously called *flans* and *tortini*) reached such a pitch of popularity and bizarre invention that the Piedmontese food writer Giovanni Goria felt compelled to plead in print, *"Basta, per favore."* ("Enough, please.") The fashion has now abated somewhat, and the *sformati* offered today are almost all worth keeping.

Of all the Piedmontese *antipasti* I serve to guests, none is received with as much delight as *sformati*. They are easily made in advance and baked just before serving. If you try just one type of Piedmontese *antipasti*, try these.

Red Pepper Flan

Sformato di Peperone Rosso

✵

The province of Cúneo, south of Turin, has a passion for sweet red peppers, which grow in that area abundantly, magnificently, and famously. Anna del Conte, in her superb *Gastronomy of Italy* (1987), notes under her entry for peppers that "the peppers most associated with Italy are the sweet ones which Americans so aptly name bell peppers. These grow everywhere in Italy, but the most highly prized ones come from around Cúneo in Piedmont."

This explains why a favorite Piedmontese *sformato* is made with sweet red peppers. It is a stunner. It is the essence of sweet red peppers and couldn't be easier or more elegant. If you can find them, look for the conical Italian sweet red peppers that some markets offer, especially in late summer and early fall. They are more intense in flavor than the regular square-shaped red pepper, which, in fairness, is plenty good.

WORTH NOTING

Hot-water bath   *Sformati* typically are baked in a hot-water bath, or *bain-marie* (in Italian, *bagnomaria*). Any ovenproof vessel will do, depending upon the size and number of molds to be placed inside. A baking dish or a deep-sided roaster works best. Simply fill the hot-water bath with enough boiling water to come two thirds of the way up the sides of the molds.

The molds   The best molds are straight-sided and plain. A four-ounce plain porcelain ramekin is ideal. A coffee cup works admirably too. Decorative molds with bas-relief designs do not work well because the texture of *sformati* is too coarse.

makes 6 servings

2 to 3 large bell red peppers, stems removed

2 tablespoons unsalted butter

2 tablespoons all-purpose flour

⅔ cup milk

3 large eggs

1½ ounces Parmigiano-Reggiano cheese, grated (6 tablespoons)

Large pinch of salt

Large pinch of freshly ground black pepper

Large pinch of freshly grated nutmeg

Boiling water for the hot-water bath

Preheat the oven to 375°F. Place the peppers on a baking sheet and bake for 30 to 45 minutes, depending on the size of the peppers. Let cool. Cut open the peppers, remove the seeds, and peel off the skin. Place in a colander set in a large bowl and let the peppers drain for an hour or so, if possible. Otherwise, blot dry with paper towels. Puree the peppers in a food processor or blender until smooth, 2 to 3 minutes.

Preheat the oven to 375°F. Generously butter six 4-ounce molds.

Place a heavy-bottomed medium-size saucepan over medium-low heat. Add the butter and, when melted, whisk in the flour. Whisk constantly for 3 minutes to allow the flour to fully absorb the butter. Then dribble in the milk, whisking constantly, to create the *béchamel*. The sauce should be thick, but not gluey. (The amount of milk added determines the consistency.)

Remove from the heat. Whisk in the red pepper puree, then whisk in the eggs. Finally, thoroughly whisk in the cheese, salt, pepper, and nutmeg. (The *sformati* base can be made ahead and refrigerated until needed.)

Pour the red pepper mixture into the prepared molds nearly up to the rim, leaving a little space. Set the molds inside the hot-water-bath vessel (see above). Pour in boiling water, to come two thirds of the way up the sides of the molds. Place the hot-water bath in the oven and bake, uncovered, until the flans puff and are firm to the touch, about 30 minutes.

Remove the bath from the oven. Lift out the molds. Let the *sformati* rest for a minute in their molds, during which time they will deflate slightly and recede from the sides of the molds. Run a thin knife around the inside of each mold. Place a small serving plate over the top of the mold and invert to unmold. Serve immediately.

Parmesan Cheese Flan

Sformato di Parmigiano-Reggiano

This is one of the best *sformati* I've come across in Piedmont, at Guido Ristorante in Costigliole d'Asti, which is Piedmont's greatest restaurant. As always, the quality of the ingredients is everything: Freshly grated Parmigiano-Reggiano is a necessity. Here, an impressive quantity is used, but to a glorious end.

makes 6 servings

2 tablespoons unsalted butter

2 tablespoons all-purpose flour

²/₃ cup milk

3 large eggs

6 ounces Parmigiano-Reggiano cheese, grated (1½ cups)

Large pinch of salt

Boiling water for the hot-water bath

Preheat the oven to 375°F. Generously butter or oil six 4-ounce molds.

Place a heavy-bottomed small saucepan over medium-low heat. Add the butter and, when melted, whisk in the flour. Whisk constantly for 3 minutes to allow the flour to fully absorb the butter. Then, slowly dribble in the milk, whisking constantly, to create the *béchamel*. The sauce should be thick, but not gluey. (The amount of milk added determines the consistency.)

Transfer the sauce to a food processor or blender. Add the eggs and process briefly. Then add the cheese and salt and process for 2 minutes to combine thoroughly. (The *sformati* base can be prepared ahead and refrigerated until needed.)

Pour the cheese mixture into the prepared molds, leaving a little clearance from the top rim. Set the molds inside the hot-water-bath vessel (see page 48). Carefully pour in boiling water to come two thirds of the way up the sides of the molds. Place the hot-water bath in the oven and bake until the flans are puffed and firm, about 30 minutes.

Remove the bath from the oven. Lift out the molds. Let the *sformati* rest for a minute or two in their molds, during which time they will deflate and recede from the sides of the molds. Run a thin knife around the inside of each mold. Place a small serving plate over the top of the mold and invert to unmold. Serve immediately.

Spinach Flan

Sformato di Spinaci

One of the niceties of Italian life is that you can go into a shop and buy a baseball-size sphere of freshly cooked spinach. You then take it home and do what you like with it. Here, our convenience takes the form of frozen spinach, which is one of the few vegetables that really does freeze well.

This popular *sformato* traditionally—and deliciously—is served with a *fonduta* sauce poured over the top (see page 57).

makes 6 servings

3 pounds fresh spinach or 1½ packages
    frozen chopped spinach, defrosted
    and squeezed dry
2 tablespoons unsalted butter
2 tablespoons all-purpose flour
⅔ cup milk

3 large eggs
1½ ounces Parmigiano-Reggiano cheese,
    grated (6 tablespoons)
Large pinch of salt
Freshly grated nutmeg
Boiling water for the hot-water bath

If using fresh spinach, slice off the stems and clean by immersing the leaves in a sink full of lukewarm water. Let the dirt settle to the bottom of the sink, then lift out the leaves. Cook by steaming or boiling for 3 minutes. Drain. When cool, squeeze dry with your hands.

For frozen spinach, heat briefly in a large skillet until warmed through.

Either way, chop the spinach very fine. If using a food processor, be careful not to puree the spinach. Set aside.

Preheat the oven to 375°F. Generously butter or oil six 4-ounce molds.

Place a heavy-bottomed saucepan over medium-low heat. Add the butter and, when melted, whisk in the flour. Whisk constantly for 3 minutes to allow the flour to fully absorb the butter. Then, whisking constantly, slowly dribble in the milk to create the *béchamel*. The sauce should be thick, but not gluey. (The amount of milk added determines the consistency.)

Remove from the heat. Thoroughly whisk in the spinach, eggs, cheese, salt, and nutmeg to taste. (The *sformati* base can be prepared ahead and refrigerated until needed.)

Pour the spinach mixture into the prepared molds, leaving a little clearance from the top rim. Set the molds inside the hot-water-bath vessel (see page 48). Carefully pour in boiling water to come two thirds of the way up the sides of the molds. Place the hot-water bath in the oven and bake until the flans are puffed and firm, about 30 minutes.

Remove the bath from the oven. Lift out the molds. Let the *sformati* rest for a minute or two in their molds, during which time they will deflate and recede from the edges of the molds. Run a thin knife around the inside of each mold. Place a small serving plate over the top of the mold and invert to unmold. Serve immediately.

Potato Flan

Sformato di Patata

This *sformato* is not, this once, "unformed," because the potato puree doesn't unmold as prettily as most others. But it does puff up nicely. So the the best thing is to serve the *sformati* in their molds. This *sformato* reminds you just how good an Idaho potato can be.

Potato *sformato* is also an ideal vehicle for oil flavored with white truffle extract or a paste of porcini mushrooms flavored with white truffle. Both are available in specialty stores. A little goes a long way.

makes 6 servings

2 pounds (about 3) Idaho-type
    (Russet Burbank) potatoes
2 tablespoons unsalted butter
2 tablespoons all-purpose flour
²⁄₃ cup milk
3 large eggs
1¹⁄₂ ounces Parmigiano-Reggiano cheese,
    grated (6 tablespoons)

¹⁄₂ teaspoon salt
2 teaspoons porcini mushroom or white
    truffle paste or 1 teaspoon
    white truffle oil (optional)
Freshly ground black pepper
Freshly grated nutmeg
Boiling water for the hot-water bath

Preheat the oven to 425°F. Bake the potatoes until tender and easily squeezed, about 1 hour. Remove and let cool. Reduce the oven temperature to 375°F.

Split the potatoes open and scoop out the interiors. Puree the potato meat in a food processor, then transfer to a large mixing bowl.

Place a heavy-bottomed small saucepan over medium-low heat. Add the butter and, when melted, whisk in the flour. Whisk constantly for 3 minutes to allow the flour to fully absorb the butter. Then, whisking constantly, slowly dribble in the milk to create the *béchamel*. The sauce should be thick, but not gluey. (The amount of milk added determines the consistency.)

Remove from the heat. Fold the *béchamel* into the potato puree. Then whisk in the eggs, cheese, salt, and mushroom paste or truffle oil, if using. Season with pepper and nutmeg. (The *sformati* base can be prepared ahead and refrigerated until needed.)

Butter or oil six 4-ounce molds. Pour the potato mixture into the molds, leaving a little clearance from the top rim. Set the molds inside the hot-water-bath vessel (see page 48). Carefully pour in boiling water to come two thirds of the way up the sides of the molds. Place the hot-water bath in the oven and bake until the flans are puffed and firm, about 30 minutes.

Remove the bath from the oven. Lift out the molds. Present the *sformati* in their molds, each one set on a serving plate.

Cabbage Flan

Sformato di Cavalo

✿❀✿

This is a "modern" *sformato* in that it employs cream rather than *béchamel* as the binding ingredient. Cabbage lends itself especially well to this approach, as the cream absorbs and amplifies the cabbage flavor. Although it is not essential, the *fonduta* sauce makes a noticeable difference to the flavor of this dish, as the cabbage taste marries beautifully with *fonduta*'s cheese flavor.

makes 6 servings

2 tablespoons unsalted butter

½ small head green cabbage, cored and
    very finely chopped

1 medium-size onion, very finely chopped

2 bay leaves

Salt

Freshly ground black pepper

4 fresh basil leaves

4 large eggs

¾ cup heavy cream

Boiling water for the hot-water bath

Fonduta Piemontese (see page 57)

Preheat the oven to 350°F. Butter six 4-ounce molds.

Add the butter to a large sauté pan placed over medium-low heat. When melted, add the cabbage, onion, and bay leaves, stirring to mix. Season with salt and pepper. Cook, stirring occasionally, until the cabbage is tender and the onion translucent, taking care to keep them both from coloring. Discard the bay leaves and set aside.

Transfer the mixture to a food processor or blender and process to a puree, 2 to 3 minutes. Put the puree through a coarse sieve, if you have one, for a finer texture. Place the puree in a large mixing bowl and whisk in the eggs and cream until well blended.

Pour the puree into the molds. Place the molds inside the hot-water-bath vessel (see page 48) and carefully pour the boiling water to come two thirds up the sides of the molds. Bake until the mixture is firm, about about 30 minutes.

Remove the bath from the oven. Lift out the molds. Let the *sformati* rest for a minute or two in their molds, during which time they will deflate and recede from the sides of the molds. Run a thin knife around the inside of each mold.

Onion Custard

Tartrà di Cipolla

One of Piedmont's classic country dishes is *tartrà*. A variation on *sformato*, this dish is a traditional specialty of the Monferrato zone, north of Asti, as well as being familiar farther south in the Langhe and Cúneo areas.

Today, *tartrà* is one of the more prized *antipasti*. It is characteristically Piedmontese in its richness and simple elegance. In the fall, when fresh porcini mushrooms are available, it often is served unmolded on top of a base of sautéed porcini. The combination is mouthwatering.

Tartrà, unlike other flans served today, is typically baked in a loaf pan, rather than individual molds. The flan is unmolded and served in slices. Unlike *sformati*, a *tartrà* does not use *béchamel* as a binder. Instead, beaten egg whites are used to give it lightness and volume.

Fifty years ago and earlier, middle-class families would serve *tartrà* with sausage links or a slice of cotechino sausage. Poor families made *tartrà* the entire meal, accompanied by polenta. Today it is considered a luxurious antipasto.

makes 6 servings

2 herb bouquets, each composed of 3 fresh sage leaves, 1 bay leaf, 1 large sprig fresh Italian parsley, and 3 small sprigs fresh rosemary

1¾ cups heavy cream

½ cup milk

2 tablespoons unsalted butter

½ onion, sliced

1 garlic clove, finely chopped

6 large eggs, separated

¾ ounce Parmigiano-Reggiano cheese, grated (3 tablespoons)

Pinch of freshly grated nutmeg

½ teaspoon salt

½ teaspoon freshly ground white or black pepper

Boiling water for the hot-water bath

Wrap one of the herb bouquets in a square of cheesecloth and tie it closed.

Pour the the cream and milk into a large mixing bowl. Add the cheesecloth-wrapped herb bouquet to the mixture. Cover and refrigerate for at least 1 hour to allow the herb flavors to infuse the milk mixture; steeping overnight is better yet.

Coarsely chop the second herb bouquet, stripping the leaves from the rosemary stems before chopping. Place the butter in a small sauté pan set over medium-low heat. When the butter has melted, add the chopped herbs, onion, and garlic and cook, stirring, until the onion is soft and translucent. Do not allow it to color.

Place the onion mixture in a food processor and process briefly to puree. Then transfer the mixture to a fine-meshed sieve and push the puree—not too vigorously—through the sieve. Add the puree to the milk mixture. Set aside.

Preheat the oven to 375°F. Butter the inside of a loaf pan (or other baking dish that can be fitted inside of a larger pan to create a water bath).

In a medium-size bowl, whisk the egg yolks together until they begin to thicken, about 2 minutes. Add the yolks to the milk mixture, whisking briefly to combine. Then whisk in the cheese, nutmeg, salt, and pepper.

With a clean whisk or a hand-held mixer, in a large clean mixing bowl, beat the egg whites until stiff peaks form. Fold the beaten egg whites into the egg yolk mixture, using a rubber spatula. Immediately pour the mixture into the buttered loaf pan. Place the pan into a larger baking pan. Pour boiling water into the large pan until it comes halfway up the sides of the smaller one. Set the hot-water bath on the middle shelf of the oven. Bake, uncovered, until the custard is fully set, about 1 hour.

To serve, run a thin knife around the perimeter of the loaf pan, shake gently, and unmold the custard onto a serving plate. Cut into 1-inch-thick slices and serve immediately on warm plates.

Fondue Piedmont Style

Fonduta Piemontese

The usual vision of a dish of melted cheese is Swiss fondue. Piedmont's version, clearly of similar origin, is *fonduta*. But there are significant differences between the two. A Swiss fondue typically is made with Gruyère; *fonduta* is made with Fontina. Gruyère is sharper tasting; Fontina is creamier and more earthy. Swiss fondue is eaten communally, with everyone dipping chunks of bread into the melted cheese dip, while *fonduta* is served individually in warm shallow bowls. Swiss fondue always has white wine incorporated in it and often a splash of *kirschwasser* (cherry brandy); *fonduta* has no such additions.

The commonality between the two is geographical. *Fonduta* originated in what is now Val d'Aosta, an autonomous region in northernmost Piedmont on the Swiss border. Formerly, Val d'Aosta was part of Piedmont. Today, it is its own entity, and French is as much its native language as Italian. Fontina cheese is Val d'Aosta's great specialty.

Over the centuries, *fonduta* became part of Piedmontese cuisine. Its greatest fans are in southern Piedmont in the Langhe and Monferrato zones. This is where Piedmont's famed white truffles are found and the locals there long ago discovered that nothing in this world (and perhaps even the next) tastes better than *fonduta* crowned with fresh white truffle shavings. This was something the natives of Val d'Aosta never could have imagined, as they have no truffles in their sparse, rocky soil.

Fonduta also became a favorite Piedmontese sauce, much as Cheddar cheese sauce is favored by broccoli lovers in this country. The Piedmontese love to spoon *fonduta* over various vegetable *sformati*, molded rice dishes, polenta, and gnocchi. Not least, it gets eaten straight—spooned up or, better yet, conveyed to the mouth by freshly made *grissini*, raw vegetables such as cauliflower, and, in early winter, the artichoke-flavored local vegetable cardoon, which has been cooked beforehand.

Although simple in its ingredients, *fonduta* can be tricky to make, if only because it is heat sensitive. If cooked too long, or at too high a heat, it becomes stringy. It should be satiny, with a smooth texture and glossy sheen. It also must be served immediately, as it does not retain this texture indefinitely.

As for the cheese, although *fonduta* classically and traditionally is made with Fontina from Val d'Aosta, the heretical fact is that today the cheese called Fontal is better. Fontal is the same type of cheese as Fontina, except that where Fontina can be made only within a geographically delimited area in Val d'Aosta, Fontal can be produced anywhere in Piedmont, as well as Lombardy. In fact, until a law was passed in 1951, all the cheese now called Fontal used to be sold as Fontina.

continued

In fairness, Fontina should be the better of the two because it is crafted from raw milk. The better ones are made on farms; lesser versions are industrially produced. Unfortunately, no legal distinction is made between the two, both being stamped with the proper name Fontina Valdostana. Fontal, in comparison, is made from pasteurized milk, in industrial quantities. Too often, Fontina Valdostana costs more, with no appreciable difference in taste from the cheaper, equally good Fontal.

WORTH NOTING

Soaking in milk One of the tricks to making *fonduta* is allowing the cheese to soak in milk for several hours or, better yet, overnight. This softens the cheese, making it less likely to become stringy when heated.

Using a double boiler The safe way to cook *fonduta* is in a double boiler, which ensures a low, even heat. However, a deft cook can also make *fonduta* easily and successfully in a heavy-bottomed saucepan, taking care about the heat.

Adding truffle paste or truffle oil Some cooks like to add the taste of white truffles to their *fonduta* with white truffle paste or oil, stirred in just before serving. If using white truffle paste, add 3 tablespoons. If using oil, add ¹⁄₂ teaspoon, then taste and continue adding a few drops at a time until the desired flavor intensity is reached.

makes 4 to 6 servings

10 ounces Fontal cheese, cut into small dice
1 cup milk

¹⁄₄ cup (¹⁄₂ stick) unsalted butter
4 large egg yolks

Soak the cheese in the milk for several hours or, preferably, overnight in the refrigerator.

Melt the butter in the top half of a double boiler set over gently simmering water. When it has completely melted, add the cheese-and-milk mixture.

Whisking constantly, add the egg yolks to the cheese one at a time. Continue whisking until the cheese is transformed into a satiny, glossy, thick-textured liquid, about 10 minutes. As soon as this texture is achieved, pour the *fonduta* immediately into warm (but not hot) shallow bowls—or over a *sformato*—and serve without delay.

Flat Omelette with Mint, Sage, and Parsley

Frittata di Erbe Aromatiche

❦

This is a classic Piedmontese frittata. The proportions of the herbs can, and should, vary depending on what you've got on hand. Fresh herbs are essential.

makes 1 serving

2 large eggs, lightly and gently beaten

1/2 ounce Parmigiano-Reggiano cheese, grated (2 tablespoons)

4 fresh mint leaves, finely chopped

4 large fresh sage leaves, finely chopped

Small handful of fresh Italian parsley leaves, finely chopped

Salt to taste

2 tablespoons olive oil

Mix together all the ingredients except the oil.

Place a nonstick skillet over medium-low heat and add the oil. When it is hot, swirl to distribute it in the pan and immediately add the egg mixture. Shake the pan to distribute the egg mixture evenly. Using a fork, expose the uncooked egg on top to the heat of the pan by gently scraping away the frittata in various spots, letting the uncooked egg flow in to fill the exposed area.

When the frittata is three-quarters cooked (about 2 minutes, depending upon its thickness and the heat), cook the top side by flipping; by inverting the frittata onto a plate and then sliding it uncooked side down back into the skillet; or by leaving the frittata in the pan and placing it under a hot broiler. Cook very briefly on the second side, no more than 1 minute. Slide the frittata onto a plate, slice into wedges, and serve.

Flat Omelette with Onions

Frittata di Cipolle

❧❦❧

The frittata is well known as Italy's version of a flat, rather than rolled, omelette. It is a staple of the Piedmontese antipasto table, typically served in wedge-shaped slices, one to a customer. Many Piedmontese don't even bother to make frittatas for themselves, preferring instead to purchase them freshly made at their local *salumeria*, or delicatessen. They then bring them home and reheat them.

Perhaps the most important feature of a frittata is that, unlike a French rolled omelette, it uses egg more as a binder for a substantial quantity of some informing flavor such as onions, parsley or other herb, or spinach. This is why the average frittata, serving one, employs just two eggs and why the amount of the flavoring ingredient almost overwhelms the quantity of egg. A spinach frittata in Piedmont is almost solid green in color.

Another green-hued specialty is the much-loved traditional frittata using a minty, leafy herb called San Pietro, the botanical name of which is *Tanacetum balsamita*. In English it goes by several names—costmary, mint geranium, or alecost.

As with rolled omelettes, tastes vary as to how well cooked and how thick or thin the frittata should be. Some Piedmontese like their frittatas well browned and even slightly dried out. Others prefer a thicker, moister rendition. My own preference is for thin but tender, so I use a large pan (nine and a half inches across at the base). Others like a small pan, half that size, which creates a thicker, smaller frittata.

Another distinguishing feature of a frittata is that the flavoring ingredient is mixed in with the eggs *before* they are poured into the pan. This means that anything requiring prior cooking, such as onions, should be allowed to cool before being added to the beaten eggs so as not to coagulate them.

WORTH NOTING

Beating the eggs It's best not to overbeat the eggs and, especially, not to be so vigorous as to create air bubbles. That can change the texture of the frittata.

The onions An onion frittata can have differing textures depending upon how the onions are chopped or sliced. The following recipe calls for relatively large slices of onion that are well cooked and lightly browned. It is a bit rustic, but the onion flavor is superb. Alternatively, the onion can be coarsely chopped, creating a smoother frittata mixture. One flavor variation is to add a large pinch of very finely chopped fresh rosemary to the onion mixture.

Heat level   Unlike French rolled omelettes, frittatas traditionally are cooked slowly over low heat, with the cook gently breaking up the egg mass with a fork while it is cooking to expose it better to the heat. If you are making a thin frittata in a large skillet, it is possible to cook over high heat, but you need to work quickly to keep the eggs from toughening.

Cooking the other side   Once the frittata is cooked on one side, the age-old challenge of cooking the flip side arises. Three options are present: flipping the frittata; inverting the frittata onto a plate and sliding it back into the pan; or leaving the frittata in the pan and placing it under a hot broiler to cook the top. All three work equally well.

makes 1 serving

1 large onion, peeled

5 tablespoons olive oil

2 large eggs

Large pinch of salt

Freshly ground black pepper

Slice the onion in half along its equator. Then slice the two hemispheres into quarters (or eighths, if the onion is very large). Place each onion quarter on its side and slice crosswise into $1/4$-inch-thick slices. Heat 3 tablespoons of the olive oil in a medium-size sauté pan over medium heat and cook the onion, stirring, until lightly browned. Set aside to cool.

In a medium-size bowl, lightly beat together the eggs, salt, and pepper to taste. Add the cooled onion slices. Mix well.

Place a nonstick skillet over medium-low heat and add the remaining 2 tablespoons oil. When it is hot, swirl to distribute it in the pan and immediately add the egg mixture. Shake the pan to distribute the egg mixture evenly. Using a fork, expose the uncooked egg on top to the heat of the pan by gently scraping away the frittata in various spots, letting the uncooked egg flow in to fill the exposed area.

When the frittata is three-quarters cooked (about 2 minutes, depending upon its thickness and the heat), cook the top side by flipping; by inverting the frittata onto a plate and then sliding it uncooked side down back into the skillet; or by leaving the frittata in the pan and placing it under a hot broiler. Cook very briefly on the second side, no more than 1 minute. Slide the frittata onto a plate, slice into wedges, and serve.

Potato Cake with Smoked Salmon
Tortina di Patata con Salmone Affumicato

I came across this dish at a country restaurant improbably named—considering it is located in the village of Ghislarengo, smack in the rice fields of northern Piedmont—Ristorante Roma. The food is traditional, the wine offerings are superb, and the specialties couldn't get more local. Ghislarengo lies between the famous wine village of Gattinara (six miles to the north) and the equally famous rice village of Arborio (two and a half miles to the south). No prizes for guessing the house food and wine specialties.

Piedmontese cooking, like all vital, living cuisines, is open to dishes that are untraditional in fact but sympathetic in spirit. This is one such. A *tortino*, or little cake, of potatoes can be found in many parts of Italy. This version is like a Russian blini: thin, smooth, and an ideal vehicle for something on top. A slice of cold-smoked salmon is an international touch, the inspiration perhaps derived from Piedmont's traditional smoked trout. The potato pancake is good enough on its own to use as a side dish. Although best served immediately, the pancake can be made ahead of time and kept warm.

WORTH NOTING

Type of smoked salmon Smoked salmon comes in two forms: cold-smoked and hot-smoked. Cold-smoked salmon is silky and thin as lingerie. Many delicatessens sell cold-smoked salmon, such as Scottish salmon. (Cold-smoked salmon is not the same as lox, by the way, which is soaked in brine and never smoked.) Hot-smoked salmon typically is marinated and sold in chunks.

For each pancake:

1 small waxy-type potato (¼ pound), peeled and boiled in water to cover until tender

1 large egg

2 tablespoons all-purpose flour

1 tablespoon unsalted butter or olive oil

1 slice cold-smoked salmon

Preheat the oven to 400°F. Lightly oil a baking sheet and put it in the oven to heat for about 9 minutes.

Puree the potato in a food processor or blender. Add the egg and flour and process again just to combine.

Melt the butter in a medium-size nonstick skillet over medium heat. When melted, add the potato mix to the pan and shake the pan to distribute it evenly. Let cook for about 1 minute, then either flip the pancake or slide it onto a plate and invert the plate over the skillet. Let cook for another minute on the second side.

To finish the pancake, slide it onto the hot baking sheet. Place it in the oven for 1 minute, to give the pancake a small but noticeable "rise." Transfer to a warm serving plate and drape the slice of cold-smoked salmon on top. Serve immediately.

Flat Omelette with Salami

Frittata Rognosa

As is true of Italians in many parts of Italy, the Piedmontese have an affection for salami. Here, it is allied to a frittata, helped along by a handful of freshly grated Parmesan. For devotees of salami and eggs, this is yet another delectable rendition.

makes 1 serving

2 ounces Italian-style salami, finely
    chopped
2 large eggs
1/2 ounce Parmigiano-Reggiano cheese,
    grated (2 tablespoons)

Salt to taste
Freshly ground black pepper
2 tablespoons olive oil

Mix together all the ingredients except the oil. Place a nonstick skillet over medium-low heat and add the oil. When it is hot, swirl to distribute it in the pan and immediately add the egg mixture. Shake the pan to distribute the egg mixture evenly. Using a fork, expose the uncooked egg on top to the heat of the pan by gently scraping away the frittata in various spots, letting the uncooked egg flow in to fill the exposed area.

When the frittata is three-quarters cooked (about 2 minutes, depending upon its thickness and the heat), cook the top side by flipping; by inverting the frittata onto a plate and then sliding it uncooked side down back into the skillet; or by leaving the frittata in the pan and placing it under a hot broiler. Cook very briefly on the other side, no more than 1 minute. Slide the frittata onto a plate, slice into wedges, and serve.

Trout Seasoned with Mountain Herbs

Trote alle Erbe di Montagna

As is well known, the best fish dishes usually are the simplest. This version of trout with herbs is magnificently flavorful. It takes little imagination to see how a native fisherman, high on an alpine stream, would catch a few trout, clean them, open a pouch of herbs and spices carried along for just this purpose, and panfry the herbed trout over an open fire.

The rest of us have to content ourselves with store-bought trout—which can be very fresh and good—prepared in an oven, which is actually both more convenient and better than panfrying, I think. The portions here are slightly large for an antipasto, but traditionally the trout are always presented whole. The trick is to secure very small trout.

makes 6 servings

Small handful of fresh thyme leaves, finely chopped

6 juniper berries, crushed and finely chopped

8 fresh sage leaves, finely chopped

6 fresh mint leaves, finely chopped

Leaves from 1 large sprig fresh rosemary, finely chopped

4 garlic cloves, finely chopped

Salt

6 small trout (about 1 pound each), cleaned and dried

6 tablespoons olive oil

6 lemon wedges

Preheat the oven to 375°F. Lightly grease a baking sheet or pan large enough to hold all 6 trout.

Divide the chopped herbs and garlic into 6 equal portions. Salt the interior of each trout. Spread a portion of the chopped herbs into the belly cavity of each trout.

Heat the olive oil in a large nonstick skillet. When the oil is hot, lightly brown the trout on both sides. Transfer the browned trout to the baking sheet or pan. Bake, uncovered, until the flesh is very firm when pressed, about 10 minutes. Serve hot, on warm plates, accompanied by the lemon wedges.

Oven-Baked Fish Bourgeois Style

Pesce al Forno al Stile Borghese

✦❦✦

This is an old, and still wonderful, dish much fancied by upper-middle-class Piedmontese in the late 1800s. Here, white sauce (*besciamella* or *béchamel*) comes into play, flavored with finely chopped Italian parsley. Only in Piedmont do you still come across this sort of rich, simple goodness. Any sort of firm-fleshed white fish, such as halibut, bass, Chilean sea bass, or flounder, works perfectly in this dish.

makes 6 servings

One 1½-pound firm, white-fleshed
   fish fillet
Milk to barely cover the fish
For the sauce:
2 tablespoons unsalted butter
2 tablespoons all-purpose flour
2 cups of the milk used to poach the fish

2 garlic cloves, very finely chopped
12 salt-packed capers, rinsed and
   crushed
3 tablespoons finely chopped fresh
   Italian parsley leaves
Freshly ground black pepper
Freshly grated nutmeg

Preheat the oven to 400°F.

Place the fish in a saucepan just large enough to hold it. Add enough milk to just barely cover the fish. Bring to a boil, then immediately reduce the heat so the the milk barely simmers. Poach in the simmering milk until the fish is very firm and bright white, about 10 minutes per inch thickness of fish. Remove the fish from the pan and set aside to drain. Reserve the poaching milk for making the white sauce.

To make the sauce, place a heavy-bottomed medium-size saucepan over medium-low heat. Add the butter and, when melted, whisk in the flour. Whisk constantly for 3 minutes to allow the flour to fully absorb the butter. Then, whisking constantly, dribble in the milk to create the white sauce. It should be thick, but not gluey. (The amount of milk added determines the consistency.)

Remove the sauce from the heat. Whisk in the garlic, capers, and parsley and season with pepper and nutmeg.

Place the poached fish in a baking pan. Spoon all of the sauce over the fish. Bake, uncovered, until the sauce begins to bubble slightly, about 8 minutes. Serve immediately.

Stuffed Cabbage Leaves

Caponèt di Cavalo

✺

Virtually every European cuisine has its version of stuffed cabbage. The Piedmontese use the beautiful, deeply crinkled Savoy cabbage. Experiment reveals that regular green and red cabbage, as well as Swiss chard, work equally well. The filling is flavorful, thanks in part to the addition of salami and Parmigiano cheese to the ground meat. Using some ground veal is very desirable as it adds a juiciness. The balance is ground turkey, chicken, or pork, each of which is equally effective, but pork is most traditional. Ground turkey, because it is so low in fat, is best moistened with a little milk beforehand.

makes 6 servings

1¾ cups water

½ cup short- or long-grain white rice

3 ounces salami

¼ pound ground veal

¼ pound ground pork, turkey, or chicken

1 ounce Parmigiano-Reggiano cheese, grated (¼ cup)

2 large eggs

2 garlic cloves, finely chopped

Small handful of fresh Italian parsley leaves, finely chopped

6 fresh sage leaves, finely chopped, or 1 teaspoon dried

¼ teaspoon salt, or more to taste

Freshly ground black pepper

6 large Savoy cabbage leaves, plus a few extra as a backup

Extra virgin olive oil

In a small saucepan over high heat, bring ½ cup of the water to a boil. Add the rice, cover, and immediately reduce the heat to low. Let cook until the rice is tender and the water absorbed, about 20 minutes. Remove from the heat and set aside.

Combine the rice, the remaining 1¼ cups water, the salami, veal, pork, cheese, eggs, garlic, parsley, sage, salt, and pepper to taste in a large mixing bowl. Using your hands, blend the ingredients thoroughly. Fry up a spoonful of the filling and taste when cooked to check the seasonings. Adjust as desired.

To make the cabbage rolls, bring a large pot of water to a boil. Lower each cabbage leaf into the water and let cook for just 30 seconds. This softens the leaf and makes it more flexible. Remove from the water, drain, and blot dry with paper towels. It's best to have a few leaves in reserve, just in case one rips while being filled: If so, wrap another leaf around the original one to create a secure wrapper.

Preheat the oven to 400°F. Butter a medium-size baking dish.

Place a cabbage leaf flat on a work surface. Place one sixth of the filling in the center of the leaf, flattening the filling slightly. Fold the bottom of the leaf up over the filling, then fold over the sides and roll it up. Place the roll, seam side down, in the buttered baking dish. Repeat with the remaining leaves and filling.

Bake until the cabbage rolls are firm and have an interior temperature of 170°F, about 30 minutes. Serve hot on warm plates, garnished with a drizzle of extra virgin olive oil.

Piedmont's Trout Salads

Piedmont's repertoire of fish dishes is quite limited. Although today you can find fish shops in all the major towns, as well as at the many weekly markets where mobile vendors come to sell their wares, the Piedmontese use recipes from other regions for this very modern availability of fresh fish.

The only fresh fish that used to be available, apart from carp and the various small fish caught in rivers (and deep-fried, like smelt), was trout. Over the years, various trout recipes emerged, many of them combining trout with traditional Piedmontese likings for anchovies, vinegar, and artichokes.

There's no sense pretending that the Piedmontese have a great deftness with fish. Theirs is a hearty appetite and fish, somehow, does not stir them deeply. But there are some Piedmontese trout recipes that are really good. They are dishes that most trout fans will likely never have previously tasted.

Typically, these dishes serve as an antipasto or as a light lunch, in the form of "salads." Except in villages high in the Alps, you will almost never simply be served a whole trout with no additional complication. That strikes the Piedmontese as too crude. Salads are the preferred vehicle in large part because trout are warm-weather fare, as that's when they are caught.

Not least, all of these recipes are amenable to other firm-fleshed fish, such as perch, cod, pike, monkfish, or salmon. What makes them so memorable is their unusual interplay of tastes.

Master Recipe for Poaching Trout

makes 4 servings

8 cups water	*1 large garlic clove, lightly crushed*
1 cup dry white wine	*1 celery stalk, thickly sliced*
¼ cup white wine vinegar	*6 black peppercorns, lightly bruised*
1 medium-size onion, thickly sliced	*2 small trout, cleaned*

Place all the ingredients except the trout in a nonreactive casserole or other large pot. Bring the poaching liquid to a boil and immediately reduce to a simmer. Let simmer for about 15 minutes to extract the flavor from the ingredients.

Raise the heat to high. Lower the trout into the simmering water. When the water returns to a simmer, adjust the heat so that the liquid just barely bubbles. Let poach until the fish is firm and flakes easily, 10 to 12 minutes. Remove the trout from the liquid and let cool. Strain the poaching liquid and reserve to use as a stock for a fish-based risotto or a fish soup or stew.

When the trout is cool, remove the skin and fins and discard. Separate the fillet on each side of trout from the spine. Gently flake the trout flesh into large flakes. Combine these pieces with any of the following to create a trout salad.

Trout Salad with Potatoes

Insalata di Trote con Patate

Effectively, this is similar to a French-style potato salad to which flakes of poached trout and a bit of garlic have been added. Depending upon my taste that day, I sometimes add a splash of red wine vinegar to the mix just before serving, as I, too, share the Piedmontese liking for acidity. Also, I sometimes add thinly sliced green onions, for both color and taste.

makes 4 servings

6 medium-size waxy-type potatoes, peeled

Extra virgin olive oil

2 large garlic cloves, sliced as thin as possible

2 green onions (scallions), trimmed and thinly sliced

2 poached trout, skinned, boned, and flaked (see page 68)

Salt

Freshly ground black pepper

Steam or boil the potatoes until a fork penetrates them easily. When cool enough to handle, cut into ⅛-inch-thick slices.

In a small amount of oil in a small saucepan, very gently cook the garlic slices over the lowest possible heat. Do not allow the garlic to color.

Combine the potatoes, garlic, green onions, and trout in a large mixing bowl. Season with salt and pepper. Drizzle a little of the olive oil used to cook the garlic (or use fresh oil) over the dish. Transfer to individual serving plates and serve at room temperature.

Trout Salad with Artichokes

Insalata di Trote con Carciofi

Nowhere else have I come across this memorably good combination of trout with arti-chokes. Not only is the pink-green color combination pretty, but the tastes are superb. This recipe is Ligurian-influenced, as Ligurian cooking abounds in artichokes.

makes 4 servings

2 globe artichokes

2 poached trout, skinned, boned, and
  flaked (see page 68)

Salt

Freshly ground black pepper

Extra virgin olive oil

Juice of 1 lemon

Place the artichokes in a large pot of boiling water. Let them cook until the leaves are easily pulled off, about 25 minutes, depending on their size. Remove and let drain. When cool enough to han-dle, remove the leaves from the base and discard; scrape the top of the base until it is completely clean. Slice the cleaned artichoke bottoms into $1/8$-inch-thick slices.

In a large mixing bowl, combine the artichoke bottoms and trout. Season with salt and pepper and drizzle extra virgin olive oil and the lemon juice over the dish to complete. Transfer to individual serving plates and serve at room temperature.

Trout Salad with Zucchini and Mustard Sauce

Insalata di Trote con Zucchine e Salsa di Senape

This trout salad truly is unusual. Not only does it make a pretty summer presentation, but the melding of mustard and zucchini with trout is especially refreshing to a palate wilted by the heat. Zucchini needs a bit of zip, and mustard does the trick.

makes 4 servings

4 small zucchini, sliced diagonally into
    $1/2$-inch-thick slices
$1/4$ cup Dijon mustard
Small handful of fresh Italian parsley
    leaves, very finely chopped
2 small garlic cloves, very finely chopped

8 salt-packed capers, rinsed and crushed
6 tablespoons extra virgin olive oil, or
    more to taste
Juice of 1 lemon, or more to taste
2 poached trout, skinned, boned, and
    flaked (see page 68)

With just a little water added, cook the zucchini slices in a large nonstick pan over medium-low heat, uncovered, tossing them from time to time so that they cook evenly on both sides. Let them cook only until just cooked through but still slightly crunchy, about 4 minutes. Set aside to cool.

To make the sauce, combine the the mustard, parsley, garlic, capers, oil, and lemon juice in a large mixing bowl and whisk to blend. Add the zucchini and trout to the sauce and toss gently to mix thoroughly. Taste for seasoning. Add more lemon juice or olive oil as desired to increase or reduce the pungency of the sauce. Transfer to individual serving plates and serve at room temperature.

Trout Salad with Anchovies

Insalata di Trote con Acciughe

Can the Piedmontese ever resist adding anchovies to anything? It's doubtful. They really *love* anchovies and find a use for them seemingly everywhere except desserts. Here, trout get the treatment and, I have to admit, the old anchovy trick works yet again, as their taste throws the more subtle trout flavor into relief.

makes 4 servings

8 whole salted anchovies, rinsed, filleted, soaked briefly in cold water, and drained

2 poached trout, skinned, boned, and flaked (see page 68)

1 tablespoon salt-packed capers, rinsed

3 tablespoons finely chopped fresh Italian parsley leaves

Juice of 1 lemon

Extra virgin olive oil

Blot the anchovies dry on paper towels, and chop into small pieces (about the size of a match head). Combine the anchovies, trout, capers, parsley, and lemon juice in a large mixing bowl. Add olive oil to taste and transfer to individual serving plates. Serve at room temperature.

Soups

*In all of Piedmont, soup was the dish most widely seen and, some years ago,
broths and soups were preferred even over pasta. To those condemned to death,
before going to the gallows, being offered a ladle of meat broth was
considered the last grant of the joy of life itself.*

Elma Schena and Adriano Ravera
La Cucina di "Madonna Lesina" (1988)

Soup is the universal food. It is filling, warming (or cooling), and satisfying and,
not least, it transforms a few basic ingredients into a proper meal. It's no surprise that every cuisine in the world has its signature soups.

Piedmont is no different. Most of its soups are what you'd expect from a region
with so many mountains and valleys, subject to a Continental climate with foggy,
chilling autumns and cold winters: soups that are filling and intensely flavorful. They
are uncomplicated yet uncommonly good. Rice figures prominently in many
Piedmontese soups, which makes sense given the extent of Piedmont's rice farming
in the Po Valley.

Chestnut Soup with Milk and Rice

Minestra di Riso, Latte, e Castagne

Chestnuts abound in many parts of Piedmont and were a staple—sometimes too much so—in many of the mountainous zones where agriculture was, literally, an uphill fight. Not surprisingly, an extensive repertoire of dishes incorporating chestnuts evolved, with Piedmont's famed *marrons glacés* representing its highest refinement and soups such as this being more approachable. Dried chestnuts were traditionally employed in this ancient dish; they are found in Asian groceries as well as Italian delicatessens.

This is an old-fashioned, filling winter soup typical of the cooking in Piedmont's mountain areas. It is the sort of consolatory soup you make on foggy fall days when the weather seems threatening.

makes 6 servings

*1 pound unshelled fresh chestnuts or
½ pound dried or vacuum-packed
peeled fresh chestnuts*

1 quart milk

1 cup Arborio rice

1 teaspoon sugar

1 teaspoon unsalted butter

For fresh chestnuts, using a paring knife, cut a small cross in the rounded side of each nut, penetrating the thick outer covering. This not only aids in peeling, but also prevents the chestnuts from bursting when heated.

Place the chestnuts in a large pot and cover generously with water. Bring to a boil and simmer for 15 to 25 minutes, until you can squeeze a chestnut easily. Drain and peel, removing both the outer shell and the papery inner peel.

For dried chestnuts, soak overnight in warm water. Drain, then place them in a saucepan of gently boiling water and cook for 1 hour before draining and adding to the soup.

In a heavy-bottomed large saucepan, bring the milk to a near-boil. Add the rice and let cook gently for 15 minutes at a near-simmer. Add the sugar and butter, stirring to blend. Add the cooked chestnuts and serve. (This soup is more flavorful if allowed to sit for several hours and then gently reheated before serving.)

Mushroom Soup
Zuppa di Funghi Porcini

All over Northern Italy you find versions of soup based on fresh porcini mushrooms. They are more similar than not, based on the sensible idea that the best thing you can do is not get in the way of all that glorious porcini flavor.

Any of a number of other flavorful mushrooms can be used, or a mix of several. Chanterelle mushrooms would be an excellent choice, as would a mix of regular supermarket mushrooms with fresh or dried shiitake mushrooms.

makes 6 servings

1 pound fresh porcini mushrooms, wiped clean

1 tablespoon unsalted butter

1 small onion, coarsely chopped

Small handful of fresh Italian parsley leaves, finely chopped, plus 1 tablespoon finely chopped fresh Italian parsley leaves

4 cups homemade chicken (see page 109), beef, or veal stock

2 large egg yolks

2 ounces Parmigiano-Reggiano cheese, grated ($^1/_2$ cup)

Extra virgin olive oil

Salt

Freshly ground black pepper

Toasted croutons for garnish

Remove the stems from the mushroom caps and reserve for making stock. Cut the caps crosswise into thin slices. Set aside.

Add the butter to a large sauté pan over medium heat. When melted, add the onion and the chopped handful of parsley, stirring to blend. Let cook, stirring, until the onion is translucent, about 5 minutes, taking care not to let it color.

Add the porcini slices and cook briefly, about 3 minutes, stirring gently to blend with the parsley and onion. Pour in the stock, raise the heat to medium-high, and bring to a simmer. Reduce the heat and let simmer for 10 minutes. Remove from the heat.

In a small mixing bowl, whisk together the egg yolks, the remaining 1 tablespoon chopped parsley, and the cheese. Slowly pour the mixture into the soup, whisking constantly. Season with salt, pepper and a dollop of olive oil. Serve with toasted croutons.

Traditional Chick-pea Soup

La Cisrà (Zuppa di Ceci)

❧

Cisrà is one of the oldest Piedmontese recipes still popular today. It is mostly wintertime fare, although some fanciers eat it in summer, served lukewarm. Traditionally, it is served on the still-revered Day of the Dead (called *I Santi*), November 2. Relatives take flowers— usually chrysanthemums—to the family mausoleum and *cisrà* is part of the lunch when everyone returns home.

In his *Gran Dizionario della Gastronomia del Piemonte,* Sandro Doglio says that *cisrà* was served in the town piazza as part of the communal celebration of the Pentecost (the seventh Sunday after Easter). The chick-pea, having three points, symbolically represented the Trinity.

The following version, which uses dried porcini mushrooms, is more elaborate (and better) than most. *Cisrà* is an exceedingly simple dish to prepare, as little need be done once the chick-peas are cooked other than combining all of the ingredients and letting them simmer together. Like so many bean soups, *cisrà* is even better the next day. This hearty soup is a meal in itself, needing nothing more than a good, rustic red wine alongside, such as Barbera.

makes 6 servings

1½ pounds dried chick-peas, soaked overnight in water to cover

1 medium-size onion, coarsely chopped

2 large leeks, white and pale green parts, sliced crosswise and thoroughly rinsed

5 garlic cloves, coarsely chopped

1 large carrot, thinly sliced

1 small turnip, peeled and thinly sliced

1 celery stalk, sliced

1 large sprig fresh rosemary

10 fresh sage leaves, coarsely chopped

3 bay leaves

1 teaspoon salt

Freshly ground black pepper

Small handful of fresh Italian parsley leaves, coarsely chopped

2 medium-size waxy-type potatoes, peeled and cut into quarters or eighths

½ ounce dried porcini mushrooms, soaked in hot water until softened and drained

4 Savoy cabbage leaves, rinsed and tough ribs removed

Extra virgin olive oil

Freshly grated Parmigiano-Reggiano cheese

Drain the chick-peas, place in a large pot, cover with fresh cold water, and bring to a boil. Immediately lower the heat to a simmer, add the onion, leeks, garlic, carrot, turnip, celery, rosemary, sage, bay leaves, salt, and pepper to taste, and stir to combine. Let simmer until the chick-peas are tender, about 2 hours.

Add the parsley, potatoes, mushrooms, and cabbage leaves. Add more water if the soup has become too dense or dry. Let simmer until the potatoes are cooked through.

Serve in large bowls, adding a generous dollop of extra virgin olive oil just before serving. Serve with Parmigiano alongside.

Potato, Bread, and Broccoli Rabe Soup

Zuppa di Patate, Pane, e Rape

Great soups, like orchestral arrangements, are more than the sum of their parts. This is a prime example. Anatomized, it doesn't look like much: potatoes, bread, and a vegetable. But combined—and admittedly enchanced by the always-elevating presence of olive oil and Parmesan cheese—this soup emerges as mouthwatering. The broccoli rabe, with its penetrating, bracing flavor, is the reason why.

Broccoli rabe, also called rape, is a stringy-looking version of broccoli. Its virtue is a more intense flavor, accentuated by a slight bitterness. With the vogue for Italian cooking, broccoli rabe has become more commonly available. It's worth searching out, as it makes a noticeable difference in this recipe. Good alternatives, if available, are mustard greens, Swiss chard, or chunks of green cabbage.

Fans of Tuscan food will find an echo of that region's famous bread soup, *ribollita*, in this dish. Here, though, beans are replaced with potatoes. Both soups are dense, thick, and filling. Worth noting is the risottolike technique of adding the stock a ladleful at a time. This ensures that the potatoes are cooked yet retain a desired firmness. This is the sort of soup that makes you pray for cold weather.

makes 6 servings

8 cups chicken or beef stock (or a mixture of both)

1 pound broccoli rabe, cut into 2-inch lengths

3 large waxy-type potatoes, peeled and thickly sliced

Homemade croutons or toasted slices of rustic bread

Salt

Freshly ground black pepper

Freshly grated Parmigiano-Reggiano cheese

Bring the stock to a simmer in a large saucepan. Place a heavy-bottomed large ovenproof saucepan over medium heat. Add the broccoli rabe and potatoes. Add ladlefuls of hot stock to the rabe and potatoes and let the vegetables cook in the stock. When nearly dry, add another ladleful of hot stock. Repeat until the rabe and potato slices are cooked through but not mushy.

Preheat the oven to 400°F.

Add the croutons or bread slices to the cooked vegetables. Pour in the remaining stock. Season with salt and pepper. The soup should be thick and dense; if it is not, reduce it over medium heat. Sprinkle a generous layer of grated Parmesan over the top.

Place the soup in the oven, uncovered, for 5 minutes to melt the cheese. Alternatively, the soup can be put into individual ovenproof bowls, sprinkled with Parmigiano, and then briefly placed in the hot oven.

Pasta and Lentil Soup
Zuppa di Pasta e Lenticchie

🙣

All over Northern Italy, lentils are a traditional New Year's dish. They symbolize a hope for wealth in the coming year. In Piedmont, especially in the mountain elevations, this hearty, warming soup is the New Year's Eve dish of choice. It can be made well ahead of time and reheated, if you add the pasta only shortly before it is served. A tray of crusty focaccia with onions is an ideal accompaniment.

makes 6 servings

8 ounces brown lentils, rinsed

8 cups chicken or beef stock

1 fresh pork hock or pig's trotter, cut in half by the butcher

2 large garlic cloves, finely chopped

¾ teaspoon salt

Freshly ground black pepper

Additional stock or dry white wine if necessary

6 ounces short dried pasta, such as rigatoni, ditali, ziti, or fusilli

Small handful of fresh Italian parsley leaves, finely chopped

¼ cup olive oil

Freshly grated Parmigiano-Reggiano cheese

Put the lentils, stock, pork hock, garlic, salt, and pepper to taste in a heavy-bottomed large saucepan over high heat. Bring to a boil and immediately lower the heat to the barest simmer. Let barely simmer, partially covered, until the meat falls easily from the bone of the hock, about 2 hours. If the soup begins to dry out, add more stock, water, or white wine.

Remove the pork from the soup, let it cool, and strip the meat from the bone. Discard the bone and chop or shred the meat, with the skin, into bite-size pieces. Return the meat to the soup.

Just before serving, raise the heat to high, bring the soup to a boil, and add the pasta. Let boil gently until the pasta is cooked, 10 to 15 minutes, depending upon the shape. Stir in the parsley and olive oil and serve in large bowls, accompanied by grated Parmigiano.

Little "Marbles" in Broth

Palline di Carne con le Mele in Brodo

This soup uses the the same chopped veal (or turkey) with apples mixture as *Polpette con le Mele* (see page 248). But instead of shaping the meat mixture into patties, you create *palline*, or large marbles. These are briefly sautéed, then added to a good chicken or beef broth and served with freshly grated Parmigiano. The combination of ground meat with grated apple is a crowd pleaser and it shows effectively in this soup.

This soup can be prepared well ahead of time, but do not add the "marbles" to the soup until just before serving, or they will get soggy. The meat mixture will keep its flavor for up to twenty-four hours, refrigerated.

makes 6 servings

½ pound ground veal

1 tart apple, such as Granny Smith,
    peeled, cored and grated or
    finely chopped

¼ cup milk

1 large egg

1 garlic clove, finely chopped

1 ½ ounces Parmigiano-Reggiano cheese,
    grated (6 tablespoons), plus extra
    for serving

Salt

Freshly grated black pepper

1 tablespoon unsalted butter

½ cup dry white wine

8 cups chicken or beef stock, preferably
    homemade

In a large mixing bowl, combine the veal, apple, milk, egg, garlic, and cheese, and season with salt and pepper. Mix with your hands to blend well. Form the meat mixture into large marbles.

In a large sauté pan over medium-high heat, melt the butter. When melted, add the "marbles" and brown on all sides. Add the wine, raise the heat to high, and let cook, uncovered, until the wine is evaporated. Set aside.

Bring the stock to a simmer in a large pot. Add the "marbles" to the stock and let simmer briefly to heat them. Serve with freshly grated Parmigiano alongside.

Garlic Soup

Zuppa d'Aglio

By now, garlic soup has become, if not well known, at least not the oddity it once was. For that we have to thank Julia Child, who popularized it. Although it is usually associated with Provence, Piedmont too has its version of garlic soup. The Piedmontese version is distinctively good, and different from the Provençal version. The difference is the use of fresh sage and a subtle but electric zip from some hot red pepper.

As in all garlic soups, the garlic taste is so tame that those who have never previously savored a garlic soup are always astonished that something as fierce as fresh garlic could emerge so civilized.

make 6 servings

6 cups cold water

2 cups chicken stock

6 heads garlic, cut in half

20 fresh sage leaves, coarsely chopped

Small handful of fresh Italian parsley
   leaves

Leaves from 1 large sprig fresh thyme

1 bay leaf

1 small dried hot red pepper, cut in half
   and seeds removed

6 tablespoons milk

Salt

Freshly ground black pepper

6 tablespoons extra virgin olive oil

Toasted or grilled slices of bread
   for garnish

Freshly grated Parmigiano-Reggiano
   cheese

Combine the water, stock, garlic, sage, parsley, thyme, bay leaf, and red pepper in a large pot. Bring to a boil, then reduce the heat to medium-low, and let simmer for 30 minutes. Let cool and strain.

Squeeze the garlic pulp into a food processor or blender, discarding the skins. Discard the red pepper and bay leaf. Add the remaining herbs to the food processor and puree. Add the milk and process to blend.

Return the broth and garlic puree to the soup pot over medium-low heat. Season with salt and pepper and add the olive oil. Stir to combine and briefly reheat. Serve with a slice of toasted bread floating in each serving bowl. Serve with grated Parmigiano alongside.

A Traditional Cauliflower Soup

Minestra di Cavolfiore

Piedmont's affection for traditional ways is seen more in its soup than in any other dish. This cream soup, for example, is a taste of the past that really deserves to be revived. Both the French and the Piedmontese had a long tradition of thickening soups with finely sieved cooked rice, which is both a binder and a texture enhancement, much like *béchamel sauce*. In recent years, such soups have been all but forgotten—except in Piedmont.

This soup tastes better if allowed to sit for a few hours before being served. It is also as good cold (on a hot summer day) as it is warm. If time is pressing, a handy shortcut is to use a few spoonfuls of Cream of Rice instead of cooking raw rice and sieving it. The flavor isn't quite as good, but the thickening effect is the same. Canned stock is fine for this dish, as so much other flavor is present.

makes 6 servings

1 medium-size head cauliflower, separated into florets

2 tablespoons unsalted butter

1 large yellow onion, finely chopped

4 cups chicken stock

1/3 cup long- or short-grain rice

1/3 cup heavy cream

Salt

Freshly ground white or black pepper

Finely chopped fresh Italian parsley leaves for garnish

Over boiling water, steam the cauliflower florets until tender but not mushy, about 10 minutes. Let cool slightly, then finely chop. Set aside.

Add the butter to a small sauté pan over medium heat. When melted, add the onion and let cook gently, stirring, until tender and translucent, about 10 minutes, taking care that it does not brown. Set aside.

Bring the chicken stock to a boil in a large saucepan. Add the cooked onion and rice. Reduce the heat to a simmer and let cook until the rice is completely soft, about 25 minutes. Transfer the soup to a blender or food processor and process until smooth. Then pour the soup into a fine-meshed sieve placed over a large mixing bowl. After the liquid has drained, push the remaining solids through with a scraper. The rice puree that is pushed through serves to thicken the soup. (It is not essential that every last bit of rice be pushed through.)

Pour the chicken stock and rice puree into a clean saucepan, whisking to blend. Add the cooked cauliflower and cream and bring to a simmer, stirring to blend. Season with salt and pepper. Serve hot, with finely chopped parsley as a garnish.

Variations

Minestra di Carote (Carrot Soup): Substitute 4 or 5 large carrots for the cauliflower. Peel and coarsely chop. Let the carrots cook in the chicken stock with the rice. Then puree the carrots with the rice as described above and proceed with the recipe.

Minestra di Verdure ("Cream of Green" Soup): Thoroughly wash 1 pound of a fresh leafy green vegetable such as spinach, lettuce, dandelion greens, sorrel, or watercress, and remove the stems. Cook the green vegetable by steaming or in boiling water until tender, just a few minutes for most. Drain and run cold water over the greens to stop the cooking. Squeeze out most of the excess water, then puree in a food processor or blender. Add the puree to the sieved chicken stock soup base along with the cream, to taste. Add a splash more cream, if desired. Serve with homemade croutons as a garnish.

An Old-fashioned Rice and Leek Soup
Antica Minestra di Riso e Porro

This centuries-old recipe is captivatingly good, the sort of winter dish that you just keep eating. And why not? Here you have a mixture of flavorful Italian rice blended with leeks and elevated by melted Fontal and Gruyère cheese. It's classic alpine fare and one of our personal winter favorites. Dense and filling, this soup doesn't require an accompaniment. Although it's possible to substitute long-grain white rice for the (more expensive) Italian Arborio variety, the resulting texture is not the same. Try short-grain rice instead, which is much closer to the soft Arborio, a special short-grain variety.

This soup can be made well ahead of time. It's best, though, to incorporate the cheeses only just before serving, as their flavor diminishes once melted.

makes 6 servings

6 large leeks or 12 small ones, white and
   light green parts, cut into ¼-inch-
   thick rounds and thoroughly washed
3 garlic cloves, finely chopped
8 cups water or very light stock
2 cups Arborio rice
2 medium-size waxy-type potatoes,
   peeled and cut into eighths or
   ½-inch-thick slices

1 tablespoon salt
Freshly grated nutmeg
3 ounces Fontal or Fontina cheese, cut
   into small pieces
3 ounces Gruyère or Emmenthal cheese,
   cut into small pieces

Over medium-low heat, cook the leeks and chopped garlic in a large pot with a little water, covered. When softened, add the 8 cups water and bring to a boil. Add the rice, potatoes, salt, and nutmeg to taste. Reduce the heat and let simmer, uncovered, until the rice and potatoes are soft, 15 to 20 minutes.

Just before serving, bring the soup to a boil. Add the cheeses, stirring constantly until melted. When the cheeses are fully integrated, the soup is ready to serve.

Rice, Celery, and Parsley Soup

Minestra di Riso al Sedano e Prezzemolo

This is a variation on the preceding soup, only here the informing ingredients are celery and parsley. I miss the cheeses, so I've added a generous quantity of freshly grated Parmigiano, which is still within the bounds of traditionalism.

makes 6 servings

¼ cup extra virgin olive oil

1 bunch celery, with leaves, coarsely
  chopped

Large handful of fresh Italian parsley
  sprigs, stems chopped, leaves left
  whole

4 cups water or stock, or more if
  necessary

1 cup Arborio rice

12 fresh sage leaves, finely chopped

1 large garlic clove, finely chopped

Salt

Freshly ground black pepper

Generous amount of freshly grated
  Parmigiano-Reggiano cheese

Add the olive oil to a large saucepan over medium-low heat. When the oil is hot, add the celery and the parsley stems and cook, stirring, until the celery is softened, for 5 to 10 minutes. Add the water and bring to a boil. Add the rice, cover partially, and cook until the rice is tender and most of the liquid has been absorbed, about 20 minutes.

Add the parsley and sage leaves and garlic. Season with salt and pepper. Let cook gently for a few minutes. Adjust the texture of the soup by adding more water if desired. Serve with freshly grated Parmigiano cheese alongside.

Fresh Fava Bean, Fettuccine, and Zucchini Soup

Minestra di Fava, Fettuccine, e Zucchine

Many regional Italian cuisines employ beans and pasta in the same dish. This is an unusual Piedmontese rendition of this practice, combining flavorful fresh fava beans with dried fettuccine.

A springtime specialty, fresh fava beans are increasingly seen here. They are always offered in their long green pods. Most often, we see mature fresh fava beans. To prepare them, remove the beans from the pods (discard the pods) and then, with your fingernail, peel off the thick inner skin of each individual bean. It's tedious, but necessary, as this thick skin prevents the bean from cooking quickly and is slightly indigestible. The flavor of fresh favas is worth the effort.

This soup, by the way, is also made in winter using dried favas. To substitute, simply soak the dried peeled beans overnight. Then cook in lightly boiling water for about two hours (depending on the size and toughness of the bean), until tender, and proceed with the recipe. The flavor is less "green" and more "beany," but delicious all the same.

This dish can be made well in advance, up to the point of putting in the pasta. Any number of pasta shapes can be used, such as orecchiette, farfalle, gnochette, or linguine, among many others.

makes 6 servings

2 pounds fava beans (in the pod)

1 medium-size onion, coarsely chopped

3 celery stalks, coarsely chopped

1 large carrot, finely chopped

2 small zucchini, sliced into 1/4-inch-thick
    rounds

3 medium-size waxy-type potatoes, peeled
    and cut into eighths

Salt

Freshly ground black pepper

6 ounces dried or fresh fettuccine

Extra virgin olive oil

Freshly grated Parmigiano-Reggiano
    cheese

Remove the fava beans from their long green pods. Then remove the outer skin of each bean. Put all of the ingredients except the fettuccine, olive oil, and Parmesan into a large pot. Cover with water. Bring to a boil and immediately reduce to a simmer. Let cook, uncovered, until the beans and potatoes are tender, about 25 minutes.

Raise the heat and bring to a boil. Add the fettuccine. When the pasta is cooked, ladle the soup into bowls, add a dollop of olive oil to each serving, and serve with freshly grated Parmigiano alongside.

The Long, Hot Summer

A lthough my wife and I had been to Piedmont numerous times, we had never visited during July or August. So it was a bit of a shock to plunk down in Piedmont in July. Actually, our first few days in early July were lullingly pleasant. It was warm, but no warmer than in mild, moderate, not-especially-humid Portland, Oregon. That spell, our Piedmontese friends later insisted, was a welcoming gift they had worked out with the local weather gods.

By the second week of July, just as we were getting comfortable, the real Piedmontese summer slammed into us. It was like being on the vent end of an unimaginably huge clothes dryer. My wife, Karen, grew up in Iowa; she knows what hot, humid summers can be like. I, for my part, was raised on Long Island—and not near the seashore. Summers in both places were sticky, muggy, and irritatingly hot. But we had forgotten these not-so-fond childhood memories. Piedmont revived them.

No one we know in Piedmont owns an air conditioner. The cost of electricity is too high. So when summer hits, the pace of life slows to a crawl. The only topic is the weather. The fact that what we experienced was, by all accounts, a perfectly normal—which is to say brutally hot and wiltingly humid—summer was beside the point. Everybody said that they just didn't know how they were going to get through it this year.

Our landlady, Lina, used to bemoan her Piedmontese fate at every opportunity. "Oh, oh, I don't know why we live here!" she would complain. When I pointed out that nowhere else in Italy does anyone speak Piedmontese, she would grunt. It was a low shot: No Piedmontese ever wants to leave the sound of her, or his, dialect. Sometimes we would call Lina to inquire about something, only to find her not at home, which was rare. So we'd leave a message and, a half hour later, she'd call back. "Where were you?" we'd inquire. "I was sitting in the car," she'd explain, "enjoying the air-conditioning."

During July and August, our daily routine varied little. We would wake up relatively late in the morning, around 9 A.M. This was because we wouldn't have been able to sleep until quite late the previous evening. You see, another characteristic of Piedmontese housing is a lack of window screens. The bugs spawned in the heat and humidity rival anything I've seen in subtropical locales. The mosquitoes do not bear mentioning in polite company. To get some sleep, you had to close the windows.

Despite, or perhaps because of, all this, our summer days were spent shopping for food in the morning. I would work on lunch, which we would enjoy with a bottle of wine under the vine-covered *pergolato* behind the house. The meals would vary. *Petti di Pollo in Carpione* (see page 42) was one of our favorites. We ate wonderful quantities of *Acciughe al Verde* (see page 18): Anchovies and basil are ideal hot-weather tastes. On Fridays we would go to the open-air market in Bra and treat ourselves to a roasted chicken, with which we had a salad alongside. And some cheese—Castelmagno and Gorgonzola for me, a few little *tomini* (soft cheeses) for Karen.

By the end of lunch, the heat would be oppressive. So we did the only reasonable thing: nothing. We took a nap. Anything that involved much energy did not happen in July and August. We ate, we slept, we went out to restaurants. It was delicious. And lazy. Also, it was rational, as the heat left you enervated.

What made the heat so maddening was the way the humidity would build. Piedmont's weather is mountain-influenced. You can see easily the Swiss Alps on a clear day. And you can just as easily see the alpine weather rolling in. There was a cycle. First, the heat would build gradually. Accompanying it was a penetrating humidity, enough to wilt dried spaghetti. Then, just when you thought that you would strangle the next person who said *buon giorno* to you—if you only had the strength—a thunderstorm would come rolling down from the Alps.

These thunderstorms were like nothing Karen and I had ever seen—and Karen had seen some impressive stuff in Iowa. This was really mountain ferocity. The sky would blacken, and you would hear the thunder, which echoed through the hills like a battle on the move. Then the lightning would appear, growing ever more frequent and violent as the storm neared. This would go on for hours before the storm—and its rain—actually reached you.

But you could be sure of one thing: At the first clap of thunder, originating probably in Zurich or someplace, the electricity would go out. We never understood this. As best we could tell, the Italian electrical system is designed to turn itself off at the first sign of a summer storm. My theory was that the entire power grid was attached to a sound sensor. With the first thunderclap—or backfire from a passing scooter—the grid would shut down. I once asked winemaker Angelo Gaja about this phenomenon, inquiring if he knew why the power went out during every storm. "Oh my God!" he shouted in frustration, "I don't know why. It's crazy. It's like Africa!"

Whatever the reason, as soon as you saw a storm coming, you learned to unplug the computer, the answering machine, fax machine, and anything else that could be harmed when the power—and its accompanying surge—returned. Then you assembled all the flashlights, candles, and matches needed for what could be an all-night siege. After that, you started closing the shutters, as the winds could bang around the windows something fierce.

Sure enough, long before the storm arrived, the power would go. So, too, usually would the telephone, although, oddly enough, sometimes it would remain alive throughout the storm. This was odd because the Italian telephone system, called SIP, is notoriously inefficient, costly, and unreliable. Fifteen years ago it was simply impossible. Today, though, it is much improved. At last report, the odds of your call going through on the first try are now as high as one in two.

Thus equipped, Karen and I would go into the kitchen, which overlooked the courtyard, and

lean out over the windowsill like a pair of kids waiting for the parade to pass by. There we forti-
fied ourselves with something good and cold, like a sweet, refreshingly acidic Moscato d'Asti.

First the winds would come, accompanied by ever-denser black clouds. If you've ever been
in a partial eclipse, you know what it was like. The thunder became, well, thunderous. Then the
lightning started. Sometimes you could hear trees cracking, either from wind damage or a lightning strike. Occasionally the phone would ring—with nobody at the other end. Once, while we
were leaning out watching the storm, a huge ball of lightning erupted in the courtyard, with an
accompanying, monumental crack. Karen and I literally jumped into each other's arms.

Blessedly, all of the heat and humidity would be flensed by the storm. The next morning, the
air would be cool, fresh, and sweet. Wandering into Bra for the first espresso of the day, you
could see the relief on everyone's face. The lilt returned to the Italian language; the banter was
lighthearted. It was delicious, if only because—as we soon learned ourselves—everyone knew
that it wouldn't last. And sure enough, in a few days the cycle of oppressive heat and humidity
would build again, only to culminate in yet another orgasmic electrical storm.

Traveling Around Piedmont

♦❧♦

There is nothing so stupid on the face of the earth as to read a book about travels in Italy—unless it be to write one!

Heinrich Heine

One of the privileges of plunking down in one place for a year is the opportunity to pick up and go whenever you like. It is an exquisite pleasure. Previously, all my trips to Piedmont had been constrained by time, jet lag, and the demands of work. Suddenly, a year stretched before us. We could do as we liked, when we liked.

Frankly, some days we did nothing at all. We ate, we drank, we checked out yet another local restaurant in search of new tastes. On other days, we would wake up, the weather would look inviting, and we would pore over our increasingly worn map of Piedmont and head out. We leisurely investigated seemingly every crevice of Piedmont's delicious landscape.

It's impossible to investigate all of Piedmont in a year, as it's the largest region on the Italian mainland, with 9,806 square miles. (Sicily is just barely larger, squeaking past Piedmont with an extra 118 square miles.) What's more, 43 percent of Piedmont is mountainous, so you can imagine how many nooks and crannies there are. But the attempt was exhilarating.

Our travels were almost continuous and rarely, if ever, were they unrewarding. We quickly sensed the sheer scale of Piedmont. It is *so* much bigger and more diverse than anywhere else on the Italian mainland. There still are countless tiny villages seemingly untouched by time or tourism, where you can find almost ritualistic dishes that have long since disappeared in more "sophisticated" areas. You must see it for yourself: the fortress at Pinerolo where, supposedly, the Man in the Iron Mask was imprisoned; the December festival at Carrù of the *grasso bue* (the huge, white beef cattle of the ancient Piedmontese breed); the little villages like Cocconato and Moncalvo in the Basso Monferrato zone, with their stage-set streets and piazzas. These, and much more, are what Piedmont holds.

Typically, our trip planning was uncomplicated. Usually I would leaf through the restaurant guidebooks, looking for a destination restaurant, some place that sounded authentic and, preferably, out of the way. In case you, too, want to do this, let me recommend two books for the purpose: Sandro Doglio's annually updated *I Buoni Indirizzi per Mangiare e Bere: Piemonte, Liguria, e Valle d'Aosta* (*Good Addresses for Eating and Drinking*) and Slow Food Editore's *Osterie d'Italia*, also updated annually. You don't need to know much, if any, Italian to get the gist of either guidebook. You will also need a good map. The best is the Touring Club Italiano's *Atlante Stradale d'Italia: Nord*. All of these can be found at any Piedmontese bookshop or, for that matter, at road-side rest stops along the pay toll *autostrada*.

Initially, our challenge was simply learning our way around home ground: the Langhe and Roero zones. You'd think that with all the visits I'd made to this section of Piedmont, it would have long since become familiar. As it happens, I did know it reasonably well for a visiting foreigner. But it is one of the world's most confusing terrains, thanks to its plunging hillsides. Langhe and Roero have hundreds of towns, each with an adjoining hamlet, called a *località*. The roads run along ridgelines, with the result that getting from one spot to another—just a few miles as the crow flies—can take as much as an hour by car.

It took two months of almost daily forays before I left confident enough to travel almost any-where without bothering with a map. This impressed not only our visitors—who were astounded at the complications of the Langhe/Roero landscape—but also our Piedmontese friends, who doubted that an outsider could grasp it. I confess that I was very pleased with myself about this.

Throughout the year, we ranged much farther afield. We lived just outside of Bra, deep inside the mountains that closet Piedmont north, south, west, and southeast. The winters there are cold, the summers hot. It is a Continental climate. Yet in little more than an hour we could reach the Mediterranean, which is another world: temperate and filled with olive trees. To do this you have to cross the *Alpi Maritime*, the mountains that separate Piedmont from Liguria.

In one sense, Langhe/Roero really is Piedmont's heartland. Living in the so-called heartland helps you to see the transitions, as the architecture and food are flavored by the demands of geography. For example, one of our favorite restaurant destinations was a place called Cacciatori in the tiny town of Cartosio, outside of Acqui Terme. There, you're in southeastern Piedmont, just a few kilometers from the Ligurian border. The food is less heavy than Langhe traditional-ism, more inflected by the vegetarian cuisine of adjoining Liguria.

You also see a difference in how the landscape is worked: stone terraces. Unusually for Italy, the steep hillsides of the Langhe are not terraced, for its soil is chalky clay, which holds itself well. But when you drive toward Acqui Terme, you pass through the Bormida Valley, which fol-lows the path of the Bormida River. The Bormida Valley is a stunning stretch of scenery, largely unknown to tourism. And the first thing you notice are the steep, carefully tended stone ter-races. You know that Liguria—which is massively terraced—is close by.

Almost directly south of our home base was another favorite destination restaurant, the Vecchia Cooperativa in the village of Nucetto, near the larger town of Ceva. Although here, too, one is close to the Ligurian border, it's a different world from mild Acqui Terme and its ancient Roman hot springs. Nucetto is in the Alpi Maritime mountains, close to several springs that supply much of the bottled water drunk in the region. The cooking at the Vecchia Cooperativa (the name comes from its former use as a local mutual aid society) is yet another midpoint Piedmontese cuisine: mountain

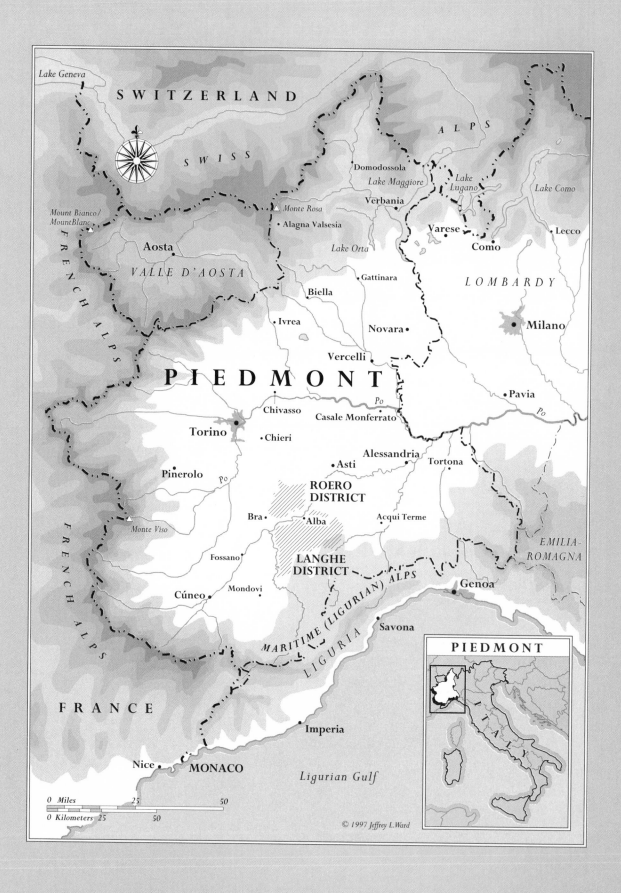

© 1997 Jeffrey L.Ward

cooking allied with Ligurian vegetarianism. The result is dishes like rabbit with vegetables, numerous dried bean soups characteristic of mountain cooking, and an abundance of mushrooms.

When you head into the high Alps, toward the ski areas, the cooking changes altogether. One destination, just because it was the village at the end of the road, was far north of us. Alagna Valsesia is right on the Swiss border, at the foot of towering Monte Rosa, at an elevation of five thousand feet. To reach Alagna Valsesia you must traverse a two-lane road that tracks the Sesia River, which roars its way down from Monte Rosa's glaciers.

In Alagna Valsesia you're deep in alpine country, with its hearty food and robust, uncomplicated flavors. This is *fonduta* and polenta country, and it's also devoted to major meat-eating. In places such as this you come across such local specialities as chamois stew flavored with juniper, goose breast, and all sorts of polenta variations. Gnocchi is a big item here as well, loved for its filling qualities—and the fact that it shows off melted cheese so well.

The disparity of the Piedmontese landscape becomes the more striking when you ease your way down from Alagna Valsesia and head directly east—little more than fifty miles by car—to find yourself at Lago d'Orta. The famous lakes of what's known as the Italian Lake Country—lakes Maggiore, Como, and Garda—all have their admirers. But the jewel in this necklace of northern lakes is tiny Lago d'Orta, easily the smallest of them all. Just fifty miles from Alagna Valsesia's alpine austerity, Lago d'Orta is a world of mild weather, elegant villas, and more refined cooking. Risotto, rather than polenta, is the ubiquitous dish.

The main town of Lago d'Orta is Orta San Giulio. No cars are allowed. You must walk into the ancient town, which is perched on a finger of land protruding into the lake. We know the place well because you can get from Lago d'Orta to Malpensa Airport (where travelers from America arrive and depart) in exactly forty-five minutes. Lago d'Orta is the ideal place to stay before departing on a transatlantic flight the next morning.

The destinations are endless. Closer to home, I frequently would strike out for the swath of land north of Asti and south of the Po River called the Basso Monferrato. It was just an hour's drive north. Sometimes it's called the Astigiana ("the area around Asti"), but that name applies to the lovely countryside south of Asti as well. In both places, the hills are spaced farther apart, in contrast to the tight cleavages of the Langhe hills. The landscape has more vistas and is somehow less mysterious.

What's more, the Basso Monferrato area has Piedmont's best collection of old houses. If you want to see the long, narrow, traditional brick farmhouses of Piedmont, this is where to go. In more prosperous Langhe, most of them were torn down in the 1960s and 1970s and replaced with god-awful boxes that look like warehouses. The Astigiana and Basso Monferrato are poorer, so the old farmhouses remain.

The Astigiana/Basso Monferrato is wine country, devoted especially to Barbera. Unfortunately, too much of what's produced under the appellation Barbera d'Asti is industrial in quality. This is where most of Piedmont's big winegrowers' cooperatives are found. But there are some really good private producers.

The food in this area is almost identical to that of the Langhe, except where risotto is concerned. The Po River divides the land of risotto from the terrain of *tajarìn*. North of the Po, risotto reigns supreme. South of the Po, its influence wanes. The Basso Monferrato is a kind of buffer zone, where both dishes are seen equally. South of Asti, risotto is a rarity.

One of our favorite trips was to the source of the Po River itself. And naturally, this being Piedmont, there's a terrific restaurant there. The source of the great Po River is one of Piedmont's most prominent peaks, the 12,602-foot jagged spire of Monte Viso. On a clear day, we could see it easily from our home. Monte Viso sits right on the Italian/French border. It has long been a favorite alpine hiking spot, which explains why the restaurant named Pian del Re ("the king's plateau") was founded in 1878, located at the end of the road in *località* Pian del Re, overlooking Monte Viso's vast glaciers. Owned since 1902 by the Perotti family, who were (and still are) alpine guides, as well as the cooks, the restaurant is at 6,693 feet in elevation.

The food and atmosphere at Pian del Re are quintessentially alpine: pine walls, trestle tables, windows steamed with wood heat and warm breaths. The food is similarly classic: abundant portions of polenta, braised meats, local mountain cheeses, and, in season, wild mushrooms.

Turin

I was born in Turin. I know what it's like to see someone else wear
silk stockings and not to have them yourself.

Cesare Pavese
Tra Donne Sole (*Among Women Only*, 1949)

In complete contrast to the rusticity of Monte Viso are the restaurants and, especially, the *caffès* of Torino (Turin). To my eye, Turin is one of Italy's most attractive cities. Many Italian cities are hardly a feast for the eye, as they are ancient, overrun with automobiles, and mostly unplanned. Turin is the great exception. Located along the Po River, Turin was planned from its earliest founding in the time of Caesar Augustus, which puts its origins back two millennia. Originally, it was an old Roman military camp called Augusta Taurinorum. You can still see one of the original gates.

What sets Turin apart from nearly all other Italian cities (except Milan) is that its streets run long, straight, and true. In this, as everyone rightly observes, Turin is much more a French city than an Italian one. That its residents spoke French natively until the late 1800s, along with their native Piedmontese dialect, only reinforced this impression. But Turin's layout was largely the work of three Italian architects, Ascanio Vitozzi in the 1500s, Guarino

Guarini in the 1600s, and Juvara—the favorite architect of the House of Savoy—in the 1700s.

What really gives Turin its French feel, however, is the grand fact that it was the seat of the House of Savoy. And that almost incomprehensibly rich family—who became Italy's royal family when the nation was unified in 1865—took its cues from the French court. Turin is truffled with Savoy palaces. Its outskirts see yet more Savoy extravagances, such as their "hunting lodge" in Stupinigi, which is surely the world's most lavish. And there's the Savoy family mausoleum, the Basilica of Superga, which is a favorite Sunday destination for the Torinese. It looms on a hill over the city and is almost preposterously huge.

Such public opulence helps explain why Turin has Italy's most decadently rich caffès, rivaled only by those in Vienna. The Torinese have a passion for coffee and chocolate, producing some of the world's best. (See the discussion and recipe for Turin's favorite local coffee, called *bicerin,* on page 262.) Visit the Caffè San Carlo on the piazza of the same name. It drips with Murano glass chandeliers, gilded pillars, and enough marble to restock a quarry. Or the Caffè Torino on the same Piazza San Carlo, another old-fashioned local favorite. To try the fabled *bicerin,* the obvious choice is the coffeehouse called Al Bicerin, on the Piazza Consolata.

As you might expect in a city devoted to no-holds-barred eating, Turin has a tremendous open-air food market, at Porta Palazzo. It's easily one of the biggest food markets in Italy. For those who find food markets better than any museum, the Porta Palazzo market is swoon-making. Everything you could ever want in a food market—including an air of ancient authenticity—is found there.

Southeast of Turin

Much as I like Turin, I confess that I prefer the smaller towns and villages of rural Piedmont. Southeast of Turin, one stop worth making is at yet another royal "hunting lodge," in the town of Racconigi. This lovely palace has not only some beautifully restored interiors, but a stupendous park. Also southeast of Turin lies the famous Langhe zone, with its major town of Alba and country villages such as Dogliani, Monforte d'Alba, Barolo, and dozens of others. Since the Langhe is mentioned elsewhere in the book, there's no need to sing its praises here, except to say that it is a landscape like no other on earth.

In the same direction are the cities of Asti and Alessandria, which lie along the Tanaro River (as does Alba). Asti lends its name to the famous sparkling muscat wine called Asti Spumante. Vineyards surround the city, yet it's nowhere near as wine-besotted as Alba. But Asti does have a beautiful cathedral and a pleasing formality. As for Alessandria, well, the less said the better. It's a dull commercial city of little appeal.

Directly south of Turin is Saluzzo, one of Piedmont's most historically significant country towns. During the Middle Ages it was the seat of the powerful Marquisate of Saluzzo, which once ruled over a goodly portion of Piedmont. Saluzzo was so powerful that, even after being conquered, it still retained the right to mint its own money.

Farther south is Cúneo, which lies astride the mountain road to Nice. Cúneo is an ancient town that saw its population grow in the 1100s as refugees from faraway Milan fled the depredations of Frederick Barbarossa, who laid waste to their city. Cúneo itself withstood at least seven sieges over the centuries, and it took no less a military foe than Napoleon Bonaparte to dismantle its fortifications. Today, Cúneo looks a bit like a miniature Turin, boasting a huge central piazza surrounded by elegant shops and restaurants tucked behind monumental pillars. But it's still a country town, one very much flavored by its proximity to the maritime Alps. Cúneo's local cuisine seesaws between two equally enticing influences: mountain heartiness and Ligurian lightness, which border is close by.

East of Cúneo is Mondovi, which is worth visiting because the old part of town sits atop a hill that offers spectacular views of the farmlands and mountains surrounding it. Mondovi is also home to an array of caves and caverns, for which tours are available.

North of Turin

The number of cities and important towns thins out north of Turin, a reflection in part of relatively sparse settlements as you get closer to the Alps and of the farmland expanse of the Po Valley, most of which is devoted to rice fields and other large-scale agriculture.

Northeast of Turin are northern Piedmont's four most significant cities: Ivrea, Biella, Vercelli, and Novara. Gastronomically, Ivrea and Biella are mountain-influenced. Their food is rustic and hearty, rich with meat. In comparison, Vercelli and Novara are creatures of the rice fields that surround them. If you want to eat risotto in its very heartland, these are the cities that celebrate it.

Of the four, Ivrea has the least to offer the visitor. It's a business city, devoted in part to the fortunes of the Olivetti computer company. Biella is prettier, though industrial as well. Biella was where Italy's Industrial Revolution occurred in the 1800s, specifically in textiles. Its wealthy bourgeoisie built Victorian wedding-cake mansions, giving the town an elegance lacking elsewhere north of the Po. To this day, Biella remains an important source of fine textiles.

Vercelli is the most interesting, if only because of its antiquity. It is the urban ornament in a sea—literally so in the right season—of rice fields. Traveling to Vercelli has sometimes reminded me of visiting France's Chartres: You traverse vast, flat farmlands and suddenly up from nowhere looms civilization. Vercelli is ancient and boasts a huge brick basilica built by the Cistercians that dates to the 1200s. It has the air of a prosperous country town, which is exactly what it is.

Novara shares with Vercelli the same air of rural prosperity. Rice fields surround Novara; like Vercelli, it is swathed in fog during the fall and winter. But Novara is centuries younger than ancient Vercelli. It's more industrial and thus richer, evidenced by the fact that Novara's cathedral is newer and grander than Vercelli's old basilica. It was designed by the same architect (Alessandro Antonelli) who created Turin's towering spire and former synagogue called La Mole, to which Novara's cathedral bears a strong resemblance.

Risotto

Frederick Barbarossa awarded [the rice] the name "risum optimum," which expression gradually vulgarized into "risoptimum" . . . "risottimum" . . . "risotto."

Livio Cerini di Castegnate
Il Cuoco Gentiluomo (1980)

Sometimes—to rework the famous lyric—a dish is not just a dish. And a sigh (of contentment) is not just a sigh. With risotto, the fundamentals of civilization itself apply. Risotto was created by insight and relentless cultivation. Unlike dishes created from wild, foraged foods, such as mushrooms, fish, game, greens, or birds, risotto did not just happen. It is more like fine wine: a coming together of plant and purpose in a very particular place.

Rice is not native to Italy. Nor is Italy especially conducive to its cultivation, except in one superb place: the Po Valley. Rice needs massive amounts of water and flat surfaces where the water can pool around the shoots. Only Northern Italy's Po Valley has both. Italy is so mountainous that, apart from the Po Valley, it has no other sizable stretch of flat land except for the Salentine Peninsula, which is the heel of the Italian boot. There it's flat, but unlike the Po Valley, there's no water. Only drought-resistant olive trees and grape vines thrive there.

Although appropriate climate is essential (rice likes it warm and humid, which the Po Valley is, swelteringly so, during the summer), the real reason that rice is cultivated in the Po Valley is the result of a geological quirk—along with massive human intervention. The geological quirk is the source of the all-important water.

At first glance, one would think that the Po River itself made rice growing possible. Its water helps, but the Po, surprisingly, is not the main source of supply. Instead the reason for all the water lies in the soil itself.

North of the Po Valley are the Alps, which are the snow reservoir for all of continental Europe. As the Alps diminish into foothills, the subsoil changes. It is a brownish, iron-filled subsoil called *ferreto* (iron in Italian is *ferro*), with the consistency of cement. Water cannot penetrate it.

What happens is that alpine snowmelt tumbles toward the Po River in seasonally engorged tributaries that stream across the surface of the land. But much of the water percolates into the topsoil. Upon reaching the impermeable stratum of *ferreto,* it just puddles up underground.

Since the land tilts toward the low point of the Po River, the puddles become underground streams. Eventually, they meet yet a different subsoil layer, equally impermeable, of compacted clay. Where the angle of the foothills intersects the flat of the Po Valley plain, this underground water is squeezed up to the surface. The result is hundreds of springs, called *fontanili*.

On a map, these *fontanili* follow a traceable line, massed along the northern edge of the Po Valley just where fading foothills meet flat plain. They gush year-round, their waters emerging at a constant temperature and unvarying flow, which make them ideal for irrigation.

Yet other water is diverted from the major tributaries leading to the Po: the Dora Baltea, Sésia, and Ticino rivers, along with half a dozen smaller feeder streams. Not to be forgotten are the substantial rains, which fall mostly in the spring and autumn, averaging about thirty inches a year.

With all this water, one would think that the Po Valley must always have been a fertile Eden. Yet the soil of the Po Valley was once barren. The brownish topsoil was thin and highly infertile. Close to the rivers, the land was swampy. Some soils in the Po Valley were literally sterile.

The ancient Romans, those masterly engineers, began the transformation of the Po Valley, largely by draining the swampy bogs. But with the fall of Rome, these efforts ended and, over time, what had been accomplished atrophied and eventually disappeared. The Po Valley reverted to wasteland.

With the arrival and expansion of the Benedictine and Cistercian abbeys between 1000 and the 1400s, the reshaping of the Po Valley commenced. Slowly, over centuries, the soil of the Po Valley was invigorated. All the rich topsoil we see today is man-made. Centuries of irrigation and careful, thoughtful, methodical cultivation—adding animal manure, cultivating meadows, and, more recently, the application of artificial fertilizers—created an entirely new, fabricated soil. The Po Valley is as much a cultural landscape as a physical one.

Fashioning canals and diverting water for irrigation were critical. All that water was seen as opportunity to the medieval world's masters of water handling: the Benedictine and, especially, the Cistercian monks. Had they not planted their abbeys in the then-barren landscape of the Po Valley, we would likely not know about risotto today. At the least, the cultivation of rice would have occurred much later.

The Cistercians, particularly, were adept at hydraulics. An early biography of Saint Bernard, the founder of the order, describes how his followers rebuilt the famous Cistercian monastery at Clairvaux, in France's Champagne district.* The monks "divided the river, set in new channels, and lifted the leaping waters to the mill wheels . . . that the river might flow fast and do good wherever it was needed in every building, flowing freely in underground conduits; the streams performed suitable tasks in every office and cleansed the abbey and at length returned to the main course and restored to the river what it had lost." As one historian (Christopher Brooke) points out, "Nothing so elaborate had been seen since Roman times."

This knowledge of, and interest in, hydraulics surely was transmitted to the abbeys of the Po Valley. One of the reasons why the Cistercian order so effectively spread knowledge wherever it settled was a requirement that the abbot of every abbey visit the Cistercian motherhouse at Citeaux, France, once a year. Moreover, the abbot of Citeaux was, in turn, required to visit all of the satellite abbeys. Eventually, this became too unwieldy as the order expanded, but visits to Citeaux were still performed frequently, for much the same spiritual—and emotional—reasons that Catholic priests today seek out St. Peter's.

You can still see the dramatic effects of the monks' labor today, although the scale is vast now compared with eight hundred years ago. When you visit the rice-growing area of Piedmont, the heart of which lies around the town of Vercelli, you see a surreal landscape. At first, the sheer flatness of the land blurs all detail: The mirrored surface of the flooded rice fields reflects only sky, giving a two-dimensional sense of the landscape. The eye finds nothing upon which to fix and calibrate scale or assess depth.

For some viewers, it is a bleak vista. Passing through the rice fields near Novara in 1789, the English agriculture writer Arthur Young recorded his dismay at the "sombre and pestiferous" scenery, calling it "a nasty country, as ill to the eye as to the health."

Then you see the old monastic abbeys, or granges, self-enclosed quadrangles like college campuses made of ancient, crumbling brick. At a distance, they don't look like much. The ratio of the landscape's horizontal to their puny vertical puts them at a dimensional disadvantage. Only when you draw near, and can measure them against a human scale, do you realize how vast these abbeys are, how many monks and laborers they must have held. And what confined, isolated worlds they must have been when measured against the isolating sweep of the rice fields.

---

*Vita Prima S. Bernardi, bk.II, ch. 5 Patrologia Latina CLXXXV, col. 285; quoted in Christopher Brooke, Europe in the Central Middle Ages, p. 71.

Even now, in an age of mechanized travel, the fields are daunting to traverse. The abbeys—and later, the granges of the big estates—must have seemed like islands, which they literally were when the rice fields were submerged. In spring, the rains would have made the few roads leading to Vercelli or Novara impassable from mud. Viewed from above, it is an archipelago of abbeys in a man-made sea.

With their multigenerational commitment, the monks helped bring fertility to the land. But it's not certain that they were responsible for planting rice. One view has it that the Cistercian monks at the awe-inspiring abbey at Lucedio (which is now privately owned and still grows and sells rice) brought rice cultivation to the Po Valley, courtesy of the spoils of the Crusades.

This much is known: The earliest written mention of rice in Northern Italy dates to about 1250, in the form of a medical prescription in the records of a hospital in Vercelli. (For centuries, Italians saw rice as a medicine rather than a food.)

The most likely, and widely accepted, theory is that the Saracens—North African Muslims—brought rice with them when they conquered Sicily. They also had conquered part of Spain and were constantly raiding the entire Mediterranean coastline of Europe, including Liguria. Somehow, surely, the Saracens were instrumental in bringing rice to Italy. (The Piedmontese still talk about the *Saracene* as if the Arab invasion of the Holy Roman Empire—of which Piedmont was a part—has only just happened.)

Spain may have had a cultural influence on rice growing in Italy. Linguists like to point out that the final addition of butter to a finished risotto—known as the *mantecazione*—comes from the Italian verb *mantecare,* to whisk or beat. Since the word for butter in Italian is *burro*, etymological conspirators like to find the Spanish hand in Italian risotto by noting that butter in Spanish is *manteca*.

Rice certainly spread through the influence of the dukes of Milan, the immensely wealthy and powerful Sforza family, which encouraged its cultivation. The House of Savoy also played a role. Rice growing leaped from one ducal estate to another. By the 1500s rice was widely, if spottily, cultivated in many parts of the Po Valley. It nevertheless remained an expensive novelty and rarity, like spices.

Various dukes and city-states did, however, follow the monastic example of canal building and irrigation. During the 1400s and 1500s, the landscape was incised with arterial canals and capillary waterways. Apart from the amazement of Venice itself, nowhere on the Italian peninsula had a landscape been subjected to such methodical engineering—or been so rewarding to such effort.

Still, civilization has its drawbacks. What happened next was unfortunate, if predictable. Flooded rice fields became pools of stagnant water. These, in turn, encouraged malarial mosquitoes. During the late 1500s and early 1600s, ducal decrees forbade the planting of rice within a few miles of towns and cities. One wonders how the workers survived. Presumably many did not; others acquired immunity if they managed to live through malaria's fearful shudderings and deadly fever.

Despite all the effort expended, rice still remained a rarity in the Po Valley. By the latter half of the 1600s, rice was planted in only two percent of the farmland. By the 1700s, it still occupied only about nine percent of the land under cultivation.

Only in the mid-1800s did rice production increase to the proportions that we know today. New estates emerged, devoted exclusively to its cultivation. These were spurred into existence by the most ambitious irrigation and canalization projects seen since the great constructions three centuries earlier. The fifty-three-mile-long Canale Cavour was constructed between 1853 and 1863. It is still one of the most important canals in use. Half a dozen other canals of scale were undertaken during the latter half of the 1800s.

The burgeoning number of rice estates also expanded human misery. Thousands of families of agricultural laborers lived subsistence lives toiling in the flooded rice fields, the women standing knee-deep in water pulling out weeds. It took two hundred hours of back-breaking labor to weed one hectare (two and one half acres) of a flooded rice field. Women did the work (88.6 percent, according to a contemporary study), while the men harvested hay and wheat grown elsewhere.

The women and families huddled in the ancient monastic abbeys and newly constructed granges (some of which look much like the old abbeys), utterly removed from contact with the outside world. Before the change in labor laws, they worked twelve hours a day, six days a week, and half a day on Sunday. At the turn of the century, and well after, their meals consisted of bread made from a mixture of half cornmeal and half wheat flour. Rice and beans comprised the typical dinner. Malaria continued to plague the workers, although by the early 1900s quinine did much to alleviate suffering. Pellagra also was a recurring problem (see page 189).

By the 1930s, the unbearably long workday had been reduced, which in turn necessitated more workers. Migrant labor performed the job. In 1931, the number of migrant workers exceeded the resident populations of the cities of Vercelli and Novara. Three quarters of these migrants were women.

Today, a visitor to Northern Italy finds it hard to imagine the poverty. I cannot recommend too strongly that you rent the movie *The Tree of the Wooden Clogs*. Although not about rice workers, it is an extraordinary (fictional) portrayal of a Po Valley agricultural estate and the life of its workers. The scenes are movingly beautiful, with only an occasional moment of heartache. It shows what I do not have the space to detail here—and could not accomplish in print, anyway.

Today, Italy is Europe's largest rice producer, growing about one and a quarter million tons of rice, slightly more than half of which is grown in Piedmont on two hundred and sixty-nine thousand acres of rice fields. This cultivation is highly concentrated: ninety-six percent of the flat plain around the city of Vercelli alone—some two hundred and twenty thousand acres—is underwater part of the year. Similar percentages apply to the area around Novara and dozens of smaller villages of the Po Valley.

Rice growing now is, thankfully, highly mechanized. Little human toil is involved, at least not without mechanical assistance. Tractors with spiked steel wheels march across the muddy or flooded fields—tilling, spraying, leveling. The flat fields (actually, they have the slightest tilt to allow water to drain) are created by tractors pulling graders that raise or lower the blade by a laser beam that determines the precise angle necessary. During the harvest, the rice is cut by huge combines that make adjustments for height and speed based upon a computer count of lost grains that slip past the hopper separating the rice from the chaff. Workers are astonishingly few. Where a large rice estate once employed more than three hundred laborers, today the entire staff numbers fewer than thirty, if that. The Po Valley has become an agricultural Disneyland: meticulously planned, controlled, and lucrative.

It should be pointed out that Piedmont is not the sole rice-growing area of the Po Valley. Rice growing extends east into the region of Lombardy and—until recently—into the Veneto region as well. The inhabitants of all three regions make risotto a way of life at the table, so it's silly to say that only Piedmont grows the best rice. What is important is to emphasize that risotto can only be made with a few distinctive types of Italian rice. And, not least, by the even more distinctive way risotto is cooked.

The Aesthetic of Risotto: The Sauce Within

One of the accusations made against Italian cooking by those trained in, or seduced by, classic French cuisine is that Italian cooking lacks refinement—as the French define it. They point, understandably, to the great French repertoire of sauces. To the French culinary mind, a dish is incomplete without an elevating sauce. This has its subtleties, to be sure.

Yet the Italian aesthetic can be even more subtle than the French. The Italian notion of saucing—although they would not choose that word—is, in essence, that a "sauce" should come from *within* the dish itself. If it is external, such as olive oil or balsamic vinegar, the added touch should serve only as something to draw out "the sauce within." Anyone who has had a plate of plain but perfectly cooked beans knows that a mere drizzle of superb olive oil unleashes an unsuspected depth of flavor in the beans themselves.

This is why, by the way, Italian winegrowers traditionally never pursued—as did the French—the use of small oak barrels to infuse their wines with the "saucing" of the vanilla scent that new oak brings. Nor did they seek to impose upon the wine the textural "polish" that these same small oak barrels provide. The sensibility about extracting intrinsic goodness made such refinements alien. It is also why the Italian wines made today using small new oak barrels seem so un-Italian. It's not just the unfamiliar flavors, it's the imposition of a foreign aesthetic premise.

The distinction of risotto—the reason why its cooking technique evolved—derives from this Italian sensibility. The intrinsic saucing of risotto is the creaminess that is teased out from the rice itself. But creaminess is not enough: The rice must still remain firm. The Italian rice varieties developed over centuries reflect this dual demand.

No other notable rice dish in the world is cooked like risotto—not in Japan or China, the Middle East, France, or Latin America. Only with risotto are grains of rice force-fed, patiently but persistently, like a *foie gras* goose. Every other rice-cooking technique, from making plain boiled rice in China to creating the wonderful broth-rich pilafs of India and the Middle East, has hot liquid applied to raw rice all at once. The pot is then covered and allowed to simmer until the liquid is absorbed.

If you cook Italian rice in a conventional fashion—water or stock added all at once and the pot covered—you will get a palatable rice dish. It will be gummy and more like a porridge, but not bad. Indeed, this was how Italian rice workers themselves made their rice, in a dish called *riso alla pilota.* (The *pilota* was the person who husked the tough, seven-layer bran from the rice.) Carol Field, in her superb book *Celebrating Italy* (Morrow, 1990), provides a description of a modern-day remembrance of this dish in a small town at the eastern end of the Po Valley where rice is no longer grown:

> The *pièce de résistance* has always been the famous *riso alla pilota,* an unusual dish in risotto-crazed Italy, since the rice is added all at once to the boiling water. . . . They fill a cauldron with water, bring it to a boil, and then drop the rice from a great funnel . . . so that it forms a perfect cone with the point just visible above the water. They shake the pot to distribute the rice and leave it to cook until most of the water has evaporated. At that point they extinguish the fire, cover the rice with heavy cloths, and let it steam under its warm blanket.

This was a cheap, filling dish that could be—and was—made in vast quantities. After all, most agricultural households comprised three generations under one roof, with the result that the meal had to feed fifteen or more people, although rarely did anyone have much to eat. If you've eaten Chinese sticky rice you know what this *riso alla pilota* is like—even to the inclusion of pork ribs, which are a traditional part of the dish on feast days.

Risotto as we know it today—the fat rice lovingly plied with yet another ladleful of valuable meat stock—clearly is not a peasant dish. Rather, it came originally from the aristocracy and later became a staple of the middle class. In fact, its diffusion to the middle classes came only when rice production expanded to industrial proportions during the mid-1800s—and when the Industrial Revolution came to Italy and created an expanded middle class. This expansion occurred, as it happens, in the same area in which rice was grown, ensuring risotto an honored place at the newly set middle-class table. In the cities, risotto was a "Sunday dish"—not surprising, considering that stock is not as cheap as water. In the rice-growing countryside it was more frequently served, as country families of some means had the poultry and livestock for their own stockpots and rice was cheap, if not grown on their farm.

But why add the stock a little at a time? No one knows who originated the risotto cooking technique. That it came from aristocratic kitchens seems likely. Rarely do recipes emerge in an Archimedean brain wave: "Eureka! I have found it!" Rather, they tend to evolve, although not just from practicality. Recipes, like music, are shaped by defining cultural sensibilities.

The originating practicality might have been a cook in an aristocratic kitchen waiting for the above-the-stairs folk to dine. As in restaurant kitchens today, the dish may have been "half-cooked" and then held. (This still occurs with risotto in some bad restaurant kitchens.) The dish was finished by adding stock, ladle by ladle, until the rice was cooked. From there, it was not much of a leap to discover the greater intrinsic goodness and refinement of a risotto where the dish is made start to finish without delay.

Whether it was the House of Savoy in Piedmont, the dukes of Milan in Lombardy, or the

Venetians in Veneto who originated risotto is unknown. What is worth noting is that differing risotto styles—but not techniques—do exist, the two extremes represented by Piedmont and Venice. Venetian *risotti* are more delicate and soupier than those of Piedmont.

Venetian cooks always say that risotto should have a consistency *all'onda,* flowing like an ocean wave. The Piedmontese *risotti* are denser. (Piedmont *is* landlocked.) Venetian *risotti* are less rich because they typically employ fish or vegetables, the flavors of which are easily overwhelmed by a meat stock. As a result, their light stocks frequently are fish- or vegetable-based. In Piedmont, meat stocks are invariable. Both schools do insist, however, that risotto be creamy. That said, the variety of rice used *will* make a difference, as some create creamier *risotti* than others. The Venetians prefer the Vialone Nano rice variety, which expands magnificently, but is not as firm-textured as Piedmont's preferred Carnaroli or Arborio varieties.

Another element of the risotto aesthetic is that, unlike most rice dishes elsewhere in the world, risotto is not a side dish, or *contorno,* as the Italians put it. Instead, rice is the focus itself, rather than a belly-filling accompaniment as in Asian cuisines.

Because of this, one important element of the risotto aesthetic is simplicity. The great risotto dishes almost always are singular in their flavoring, employing just one informing ingredient, such as a particular cheese (*risotto al Gorgonzola*), or a spice (the saffron-infused *risotto alla Milanese*), or an added ingredient such as mushrooms (*risotto ai funghi porcini*), vegetables (*risotto alla zucca*), or even just a lemon (*risotto al limone*). The exaltation of the rice itself is why this aesthetic emerged—and why overly complicated *risotti* are somehow unsatisfying, even flawed.

The Language of Italian Rice

Reading a package of Italian rice can be confusing until you have the terminology sorted out. The package tells us two things about the rice inside: the grade of the rice and its variety.

The Size and Grade

Rice, like eggs, comes in different sizes and grades. Larger grains are more prized. Italian rice is graded according to length (short or long), shape (round or oval), and size (small, medium, or large), as well as wholeness (broken grains are appropriately downgraded). What results are the following grades, which are marked on the packages.

Commune od originario The cheapest, most basic rice, typically short and round. It is used mostly for soups and desserts, never risotto. The rice most often seen with this grade is the Balilla variety. It cooks faster than other grades.

Semifino This grade represents a medium length and maintains some firmness when cooked. Risotto can be made with a *semifino* grade, although it is better employed in soups. The rice variety most often seen with a *semifino* grade is Maratelli.

Fino Here we arrive at genuinely fine rice, as the name says. The grains are relatively long, large, and taper at the tips, creating an oval shape. *Fino*-grade rice remains firm when cooked. Several varieties commonly are sold with the *fino* grade, such as Vialone Nano, Razza 77, San Andrea, and Baldo.

Superfino Just what you'd expect, the end of the line. This grade represents the fattest, largest grains. *Superfino* is the province of the two best risotto varieties, Carnaroli and Arborio. They take the longest to cook, as they can absorb more liquid than any of the others while still remaining firm. I have never seen Arborio and Carnaroli graded anything other than *superfino*.

Italian Rice Varieties

As is well known, rice is divided into short-, medium-, and long-grain varieties. But within that enormously broad categorization are an estimated eight thousand varieties or strains of rice. The vast majority of these strains are hybrids, created by rice growers to improve yields or disease resistance or to deliver enhanced textural or flavor qualities.

So it is with the various Italian rices. There *are* noticeable differences among the Italian rice varieties. These differences are not a matter of flavor, but rather of size, creaminess (when cooked), and texture. All Italian rice varieties are strains of a thick, short-grained rice called "japonica," botanically, *Oryza sativa japonica*. (The long-grain rice popular in the United States is *Oryza sativa indica*.)

Italian rice varieties were distinctive enough even two hundred years ago to give rise to a bit of agricultural espionage involving no less a figure than Thomas Jefferson. Seeking to improve the rice production of South Carolina (in hopes of greater foreign trade with France), Jefferson forayed to Piedmont in 1787 to discover why Italian rice was so prized. Initially, he supposed it was because of superior processing. Italian rice had fewer broken grains, which was a common complaint against the American product. He quickly came to a different conclusion: "It is a difference in the species of grain, of which the government of Turin is so sensible that . . . they prohibit the exportation of rough rice on pain of death."[*]

The death penalty, as criminologists are forever pointing out, is no deterrent. Nor was it for Jefferson. He stuffed his pockets with "rough" (unmilled) rice and smuggled some out of Italy. But that was only as a backup in case his main scheme failed. Jefferson had hired a mule driver to transport to Genoa two sacks of illegally acquired unmilled rice for shipment to South Carolina. No one knows what happened to the muleteer. The rice, however, did arrive. We also know what happened to it: The Carolinians dutifully planted the Piedmontese variety and subsequently pronounced it inferior to their own. They never bothered with it again. America was not destined for risotto—at least not until now.

[*]The Papers of Thomas Jefferson, Vol. 11, pp. 587–88. Letter to Edward Rutledge, July 14, 1787.

As mentioned previously, all of the rice grown in Italy is a variation on the short-grained *japonica* species. But new hybrids are forever under development, which has led to what might be called (using wine jargon) varietal rices. They take the commercial name of the hybrid. None, to my palate, taste different. They do, however, offer noticeably different textures and different degrees of creaminess when cooked. Which variety you use will make a difference, although not critically so. All of the following can be used successfully (and interchangeably) for risotto.

Carnaroli This is the supreme variety for risotto and the one preferred by every restaurant chef I talked to in Piedmont. It has the largest grain of any of the rice varieties, retains a rewarding "bite" even when fully cooked, and, best of all, rewards the cook with a satiny creaminess while keeping a firm mass.

Carnaroli is an old variety that almost went out of commercial existence because it yields less than newer strains. It has been revived in recent years and now is in widespread production, thanks to the unstinting celebration of its qualities by many Northern Italian chefs. The demand for Carnaroli is such that dark rumors percolate that some rice sold as Carnaroli really isn't. This is possible, maybe even likely. Unfortunately, it is impossible to distinguish raw Carnaroli from another good variety such as Arborio—until you finally cook it. Then the sheer size and plumpness of cooked Carnaroli reveals its authenticity.

Carnaroli is the rice I use for all of my *risotti*. Because it is not anywhere near as commonly available as Arborio (my second choice), I buy it by mail order. This is a handy way to buy rice and doesn't cost much more than hauling it home from the store. If you cannot locate Carnaroli in your town, it is worth the effort to mail-order it. One source is Corti Brothers, 5810 Folsom Boulevard, Sacramento, California 95819 (telephone: 916-736-3800). Carnardi is exported by Beretta, an excellent company in Vercelli. Beretta can be found in other parts of the country as well.

Arborio The most famous of all Italian rice varieties, it takes its name from the Piedmontese village of Arborio, which lies near the famous Gattinara wine zone. Like Carnaroli, Arborio can absorb a lot of liquid while still retaining a firmness when fully cooked. It also is generous in size. This is the "standard" risotto rice and with good reason: It works wonderfully well. It is widely available.

Baldo You don't see Baldo much outside of Italy. Derived from the Arborio strain, it is a recent innovation that offers quite a bit of creaminess but not as much firmness as either Arborio or, especially, Carnaroli. It's not worth going out of your way for.

Vialone Nano An old variety more appreciated in Lombardy and Veneto than in Piedmont. Vialone Nano probably expands more than any other variety, tripling in size when cooked. However, it becomes slightly mushy in the process, which makes it ideal for the lighter, soupier style of risotto, but less good for achieving Piedmont's preferred density. Its absorptive capacity, though, makes it a terrific choice for seafood *risotti,* the taste of which is better infused in Vialone Nano, thanks to its flavor-welcoming texture.

Other Italian rice varieties include Roma, Razza 77, Maratelli, San Andrea, Padano, and Ballila.

Tailoring the Perfect Risotto

However odd it may appear, the term *tailoring* is used simply because the perfect risotto is not something that gets thrown together. Instead, like a fitted dress or suit, it requires a certain kind of attention, a recognition about when something is "just so." The nature of adding stock incrementally is nothing less than a proper fitting—in this case, stock to rice to achieve creaminess with firm texture. It's hardly difficult, but as with tailoring, you can't be haphazard either. Above all, it is pleasurable.

The Stock

Apart from the rice, the key ingredient to the perfect risotto is the stock. Risotto is one of those dishes that can be abused, the self-deluding cook (or corrupted professional chef) pretending that he or she is making risotto simply by virtue of using the risotto technique. It is vulnerable to corner-cutting and shortcuts, nowhere more so than in the quality of the stock. The availability of bouillon cubes and canned stock makes this tempting. The result, it must be said, is acceptable, especially for *risotti* where a strong informing ingredient such as wine or a squash puree can mask the one-dimensional flavor of the bouillon cube or canned broth. In a pinch, use them. (Canned broth is the better choice. Swanson's No-Salt chicken broth is a good brand.)

But do not be deceived by professional chefs—who should know better—who endorse bouillon cubes as being "just as good" as homemade stock. Too many chefs use dried bouillon powder. They buy it, literally, by the bucketful. If a dish calls for stock, no problem: They scoop up what they need from the bucket like so much laundry detergent and toss it into hot water. Apart from a metallic, heavy-handed flavor, one of the giveaways is excessive saltiness.

Make your own stock. Since so much depends, in effect, on so little, the loss of goodness in one of just a few critical ingredients makes the dish increasingly opaque in flavor. It loses vibrancy, clarity, depth—like viewing a coral reef in murky water.

Making Stock

The most useful stock for risotto, in my opinion, is chicken stock. It delivers a lighter, clearer flavor than other meat stocks, including veal. Besides, you can transform chicken stock into a convincing meat stock simply by adding some beef—or even just mushrooms. Just let the beef simmer in the chicken stock for a few hours. A typical Italian *brodo,* it should be noted, is made with a mixture of both beef and chicken. Too often, it winds up muddy-tasting. (I was gratified to see the superiority of chicken stock as an ideal base confirmed by a comparative tasting of onion soups in Paris, where the version judged best employed chicken stock rather than the famously traditional beef stock.)

Quantity of chicken This stock recipe uses more chicken than most. The reason? American chicken is wonderfully cheap, but it doesn't have much flavor. So adding more chicken than might seem reasonable is desirable. Ideally, it's best to use as old a chicken as you can find, which these days means a roaster. But the best deals are always with young fryers, so I buy those.

Chopping up the chicken In order to extract the flavor from any kind of meat, especially with bones, you have to cut up the meat and break open the bones. With chicken, this means not only cutting up the chicken into parts (wings, thighs, back, breast), but then, using a cleaver, chopping up each section into smaller pieces, the better to expose the meat and open the bone to the simmering water. Once I made stock without doing this, just to see if there really was a difference. It was astounding to discover just how flavorless the stock was.

Length of cooking Stock should always be cooked longer than usually is recommended. In professional kitchens the stockpot sits on the back of the stove and is simmering all day and half the night, replenished with bones and scraps. Time makes a difference. Experiment reveals that stock simmered for only three hours is not as rich and flavorful as that simmered for ten to twelve hours. This is especially true if you are using a generous quantity of chicken. Common sense tells us that the more meat used relative to the amount of water, the longer it will take for everything to be extracted. So I recommend that you simmer your stock for eight to twelve hours.

Oven-simmering The easiest way to cook stock for a long stretch is to let it simmer in the oven. It probably falls under the category of a phobia, but I don't like to leave my gas cooktop going when I'm not in the room. So I let my stock simmer in the oven, which is wonderfully handy. A twenty-quart stockpot fits perfectly in my oven, which is a standard size. It just slides right in on the lowest rack. I start the stock in the evening: I bring it to a boil on the stove and then transfer it, covered, to a 275°F oven. When I get up the next morning, the house is perfumed with the scent of stock. (This is a good use for the "timed bake" gizmo, if your oven has one, if you prefer to do this during the day while at work.)

The stock is allowed to cool—with the meat still in there—on a heatproof surface. After cooling, it gets drained, strained, and transferred to half-gallon plastic freezer containers. The fat rises to the top. Leave it there. Remove it when you use the stock.

Fresh rosemary One of the informing flavors of Piedmontese cuisine is rosemary. Fresh rosemary adds a noticeable dimension to chicken stock. Add several good-size sprigs to a twenty-quart stockpot. Use dried rosemary if you can't find fresh, but fresh does make a difference.

No salt Don't add salt to the stock—add it instead to the risotto while cooking. This gives you more precise control. Also, if you choose to reduce the stock to make it more concentrated or to decrease the amount of space it takes up (by concentrating further into a glaze), the absence of salt is essential.

Chicken Stock

makes about 12 quarts

4 whole fryers or other chickens	3 bay leaves
1 bottle cheap dry white wine (optional)	4 large carrots, cut into chunks
2 or 3 large sprigs fresh rosemary, each about 4 inches long	2 large onions, cut into chunks
	4 to 6 garlic cloves, crushed but not peeled
About 15 black peppercorns	

Cut the chicken into parts. Bone the breasts and reserve the breast meat for another dish. (My favorite use is in *Petti di Pollo in Carpione,* on page 42.) Using a cleaver, chop the wings, thighs, breast bones, backs, and necks into smaller chunks.

Toss everything, including the skin, into the stockpot. Add water to cover within 3 inches of the rim of the stockpot. (No higher, or the pot could overflow as the simmering water pushes up the floating ingredients, such as the onion chunks.) Place over the highest heat and bring to a boil.

When the stock is nearing the boiling point, preheat the oven to 275°F. Set one oven rack on the lowest level and remove the other rack. When the stock begins to boil, lower the heat to a simmer. Skim the froth from the stock if you like, but it's really not necessary. Transfer to the oven.

Let the stock simmer, covered, in the oven for anywhere from 8 to 12 hours. Or simmer it over low heat on the stove. Remove the stockpot from the oven or the heat, and place on a heatproof surface to cool. When cool enough to handle safely, strain the stock to remove all the solids. The stock will be a light amber color. Some liquid will be lost from evaporation. Just top it up with water, if desired, as this is a concentrated stock after such long cooking.

Transfer the strained, cooled stock to plastic freezer containers, leaving 1 inch of air space, as the stock will expand as it freezes. Do not be concerned about the fat. It will float to the top and freeze there. Its presence provides that much more protection against oxidation. The fat can easily be removed later before use. Seal tightly and freeze. It will keep well, frozen, for up to 6 months.

The Master Recipe

The best advice for making a perfect risotto is found in fairy tales. Would-be suitors for the hand of the princess are told that they must go out and slay the dragon. They sharpen their swords, polish their armor, saddle up, and ride forth to do battle. If they return at all, it is empty-handed. Finally, some love-smitten fellow seeks advice from the local shaman. *"Mahatma,"* he says. "What do I have to do to slay the dragon and win the hand of the princess?" The *mahatma,* a trying sort in the best of circumstances, replies cryptically, "All you need is a pure heart." Our hero, unsullied to his bones, rides forth and whacks the dragon with little more than a butter knife.

All of which is a (long-winded) way of saying that to create the perfect risotto you don't need any fancy equipment or cooking wizardry. You need only be pure of heart: good stock, Italian rice, Parmigiano-Reggiano, and warm plates. Then you can sally forth with perfect assurance that all *risotti* are yours to conquer. And that's no fairy tale.

About butter It *is* possible to make risotto without using any fat at all. In fact, fat is really not necessary. The traditional "toasting" of the raw rice in butter before adding the first ladle of stock doesn't demand butter or oil. It can be done in a dry pan or with the cooked chopped onions (which also don't need any butter). The result is identical at the end.

The stock need not have any fat in it either. A good, concentrated stock carries plenty of flavor on its own without any fat.

Traditionally, a classic risotto has a dollop of butter vigorously stirred in just before serving. This is called the *mantecazione*. It makes the risotto that much creamier and we all know about the taste. But, again, it's not necessary. What *is* necessary—for flavor and creaminess—is freshly grated Parmigiano. You can eliminate all the other fat in risotto, but not the cheese.

About Parmesan Rice being bland, the flavorfulness of risotto is critically dependent upon the quality of the stock and, almost equally so, that of the Parmesan cheese added at the end. This is not the place to stint. Buy the real thing: Parmigiano-Reggiano.

Economy-minded sorts recommend a Parmesan-like Italian cheese called Grana Padano (*grana* means granular; *padano* is, literally, "of the Po"). Some Granas, as they are called, can be pretty good. But none offers the same quality of flavor as Parmigiano-Reggiano. Like wines, two cheeses can be made identically, but their character, their "breed," derives not from technique, but from the origins of the milk itself. Parmigiano-Reggiano has got it; the others don't. I don't know why. But I do know that anyone can taste the difference.

As for the business of fat mentioned previously, 1½ ounces Parmigiano-Reggiano (½ cup grated Parmesan) has just 10.5 grams of fat. Butter, in comparison, has more than three times as much (34 grams). So, if you're making a low-fat risotto, don't shortchange yourself. Parmigiano-Reggiano is essential. Its flavor impact is mighty. Grate it only when it is ready to be used; it loses flavor rapidly once grated.

About stirring   Some cooks insist that you must stir risotto frequently. It brings out the starch, they say. Others, such as myself, find frequent stirring unnecessary, although not harmful. It does ensure that the top layer of rice doesn't get overly dry. Still, I don't know why this matter of stirring risotto has become an issue. I've made hundreds of *risotti*. I've stirred and I've refrained from stirring. I can only tell you, based on experience, that it doesn't matter. When I add a ladleful of stock, I give it a good stir. Then I leave the risotto alone until the next ladleful. That works just as well as incessant stirring.

About the quantity of stock   The amount of stock needed varies with the kind of rice used, as well as with how high the heat is, how much moisture is in the raw rice, and the desired texture of the cooked rice. With those caveats out of the way, figure on this:

Using a scale/For each ounce of raw rice: ½ cup of stock

Using cup measures/For each cup of raw rice: 1 quart of stock

About the quantity of rice   If you ask an Italian cook how much raw rice to use per person, they say *"due manciati"*—two handfuls. That means about ½ cup rice. This is a good guide, but unless you've got a huge appetite, plan on a light main course, or *secondo,* afterward. I often serve an ample portion of risotto followed by a salad and maybe dessert and call it a meal. In Piedmont, where appetites can be as heroic as their Barolos, that would be almost scandalous.

About washing the rice   Don't. It will wash away the starch. All imported Italian rice is ready for use straight from the package.

About wine   The most frequently recited risotto maxim is that "rice is born in water and dies in wine." Like so many Italian sayings, it sounds charming, affirms the primal importance of wine, and is only half-true. It was probably said by peasants who made their rice using only water; wine certainly would have added valuable flavor.

Whether wine should be incorporated into a risotto is strictly a matter of taste. If you do add it, use a dry white wine and add it not directly to the rice, but to the boiling stock. Be sure the wine-infused stock boils briefly, or the risotto will taste a little too much like wine, which you don't want. (The exception to this is *Risotto al Vino Rosso*, on page 116.) Figure a quarter of a bottle of dry white wine to a quart of stock, maximum.

About the pan   Nothing special is needed. Most cooks use a straight-sided sauté pan. I use a heavy copper sauté pan about ten inches in diameter. But you can make a risotto in just about anything.

About serving immediately   Risotto is a dish that cannot wait, as the all-important creaminess is achieved when the risotto is still very hot and the starch that has so carefully been coaxed from the grains remains liquefied and suspended. It doesn't take long for a risotto to lose this state of grace. Very warm plates are vital, the better to prolong the moment.

Risotto with Parmesan

Risotto al Parmigiano

✿✵✿

This risotto also is known as *risotto al bianco* (white risotto), as it is the classic "parent" of which all other *risotti* are descendants. Like a commoner awarded a knighthood, this risotto undergoes a name change when given the magical tap of freshly shaved white truffles, becoming *risotto alla piemontese*. But that title is much in dispute, as there are other pretenders, each insisting that their additions (pieces of chicken, various herbs, one or another mushroom) make it the one true *risotto alla piemontese*. All of which explains why no risotto in this book parades under that name. It's a matter of frank cowardice.

makes 4 to 6 servings

8 cups chicken stock

2 tablespoons unsalted butter or olive oil

1 medium-size yellow onion or 4 large
    shallots, very finely chopped

2 1/2 cups Arborio or Carnaroli rice

Salt

To finish the risotto:

4 ounces Parmigiano-Reggiano cheese,
    grated (1 cup), plus extra for garnish

2 tablespoons unsalted butter (optional)

Bring the stock to a boil and immediately reduce to a simmer.

Put the butter or olive oil in a heavy-bottomed sauté pan over medium heat. When the oil is hot, add the onion. Cook, stirring, until the onion is translucent, about 3 minutes. Do not allow it to color.

Raise the heat to high. Add all of the rice at one time. Cook, stirring vigorously, exposing all of the rice to the heat, for about 1 minute. It will turn translucent, revealing an opaque "pearl" in the center of each grain. When you see this, the rice is sufficiently "toasted," which makes it better able to absorb the stock.

Immediately reduce the heat to low and add enough stock so that the rice is covered by the thinnest veil of stock—between two and three ladles' worth. Stir to distribute the stock throughout the pan. Season with salt. Adjust the heat so that the stock is barely bubbling. In about 2 minutes, the rice will look dry, with airholes in a creamy, wet surface, like a tide pool where the water has just ebbed out. Add a ladleful of simmering stock. Stir it in briefly. If the rice is sticking to the bottom of the pan, either the heat is too high or you've waited too long to add the ladleful of stock. No harm done. Adjust the heat accordingly. Continue to taste for salt as you go, adding it along with the stock.

As the risotto absorbs stock, it will increase in mass. Increase the heat slightly but progressively to compensate. The heat intensity necessary to keep the rice hot at the beginning isn't enough to do the same trick when the mass is two to three times bigger 15 minutes later.

After 18 to 20 minutes, the rice should be close to the tender-but-firm stage. Only a ladleful or two worth of stock remains. This is where a judgment must be made. The rice should not be hard. Neither should it be mushy. Taste for salt. The risotto is done when you decide that *just one more ladleful* will bring it to its full glory. With that final ladleful, it will be done. How firm or liquid its body is another judgment call. It is better to err on the slightly liquid side, as the rice will continue to absorb stock. Modify the body of the risotto, if necessary, by stirring in some more simmering stock, then immediately remove the pan from the heat.

To finish the risotto, add the Parmigiano and stir it in vigorously. The risotto will take on a satiny sheen. Finally, add the optional butter (the *mantecazione*) and stir it in vigorously. Cover and let the risotto rest for about a minute. Transfer to very warm individual serving plates, grate some more Parmigiano over each serving as a garnish, and serve immediately.

To make a low-fat risotto: Remove all of the fat from the stock (this is easiest if the stock has been chilled so you can just scrape off the fat). Follow the recipe for *Risotto al Parmigiano*, but do not add any butter. Instead, cook the chopped onions in a little water, stock, or dry white wine, covered, until tender. Uncover and cook, stirring constantly, until the pan is dry and the onions are translucent but not colored. Then add all of the rice. Over high heat, stir the rice constantly until it is translucent and the "pearl" in each grain appears clearly, 2 to 3 minutes. The bottom of the pan will be slightly sticky from the starch adhering. This is the time to start adding the stock. Lower the heat and proceed as in the master recipe, omitting the addition of butter at the finish.

Risotto with Blue Cheese

Risotto al Gorgonzola

Gorgonzola is one of the greatest blue cheeses ever created, and it's pure Piedmontese. Every commercial Gorgonzola emerges from just one giant aging facility, a huge temperature-controlled structure in Novara. Each producer has a section where he or she matures the Gorgonzola for his or her brand.

Gorgonzola is offered in two strengths: *dolce* (mostly white with only a little blue) and *naturale* (very blue). Gorgonzola fanciers gravitate to *naturale*, but experiment reveals that it's too strong for a risotto. Similarly, French Roquefort cheese doesn't serve well either.

Gorgonzola *dolce* is the ticket. Make sure that your piece of Gorgonzola *dolce* is freshly cut, and use it within a day or two of purchase. Gorgonzola is a fragile cheese and it quickly takes on a stale taste that transfers to the risotto.

One last point: The milk called for is essential, as it thins out the otherwise too-dense Gorgonzola. This risotto should definitely be made on the soupy side and served on the hottest possible plates.

makes 4 to 6 servings

8 cups chicken stock

2 tablespoons unsalted butter

1 medium-size yellow onion or 4 large shallots, very finely chopped

2½ cups Arborio or Carnaroli rice

Salt

To finish the risotto:

8 ounces Gorgonzola **dolce,** *rind trimmed and crumbled into small bits*

⅓ cup milk, or more if necessary

Bring the stock to a boil and immediately reduce to a simmer.

Melt the butter in a heavy-bottomed, large sauté pan over medium heat. Add the chopped onion and cook until translucent. Raise the heat and add the rice. Stir vigorously until the grains are translucent and the "pearl" in each grain appears clearly. Immediately reduce the heat and add two or three ladles' worth of simmering stock, just barely enough to cover the rice. Season with salt. Stir briefly. When airholes start to appear in the surface, add another ladleful of stock. Continue to cook and add the stock, tasting for salt from time to time.

To finish the risotto, when the rice is almost fully cooked, add the Gorgonzola and milk. Raise the heat slightly and stir vigorously to combine. The texture should be almost a quivery mass.

When the risotto is cooked, immediately remove it from the heat. If the consistency is too dry, stir in a little more milk or stock. Serve immediately on hot plates.

Risotto with Melted Cheese

Ris an Cagnon

꧁꧂

This is a traditional dish of northern Piedmont, especially around the city of Biella. There, they use two different types of toma cheeses: a younger toma, called *toma del Macagno*, and an older version generically called (in dialect) *toma veja.*

Here, we can substitute any of a number of similar soft, creamy-style cheeses. The trick would be to blend a fresh, very soft, creamy cheese such as mascarpone with something a little older and more forceful tasting, such as Muenster. This is a rich winter risotto that is immensely rewarding when accompanied by a big Piedmontese red wine such as Barolo, Barbaresco, or Gattinara.

makes 6 servings

8 cups chicken stock

2 tablespoons unsalted butter or olive oil

1 medium-size yellow onion or 4 large
    shallots, very finely chopped

2½ cups Arborio or Carnaroli rice

Salt

To finish the risotto:

6 ounces young, fresh creamy cheese,
    cut into thin, narrow slices

6 ounces older, stronger-tasting creamy
    cheese, cut into thin, narrow slices

Freshly ground black pepper

Bring the stock to a boil and immediately reduce to a simmer.

Melt the butter in a heavy-bottomed sauté pan over medium heat. Add the onion and cook, stirring, until translucent. Do not allow the onion to color.

Raise the heat to high. Add all of the rice at one time. Cook, stirring vigorously to expose all of the rice to the heat for about 1 minute. The rice will turn translucent, revealing an opaque "pearl" in the center of each grain. When you see that, the rice is sufficiently "toasted," which makes it better able to absorb the stock.

Immediately reduce the heat to low and add enough stock so that the rice is covered by the thinnest veil of stock—between two and three ladles' worth. Stir to distribute the stock throughout the pan. Season with salt. Adjust the heat so that the stock is barely bubbling. In about 2 minutes, the rice will look dry, with airholes in a creamy, wet surface, like a tide pool where the water has just ebbed out. Add a ladleful of simmering stock and stir it in briefly. Repeat these steps until the risotto is finished.

When the risotto is cooked, remove it from the heat. To finish the risotto, add the cheese and pepper, stirring vigorously to blend. Serve immediately on warm plates.

Red Wine Risotto

Risotto al Vino Rosso

✺

The idea of a scarlet-colored, red wine–infused risotto can initially seem a little odd. At least some of our friends thought so. Yet not only is it one of the great Piedmontese classics, it's one of the best *risotti* you'll ever eat. Traditionally, the dish sails under the name of *risotto al Barolo* or *risotto al Barbera*, two classic Piedmontese wines. In the old days, Barolo was so inexpensive that you could devote three quarters of a bottle to a risotto and not feel profligate. These days, forget it: Barolo is way too expensive. Even Barbera is getting a bit too pricey, although there still are a few decent cheap ones out there.

All of which explains why I renamed this dish *Risotto al Vino Rosso*. Use whatever red wine you've got that's good enough to drink but not so expensive that you feel a pang when cooking with it. If you want to be authentic, by all means use a Barbera (my choice) or a Nebbiolo d'Alba or Spanna. But don't waste a good Barolo or Barbaresco. I have tested this recipe using a first-class Barolo and an ordinary, but drinkable, Cabernet Sauvignon. There was little flavor difference.

As for the marrow, it's essential. Marrow provides a flavor that elevates the dish to something truly remarkable. Many supermarkets sell sliced beef marrow bones. To get at the marrow, just scoop it out with a butter knife. Because of the fat in the marrow, there's no need for additional butter or oil. Give the bone to your favorite dog.

makes 4 to 6 servings

6 cups chicken stock

2 ounces beef marrow (about 4 or 5 bones' worth), coarsely chopped

1 medium-size yellow onion or 4 large shallots, very finely chopped

2½ cups Arborio or Carnaroli rice

Salt

½ to ¾ bottle dry red wine

2 teaspoons tomato paste

To finish the risotto:

Large pinch of freshly ground black pepper

Large pinch of freshly grated nutmeg

2 ounces Parmigiano-Reggiano cheese, grated (½ cup)

2 tablespoons unsalted butter (optional)

Bring the stock to a boil and immediately reduce it to a simmer.

Place the marrow in a large heavy-bottomed sauté pan over medium heat. When most of the marrow has melted, add the chopped onion and cook, stirring, until transculent. Raise the heat and add the rice. Stir vigorously until the grains are translucent and the "pearl" in each grain appears clearly. Immediately reduce the heat to low and add two or three ladles' worth of simmering stock, just barely enough to cover the rice. Season with salt. Stir briefly. When airholes start to appear, add another ladleful of stock.

Continue to cook, adding more stock as necessary; each time you add stock, pour in a dollop of red wine. Do not add too much wine at any one time, however, as it is necessary to keep the heat of the risotto unchanged. (You don't want to boil the wine, as that would mute its flavor.) After about 10 minutes, when the risotto is about half-cooked, add the tomato paste along with some stock.

When the risotto is cooked, remove from the heat. To finish the risotto, stir in the pepper and nutmeg. Add the grated Parmigiano, stirring again. Check for texture. If the consistency is too dry, stir in a little stock. Add the butter, if you wish, stirring it in. Serve immediately on very hot plates.

Risotto with Squash

Risotto alla Zucca

❧

Risotto lends itself extraordinary well to all sorts of vegetable purees. The technique in all cases is the same: The vegetable is first fully cooked and pureed. It is then incorporated into a partially cooked risotto, the moisture of the puree helping to finish the cooking of the rice. Frequently an egg yolk is whisked in as a binder.

Risotto alla zucca is one of the most successful vegetable *risotti*, in that the flavor of the pureed squash shines. Squash puree loses flavor after two days, so it's best to make the puree on the day you are serving the risotto.

All kinds of pumpkins and squashes can be used. The Piedmontese typically use a large, round, greenish-gray squash with a warty rind and bright orange-red flesh called a Chioggia. Because of its large size, it's bought in wedges. My own preference among the American assortment (which is becoming impressively diverse) is butternut squash, which delivers a lovely flavor. Because of the squash puree, the consistency of this risotto is particularly "juicy."

makes 4 to 6 servings

For the puree:

1 pound butternut or other squash

2 medium-size yellow onions

1 celery stalk

1 carrot, peeled

1 leek, white part only, thoroughly washed and trimmed

1 small fennel bulb, including the stalks and feathery fronds

Handful of fresh Italian parsley sprigs

One 3-inch sprig fresh rosemary

For the garnish:

Olive oil as needed

4 to 6 pieces peeled butternut squash, the length and thickness of a French fry, per serving

For the risotto:

6 cups chicken stock

2 tablespoons unsalted butter or olive oil

1 medium-size yellow onion or 4 large shallots, very finely chopped

2 1/2 cups Arborio or Carnaroli rice

Salt

1/2 cup milk

2 large egg yolks

2 large pinches of freshly grated nutmeg

Grated zest of 1/2 lemon

To finish the risotto:

2 ounces Parmigiano-Reggiano cheese, grated (1/2 cup)

To make the puree, slice the squash lengthwise and scoop out the seeds. Cut the squash crosswise into 1-inch-wide slices. Steam the squash until the meat is easily penetrated by a fork, about 20 minutes. Let cool, then scoop out the meat, discarding the skin. Set aside.

Cut the onions, celery, carrot, leek, and fennel into small chunks or slices. Put the vegetables and the herbs in a large flameproof casserole. Add just enough water to cover the bottom of the pot, cover, and cook over medium-low heat until the fennel (the toughest item in the collection) is tender and cooked through, about 1 hour. Check the water in the casserole from time to time to ensure that the vegetables are not drying out. Drain any remaining water into the stock to be used for the risotto. Remove the leaves from the rosemary sprig and discard the stem.

Place everything, including the squash, in a food processor or blender and process until smooth. Set aside.

To make the garnish, add a generous quantity of olive oil to a large sauté pan over medium-high heat. When the oil is hot, add the squash sticks and cook until all the sides are medium-deep brown, 10 to 15 minutes. Drain the fries on paper towels and keep warm in a low oven until needed.

To cook the risotto, bring the stock to a boil and immediately reduce to a simmer. Melt the butter over medium-low heat in a large heavy-bottomed sauté pan. Add the chopped onion and cook, stirring, until translucent. Raise the heat and add the rice. Stir vigorously until the grains are translucent and the "pearl" in each grain appears clearly. Immediately reduce the heat to low and add two or three ladles' worth of simmering stock, just barely enough to cover the rice. Season with salt. Stir briefly. When airholes start to appear in the surface, add another ladleful of stock. Continue to cook and add stock, tasting for salt from time to time.

Meanwhile, heat the puree in a nonstick pan over medium-low heat. When the risotto is three-quarters cooked, after about 15 minutes, raise the heat slightly and add the warm puree, stirring vigorously to blend. Whisk together the milk and egg yolks and pour into the risotto, stirring to blend. The risotto texture will be quite wet, but the egg yolks will serve as a binder. Raise the heat slightly and let cook, stirring frequently, without any further additions of stock. Add the nutmeg and lemon zest, stirring to combine.

When the rice is cooked through but still slightly firm, remove from the heat. To finish the risotto, add the grated Parmigiano, stirring it in. Transfer to very warm plates and garnish each serving with the fried butternut squash sticks, arrayed in a starburst pattern. Serve immediately.

Lemon Risotto

Risotto al Limone

⚜

This risotto was a hit every time we served it to Piedmontese friends. They all insisted that they had never before had a *risotto al limone*, and that it certainly couldn't be Piedmontese, but that it was wonderful and could I please tell them how it was made?

Far be it from me, a *straniero* (foreigner), to tell native-born Piedmontese what is, or isn't, authentically Piedmontese. But I was able to point out that Giovanni Goria, in his book *La Cucina del Piemonte*, has a recipe for a *risotto alle erbe profumate all'uovo e al limone*—with rosemary and sage, egg, and lemon. So it *must* be Piedmontese. No matter. I prefer my own version below, which is simpler and purer. This is a terrific risotto, particularly so in warm weather, when it tastes especially refreshing.

makes 4 to 6 servings

8 cups chicken stock

2 tablespoons unsalted butter or olive oil

1 medium-size yellow onion or 4 large shallots, very finely chopped

2½ cups Arborio or Carnaroli rice

Salt

To finish the risotto:

1 large egg yolk

Grated zest and juice of 1 medium-size lemon

2 ounces Parmigiano-Reggiano cheese, grated (½ cup)

2 tablespoons unsalted butter (optional)

Bring the stock to a boil and immediately reduce to a simmer.

Melt the butter in a large heavy-bottomed sauté pan over medium heat. Add the chopped onion and cook, stirring, until translucent. Raise the heat, add the rice, and stir vigorously until the grains are translucent and the "pearl" in each grain appears clearly. Immediately reduce the heat to low and add two or three ladles of the simmering stock, just barely enough to cover the rice. Season with salt. Stir briefly. When airholes start to appear in the surface, add another ladleful of stock. Continue to cook and add the stock, tasting for salt from time to time.

Meanwhile, in a small bowl, whisk together the egg yolk and lemon zest and juice. Set aside.

When the risotto is cooked, remove it from the heat. To finish the risotto, slowly swirl in the egg yolk mixture, stirring it in thoroughly. Add the grated Parmigiano, stirring again. Check for texture. If the consistency is too dry, stir in a little stock. Add the butter, if you wish, stirring it in. Serve immediately on very hot plates.

Risotto with Sweet Fennel

Risotto ai Finocchi

🖾

One bite of this fennel-infused risotto can bring back memories of Italy with Proustian intensity. Something about sweet fennel is profoundly Italian and *risotto ai finocchi* is a superb vehicle for its persuasive taste and scent. Fennel can be cooked various ways, but it is especially tasty when simply braised in a little olive oil and water, with whole, unpeeled garlic cloves. The fennel and garlic are pureed, with the fennel-scented oil left in the pan. One of the great pleasures of cooking fennel this way is the cook's secret sopping up of the leftover braising liquid with some good bread, enjoyed with a glass of red wine, when nobody's looking. The fennel puree can be made well in advance, as it holds its flavor well.

Alternatively, you can just steam the split fennel until it is tender, and it will still deliver superb flavor.

A little more Parmigiano than usual is suggested in this risotto, because it helps bind this somewhat liquid risotto (rather than the more typical egg yolk) and because its flavor so enhances that of the fennel.

makes 4 to 6 servings

For the puree:

1 medium-size fennel bulb (about
    1 pound; feathery fronds to use
    as a garnish)

¼ cup olive oil

6 garlic cloves, unpeeled

Large pinch of cumin seeds or ground
    cumin

Salt

Freshly ground black pepper

½ cup water

For the risotto:

6 cups chicken stock

2 tablespoons unsalted butter or olive oil

1 medium-size yellow onion or 4 large
    shallots, very finely chopped

2½ cups Arborio or Carnaroli rice

Salt

To finish the risotto:

3 ounces Parmigiano-Reggiano cheese,
    grated (¾ cup)

Place the fennel bulb on end and split it in half lengthwise. This will expose the interior and help it to cook more evenly. Add the oil to a sauté pan or casserole with a tight-fitting cover large enough to hold the two halves of the fennel side by side. Place the pan over medium-high heat. When the oil is hot, add the fennel halves, side by side. When both sides are golden brown, add the remaining puree ingredients. Bring to a boil, then immediately reduce the heat to low, so that the liquid is just barely simmering. Cover tightly and let the fennel braise until it is meltingly tender, about 1 hour.

continued

Remove the fennel and the garlic from the pan. Peel the garlic. Put the peeled garlic and the fennel in a food processor or blender and process until smooth. Set aside.

Bring the stock to a boil and immediately reduce to a simmer.

Melt the butter in a large heavy-bottomed sauté pan over medium-low heat. Add the chopped onion and cook, stirring, until translucent. Raise the heat slightly and add the rice. Stir vigorously until the grains are translucent and the "pearl" in each grain appears clearly. Immediately reduce the heat to low and add two or three ladles' worth of simmering stock, just barely enough to cover the rice. Season with salt. Stir briefly. When airholes start to appear in the surface, add another ladleful of stock. Continue to cook and add stock, tasting for salt from time to time.

Meanwhile, heat the puree in a nonstick pan over medium-low heat. When the risotto is three-quarters cooked—about 15 minutes into the process—raise the heat slightly and add the warm puree, stirring vigorously to blend. Raise the heat slightly and let cook, stirring frequently, without any further additions of stock.

When the risotto is cooked, remove from the heat. To finish the risotto, stir in the the grated Parmigiano. Just before serving, garnish with the reserved fennel fronds.

Mushroom Risotto

Risotto con Funghi

In Piedmont, there would be no question about which *funghi* would go into this risotto: porcini, or "little pig," mushrooms. The area where I lived abounded in porcini because of its extensive woods. I never found any porcini myself, but then, by the time I would have figured out where to look, the locals would have long since scoured the spot.

I bought locally harvested porcini at the Friday market during the autumn and early winter months. The seller—always the same unshaven man—sliced a few porcini lengthwise to prove that their thick, meaty caps were not worm-riddled, a common problem.

Here in the States, getting fresh porcini is neither quite so easy nor so colorful. The Pacific Northwest, my native haunt, is happily a prime American source for what is more often referred to as the boletus mushroom, from the porcini's Latin name, *Boletus edulis*. (In France, this mushroom is called the *cèpe*.) *Boletus, porcini, cèpe:* They are one and the same. Specialty markets in major American cities carry them during the autumn and, sometimes, the spring. Dried porcini are commonly available year-round. They retain an amazing amount of flavor.

Any fresh mushroom works with risotto. Fresh shiitake mushrooms are ideal. A few of them go a long way and they have superb flavor and texture. I'm certain that the Piedmontese would love them—as long as they could find them for free in the woods.

makes 4 to 6 servings

1/2 to 3/4 pound fresh porcini mushrooms, wiped clean

8 cups chicken stock,

1/4 cup (1/2 stick) cup unsalted butter or 1/4 cup olive oil

1 medium-size yellow onion or 4 large shallots, very finely chopped

2 1/2 cups Arborio or Carnaroli rice

Salt

To finish the risotto:

4 ounces Parmigiano-Reggiano cheese, grated (1 cup)

Remove the porcini stems and add them to the stock. Slice the caps crosswise about 1/4 inch thick. If the caps are very large, slice in half lengthwise. In a medium-size sauté pan over medium-low heat, melt 2 tablespoons of the butter. Add the mushroom slices and cook, stirring frequently, until soft, about 5 minutes. Set aside.

Bring the stock to a boil and immediately reduce to a simmer.

In a large sauté pan over medium heat, melt the remaining 2 tablespoons butter, then add the onion and cook, stirring, until translucent. Raise the heat and add the rice and stir vigorously until the grains are translucent and the "pearl" in each grain appears clearly. Immediately reduce the heat to low and add two or three ladles' worth of simmering stock, just barely enough to cover the rice. Season with salt. Stir briefly. When airholes start to appear in the surface, add another ladleful of stock. Continue to cook and add stock, tasting for salt from time to time.

When the risotto is about two ladles' worth of stock from being fully cooked, stir in the mushroom slices and continue cooking. When fully cooked, remove from the heat. To finish the risotto, add the grated Parmigiano, stirring again. Serve immediately on hot plates.

Risotto with Hops
Risotto al Luppolo

Risotto with fresh hops is a wonderful, haunting dish. Italians are great foragers and the Piedmontese—long used to scouring the woods for mushrooms—are world class at finding free food in the forests, meadows, and fields. As a result, if you're lucky enough to be served this risotto in Piedmont, it's likely to be called *risotto al luvertin, luvertin* being Piedmontese dialect for wild hops.

Wild hops (*Humulus luppulus*) abound in many parts of Piedmont, as well as in many other places in Italy. The shoots are harvested in the spring when they are about three inches long, when the bud has yet to flower. In the kitchen, they find their way into soups, are mixed into frittatas, and, very often, are served like asparagus—briefly steamed or blanched in boiling water and anointed with melted butter and grated Parmigiano cheese. But the best vehicle of all, I think, is risotto, as it offers a subtle backdrop for the slightly bitter, penetrating quality of hops, whether cultivated or wild.

I include this recipe not in the belief that readers will rush out to secure hops at great effort. Rather, it's because occasionally hops do appear, especially now that home-brewed beers are becoming so popular. It is (dried) hops that give beer flavor. Some states, such as Oregon and Washington, grow hops extensively, so it is possible to find fresh hops out there. These days you never know what might come your way in specialty markets.

Like many risottos made with additions of greens, this one is effectively *Risotto al Parmigiano* (see page 112) to which hop shoots are added when the risotto is nearly finished cooking.

makes 4 to 6 servings

8 cups chicken stock

2 tablespoons unsalted butter or olive oil

1 medium-size yellow onion or 4 large
    shallots, very finely chopped

2½ cups Arborio or Carnaroli rice

Salt

Large handful of fresh hop shoots

To finish the risotto:

4 ounces Parmigiano-Reggiano cheese,
    grated (1 cup)

Bring the stock to a boil and immediately reduce to a simmer.

Add the butter to a heavy-bottomed sauté pan over medium heat. When the butter is melted, add the onion and cook, stirring, until translucent. Do not allow the onion to color or burn.

Raise the heat to high. Add all of the rice at one time. Cook, stirring vigorously to expose all of the rice to the heat, for about 1 minute. The rice will turn translucent, revealing an opaque "pearl" in the center of each grain. When you see that, the rice is sufficiently "toasted," which makes it better able to absorb the stock.

Immediately reduce the heat to low and add enough stock so that the rice is covered by the thinnest veil of stock—between two and three ladles' worth. Stir to distribute the stock throughout the pan. Season with salt. Adjust the heat so that the stock is barely bubbling. In about 2 minutes, the rice will look dry, with airholes in a creamy, wet surface, like a tide pool where the water has just ebbed out. Add a ladleful of simmering stock and stir it in briefly. Repeat these steps until the risotto is almost finished.

While the risotto is cooking, steam the hop shoots or blanch in boiling water. Let cook only until the shoots begin to droop, about 2 minutes. Remove from the heat and drain thoroughly.

When the risotto is three-quarters cooked—about 15 minutes into the process—add the shoots and stir vigorously to blend. Add another ladleful or two of stock and complete the cooking.

Remove from the heat. To finish the risotto, stir in the Parmigiano. Serve immediately on warm plates.

Sweet Pepper and Prosciutto Risotto

Risotto con Peperone e Prosciutto

Sweet red and yellow peppers figure prominently in Piedmontese cooking, as they do in many other regional Italian cuisines. In the markets you can buy all sorts of red and yellow sweet peppers, their sizes and shapes varying depending upon the intended use. In Piedmont, as elsewhere, some varieties are long and boxy, almost rectangular, with straight, smooth sides (called *peperone quadrata*). These are to be stuffed and baked. Yet other peppers are conical, for slicing into strips.

Peppers need to have their skins removed for digestibility. Several techniques can be used, such as baking or charring them, then removing the softened or blistered skin. Less frequently mentioned is simply peeling them with a vegetable peeler. It's quick and easy and is the technique recommended here.

makes 4 to 6 servings

4 medium-size red or yellow bell peppers
    (preferably 2 of each)
¼ cup olive oil
2½ cups Arborio or Carnaroli rice
8 cups chicken stock
1 medium-size yellow onion or 4 large
    shallots, very finely chopped
Salt

To finish the risotto:
4 to 6 ounces Italian prosciutto or a good
    American country ham, thickly sliced
    and cut into small cubes
4 ounces Parmigiano-Reggiano cheese,
    grated (1 cup)

Using a vegetable peeler, peel the skins from the peppers. Remove the stem and the seeds from each pepper. Cut the peppers into medium-size dice.

Add 2 tablespoons of the oil to a large nonstick skillet over medium-high heat. When hot, toss in the peppers. Cook, stirring and tossing frequently, until the pepper dice is cooked through but still slightly crunchy, about 5 minutes. Remove from the heat and set aside.

Bring the stock to a boil and immediately reduce to a simmer.

To make the risotto, heat the remaining 2 tablespoons oil in a large heavy-bottomed sauté pan over medium heat. Add the chopped onion and cook, stirring, until translucent. Raise the heat and add the rice, stirring vigorously, until the grains are translucent and the "pearl" in each grain appears clearly. Immediately reduce the heat to low and add two or three ladles' worth of simmering stock, just barely enough to cover the rice. Season with salt and stir briefly. When airholes start to appear in the surface, add another ladleful of stock. Continue to cook and add stock, tasting for salt from time to time, taking care not to use too much if you are using a salty ham such as an American country ham.

When the risotto is three-quarters cooked—about 15 minutes into the process—add the cooked peppers, mixing them in thoroughly. Continue cooking the risotto, adding stock as needed. When the risotto is cooked, remove from the heat.

To finish the risotto, add the prosciutto, mixing it in thoroughly. Add the grated Parmigiano, stirring again. Serve immediately on very hot plates.

Risotto with Sausage and Rum

Risotto alla Salsiccia e Rhum

⁂

This is an ancient recipe resurrected by the Piedmontese food writer Giovanni Goria. At first glance, the combination seems odd. But upon tasting it, you'll find that the flavor of rum—which is noticeable but not intrusive—adds an unsuspected dimension. This is a particularly hearty risotto, ideal for serving to family and close friends, preferably on a cold winter day.

makes 6 servings

8 cups chicken stock

1/4 cup oil

2 onions, finely chopped

1 small carrot, finely chopped

2 garlic cloves, finely chopped

Leaves from 1 sprig fresh rosemary, finely chopped

1 sprig fresh sage, finely chopped

1/2 pound very mild sausage meat

1 cup light or dark rum

1/4 cup tomato paste, diluted with 1 ladleful stock

2 cups Carnaroli or Arborio rice

Salt

To finish the risotto:

2 1/2 ounces Parmigiano-Reggiano cheese, grated (about 2/3 cup)

Bring the stock to a boil and immediately reduce to a simmer. Meanwhile, add the oil to a large sauté pan over medium heat. Add the onions, carrot, garlic, rosemary, and sage and cook, stirring until the onions have softened. Add the sausage meat and stir. When the sausage is browned and cooked through, raise the heat to high, add 1/2 cup of the rum, and let it reduce until only a few tablespoons of liquid remain in the pan. Stir in the diluted tomato paste and let reduce until almost no liquid remains in the pan.

When the ingredients are nearly dry, add the rice and stir vigorously until the grains are translucent and the "pearl" in each grain appears clearly. Immediately add two or three ladles' worth of simmering stock, just barely enough to cover the rice. Season with salt. Stir briefly. When airholes start to appear in the surface, add another ladleful of stock. Continue to cook and add stock, tasting for salt from time to time.

When the risotto is about two ladles' worth of stock away from being fully cooked, add the remaining 1/2 cup rum and continue to cook. When the risotto is fully cooked, remove from the heat. To finish the risotto, stir in the grated Parmigiano.

Fried Risotto

Risotto Fritto

✥✥✥

Risotto fritto is just what the name suggests: pan-fried risotto. More than a few Italians will privately confess that what they most like about risotto is having the leftovers the next day for lunch in the form of *risotto fritto*.

Making this dish couldn't be simpler: Use a large nonstick pan, heat up a few tablespoons of olive oil, and fry a thin, flat "cake" of leftover risotto until it is brown on both sides.

But for those of us who didn't have an Italian mother to observe making *risotto fritto*, that description—although accurate—is not enough. The technique that follows will result in a successful *risotto fritto* the first time out. Because the amount of leftover risotto will vary, there's no sense in providing precise measurements.

Olive oil	*Salt*
Leftover risotto (any quantity)	*Lemon wedges*

A large nonstick skillet with sloping sides works best. Place the pan over high heat. Add a few tablespoons of olive oil. When the oil is hot but not smoking, add enough leftover risotto to create a cake that, when flattened, is no more than $1/3$ inch thick.

Using a broad wooden spatula, forcefully flatten the risotto in the pan to create this flat cake. (The oil will splatter a little, so be sure to wear an apron.) The rice will become easier to work as it warms up. Making a *risotto fritto* is as close to making a mud pie as a grown-up can get. Just keep patting away until it takes the shape and thickness you want. Keep spreading it out, tucking in the sides as they straggle out. This is a very forgiving dish, as it takes time to cook through.

When the risotto cake is suitably flat, let it fry until the edges are brown.

To flip the *risotto fritto*, place a plate slightly larger than the pan over the top and invert the pan. Then slide the *risotto fritto*, uncooked side down, back into the pan. If the cake breaks apart as it is returned to the pan, no worries: Just press it firmly together with the back of the spatula and continue cooking.

The *risotto fritto* is cooked when it really is *fritto* on both sides. I usually flip mine over three times to get it properly crisp on both sides. But this is a matter of taste and heat level—and whether I need to reassemble a less-than-successfully flipped *risotto fritto*.

To serve, slide the hot *risotto fritto* onto a serving plate and slice into wedges. Sprinkle generously with salt and serve with lemon wedges alongside.

Rice Croquettes

Crochette di Riso

❧

Rice croquettes are a variation on *risotto fritto*. As with that dish, precise measurements are not needed, as this is also an inventive way of transforming leftover risotto into something as good as—maybe even better than—the original risotto.

Fine dried bread crumbs
Freshly grated Parmigiano-Reggiano
  cheese

Leftover risotto (any quantity)
Olive oil
Salt

Assemble two plates, one holding finely ground bread crumbs, the other with freshly grated Parmigiano. Take about 2 tablespoonfuls of leftover risotto for each patty. Using your hands, make a small, flat patty of the rice. Dredge both sides of the patty first in the grated Parmigiano, then in the bread crumbs.

Add a little olive oil to a large sauté pan over medium-low heat. When the oil is hot, cook the patties until the bread crumbs are browned on one side. Flip the patties and repeat. Remove from the pan and blot the patties on both sides with paper towels. Sprinkle with salt and serve hot.

❧

The Cult of
Bagna Caôda

Perhaps the most famous of all Piedmontese dishes is *bagna caôda* (the proper dialect spelling), or *bagna cauda* (which is how it is pronounced): "hot bath." The bath in this instance is olive oil, garlic, and anchovies that have been chopped to a fine paste. Although *bagna caôda* is conventionally classed as Piedmontese, it might more accurately be attributed to just one section of Piedmont, the province of Cúneo, which encompasses the famous winegrowing zone called the Langhe. Dishes never are confined to precisely delimited borders, but the *cult* of *bagna caôda* is more ardent in the Cúneo province, especially in the Langhe hills, than anywhere else in Piedmont.

Bagna caôda is a taste of another time. A peasant's dish, its original use was as a morning snack for chilled-to-the-bone vineyard workers pruning the vines in midwinter. They would make a small fire from vine cuttings and heat the *bagna*; hence the name. What got dipped into this tasty bath was whatever was on hand: *grissini* (breadsticks) for certain, and any available vegetables, such as carrots, cardoons, celery, red peppers, sweet fennel, mushrooms, onions, and anything else on hand in late fall and through the winter.

For the food historian, *bagna caôda* is an extraordinary dish. It was a food of poverty, yet two of its three informing ingredients—olive oil and anchovies—were neither local nor indigenous. This is highly unusual. Rarely do you come across a ubiquitous peasant preparation not made from ingredients locally grown or found for free by foraging. (The third critical ingredient, garlic, was local. It was so widely grown and used in the Cúneo province, especially around the town of Bra, that the synonym for garlic in Turin was *vaniglia di Bra*, "vanilla of Bra.")

Bagna caôda tells us just how cheap olive oil and anchovies were centuries ago. So how did a faraway item such as anchovies become such a staple of the Piedmontese kitchen, even in the poorest kitchens? The answer goes back five hundred years, to the expulsion of the Jews from Spain in 1492, a consequence of the Spanish Inquisition. Dispersed through Europe, the Spanish Jews—many of whom were traders and merchants—sought new homelands. Piedmont became one of them, notably the town of Cherasco, which for centuries had been a major stop on itinerant traders' routes through Europe. It was one of Piedmont's significant trading centers.

Jews settled in Cherasco, and elsewhere, bringing with them their tastes and trade connections. One such taste was for anchovies. They were easily imported as they shipped well, packed in salt. And they were cheap, as the popularity of *bagna caôda* attests.

As for olive oil, it was an ancient item of commerce. Liguria was the predictable source. The lowest, and most easily traversed, of the Piedmont's mountain passes is across the Maritime Alps to Liguria. Even by mule, a trader could get from Mediterranean Liguria to inland Piedmont in about one week. Piedmont, especially the famous Langhe area, had abundant, cheap, and wonderfully good red wines. Liguria had abundant, cheap, and wonderfully good olive oil. The exchange soon became institutionalized. Traders crisscrossed the Maritime Alps with metronomic frequency. Olive oil, like anchovies, effectively became an honorary indigenous ingredient.

Bagna caôda is a spiritual meal: a ritual, a rite. It is a dish designed for the despair-inducing fogs that settle into Piedmont in late autumn and through the winter. Not only is it warming and nourishing to bone-chilled bodies, but its communal nature warms the spirit.

It takes little imagination to understand how for many Piedmontese, including those well outside of the Langhe zone, *bagna caôda* became a ritual dish—an affirmation of Piedmontese-ness. The eating of it is tribal. Traditionally, the anchovy bath is served in a large pottery bowl placed over a candle warmer put in the center of the table.

Today, the fashion is for each participant to have his or her own little glazed pottery bowl set atop a matching stand (a *fornelletto*) that contains a small candle to keep the bath hot. A platter of foods to be dipped is always placed in the center of the table.

The wine is always Barbera—the peasant's grape whose high acidity knifes through the strong, rich flavors of the anchovy dip.

Bagna caôda is still widely and avidly eaten, if not with the frequency that farm laborers once did. In November and December, the height of the white truffle season, *bagna caôda* is garnished at the table with shavings of fresh white truffle. Frankly, that's a bit of a waste, but it does show the affection held for the dish. (It also reveals how cheap white truffles once were, as this is a traditional practice.) When the Piedmontese want to feel and celebrate being Piedmontese, they eat *bagna caôda*. It is one of the tastiest, most elementally satisfying of winter dishes. *Bagna caôda* is a meal in itself that, like a good cassoulet, needs nothing more afterward than a long walk.

Hot Anchovy Bath
A Traditional *Bagna Caôda*

The following recipe is for a truly classic, traditional version. Not only is the quantity of garlic more substantial than what is normally suggested in "modern" renditions, but there is the inclusion of milk in the olive oil bath.

According to tradition, when each participant is down to his or her last bit of *bagna caôda* (or at least as much as can be eaten), a whole egg is stirred into the little remaining in the hot bowl and cooked in the hot bath.

WORTH NOTING

The garlic Unless the garlic is very fresh, it may have a green germ growing inside. This creates a bitter taste, especially in dishes such as this where the garlic is cooked for a long time and is so fundamental to the taste of the dish. If the garlic does have this green germ, remove it by slicing each clove lengthwise and pulling it out.

The cooking time Although *bagna caôda* is put together quickly, it takes an hour of slow cooking to tease out the flavor of the anchovies and moderate the sharpness of the garlic. Because both the anchovy and the garlic can easily burn, it is vital that the dish be cooked over low heat throughout the process.

continued

What to serve with *bagna caôda*   Some of the best items to dip into a *bagna caôda* are breadsticks, raw sweet fennel and carrots, green onions, slices of red bell pepper, raw Jerusalem artichokes, cooked potatoes, and raw or cooked cauliflower. Raw cardoons—celerylike white stalks that taste like artichoke—are a classic accompaniment in Piedmont, but they are hard to find in this country. Less commonly seen in Piedmont, but delicious, are thick strips of peeled and seeded cucumber and cherry tomatoes. All of the vegetables should all be sliced into manageable-size strips or pieces and prettily arranged on a communal platter.

Per person:

1 tablespoon unsalted butter

1 small head garlic (about 2 ounces),
    separated into cloves, peeled, and
    very finely chopped

½ cup extra virgin olive oil

2 whole salted anchovies, rinsed, filleted,
    soaked in cold water briefly, drained,
    and chopped into a paste

¼ cup milk

Melt the butter over low heat in a heavy-bottomed saucepan large enough to hold all the ingredients. Add the garlic and cook for 10 minutes. Take care that the garlic does not burn. Add the remaining ingredients and let cook, whisking occasionally, for 1 hour. (The *bagna caôda* can be set aside and gently heated when needed.)

To serve, place the *bagna caôda* in one or more bowls set over a warmer to keep it hot.

Hot Anchovy Bath with Red Wine

Bagna Caôda con Vino Rosso

✹✸✹

This *bagna caôda* is adapted from a version popularized by Cesare Giaccone, the owner/chef of the restaurant Dei Cacciatori da Cesare, high in the Langhe hills, what's known as the Alta Langhe. The red wine adds a new dimension of flavor.

Per person:

1 tablespoon unsalted butter

*1 small head garlic (about
    2 ounces), separated into cloves,
    peeled, and sliced lengthwise into
    very fine strips*

⅓ cup extra virgin olive oil

½ cup milk

*½ bottle Nebbiolo wine (Cesare
    Giaccone uses Barolo or Barbaresco)
    or Barbera*

*2 whole salted anchovies, rinsed, filleted,
    soaked in cold water briefly, drained,
    and chopped into a paste*

Melt the butter over low heat in a heavy-bottomed saucepan large enough to hold all the ingredients. Add the garlic and cook for 10 minutes. Take care that the garlic does not burn. Add the remaining ingredients and let cook, whisking occasionally, for 1 hour. (The *bagna caôda* can be set aside and gently heated when needed.)

To serve, place the *bagna caôda* in one or more bowls set over a warmer that will keep it hot.

✹✸✹

A Creamy Bagna Caôda
Crema di Bagna Caôda

✢❀✢

This untraditional, undeniably rich *bagna caôda* is delectable. It has become a standby in our repertoire for dining with friends on midwinter Sunday afternoons. We move a small table in front of our living room fireplace and put a communal *bagna caôda* in the center. It drips, of course, but that's part of the intimacy. This version is much less garlicky than the traditional version, but it has as much anchovy. The consistency will thicken as the cream is allowed to reduce. If it become too thick, simply thin it with milk or more cream. This dish can be made well ahead of time. Indeed, the flavor improves as the anchovies and garlic steep in the cream.

Per person:

1 tablespoon unsalted butter

1 large garlic clove, very finely chopped

1 whole salted anchovy, rinsed, filleted,
   soaked in cold water briefly, drained,
   and chopped into a paste

½ cup heavy cream

Melt the butter over low heat in a heavy-bottomed saucepan large enough to hold all the ingredients. Add the garlic and cook for 10 minutes. Take care that the garlic does not burn. Add the anchovy and cream and bring to a simmer, whisking frequently; do not let boil. Let barely simmer for 20 to 30 minutes. (The *bagna caôda* can be set aside until needed. Reheat gently, thinning it with additional milk or cream as desired.)

Serve the *bagna caôda* in a bowl placed over a warmer.

✢❀✢

Sweet Peppers with Anchovy Sauce
Peperoni con Bagna Caôda

✸⚜✸

This dish is the confluence of two of Piedmont's favorite tastes: peppers and anchovies. If you visit a Piedmontese home, the odds are good that one of the *antipasti* served will be *peperoni con bagna caôda*. The idea couldn't be simpler: baked red peppers brought to room temperature, torn into wide strips, and liberally sauced with warm *bagna caôda*. Both red and yellow sweet peppers are used.

Per person:

1 large red or yellow bell pepper, stem removed

1 tablespoon unsalted butter

1/2 small head garlic (about 1 ounce), separated into cloves, peeled, and very finely chopped

1/4 cup extra virgin olive oil

1 whole salted anchovy, rinsed, filleted, soaked in cold water briefly, drained, and very finely chopped to a paste

Preheat the oven to 400°F.

Place the peppers stem side down on a baking sheet and bake for approximately 30 minutes if the peppers are hothouse grown and 45 minutes to 1 hour if field grown. The peppers are sufficiently cooked when the skins balloon from the bodies of the peppers. Remove from the oven and let cool.

Slice off the top and bottom of each pepper, remove the seeds, and slice the pepper into 2 or 3 wide strips. Blot dry with paper towels.

To make the sauce, add the butter to a small heavy-bottomed saucepan over low heat. When the butter has melted, add the garlic and cook for 10 minutes. Then add the olive oil and anchovy and cook, whisking occasionally, for at least 15 minutes, preferably longer. (The *bagna caôda* can be set aside and gently reheated when needed.)

Place the pepper strips on individual plates or one large platter. Spoon the *bagna caôda* over the peppers and serve.

Jerusalem Artichokes with Creamy Anchovy Sauce, Boccondivino

Topinambur con Crema di Bagna Caôda, Boccondivino

Although still relatively unknown in this country, Jerusalem artichokes are popular in Piedmont, where they are often sliced and eaten raw, dipped into *bagna caôda*. This baked dish, a variation on that theme, adds cream to the anchovy sauce to give it body. The Jerusalem artichokes are sliced, mixed with the creamy *bagna caôda*, and baked. The artichokelike taste of the root vegetable is an ideal counterpoint to the sauce. This dish is one of the specialties of Maria Pagliasso of Arcigola's restaurant, Boccondivino.

makes 4 servings

1 pound Jerusalem artichokes, peeled

1 quart milk

Juice of ½ lemon

3 tablespoons extra virgin olive oil

3 large garlic cloves, very finely chopped

6 whole salted anchovies, rinsed, filleted, soaked in cold water briefly, drained, and chopped almost to a paste

¼ cup heavy cream

Slice the peeled Jerusalem artichokes crosswise as thin as possible. (The thin slicing blade of a food processor works well, as does a mandoline.) Add the milk and lemon juice to a large heavy-bottomed saucepan and bring to a simmer. Add the Jerusalem artichoke slices and let simmer until cooked through but not soft, 6 to 8 minutes, depending upon the thickness of the slices. Drain the slices and set aside.

Preheat the oven to 375°F.

To make the the sauce, add the olive oil to a small heavy-bottomed saucepan over low heat. When the oil is warm but not hot, add the garlic and cook for 10 minutes. Take care that the garlic does not burn. Whisk in the anchovies and heavy cream. Let cook, whisking occasionally, for 15 minutes.

In a 1-quart baking dish, thoroughly combine the Jerusalem artichoke slices with the *bagna caôda* cream. Bake, uncovered, until the artichoke slices are tender and the liquid is reduced and creamy, about 20 minutes, depending upon the depth of the baking dish. Serve hot on warm plates.

Lidia Alciati and Ristorante Guido

✦✦✦

Every eater has his or her dream restaurant. Mine is Ristorante Guido. It is, for me, and many others, the supreme restaurant in Piedmont. If I had only one last restaurant meal on Earth, I would choose to go to Guido.

Ristorante Guido is located in an odd, lower-level room in a nondescript row of buildings in Costigliole d'Asti, a country town surrounded by vineyards about ten miles south of Asti. Nothing about its appearance gives a hint to the glories within. Italian restaurants are like that.

You go downstairs and discover a slightly formal room arrayed with Oriental rugs and attractive paintings, seating fifty people in a single open space. The room is pleasant but unexceptional.

But when dinner begins—actually, *before* it commences—you discover that Guido is unlike any other restaurant you know. There is no menu and a small wine list that gives not a hint of the treasures that lie, literally, below your feet. Ristorante Guido has one of the largest wine cellars of any restaurant in Italy.

At a time when Piedmont was a backwater of rusticity, Guido Alciati had a vision of perfection that no one in Piedmont dared to imagine: something as sophisticated and refined as a three-star French restaurant—but not French. The food would be pure Piedmontese, refined to a degree previously unseen. To this day, no one else has equaled his achievement, although a growing number have tried, inspired by his example.

Guido Alciati, who died at age sixty-six in September 1997, was a perfectionist. But unlike some of the most famous French restaurant owners, he was not an egoist. I never saw him bully a client, nor refuse to admit someone because of how he or she was dressed. Or refuse to accept a reservation from a foreigner in the name of keeping the restaurant "Italian." All of these sins, and worse, are commonly, even proudly, committed by the most glamorized and praised restaurateurs in Paris and Manhattan. For Guido, such posturing and bullying were absurd. He never confused his private dream of a great restaurant with the misplaced arrogance of reforming his guests.

For years, Guido was in fragile health, enfeebled by a series of heart attacks. His son Piero has taken his father's place in watchful command of the dining room, assisted by his younger brother, Andrea. The third son, Ugo, works in the kitchen with Guido's wife, Lidia.

By all accounts Lidia has always been a remarkable cook. Yet longtime acquaintances suggest that it was Guido's drive that pushed Lidia to a level of accomplishment that she might not have pursued on her own. Whatever the motivating force, she long ago arrived at a pinnacle of

Piedmontese culinary sophistication no one else had reached. To this day, her accomplishment is unrivaled.

Nearly all the best Piedmontese cooks are women. Exceptions exist, but it is a defensible assertion. I point this out because these women, as the foundation and continuing force of professional Piedmontese cuisine, are openly content to pursue traditional cooking. Not for them are the flights of fancy and dazzling displays of technique so common among some male chefs, including those in Piedmont. Instead, the superb quality of so many Piedmontese kitchens, professional and personal, comes from a quiet, modest but nevertheless forceful insistence on traditional foods, rather than novelty.

There's a restaurant in the obscure *località* of Caniglie, a few miles north of Asti, called Da Dirce. Two women run Da Dirce: the mother (Luciana), who is the chef, and her daughter (Marisa), who attends to the clients. Dictated by the constraints of the seasons, the menu at Da Dirce never changes. If it is fall or winter, there will be a meltingly classic *finanziera*, a stew replete with the cockscombs and various innards that made this dish a taste sensation of a century ago. Luciana is content to make it a hundred times, indeed a thousand times, insisting only that it be as authentic and perfectly executed as possible. Her repertoire is small, but each dish is polished with lapidary care.

This is the tradition to which Lidia Alciati, now in her mid-sixties, was born and adheres to with quiet fervor. For example, nearly every restaurant in Piedmont makes agnolotti, the Piedmontese ravioli. Most are very good; a few are stupendous. Yet everyone concedes that Lidia's are the best of all. How do you improve on something so simple? Especially when the competition is hardly a bunch of slackers?

I have stood in Lidia's kitchen asking such questions. Partly it is technique, the sort born of thirty years of professional cooking and a lifetime of cooking and eating at home. But partly it is Guido's insistent perfectionism. For it was Guido, in the beginning, who obsessively secured Lidia's exemplary raw ingredients, what the Italians evocatively call the *materia prima*, the foundation foods.

"We get our veal from a small breeder who lives high in the mountains," Guido once told me, by way of explaining why Lidia's veal dishes are so good. "This man has a very small number of calves. He raises them more carefully than anybody I've ever met," he said. "And we pay him more money than anyone else gets." Guido said that ruefully, for no country Italian wants to be seen as profligate. Yet the truth is that Guido cared nothing about money. "I don't know if this veal is really worth the premium we pay. I only know that I've never seen better. So that's what we get—only his."

The nature of Lidia's accomplishment can be difficult for those unfamiliar with classic Piedmontese dishes to recognize. Her cooking pleases everyone. But, as in deciding which of an artist's paintings are the masterworks, it helps to know the body of work. In Lidia's case, the people most impressed are those who have tasted other versions of the same traditional dishes she presents.

This was brought home to me a few years ago at a lunch given in honor of the English wine auctioneer Michael Broadbent. He and his wife, Daphne, were invited to Piedmont as the weekend guests of Angelo Gaja, Piedmont's most acclaimed wine producer. Broadbent's professional specialty is auctioning old and rare wines, especially Bordeaux and Port, for Christie's auction house. Piedmontese wines are not much in demand at the Christie's "Fine and Rare" wine auctions over which Broadbent presides. As a result, Broadbent had not been in the region, he said at the time, for at least twenty years. Getting him to visit, if only for a weekend, was clearly something of a coup for Gaja.

Anyway, Gaja had arranged for a monumental tasting of other producers' wines—with the winemakers in attendance, as well as local political dignitaries—at the palatial quarters of the publicly owned Castello di Costigliole d'Asti, one of the area's grandest old castles. The tasting took place in the morning. Then, for lunch, everyone was invited to Guido, which was opened specially for the occasion.

Virtually every winemaker who was anybody in the Langhe was present, serving their most stupendous wines. It was an unprecedented wine fest, with some fifty producers and three times as many wines put forth. All morning long, I wondered what Lidia would cook for the occasion. After all, this was an assemblage of virtually every great winegrower in the zone. They were serious men, whose lives were dedicated to taste. And they knew all the great restaurants of the region.

What Lidia chose to do was daring. And triumphant. Lidia served them *the* most traditional Piedmontese dishes, such as *pate di tonno*, agnolotti, *brasato di Barolo*, and half a dozen others. As each dish was brought out and tasted, you could hear the murmurs of approval, even awe. This wasn't the usual clamorous Italian fanfare, which is offered out of obligatory courtesy. Instead, this was real appreciation. Everyone was unusually quiet. These were serious eaters, eating the food of—literally—their lives.

After lunch, I took an informal poll among some of the winegrowers I knew, asking them all the same questions: Did you ever have better agnolotti? Better *brasato*, that oh-so-simple dish of braised veal? Better *pate di tonno*?

These are the classics. These men had eaten these dishes hundreds of times. Their mothers made them; their wives and daughters continue to prepare them weekly. Their answers, voiced sincerely, consistently, were "No, I've never had better. That was the best *brasato*/agnolotti/*pate di tonno* I've ever eaten." It was a tour de force.

I've thought often about what sets Ristorante Guido apart from all others. The food, certainly. Also, the manner in which the dinner unfurls. You are served what Lidia chooses to cook, with wines that once Guido, and now Piero, suggests goes with the dish.

And you don't think about money. The price of the meal is fixed in advance, typically about a hundred and twenty thousand lire. The price of the wines varies, but you never worry about the cost because you know that the Alciatis take a very small markup. Guido once lamented, "If they break a glass, I've lost my profit." Granted, going to Guido is not cheap, but it's really not much more expensive than any of a number of other, lesser restaurants in the area.

But in the end, what makes it an extraordinary experience is something unseen but deeply felt by both patron and client: They have courage. No one else had pursued such perfection in Piedmont without simply becoming French. For his part, Guido took the act of dining in a restaurant, with its menus, wine lists, and tensions, and stood it on its head. He dispensed with most of the trappings and most of the guideposts we know and expect. For some, a first visit to Ristorante Guido can be disorienting, especially for those who are uncomfortable when not in control.

This element of courage is increasingly important. It's easier to be a chip off someone else's block. Thirty years ago Guido and Lidia created a genuinely local restaurant that not only surpassed the standards of what was then offered, but invented a wholly new one—without betraying tradition. This is why Ristorante Guido is so significant.

Piedmont's Pasta

When the Piedmontese sit down to eat pasta—which they do almost daily—they eat the usual assortment of dried pastas: Spaghetti, bucatini, and the like are all standard fare in Piedmontese homes, as elsewhere in Italy. The cuplike "little ears" called orecchiette, a Southern Italian dried pasta from Apulia, is now enjoying a great vogue in Northern Italy.

But when it comes to fresh pasta, you could defensibly say that Piedmont has just two forms: *tajarìn* and agnolotti. *Tajarìn* (pronounced tie-yah-REEN) is Piedmontese dialect for tagliatelle; agnolotti are Piedmont's ravioli. It's true that other fresh pastas do pop up (usually wider versions of *tajarìn,* such as pappardelle), but the Piedmontese are a stubborn lot. They love their *tajarìn* and can happily eat it—and do—every week. Ditto for agnolotti.

Like Islamic artists who create ever-more-complicated abstract designs because their religion forbids graven images, the Piedmontese appear to have happily restricted their range in exchange for an ever-greater perfectionism of *tajarìn* and agnolotti. Piedmontese cooks have pushed the limits of these two pasta forms.

Tajarìn, for one, is about as simple as pasta gets. You combine flour, water, and eggs, roll it out, and slice it into narrow ribbons. There is only one avenue for improvement: more eggs. And so it has crept up. A good pasta dough for tagliatelle from, say, Bologna (which is known for its fine egg pasta) uses two eggs for every hundred grams of Italy's soft white flour. That works out to twenty eggs per kilogram (2.2 pounds) of dough, which is pretty rich.

In Piedmont, such a ratio is the *starting* point. Some of Piedmont's best professional cooks push it way beyond that. The current record holder (to my knowledge) is Maria Pagliasso, the grandmotherly head chef of Arcigola's Boccondivino restaurant in Bra. She uses *forty* egg yolks per kilogram of dough. Several other cooks in the area are close behind, typically employing about thirty egg yolks.

Does this extremism make a taste difference? You bet. When American friends came to visit us in Piedmont, we always took them to restaurants such as Boccondivino and Il Giardino da Felicìn in Monforte d'Alba, both of which make superb *tajarìn.* Invariably, the pasta was raved over, but I was always afraid to reveal why it was so good, given America's cholesterol consciousness.

But now I have to reveal the truth about Piedmont's pasta goodness. The average portion of fresh, ultrarich Piedmontese pasta dough is a three-ounce portion. If you throttle down to a mere thirty egg yolks per kilogram of dough (which is the way I make it), it works out to only three egg yolks per immensely satisfying plate of pasta. Even if you go wild, pursuing the forty-egg-yolk madness, each diner will consume just three and a half egg yolks. For a special treat, it's well worth it.

Making such rich pasta dough requires a little more care, as the dough is softer than ordinary pasta dough. You'll certainly want to use a pasta machine for rolling. Everyone in Piedmont does. With one of these, you can easily make *tajarìn* that tastes as good as any in Piedmont.

A selection of *antipasti*: a *frittata* (flat omelette), *Peperone con Ripieno di Tonno* (Sweet Peppers with Tuna Stuffing), and *Sformato* (flan)   MAURA McEVOY

Grissini   MAURA McEVOY   Salt-dried anchovies   MAURA McEVOY

ABOVE: Fresh truffles stored in raw rice MAURA MCEVOY   RIGHT TOP: *Trifolau* (truffle hunter) Aldo Drago and his favorite truffle dog, Pulìn. Note that Pulìn is mostly white, which is typical of truffle dogs, the better to be seen at night when truffles are hunted.   RIGHT BOTTOM: Signs are everywhere in Piedmont warning truffle hunters off private property. This one reads "Private Property. Truffle Harvesting Is Forbidden." MATT KRAMER

LEFT: The rakish Fiorenzo Giolito, the master cheese merchant of Bra, at his regular booth in the outdoor market. Giolito has a proper shop in town as well. RIGHT: The large street market of Bra near where we lived. Not only is it a sizable food market, but merchants of all sorts display their wares for shoppers from dozens of small nearby villages. MATT KRAMER

Gorgonzola cheese, Piedmont's "Big Blue"   MAURA McEvoy

Polenta   MAURA McEvoy

Cavolfiori e Zucce in Salsa d'Acciuga (Cauliflower and Winter Squash in Anchovy Sauce)   MAURA McEvoy

Agnolotti (Piedmontese ravioli) MAURA MCEVOY

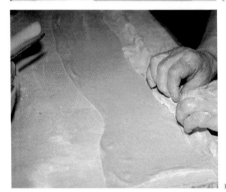

1. Lidia Alciati, chef of Ristorante Guido, with a sheet of uncut pasta ready to be filled and transformed into agnolotti 2. Lidia's two-spoon technique for adding the filling for her agnolotti. Note the small amount of filling used for each one. 3. Crimping the pasta around each filling 4. A golden, humped row of filled agnolotti, just before they are cut into individual pieces 5. A plate brimming with finished agnolotti lightly dusted with flour and lightly dried, ready to be plunged briefly into boiling water MATT KRAMER

Tajarìn con Sugo di Carne (Tagliatelle with Meat Sauce)   MAURA MCEVOY

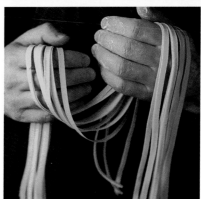

Tajarìn (tagliatelle)   MAURA MCEVOY

Gnocchi   MAURA MCEVOY

Risotto con Vino Rosso
(Red Wine Risotto)
MAURA MCEVOY

Pan-fried trout   MAURA MCEVOY

Pollo alla Cacciatora
(Chicken Hunter's Style)
MAURA MCEVOY

Quartetta (Rolled Pork Loin)   Maura McEvoy

Palline di Carne con le Mele in Brodo
(Little "Marbles" in Broth)   Maura McEvoy

A typical eighteenth-century village
church. This one was near our home
in Ioalita America dei Boschi.
Matt Kramer

Torta di Farina Gialla (Sweet Cornmeal Cake)   MAURA MCEVOY

Nonna (Grandmother) Milano of
Ristorante Cacciatori in the hamlet of
Cartosio near Acqui Terme shaping dough
for one of her desserts   MATT KRAMER

Bicerin (Turin's Coffee and
Chocolate Drink)   MAURA MCEVOY

Tajarìn

❧❧❧

Fresh pasta has acquired an aura of inevitable superiority over dried pasta. It's not so. Most commercially made fresh pastas are not especially good, largely because of the difficulty in handling really thin, soft dough. Many of them are overly thick, dense, and chewy. That's not what *tajarìn* is all about, at least not in Piedmont's best restaurants and private homes.

Making fresh pasta at home is simple. You mix up the dough by hand or in a food processor (a few minutes either way), let it rest briefly, and then run it through the rollers of a hand-cranked pasta machine. The ultrapurists insist that pasta rolled out with a rolling pin is superior (nubby texture, they say), but no one I met in Piedmont does it that way any more. It's just not necessary.

The pasta machine The most commonly available pasta machine is a hand-crank job made by Atlas. However, if you're planning on buying a pasta machine, I suggest you investigate a brand called Imperia. Every restaurant kitchen I saw in Piedmont uses an Imperia. (Perhaps that's because Imperia is made in Turin.) The restaurants use the R220 model, which has wide rollers and is put together like a chronograph, but it is prohibitively expensive, upwards of $600. The one to get is the Imperia SP 150. It looks just like the little Atlas job, but it's better built.

The Imperia machine takes a bit of looking for. One source that sells it at an especially good price is Figoni Hardware Company, 1351 Grant Avenue, San Francisco, California 94133 (telephone: 415-392-4765). Vince Figoni, the owner, says that he always stocks the Imperia SP 150. "It's one of those things I've got to have in stock at all times, like bocce balls." He will ship anywhere.

Dusting with flour Flour acts as a lubricant, allowing the dough to pass easily through the rollers and cutters, so it is necessary to dust the dough occasionally. The easiest, and most effective, way to dust the dough is to toss some flour on a countertop or cutting board and swipe the dough ribbon across it. This will leave just the lightest coating of flour. Do on both sides and then brush off the flour. What adheres will be just right.

Vince Figoni suggests this trick: "Use rice flour for dusting the pasta dough. When my wife was alive, I used to help her make pasta and sometimes it would stick a little. I said, 'You're making it too thin.' But she insisted. So I went across the street to a local macaroni factory here and I said, 'How do you guys roll out those huge sheets of pasta so thin?' They told me to use rice flour for dusting the dough. And I did. It works great."

Tajarìn **thinness and length** Like the Chinese, professional Piedmontese cooks take great pride in concocting ever-longer lengths of *tajarìn*. This is nothing more than bravado. The length of the *tajarìn* is unimportant, especially compared to the richness and thinness of the dough. However, the Piedmontese do agree with the Duchess of Windsor: No *tajarìn* can ever be too rich or too thin.

continued

Drying time Before the finished *tajarìn* can be cooked, they must be relatively dry. "Dry" in this instance means that the strands do not stick together easily. This can take anywhere from thirty minutes to several hours, depending upon how the *tajarìn* is stored and, above all, the heat and humidity of the kitchen. Ideally, they should be slightly stiff when handled. The important thing is that they not be so moist that they stick together when put into boiling water. Use an extra large pot of water if the pasta is still a bit damp.

For each 3-ounce serving (multiply as needed):	1 cup (3½ ounces) plus 1 tablespoon
1 large egg plus 2 large egg yolks	*unbleached all-purpose flour*
	Large pinch of salt

Place all the ingredients except the 1 tablespoon flour in a food processor. Pulse on and off for just a few seconds. The dough will clump and look fairly wet. Add the remaining 1 tablespoon flour. Pulse for another couple of seconds. Stop just when the dough is about to ball up.

Remove the dough to a lightly floured cutting board. Knead briefly by hand. The dough should feel very slightly moist but still smooth. Pat into a rectangular shape.

To roll out the dough, set the rollers of the pasta machine to the widest setting. Dust both sides of the dough lightly with flour, brushing off any excess. Slowly run the dough through the rollers. Cut the thick ribbon of dough in half crosswise. Wrap one half in plastic wrap to keep it from drying out, and set aside. Lightly flour the countertop area where the dough will emerge.

Fold the ribbon in overlapping thirds, as if you were folding a letter. Lightly dust it on both sides with flour. Turn it lengthwise, inserting the open edge of the "letter" into the rollers, still at the widest aperture. Repeat the rolling, folding, and turn-and-insert process several times until the dough is silky smooth.

Reduce the opening of the rollers to the next setting. Run the ribbon slowly through. Dust the dough with flour as necessary to prevent sticking. Feed the dough into the rollers, with the ribbon resting along the length of your forearm, cranking slowly. The ribbon will be quite long, so let it lie flat on the flour-dusted countertop, moving it down the line as more dough emerges.

Repeat the rolling process, reducing the space between the rollers with each succeeding pass, until the dough has passed through the narrowest (or second-narrowest) opening, depending on the machine. Let the dough rest on a floured surface for 10 minutes before cutting it.

Repeat the procedure with the other half of the dough.

To cut the dough into *tajarìn*, lightly dust each ribbon of dough with flour. Put the thin dough ribbon through the medium-width cutters of the machine (tagliatelle width), cranking very slowly. Gently cradle the strands as they emerge from the cutters, like a hairdresser carefully keeping strands of hair in alignment. When all of the strands have emerged, loop the strands over your hand and let them dry on a lightly floured countertop (or tablecloth) in straight rows or in a gentle loop. Let dry until the ribbons begin to stiffen, at least 30 minutes. Much depends upon heat and humidity.

To cook, bring a large pot of salted water to a boil. Gently lower the *tajarìn* into the water, taking care not to press the strands together, so as to keep them from sticking and clumping. Stir the pasta vigorously to separate the strands. When the water returns to a boil, let cook for just 1 minute. Drain quickly. Place on warm plates and spoon on the desired sauce. Serve immediately.

Cornmeal Pasta

Stradette

Although *tajarìn* traditionally is made with white wheat flour, an old version uses corn-meal. This makes sense when one realizes that, for centuries, cornmeal was cheaper than wheat flour. *Stradette*, also called *tajarìn di granoturco* (cornmeal), is rarely seen anymore, but it deserves a comeback, as it's so tasty. The texture is different from regular *tajarìn*, as is the flavor. This is one of the most unusual fresh pastas that I know. The ideal sauce for stradette is the *Sugo di Porro*, or Leek Sauce, on page 150.

For each 3-ounce serving (multiply as needed):

1 large egg plus 2 large egg yolks

²⁄₃ cup unbleached all-purpose flour, plus more if needed

¹⁄₃ cup fine-ground cornmeal

Pinch of salt

Place all the ingredients in a food processor. Pulse on and off for just a few seconds. The dough will clump and look fairly wet. Add additional wheat flour if needed. Pulse for another couple of seconds. Stop just when the dough is about to ball up.

Remove the dough to a lightly floured cutting board. Knead briefly by hand. The dough should feel slightly moist, but still smooth. Pat it into a rectangular shape.

Roll out and cut the pasta as described on page 146.

Sauces for Tajarìn

Tajarìn sees just a few sauces, with each cook adding his or her little fillip. A Piedmontese favorite is so simple that it hardly warrants a recipe: melted butter combined with finely chopped fresh sage. The other two classics are *sugo di fegatini* (a chicken liver sauce) and *sugo di carne* (a meat sauce).

The amount of sauce per serving Italians do not use anywhere near as much sauce on their pasta as we Americans do. Their reason is straightforward: They want to taste the pasta. This is true with *tajarìn* especially, given its rich flavor. In Piedmont, a standard serving of sauce is just three or four tablespoons heaped in the center of the pasta, the better to display the pasta's golden beauty.

Tomatoes Several sauces employ finely chopped tomatoes as a binder for the meat. If good, fresh tomatoes are unavailable, the best alternative is a relatively new Italian import sold under the brand name Pomi. It is a modern-day product, fine- or coarse-chopped fresh Italy-grown tomatoes packed with no preservatives in special cardboard packages, like fruit juice. The giant Italian food processing company Parmalat makes this item and it is better than any canned tomato and, for that matter, many fresh ones. The package keeps without refrigeration until opened, then it's good for ten days if refrigerated. The 17.5-ounce pack is equivalent to two medium-size fresh tomatoes.

Butter and Sage Sauce
Sugo di Burro e Salvia

Fresh sage and good butter are all you need. Fresh sage is essential, as the dried version tastes a little too musty for a sauce this flavor-transparent. This is my wife's favorite *tajarìn* sauce; considering all that she has sampled, that's says something.

For each serving (multiply as needed):

2 tablespoons unsalted butter

2 large fresh sage leaves, very finely
   chopped

Freshly grated Parmigiano-Reggiano
   cheese

In a small heavy-bottomed saucepan over low heat, melt the butter, then add the sage and remove from the heat. The longer it sits, the more the sage flavor infuses into the butter. If necessary, remelt the butter just before serving. Serve with Parmigiano alongside.

Piedmontese Tomato Sauce

Bagnet Ross

Bagnet ross is dialect for "red bath." It is one of the traditional garnishes for the mixed boiled meats feast called *bollito misto*. I prefer it as a tangy sauce to use over pasta or polenta. It's also terrific, used sparingly, over fresh tuna, mackerel, salmon, or other strong-flavored, oily fish. This sauce can be made well ahead of time and keeps, refrigerated, for at least a week. It also freezes well.

makes 4 servings

2 pounds ripe tomatoes, peeled, seeded, and coarsely chopped

1 medium-size onion, thinly sliced

1 large carrot, thinly sliced

1 celery stalk, thinly sliced

2 garlic cloves, finely chopped

4 fresh sage leaves, finely chopped, or ½ teaspoon dried

1 small sprig fresh rosemary, finely chopped, or ½ teaspoon dried

Small handful of fresh Italian parsley leaves, finely chopped

1 small dried hot red pepper

Salt

1 teaspoon red wine vinegar

1 teaspoon tomato paste

Pinch of ground cinnamon

2 teaspoons sugar (optional)

In a large saucepan over medium heat, combine the tomatoes, onion, carrot, celery, garlic, sage, rosemary, parsley, hot pepper, and salt to taste. Bring to a simmer. Reduce the heat to low and let cook very gently, stirring occasionally, until it is reduced to a dense but still fluid consistency, about 30 minutes.

Transfer the sauce, including the hot pepper, to a food processor or blender and puree. Return the puree to the saucepan over low heat. Stir in the vinegar, tomato paste, and cinnamon. Cook, uncovered, until the sauce is thick, stirring occasionally. Taste and adjust the seasoning. If the sauce is too spicy, add the sugar, a little at a time, until the desired counterbalance is achieved.

Serve warm or at room temperature.

Leek Sauce

Sugo di Porro

✤

Sugo di porro is an unusual, subtly flavorful sauce refined by Cesare Giaccone, the chef/owner of Dei Cacciatori da Cesare, high in the Langhe hills in the minuscule town of Albaretto della Torre. He uses this sauce for his resurrection of the cornmeal pasta called *stradette*. And indeed, the melding of the mild cornmeal flavor with that of the leeks is sublime. That said, I've found this a wonderful winter saucing for virtually any pasta shape. I like it especially with the fat hollow spaghetti shape called perciatelli or bucatini.

WORTH NOTING

The stock Because the stock in this recipe is reduced to almost a glaze, it is important that it be unsalted. Otherwise, the resulting sauce will be too salty.

Quantity of sauce This is a rich sauce, intended to be used sparingly. Two tablespoons of sauce per serving is all that's needed, the better to let the taste of the cornmeal pasta shine through.

Preparing ahead This sauce can keep well for hours, or even overnight if refrigerated. Over time, the leek flavor becomes more pronounced, although the texture suffers slightly. The sauce may need to be thinned slightly upon reheating. A tablespoon of stock or dry white wine is ideal for this.

makes 6 servings

8 medium-size leeks, white part only	1 1/2 cups chicken or veal stock
6 tablespoons (3/4 stick) unsalted butter	Freshly grated Parmigiano-Reggiano
3/4 cup heavy cream	cheese

Slice the leeks in half lengthwise, then rinse under cold running water to remove any dirt lodged between the layers. Slice the leek halves into quarters. The resulting strips should be about 1/2 inch wide.

Place the butter in a large heavy-bottomed sauté pan over medium-low heat. When the butter is melted, add the leek strips. Cook the leeks over low heat for about 15 minutes, stirring occasionally. The butter should just barely bubble, slowly drawing out the leek flavor. The leeks will color slightly, but do not allow them to brown noticeably.

Add the heavy cream, stirring to combine. Let the cream reduce over medium-low heat until most of it has evaporated, 5 to 10 minutes. Then add the stock. Raise the heat to medium-high and bring the stock to a vigorous simmer. Let simmer until the sauce is reduced to little more than 4 or 5 tablespoons. Keep warm until needed.

To serve, spoon about 2 tablespoons of sauce over each serving of pasta. Garnish with Parmigiano and serve immediately.

Meat Sauce

Sugo di Carne

This is the classic sauce for *tajarìn*. Traditionally, *sugo di carne* is a mix of ground veal and ground pork, but there's no reason why it can't be all of one or the other. Some Piedmontese cooks use rabbit instead, which is a great favorite. Ground turkey works reasonably well, but its flavor is muted. Ground lamb, however, although utterly untraditional, is swell.

makes 4 to 6 servings

3 tablespoons olive oil

1 medium-size onion, finely chopped

1/4 pound ground pork

1/4 pound ground veal

1 large carrot, finely chopped

2 garlic cloves, finely chopped

Leaves from 1 large sprig fresh rosemary,
    finely chopped

2 medium-size fresh tomatoes, peeled,
    seeded, and finely chopped
    (see Note on tomatoes on page 156)

Salt

Freshly ground black pepper

Extra virgin olive oil for garnish

Freshly grated Parmigiano-Reggiano
    cheese

Add the olive oil to a large saucepan over medium heat. When hot, add the onions and cook briefly, stirring. Add the pork and veal. Break up the chunks into the smallest possible pieces and cook, stirring, until browned. Stir in the carrot, garlic, rosemary, and tomatoes and season with salt and pepper. Reduce the heat and let simmer for 1 hour, partially covered. The sauce should be dense, with little wateriness.

To serve, spoon the sauce into the center of each serving of just-cooked *tajarìn*. Drizzle a generous amount of extra virgin olive oil over the sauce and serve Parmigiano alongside.

Chicken Liver Sauce

Sugo di Fegatini

✤

When you first taste this sauce, especially if it's been allowed to sit overnight, it takes a bit of attention to recognize that the meat is chicken livers. Even those who insist that they don't care for chicken livers find this sauce the exception to their exclusionary rule. Those who like chicken livers think this is one of the all-time great pasta sauces.

makes 4 to 6 servings

½ pound chicken livers, trimmed of fat

2 tablespoons olive oil

½ medium-size yellow onion, finely chopped

Leaves from 1 large sprig fresh rosemary, finely chopped

2 medium-size tomatoes, peeled, seeded, and finely chopped (see Note about tomatoes on page 156)

½ cup chicken or beef stock (canned is fine), plus more if necessary

Salt

Freshly ground black pepper

Extra virgin olive oil for garnish

Freshly grated Parmigiano-Reggiano cheese

Finely chop the chicken livers by hand, as a food processor would puree them. Add the olive oil to a medium-size nonstick skillet over medium heat. When the oil is hot, add the onion and cook briefly, then add the chopped chicken livers. Cook, stirring, until the livers are browned. Add the rosemary, tomatoes, and stock, season with salt and pepper, and stir well to blend. Reduce the heat to medium-low and let simmer gently for 30 minutes. If necessary, moisten the sauce with more stock or water. The sauce should be dense and just barely liquid enough to drop heavily off a spoon.

To serve, spoon some sauce into the center of each serving of just-cooked *tajarìn*. Drizzle a generous amount of extra virgin olive oil over the sauce and serve with Parmigiano.

Dried Porcini Mushroom Sauce

Salsa di Porcini Secci

The Piedmontese are fanatical about porcini mushrooms, which grow almost everywhere in the region. The fresh mushrooms are the high point, along with truffles, of the fall months. But great use is also made of dried porcini, which have superb flavor in their own right. So common are dried porcini that you can buy big bags of them at roadside rest stops along the Piedmont stretch of the *autostrada*, or toll road. Happily, dried porcini are widely available in this country too.

The following sauce is one of the great all-purpose sauces. It is a superb saucing for almost any kind of pasta, especially *tajarìn,* as well as an ideal finishing touch to broiled or sautéed chicken, steak, veal, or pork.

WORTH NOTING

Dried porcini typically are priced according to the size of the slices, the larger being the more expensive. But size makes no difference in flavor. Since the mushrooms are coarsely chopped in the following recipe, there's no reason to pay the premium for larger-size dried porcini.

makes 4 servings

1 ounce dried porcini mushrooms, soaked in hot water for 30 minutes	1 garlic clove, finely chopped
1/4 cup (1/2 stick) unsalted butter	1/3 cup heavy cream
2 tablespoons finely chopped fresh Italian parsley leaves	1/3 cup dry white wine
	Salt
	Freshly ground black pepper

Drain the soaked porcini in a fine-meshed sieve, reserving the flavorful soaking water. If the mushrooms seem gritty, rinse them well. Coarsely chop the mushrooms. Set aside.

Add the butter to a large nonstick sauté pan over medium-low heat. When the butter has melted, add the parsley and garlic, stirring to combine. Stir in the mushrooms. Moisten the mixture with a few tablespoons of the mushroom soaking water. Cook, uncovered, for 5 minutes, stirring a few times.

When the moisture has largely evaporated, add the cream and wine, stirring to combine. Cook for 5 minutes at the barest simmer to the reduce the liquid slightly. Season with salt and pepper and use as you wish.

Gorgonzola Sauce

Salsa al Gorgonzola

※

This sauce is known in my house by the code name of TDF—To Die For, as in: "What's for dinner tonight?" "Oh, pasta with TDF sauce." The fearful (or cynical) might look at the cheese and cream in the sauce and suggest that TDF might better stand for "To Die From." Don't listen to these fearmongers. Yes, *salsa al Gorgonzola* is rich. But you don't want to use too much of it. And once you've put a spoonful or two of this devastatingly good sauce over pasta, *gnocchi*, broccoli, or a slice of veal pork or even a small steak—well, the world is a better place.

makes 1 cup; serves 6

2 tablespoons unsalted butter

6 fresh sage leaves, very finely chopped

1 garlic clove, very finely chopped

3 ounces Gorgonzola **naturale** *or* **dolce**, crumbled

½ cup heavy cream

Freshly ground black pepper

Milk, if needed

Place the butter in a small nonstick saucepan over medium-low heat. When the butter is melted, add the sage and garlic. Let cook for several minutes, taking care that the garlic does not color. Add the Gorgonzola, cream, and a few grinds of black pepper. Stir constantly until the cheese is completely melted. Let cook for another minute or two, then keep warm until needed. If, before serving, the sauce has become overly thick, stir in a small amount of milk. Serve hot.

※

Roast Veal Sauce

Sugo di Arrosto

✦

This is used as both a filling and a sauce (*sugo*) for agnolotti and *tajarìn*. Many Pied-montese restaurants use this as a kind of "master sauce" or filling, with each cook adding a seasonal fillip such as fresh beet greens (instead of spinach), a dollop of pesto, or just a final swirl of extra virgin olive oil when used as a sauce.

If you're using it as a filling for agnolotti, add the optional rice to "lighten" the mixture.

makes 6 servings

2 tablespoons olive oil

1 medium-size onion, finely chopped

Leaves from 1 large sprig fresh rosemary, finely chopped

1 pound pork loin, in one piece

1 pound veal loin or boneless leg, in one piece

2 cups dry red wine

About 1 cup stock of your choice

Salt

Freshly ground black pepper

1 pound cooked spinach, tough stems removed and leaves finely chopped

8 ounces Parmigiano-Reggiano cheese, grated (2 cups)

2 large eggs

Freshly grated nutmeg

2 cups cold water (if cooking the rice)

1 cup long- or short-grain rice (for use as agnolotti filling; optional)

Heat the olive oil in a small saucepan over medium-high heat and sauté the onion and rosemary until softened.

Place the pork and veal in a 3- to 4-quart casserole with a tight-fitting cover. Add the wine, onion, and stock and season with a large pinch of salt and pepper to taste. Cover tightly and cook over low heat or in a preheated 300°F oven until the meat is tender, about 2 hours.

Let the meats cool in the braising liquid, then remove them and finely chop by hand. Place the chopped meats in a large mixing bowl and add the spinach, Parmigiano, and eggs. Blend thoroughly, then season with salt, pepper, and nutmeg.

If using the sauce as a filling for pasta, cook the rice: Put the water in a 2-quart saucepan with a tight-fitting cover. Bring to a boil, then add the rice, cover tightly, and immediately lower the heat to as low as possible. Cook, covered, until the water is absorbed, about 20 minutes. Remove from the heat and let cool.

When the rice is cool, add it to the meat mixture and blend thoroughly to combine.

Tagliatelle with Veal and Fresh Tomatoes

Tajarìn con Vitello e Pomodori

꧁꧂

This is one of those classically simple, transparent dishes at which Italy in general, and Piedmont in particular, excel. Really, there's not much to it—basic egg noodles, a little ground veal, fresh herbs, and a couple of good tomatoes—yet a plate of pasta is transformed into a memorable dish.

The final garnish of Parmigiano is more appealing if the cheese is shaved over each plate in thin slices. A cheese plane does the trick. Otherwise, conventional grating is fine. And if homemade or fresh tagliatelle is unavailable, a good dried version is equally rewarding, in its fashion.

WORTH NOTING

About tomatoes The consistency of the tomatoes in the sauce will depend upon the type of tomatoes used. A chunkier consistency is achieved using regular tomatoes. But a smooth, nonchunky effect is created by using plum or Roma tomatoes. These break down quickly during cooking (they are used commercially for making tomato paste). Also, if the season doesn't offer good, fresh tomatoes, I find the chopped "fresh-pack" tomatoes that come unrefrigerated in special cardboard packages (Italy's Parmalat is the leading producer) a worthy substitute. Indeed, they are better than some growers' fresh tomatoes.

makes 6 servings

1/4 cup extra virgin olive oil

1 medium-size onion, finely chopped

1 medium-size carrot, finely chopped

1 large garlic clove, very finely chopped

Small handful of fresh Italian parsley leaves, chopped

Leaves from 1 small sprig fresh rosemary, finely chopped, or 1 teaspoon dried

2 large ripe tomatoes, peeled, seeded, and coarsely chopped

1/2 pound ground veal

Salt

Freshly ground black pepper

For the dish:

2 1/2 pounds **tajarìn** (see page 145) or fresh tagliatelle

10 fresh basil leaves, sliced lengthwise into "streamers" 1/8 inch wide

Shaved or freshly grated Parmigiano-Reggiano cheese

Place a large sauté pan over medium heat and add the olive oil. When hot, add the onion, carrot, garlic, parsley, and rosemary, and stir vigorously to blend. Lower the heat to medium-low and let cook, stirring occasionally, until the onions are translucent, about 5 minutes. Add the tomatoes, stirring to combine. Let cook another 10 minutes, stirring from time to time. Add the ground veal and season with salt and pepper. Reduce the heat to low and let the sauce barely simmer for 30 minutes, stirring occasionally. Taste for seasonings and adjust accordingly.

To create the dish, bring a large pot of salted water to a boil. Add the pasta to the water and, when it reaches a boil, let cook until cooked through but still firm, about 1½ minutes. Drain.

Place the pasta on warm serving plates. Add a few spoonfuls of sauce to each serving. Garnish each plate with the streamers of fresh basil for a colorful effect, then lightly shower each plate with broad shavings of Parmigiano on top. Serve hot.

Tagliatelle with Garlic and Walnut Sauce

L'Aja

≋

This is an old-fashioned mountain sauce once much loved among Piedmontese in the northern reaches of the region, especially around the city of Biella. Originally, everything was pounded in a large mortar or with a pestle, ground until a creamy sauce was created. If you have a good-size mortar and pestle, and the inclination to do things the old-fashioned way, I recommend it. Wonderful as the food processor (or blender) is, it doesn't extract as much flavor from the nuts and garlic as does grinding them in a mortar with a pestle. That said, the result from a food processor or blender still is wonderfully flavorful.

makes 6 servings

For the sauce:

48 walnut halves (about 3 ounces), very
    finely chopped or ground

3 large garlic cloves, very finely chopped

1/3 cup extra virgin olive oil

Salt

Freshly ground black pepper

1 cup dried bread crumbs, soaked in
    1/2 cup milk

For the dish:

1 pound **tajarìn** (see page 145) or fresh
    tagliatelle

1 tablespoon unsalted butter

Freshly grated Parmigiano-Reggiano
    cheese

Place all the sauce ingredients in a food processor or blender. Process until well blended, about 2 minutes.

Bring a large pot of salted water to a boil. Cook the pasta until al dente about 1 1/2 minutes. Drain and immediately transfer to a large, warm bowl. Add the butter and sauce and mix until the pasta is thoroughly coated. Serve with Parmigiano on top.

Oven-Baked Penne with Mushrooms

Penne con Funghi al Forno

ᴥᵂᶜᴬ

This is an undeniably rich, satisfying pasta dish. It's the sort of winter fare that cries out for a comparably rich red wine such as Barolo, Barbaresco, or a good Barbera. A green salad afterward completes the meal.

Although the usual supermarket mushrooms work well here, I like to splurge and mix them with some dried porcini mushrooms that have been soaked in very hot water for thirty minutes, then drained. Of course, other mushrooms can be used. A fine choice would be the large brown portobello mushrooms. (They are, in fact, the very same supermarket mushroom [*Agaricus bisporus*] called for in the recipe—but allowed to grow to a huge size, gaining flavor all the way.)

makes 4 servings

¼ cup (½ stick) unsalted butter

1 garlic clove, finely chopped

1 pound mushrooms, wiped clean and thinly sliced

10 ounces dried penne

1 tablespoon olive oil

10 ounces Fontal or Fontina cheese, coarsely grated (about 2½ cups)

Salt

Freshly ground black pepper

1 cup heavy cream

Put the butter in a large nonstick sauté pan over medium heat. When the butter is melted, add the garlic and cook for 1 minute. Add the mushrooms and, tossing thoroughly, cook until the mushrooms are tender, about 5 minutes. Set aside.

Bring a large pot of salted water to a boil. Add the pasta and cook until cooked through but still firm. Drain thoroughly. Transfer to a large mixing bowl, add the olive oil, and toss to coat the pasta.

Preheat the oven to 400°F. Butter a 2-quart ovenproof baking dish.

Cover the bottom of the baking dish with a thin layer of the pasta. Distribute one quarter of the mushrooms over the pasta, cover with one quarter of the cheese, and sprinkle with salt and pepper. Repeat until all the ingredients are used, finishing with a layer of cheese.

Pour the cream over the assembled dish. Cover tightly with a sheet of aluminum foil dull side out, and bake for 15 minutes. Remove the foil and bake for an additional 10 minutes. This creates an attractive crust on the surface. Remove from the oven and let sit for 5 minutes before serving.

Penne with Roe

Penne con Uova di Pesce

꧁꧂

This is an unusual pasta dish by anybody's standards. In Piedmont it certainly is a rarity. A specialty of northernmost Piedmont, in the area near Lake Maggiore, the dish is properly called *penne con uova di luccio*—with pike eggs. Lake Maggiore shelters a good number of pike, the tasty roe of which are incorporated into this simple, flavorful dish.

I have substituted shad roe instead, which works wonderfully well. Fresh shad roe can be found on both the East and West coasts during the spring. It's also available canned all year round. Canned shad roe also works well, although fresh, as always, is better.

Other forms of dried pasta can be used to equally good effect. I particularly like the cup-shaped orecchiette, which cradles the chunks of roe. This is a dish for which everything can be prepared well ahead of time. Cook the pasta, drain it, toss it in with all the other ingredients, and it's ready. Traditionally the tomato used is in the form of a sauce, but I prefer the freshness and look of coarsely chopped raw tomatoes instead.

makes 4 servings

1 pair (2 lobes) fresh or canned shad roe

2 tablespoons olive oil

1 large onion, coarsely chopped

8 ounces dried penne

1 tablespoon extra virgin olive oil

2 ripe tomatoes, seeded and coarsely chopped

Small handful of fresh Italian parsley leaves, finely chopped

Salt

Freshly ground black pepper

To prepare the shad roe

If fresh: Separate the two lobes. Bring a pot of water to a simmer. Gently lower the lobes into the simmering water. Let simmer very gently for 10 to 15 minutes, depending upon the size of the lobes. Remove from the pot with a skimmer or slotted spoon and set aside to cool.

If canned: Rinse the roe—which are already cooked in the canning process—and revitalize them by poaching or steaming with a little dry white wine. Set aside to cool.

When cool, slice the roe into small chunks roughly the same size as the pasta.

Heat the 2 tablespoons olive oil in a small sauté pan over medium heat. When hot, add the onion and cook, stirring, until translucent and just slightly golden; do not let brown. Remove from the heat and set aside.

Bring a large pot of salted water to a boil. Add the pasta and cook until cooked through but still firm to the bite. Drain.

To assemble the dish, place the drained pasta in a large bowl. Stir in the extra virgin olive oil and toss to distribute. Add the shad roe chunks, sautéed onion, the tomatoes, and parsley and season with salt and pepper. Toss to distribute. Taste for seasoning and serve immediately.

Pesto

Pesto is an unforgettably aromatic sauce of a green hue of the sort found on British racing cars. The taste is equally green, like swallowing a rain forest.

Although pesto is rightly associated with Liguria—whose vegetable-deprived mariners longed for pesto's fresh vibrancy—the fact is that pesto has long been a Piedmontese passion as well. No one seems to know when pesto slipped across the Ligurian border into southern, or *meridionale*, Piedmont, but by all accounts it's been there for centuries. What's interesting is the ancient Piedmontese dialect word for pesto, which means paste. In Piedmontese, it's called *aja*, a reference to garlic, or *aglio*. (The same root is found in the name of the Provençal garlic mayonnaise *aïoli*.)

Not surprisingly, pesto appears most frequently in those towns and villages nearest the Piedmont/Liguria border. It's seen in its expected use—as a sauce for pasta and a finishing touch for minestrone—but also in less expected ways, such as a delectable sauce for eggplant. I've even seen it judiciously added to sautéed wild mushrooms, to great effect. Another superb dish is pesto added to warm fresh fava beans mixed with chunks of potato.

Though pesto is a very familiar taste, visitors to both Liguria and southern Piedmont are struck by just how good the pesto is there. Although classic Ligurian pesto employs Sardinian pecorino cheese (and nowadays, Parmigiano), some Piedmontese cooks instead use the aged version of the cheese called Bra (after the town). That peculiarity aside, when visitors ask for the ingredients of a profoundly good pesto, they are told what they already know: Pesto is made from fresh basil leaves, olive oil, ground pine nuts, garlic, and grated pecorino or Parmigiano cheese. When this happens, as it often did when visiting food-loving friends arrived, they were understandably dissatisfied with the restaurateur's response. "There's got to be a reason why it's so much better here," declared one such friend. She was right. The reasons, taken individually, seem minor. But added up, the sum is greater than the parts.

The basil Although pesto can be delicious made with any variety of basil, the basil used by the best home cooks in Liguria is a sort too rarely seen in America. This basil delivers a gentle, light taste, devoid of pungency. Some basil varieties can be very peppery or sharp-flavored. When a large quantity of such basil is pounded into a *pesto*, or paste, the intensity gets compounded too.

The best basil to use for pesto is the one with the smallest leaves, what's usually called *piccolo* basil. It's also known as *basilico fino verde compatto*. Ligurian housewives grow this shrublike, small-leaved basil in multiple pots (or brightly colored old cans) on their terraces. The leaves are no more than one inch long and the flavor is subtle yet perfumed.

Alternatively—and more useful for making large quantities of pesto—is another Ligurian variety called *basilico Genova*, the basil from Genoa. The leaves of this variety are large but narrow. It is mild and perfumey, although not quite as delicate as the piccolo variety. The Genoa variety is also a larger, more stalky plant. This is the basil you most often see in Ligurian and Piedmontese open-air markets, as it's the type that is commercially grown.

Both of these basil varieties are available in the United States and are easily grown just about anywhere during the summer. Seeds for both, as well as a vast assortment of other European vegetable varieties, can be obtained from Shepherd's Garden Seeds, 30 Irene Street, Torrington, Connecticut 06790 (Connecticut telephone: 203-482-3638; California telephone: 408-335-6910).

The olive oil The other informing reason why the "true" pesto tastes so refined, so delicate, is the olive oil. Not surprisingly, the olive oil used is Ligurian. Here, the Piedmontese are in complete accord: Ligurian olive oil has been traditional everywhere in Piedmont for centuries, for no other reason than proximity.

Ligurian olive oil is Italy's most delicate. It's extraordinary olive oil, rivaled only by that produced farther south in Tuscany's Chianti Classico zone, which is more peppery. Ligurian olive oil is "sweeter," with a lighter texture. With Ligurian olive oil, the delicate taste of the piccolo or Genoa basil shines through, along with those of the cheese and pine nuts. It's worth seeking out. One of the best producers, whose oils are available in the United States, is called Ardoino, which offers as many as six different varieties of Ligurian olive oil, depending upon the picking times and the olive varieties.

The cheese Traditionally, pesto was made with pecorino, or hard sheep's milk cheese from Sardinia (which, in turn, got coal from Liguria). Sardinian pecorino is milder than the more commonly seen pecorino Romano, which is sharper. Today, many cooks use Parmigiano-Reggiano (the best) or the less expensive (and pretty good) Parmesan look-alike called grana Padano. Many cooks prefer a mixture of half pecorino and half Parmigiano. And, as mentioned previously, some Piedmontese cooks like to used aged Bra cheese, which is hard and easily grated.

The nuts Traditionally, pine nuts are used in pesto simply because they are local to Liguria. In Piedmont, hazelnuts are sometimes used, as they are locally grown. The same applies for walnuts. Sometimes nuts aren't used at all, especially when the pesto is intended as a sauce for vegetables such as roasted red and yellow peppers, where the flavor of the nuts would muddy the counterpoint between the basil and the vegetables.

Mortar versus blender Pesto purists insist that using a mortar and pestle is the only way to achieve the transcendent flavor of the "true" pesto. That sounds good. And there is something gratifying about pounding everything in a mortar with a pestle. But in my blind taste tests, I confess to not being able to tell the difference between the pounded and the blended. If there's a difference, it's a matter of texture. Pounded pesto seems to be creamier textured. The trick is in incorporating most of the olive oil and all of the grated cheese by hand at the end of the process. This ensures an ideal texture. Ultimately, though, the key to pesto perfection lies in the quality of the ingredients, rather than the technique.

Pasta types Pesto can be served on virtually any shape pasta you like. Traditionally, it is employed with spaghetti, linguine, and a Ligurian type of linguine called trenette. But it's terrific over fettuccine, radiatore, chewy gnocchette pasta, and even on large, flat, plate-size squares of very thin pasta, another Ligurian specialty. Not least, it's a classic sauce for potato gnocchi and vegetable- or cheese-filled (never meat) ravioli.

Ligurians—especially the Genoese—add a waxy potato cut into chunks to the boiling water when cooking the pasta. Later, a cooked piece of the potato is added to each pasta serving. Nobody seems to know why the Ligurians do this (it's not done in Piedmont). Some say it's to stretch the pasta dish. Others submit that the potato helps sop up the olive oil.

Pesto

✦✦✦
makes 1⅓ cups; 6 servings

½ teaspoon salt, or more to taste	¼ cup pine nuts
3 cups loosely packed fresh basil leaves (about 2 bunches), well washed and patted dry	8 to 10 tablespoons extra virgin olive oil
	1 ounce Parmigiano-Reggiano cheese, grated (¼ cup)
3 large garlic cloves, crushed	1 ounce pecorino cheese, grated (¼ cup)

Place the salt, basil, garlic, and pine nuts in a food processor or blender. Process until the mixture is finely pureed. Add a little olive oil if necessary to facilitate the process.

Transfer the mixture to a serving or mixing bowl. Using a whisk, gently add the remaining olive oil a tablespoon at a time, saving a few spoonfuls to be added after folding in the grated cheeses.

Fold in the grated cheeses with a rubber spatula. If the mixture is too thick (tastes differ on this matter), adjust the the texture by folding in a little more olive oil. Taste for salt and adjust as needed. The sauce is best when the flavors are allowed to marry for 15 minutes to 1 hour, but it's also great served right away.

To serve, arrange individual portions of cooked pasta on warm plates. Spoon about 3 tablespoons of the pesto into the center of the pasta. Let the diners mix the pesto with the pasta as they eat.

Preserving pesto Pesto is at its most flavorful when used immediately. However, it will keep well, refrigerated, for several days. The trick is to omit the addition of the grated cheeses until just before using the pesto. Also, a thin layer of olive oil on top helps prevent excessive darkening of the basil leaves.

To refrigerate: When making the pesto, do not add the grated cheeses. Cover and chill until it is very firm. Uncover, pour a layer of olive oil on top of the firm pesto, and reseal tightly. Before serving, bring the pesto to room temperature. Stir in the freshly grated cheeses and serve.

To freeze: Omit the grated cheeses when making the pesto. Cover and chill the pesto first to firm it, then add a protective layer of olive oil on top. Seal tightly before freezing. To serve, defrost the pesto overnight in the refrigerator. Before serving, bring it to room temperature, then stir in the freshly grated cheeses and serve.

Variations

For an earthier, nuttier taste (ideal for saucing chicken or turkey breasts): Substitute hazelnuts for the pine nuts. Toast the hazelnuts for 10 minutes at 350°F on a baking sheet. Let cool completely, then add to the other pesto ingredients.

For a more restrained, silkier pesto (ideal for grilled fish or vegetables): Add 1 tablespoon heavy cream or plain yogurt and ¼ cup (½ stick) unsalted butter, melted, after preparing the basic pesto.

Gnocchette, Favas, and Potatoes with Pesto
Gnocchette con Fave e Patate al Pesto

A mixture of pasta and potatoes, along with fresh fava beans, this is a showstopper dish that reveals the possibilities of pesto. If fresh favas are unavailable (they are a springtime specialty), you can use fresh (or frozen) lima beans. Or use fresh green beans cut to the same length as the gnocchette pasta.

Gnocchette, or little gnocchi, is a thick, chewy pasta shape. These are ideal not only because they mimic the shape of the fava beans, but because their chewiness somehow enhances the pesto pleasure. Any number of other chewy-type pastas, such as orecchiete, could be employed as well. Dried gnocchette pasta take longer to cook than most other shapes, typically between fifteen and twenty minutes.

makes 6 servings

continued

2 pounds fresh fava beans in the pod

1 pound waxy-type potatoes

8 ounces dried gnocchette

6 tablespoons Pesto (see page 164)

Freshly grated Parmigiano-Reggiano
cheese

Fresh fava beans are cushioned inside thick green pods. To prepare them, split open the green pod. Strip the beans and discard the pod. Each fava bean is covered by a pale green, waxy-looking cover. This, too, should be removed. To do so, run your thumbnail between the cleft at one end of the bean. This will split the covering, allowing you to peel it off; the fava bean will have the lime-green tint of a freshly cut avocado. It's tedious work, but desirable, as it makes the fava bean more digestible and better-tasting. Set aside.

Peel the potatoes. Depending on their size, cut them either into quarters or into eighths. The potato pieces should be not much more than two or three times the size of the pasta. Cook the potatoes by boiling or steaming until they are slightly undercooked. You will finish the cooking by adding them to the pasta water.

Bring a large pot of salted water to a boil. Add the pasta. Boil until the pasta is nearly cooked through. About 2 minutes before the pasta is cooked, add the potatoes. Continue cooking until the pasta is slightly chewy, but not "chalky," to the bite. Drain.

While the pasta is cooking, place a steamer rack in another large pot. Bring the water to a boil. Add the fava beans and steam for 5 minutes. Check to see if they are cooked through. Fava beans differ in size, so the time is exact. When the beans are cooked, remove from the steamer and set aside. It doesn't matter if they cool, as they will rewarm when combined with the still-warm pasta and potatoes.

To assemble the dish, in a large mixing bowl or on a serving platter, gently mix together the warm drained pasta and potato chunks with the steamed fava beans. Add the pesto, mixing gently to distribute it evenly. Serve immediately on warm plates, adding a shower of freshly grated Parmigiano over each serving as a garnish.

Agnolotti

With the possible exception of *bagna caôda,* no dish is more symbolically Piedmontese than agnolotti. Outsiders may note, justifiably, that they're just ravioli. But that's like saying to a Frenchman that "La Marseillaise" is just another national anthem.

The origin of agnolotti is the same as for every other form of ravioli: It's a way of using up leftovers. One odd thing about agnolotti is the name itself. According to Sandro Doglio in his authoritative *Gran Dizionario della Gastronomia del Piemonte,* the origin of the name legendarily refers to that of the cook of an ancient Marchese di Monferrato who presided over a significant portion of Piedmont up to the early 1800s.

Anyway, the Marchese's castle had been unsuccessfully laid siege to by an enemy. Upon the enemy's withdrawal, the nobleman declared that a banquet should be prepared to celebrate the victory. The only problem, replied his cook (in Piedmontese, of course), was that the siege-depleted larder had just "*quat'oss e quat'brindej 'd carn*"—four bones and four pieces of meat.

You know what happened next. The cook, named Angeloto, chopped up the meat as fine as possible, rolled out some pasta, and fashioned little pockets of pasta stuffed with chopped meat. These were cooked in a broth made with the four bones. The resulting dish was christened *piat d'Angelot.* The rest, as they say, is linguistic history.

Today, surprisingly little consensus exists about exactly what a true Piedmontese agnolotti should be. Actually, that's not surprising. This is Italy, after all. So what happens is that you order agnolotti in one restaurant and receive agnolotti in a crescent shape, curled up like a defensive armadillo. This, you are told, is the true agnolotti. But then you wander farther afield and you discover that what someone else calls agnolotti, everyone else knows as ravioli. With extravagant courtesy you are disabused of this foolish notion. The true agnolotti are not curled, but square: agnolotti *quadratri* (square-shaped). Then there's the matter of size, ranging from the pasta equivalent of doing needlepoint to something large enough that a few agnolotti *quadratri* fill your plate.

As for fillings, well, the field is wide open. Some say that it's a ravioli when meat-filled, agnolotti when filled with greens or cheese. Others assert the opposite. There are agnolotti plumped with *fonduta,* often flavored with white truffle oil (also known as *agnolotti della Bela Rosin,* the morganatic wife of King Vittorio Emanuele II and as scrumptious as she was reported to be); agnolotti stuffed with ham, salami, endive, and parsley (an old specialty of the Susa valley); and even *agnolotti di asino* (donkey meat), a Carnival specialty in the town of Calliano, just north of Asti. (I never did get there in time to sample it.) In truth, agnolotti can—and should—be filled with whatever is handy. *That* is the one true agnolotti.

Making Agnolotti

There's no sense in pretending that fashioning agnolotti isn't a lot of work. It is. As a friend of mine once put it, "You know that someone really loves you if they make you agnolotti." They also must love to work with their hands. The trick, so-called, is to make it easy on yourself. Put the filling together on one day—when, for example, some leftover meat presents itself—and make the pasta dough on a different day. A really smart cook whips up a filling and freezes it until ambition takes hold. This is worth doing when you've made a big roast and the leftovers seem endless.

As for the shape of agnolotti, it's up to you. Yes, you can use your ravioli form to make agnolotti. Just call them agnolotti *quadrati* and hold your head up high. That said, in my heart I believe that real agnolotti are formed by hand in crescent shape. But then I lived in that part of Piedmont where those are ubiquitous and I surely was brainwashed.

However, by almost universal acclamation the best agnolotti in Piedmont—square-shaped, no less—are made by Lidia Alciati of Ristorante Guido in Costigliole d'Asti. So for the definitive lesson in agnolotti making, I asked Lidia to show me her technique. This is the basis of the instructions to follow, but I can tell you right now that good as the result is, it's still not quite what she achieves. It's the old story: All you need are forty years of experience, plus Piedmont's superb raw ingredients. That said, the result on these shores is still superb.

Agnolotti di Lidia Alciati

makes about 150 agnolotti, depending on
their size (15¼ ounces)

4½ cups plus 1 tablespoon unbleached all-purpose flour	5 tablespoons water
2 large eggs	1 tablespoon olive oil
5 large egg yolks	Pinch of salt

Lidia Alciati mixes the dough by hand, making a cone-shaped mound of flour and adding the eggs, water, olive oil, and salt to a crater-shaped depression at the top of the cone. These ingredients are gradually and methodically mixed together, first with a fork and then worked by hand. It's easy enough to do, but a food processor can be substituted.

To use a food processor   Place 4½ cups of the flour and all of the remaining ingredients in a food processor. Pulse on and off for just a few seconds. The dough will clump and look fairly wet. Add the additional 1 tablespoon flour. Pulse for another couple of seconds. Stop just when the dough is about to cohere into a ball.

Remove the dough to a lightly floured cutting board. Knead briefly by hand. The dough should feel very slightly moist but smooth. Pat into a rectangular shape.

Rolling out the dough   Set the rollers of the pasta machine to the widest setting. Dust both sides of the dough lightly with flour, brushing off any excess. Slowly run the dough through the rollers. Cut the thick ribbon of dough in half crosswise. Wrap one half in plastic wrap to prevent it from drying out, and set aside. Lightly flour the countertop area where the dough will emerge.

Fold the ribbon in overlapping thirds, as if you were folding a letter. Lightly dust it on both sides with flour. Turn it lengthwise, inserting the open edge of the "letter" into the rollers, still at the widest aperture. Repeat the rolling, folding, and turn-and-insert process several times until the dough is silky smooth.

Reduce the opening of the rollers to the next setting. Run the ribbon slowly through. Dust the dough with flour as necessary to prevent sticking. Feed the dough into the roller, with the ribbon resting along the length of your forearm, cranking slowly. The ribbon will be quite long, so let it lie flat on the flour-dusted countertop, moving it down the line as more dough emerges.

Repeat the rolling process, reducing the space between the rollers with each succeeding pass, until the dough has passed through the narrowest (or second-narrowest) opening. Let the dough rest on a floured surface for 10 minutes before cutting it. Repeat the procedure with the other half of the dough.

Place the sheets of dough (they should be about 5 inches wide and about $2\frac{1}{2}$ feet long if rolled out very thinly) on a flour-dusted cloth (Lidia uses hard semolina flour for this purpose) placed on a baking sheet and fold the cloth over the pasta sheets to cover them fully. The sheets are best fashioned immediately into agnolotti but can rest, covered, for several hours in the refrigerator.

Filling and shaping the agnolotti   Lay one sheet of dough on a lightly floured surface, with a long side facing you. Put a row of heaping $\frac{1}{2}$ teaspoonfuls of filling (see the recipes that follow) on the dough, slightly off-center towards you, leaving a 1-inch space between each dollop of filling. Fold the top half of the dough over the filling, lining up the bottom and top edge. Press the two edges firmly together with your fingers. Then seal the dough around the spoonfuls of filling by using the sides of your hands and coming down on both sides of the filling (like a gentle karate chop) to make a tight fit that prevents too big an air pocket from forming inside.

Dividing the agnolotti   A ravioli crimper is wonderfully handy and I urge you to use one. Otherwise, use a fluted pastry wheel, taking care that the edges of the dough are firmly pressed together after cutting. Pressing firmly, run the ravioli crimper along the two overlapping edges of dough, cutting off a silver of dough. This fully seals one side of each agnolotto. Then run the ravioli crimper between each mound of filling, cutting fairly close to the filling. Reserve the scraps of pasta dough, as these can be rolled out again and reused. Trim off any excess dough from each agnolotti. Cover with a flour-dusted cloth and refrigerate until ready to cook.

Cooking the agnolotti   At Guido, the average serving is thirty small agnolotti. These are served in a large, shallow white porcelain soup bowl.

Bring a large pot of salted water to a boil. Gently slide some agnolotti into the boiling water. Cook in batches for 5 minutes, or until the agnolotti puff and float to the surface. Remove with a large perforated strainer and transfer to a large nonstick skillet for saucing.

Fillings for Agnolotti

As mentioned previously, fillings for agnolotti were, and still are, created from leftovers, especially roasted meats. The classic filling employs leftover *brasato*, or braised meat, typically veal. This is not the moment to be slavish to a precise recipe, which is inimical to the spirit of agnolotti.

Lidia Alciati's Three-Meat Agnolotti Filling

Ripieno del Tre Carni di Lidia Alciati

Guido is one of Italy's luxury restaurants. Not surprisingly, Lidia Alciati's filling for agnolotti is like no other. It also takes advantage of the meats that usually are served at Guido: veal, rabbit, and, less frequently, pork.

One of the disadvantages of gleaning recipes from professional chefs is not that the chefs are unforthcoming or secretive. Rather, it's that professional chefs everywhere (except for pastry cooks) do not bother with precise measurements. Why should they? They know when something looks "about right." Never is this truer than with a filling for agnolotti. I doubt if Lidia Alciati has bothered to measure the precise quantities of the three meats she uses for her filling in twenty or thirty years. So in talking about her agnolotti filling, she is understandably vague.

In essence, Lidia Alciati uses roughly equal amounts of roast pork, roast veal, and roast rabbit. It's not exact, nor need it be: What is true for her is true for us, too.

makes 4 cups, enough to fill about 125 agnolotti, depending upon their size

Olive oil

$1/2$ pound ground veal (or leftover veal roast or, especially good, veal shanks)

$1/2$ pound pork loin (or better yet, leftover pork loin roast)

1 rabbit hindquarter (about $1/2$ pound)

1 medium-size onion, thickly sliced

1 large carrot, sliced into chunks

Leaves from 1 sprig fresh rosemary, finely chopped

$1/2$ cup chicken stock (canned is fine)

$1/2$ bottle dry white wine

2 ounces Parmigiano-Reggiano cheese, grated ($1/2$ cup)

1 pound fresh spinach, thoroughly washed, tough stems removed, and finely chopped, or 1-pound package frozen chopped spinach, thawed

3 large eggs plus 2 large egg yolks

$1/4$ teaspoon freshly grated nutmeg

Salt

Freshly ground black pepper

Lidia Alciati cooks each meat separately, although it's really not necessary. In a large saucepan or casserole, place the pork loin, rabbit hindquarter, onion slices, carrot chunks, and rosemary. Add the chicken stock and wine; the liquid should barely cover the solids (augment with water if necessary). Bring to a boil, then immediately reduce the heat to a bare simmer. Cover tightly and braise for 2 hours. (If using leftover meats, cook the vegetables in the broth until tender, drain, and set aside until needed.)

While the meats are braising, heat a little olive oil in a small sauté pan over medium heat and sauté the veal until no longer pink. Set aside.

Remove the meats from the braising liquid. Debone the rabbit, discarding the bones. Strain the braising liquid, reserving the onions and carrot. Reserve the braising liquid for another use (such as a base for the stock reduction sauce on page 150). Let the meats cool completely.

Combine the cooled braised meats with the reserved onion and carrot and the veal and finely chop or grind, by hand, in a meat grinder, or with a food processor. When the meat is finely chopped, add the remaining ingredients, mixing very thoroughly to combine. Taste for seasoning. Refrigerate and use for filling agnolotti.

Cheese Filling for Agnolotti
Ripieno di Fonduta

அஜ்க

This filling creates what some restaurants like to call *agnolotti della Bela Rosin*. It is a simple filling that frequently, although not necessarily, admits the addition of fresh herbs (sage is usual) or a judicious amount of white truffle oil or white truffle paste. Saucing for *fonduta*-stuffed agnolotti almost always is *burro e salvia*, butter and fresh sage.

makes 1¼ cups, enough to fill about 50 agnolotti,
depending upon their size

5 ounces Fontal cheese (or an equal mix of Fontal and Fontina), cut into small dice	*½ cup milk* *2 tablespoons unsalted butter* *2 large egg yolks*

Soak the Fontal in the milk for several hours or overnight in the refrigerator.

In the top half of a double boiler set over gently simmering water, melt the butter. When the butter is completely melted, add the Fontal-and-milk mixture. Whisking constantly, add the egg yolks one at a time. Continue whisking until the cheese has melted and the mixture has been transformed into a satiny, glossy, thick-textured liquid; this will take about 10 minutes. Immediately remove the fonduta from the heat. Let cool and refrigerate until needed. The fonduta should be cool and firm before using it as a filling for agnolotti.

Ravioli with Potato and Spinach Filling

Ravioli di Patate e Spinaci

✿❀✿

This is one of those subtle, flavorsome ravioli fillings that make attentive eaters pause briefly to analyze what makes it so good. Then it dawns on you: It's the potatoes. Because of that, the choice of potatoes is important. You can use baked Russet Burbank (Idaho-type) potatoes to great effect, minus the skins. In Piedmont, however, they use waxy-type potatoes. The best sorts here are Yellow Finnish or Yukon Gold, which are sweeter tasting than the usual red- and white-skinned varieties.

WORTH NOTING

Do not use a food processor to mash the potatoes, as it will make them gluey. That old-fashioned and indispensable utensil, the potato ricer, is the ticket here.

makes enough to fill about 60 agnolotti,
depending upon their size

2 pounds waxy-type potatoes, peeled and quartered, or 3 medium-size Russets, baked and insides scooped out and reserved

2 pounds fresh spinach or 1 package frozen chopped spinach, thawed

2 tablespoons olive oil

1 leek, white part only, coarsely chopped and thoroughly washed

3 garlic cloves, very finely chopped

Leaves from 1 sprig fresh rosemary, finely chopped

1 large egg

1½ ounces Parmigiano-Reggiano cheese, grated (6 tablespoons) or more if needed

Salt

Freshly ground black pepper

Freshly grated nutmeg

Dried bread crumbs (optional)

Cook the potatoes by steaming them or cooking them in boiling water to cover. When the potatoes are tender, drain and let cool. Put the cooled cooked potatoes through a potato ricer or chop very fine. Set aside.

If using fresh spinach, trim the stems and immerse the leaves in a sinkful of cold water. Swish the leaves to dislodge any sand, then pull them from the water. Plunge the leaves into a large pot of boiling salted water. Let cook for just 1 minute. Drain in a colander. Run cold water over the spinach to stop it from cooking further. Let drain again, pressing down on the spinach to extract excess moisture. Finely chop and set aside.

If using frozen spinach, squeeze out any excess moisture. Finely chop (if necessary) and set aside.

Place a large, nonstick sauté pan over medium-low heat. Add the olive oil. When hot, add the leeks, garlic, and rosemary and cook briefly, stirring, taking care not to let the garlic brown. Add the spinach, tossing and stirring vigorously to evaporate any excess moisture. When the spinach seems reasonably dry, remove from the heat. Transfer to a large mixing bowl and let cool.

When the spinach mixture is cool, add the potatoes, egg, and Parmigiano and season with salt, pepper, and nutmeg. Blend the mixture thoroughly, using your hands. If the mixture seems overly moist, add some very fine bread crumbs or more grated Parmigiano. Use as a filling for agnolotti.

Sauce the cooked agnolotti with nothing more than a drizzle of melted unsalted butter, accompanied by grated Parmigiano.

Herb-Filled Agnolotti with Marjoram Sauce

Agnolotti Ripieni con Erbe, Profumo di Maggiorana

This is a Ligurian-influenced pasta that relies on fresh herbs. The mixture of herbs for the filling should vary with availability and the season. What's important is that the mixture not be dominated by any single herb. Some cooks like to add small amounts of finely chopped strong-flavored greens such as dandelions or unusual lettuces. Whatever the mix, the result is fresh tasting and vibrant. The marjoram-infused butter sauce is a subtle counterpoint.

makes about 50 agnolotti, depending upon
size; 4 to 6 servings

For the sauce:

$^1\!/_4$ cup ($^1\!/_2$ stick) unsalted butter

2 large sprigs fresh marjoram

For the filling:

6 tablespoons finely chopped mixed fresh
    herbs, such as thyme, rosemary,
    borage, mint, and sage

$^3\!/_4$ cup ricotta cheese

3 ounces Parmigiano-Reggiano cheese,
    grated ($^3\!/_4$ cup)

2 large eggs

Salt

Freshly ground black pepper

For the pasta:

3 to $3^1\!/_2$ cups ($10^1\!/_2$ to $12^1\!/_4$ ounces)
    unbleached all-purpose flour

3 large eggs

Large pinch of salt

To serve:

Freshly grated Parmigiano-Reggiano
    cheese

To make the sauce, melt the butter in a small pan over low heat. Remove from the heat, add the marjoram, and let steep for 1 hour or more.

To make the filling, bring a small pan of water to a boil. Add the herbs and blanch for 1 minute. This heightens the color and taste of the herbs. Drain immediately in a strainer and set aside.

In a medium-size mixing bowl, combine the herbs with the ricotta, Parmigiano, and eggs and season with salt and pepper. Mix thoroughly to blend. Set aside.

For the pasta, make the dough with the flour, eggs, and salt as described on page 146. Roll out the pasta dough into sheets as described on page 146, and fill and firm agnolotti using the herb filling, as on page 169, taking care that they are well sealed.

To serve, remove the marjoram sprigs from the herb butter and reheat the butter. Place the cooked agnolotti on warm plates and sauce with the marjoram-infused butter. Sprinkle with Parmigiano and serve immediately.

Lidia Alciati's Sauce for Agnolotti

Sugo di Lidia

What to put on agnolotti is a vexing question for some Piedmontese. The classic is simply butter and freshly grated Parmigiano cheese. For great agnolotti, this is ideal. Some like to use the tomato-based *sugo di carne* traditional to *tajarìn*. This offends agnolotti connoisseurs, with reason. Giovanni Goria, one of Piedmont's food authorities, declares with undisguised dismay that "In the countryside many use a meat sauce on their agnolotti. This is an error. It vulgarizes the dish. True Piedmontese agnolotti needs only meat stocks and no 'outside' meat."

That is, essentially, the sauce that Lidia Alciati uses: a reduced meat stock to which is added a little enriching butter. It really is *the* best sauce. The stock must be homemade, as no sauce is more transparent in flavor. Lidia Alciati says she always uses veal stock. "But sometimes I use rabbit," she adds quickly.

For my own cooking, I prefer chicken stock. When I mentioned that to Lidia, she nodded and said, "Yes, that would be very good, too." With that absolution, I suggest you do the same, as it tastes great.

For each serving:

½ cup homemade chicken stock (see page 109; it must be salt-free)

1 to 2 tablespoons unsalted butter

Freshly grated Parmigiano-Reggiano cheese

Place a large nonstick skillet over high heat. Add the stock and reduce to a slightly liquid glaze. Remove from the heat and swirl in the butter. When the butter is completely incorporated, add a serving of just-cooked agnolotti to the skillet and gently turn them until fully glazed. Slide the agnolotti into a heated shallow soup bowl or warmed plate. Serve immediately with freshly grated Parmigiano.

Count Barbaroux's Lavish Stuffed Pasta

Cannelloni alla Conte Barbaroux

❧

This is an ancient, and elaborate, stuffed pasta named in honor of Count Giuseppe Barbaroux (1772–1843), who supposedly invented the dish. More likely, his cook created it and named it in his honor. Barbaroux was from Cúneo and was known in his day as a jurist and author of a revised civil code.

This dish is the taste of another time and might be, for some, too much of a good thing. It certainly is, well, stuffed with goodies. Nevertheless, I like it as a midwinter treat. In the old days it was brought out with great fanfare in honor of a special guest. By the way, this is an unusual dish in that, although it is irreproachably Piedmontese, most Northern Italian stuffed pasta recipes (ravioli excluded) come from the Emilia region farther east.

One feature of this time-honored dish that makes it so Piedmontese is the fact that the cannelloni are made not with pasta dough, but rather with a wrapping that is, effectively, a crêpe. Here, the French influence on Piedmont makes itself felt.

Actually, creating the dish is quite simple, if a bit time-consuming. In essence, it's a matter of freshly made crêpes (*crespelle* in Italian) into which a spoonful of a meat mixture is added. The crêpes are then rolled up into a tube shape (hence the name cannelloni), arrayed in a baking dish, napped with white sauce, and baked. The dish cries out for just the sort of penetrating, invigorating red wine at which Piedmont excels: Barbera, Barolo, or Barbaresco.

The idea of this dish is a good one. And there's no reason not to create your own, simpler filling. Ground veal combined with chopped ham, for example. Or a straight vegetarian version using just spinach and *béchamel*. Whatever you do, this is a dish that can be prepared well ahead of time, very tightly wrapped, and kept refrigerated until just before baking. Once cooked, though, of course, it should be served straightaway.

makes 8 servings

For the *crespelle:*

1 large egg plus 1 large egg yolk

2 cups milk

2 tablespoons olive oil

1½ cups all-purpose flour

Large pinch of salt

For the filling:

½ pound sausage meat

½ pound ground pork

1 pound ground veal

1 large garlic clove, finely chopped

Leaves from 1 large sprig fresh rosemary,
    finely chopped

3 pounds fresh spinach or 1½ packages
    frozen chopped spinach, thawed

Salt

Freshly grated black pepper

1 ounce Parmigiano-Reggiano cheese,
    grated (¼ cup)

For the *béchamel:*

2 tablespoons unsalted butter

2 tablespoons all-purpose flour

2 cups milk

Generous pinch of freshly grated nutmeg

Salt

Freshly ground white pepper

Olive oil for cooking the **crespelle**

To make the *crespelle* batter, in a medium-size mixing bowl, whisk together the whole egg and egg yolk, then whisk in the milk and oil. Slowly whisk in the flour a little at a time. Continue whisking for several minutes after the flour is completely incorporated to ensure that it is well blended. Add the salt. Cover tightly and refrigerate for at least 2 hours, to allow the gluten in the flour to relax. (Gluten is the protein in flour that gives dough elasticity.)

To make the filling, in a large mixing bowl, combine the sausage, pork, veal, garlic, and rosemary. Blend thoroughly, using your hands.

Place a large sauté pan over medium heat. Add the meat mixture to the pan (no oil is necessary, as the fat in the sausage will serve to grease the pan soon enough) and stir constantly with a wooden spatula constantly to expose all of the meat to the heat. Use the spatula to break up any large chunks. When the meat is fully cooked, remove from the heat and set aside.

If using fresh spinach, trim the stems and immerse the leaves in a sinkful of cold water. Swish the leaves to dislodge any sand, then pull them from the water. To cook, plunge the leaves into a large pot of boiling salted water. Let cook for just 1 minute. Drain in a colander. Run cold water over the spinach to stop it from cooking further. Let drain again, pressing down on the spinach to extract excess moisture. Finely chop and set aside.

If using frozen spinach, squeeze out any excess moisture. Finely chop (if necessary) and set aside.

continued

When the meat mixture is cool, finely chop it to ensure an even texture and to eliminate any over-large lumps. Blend in the chopped spinach, combining the ingredients thoroughly with your hands. Season with salt and pepper. Add the Parmigiano and set aside.

To make the *béchamel*, place a small heavy-bottomed saucepan over low heat. Add the butter and when melted, whisk in the flour. Let the butter and flour cook for about 2 minutes, whisking constantly. Then slowly dribble in the milk, whisking constantly. Add the nutmeg, salt, and pepper, whisking to combine. This will create a fairly thin *béchamel*, which will thicken somewhat when baked. Stir ¼ cup of the *béchamel* into the filling, to act as a binder, and set the remainder aside.

To make the *crespelle,* gently whisk the batter for a few seconds to recombine it. Place a 9-inch non-stick frying pan over low heat. Add ½ teaspoon of olive oil to the pan. When the oil is warm, add 1 tablespoon of the batter and swirl it quickly around the pan to spread it out. Let it cook for 30 seconds or so, flip it over (or use a rubber spatula to help turn it), and let it cook for just 10 seconds or so. Transfer to a plate. Repeat the process until all of the batter is used up.

To create the cannelloni, preheat the oven to 375°F. Lightly butter or oil a large baking pan or a baking sheet with sides.

Place a *crespelle* on a clean work surface. Put a heaping tablespoonful of the filling in the middle of it. Flatten the filling out slightly. Roll up the *crespelle* into a tubular form. Place it seam side down in the greased roasting pan. Repeat until all of the *crespelle* are filled, rolled, and arranged in the baking pan.

Distribute the remaining *béchamel* in wide-ribboned strips across the cannelloni in the baking pan. Bake, uncovered, until golden brown and bubbling, about 1 hour. Carefully lift the cannelloni from the pan with a spatula and serve hot.

In Search of Truffles

The white truffles of Piedmont are recognized by everyone as the most valuable.

Pellegrino Artusi
La Scienza in Cucina e l'Arte di Mangiar Bene (1913)

Once I was the guest at a small dinner where a bowl of fresh white truffles was passed around for each person to shave over his risotto. As a foreigner, I was given the privilege of being first. I looked at this trove of truffles and, I confess, all I could think about was their worth. The down payment on my house was probably less than what these truffles cost. So I gingerly picked up the smallest truffle in the pile and sparingly gave my risotto a dusting of truffle shavings, like whittling a piece of ivory.

My host looked at me disapprovingly and inquired, "You don't like truffles?" I replied that I liked them very much. She instantly discerned the difficulty. In a display of the sort of easy but exquisite manners that sets Italians apart from all others, she absolved me of responsibility. She turned to her daughter and commanded her to attend to the matter for me. The daughter walked over to my plate, picked up the largest truffle in the bowl, and showered my risotto with a pile of shavings that actually formed a peak. *"Ecco,"* said my hostess with undisguised satisfaction. *"Mangia!"*

Probably no food has been subject to more fantasy than truffles. The reason is simple: Truffles are the perfume of the earth itself. Until very recently, no one really knew how they were formed, or why, or even where. Even now, there still are mysteries yet to be divined. Not least is the price, which excites people even more. Truffles are close to gold—except that gold is more abundant than truffles, especially Piedmontese white truffles.

Finding Piedmontese truffles is increasingly difficult. They have become, to mix a metaphor, fished out. "You probably won't believe this," said the sixtyish Lorenzo Scavino of Azienda Azelia, a wine estate in the heart of the Langhe in Castiglione Falletto, "but when I was a boy, not only were truffles cheap, they were abundant. I remember how our fields used to smell in the early winter when we would plow them. The plowshares would rip through the soil and cut through heaven knows how many truffles. The smell enveloped you."

Today you know it's truffle season as soon as you enter a restaurant in the Langhe zone, where Barolo and Barbaresco wines are grown. The Langhe, and the neighboring Roero zone, are famous for the quality of their white truffles. The scent of truffles very nearly permeates the wallpaper. The supply, however, keeps dwindling. Still, the best restaurateurs get what they want. It's a matter of honor, to say nothing of the most important business of the year.

This aroma, by the way, is considered by many—although, regrettably, not all—to be sexually arousing. Chemical analysis reveals, rather unappetizingly, that one of the scents in truffles is the same as is found in the saliva of male pigs (who expectorate during mating). Another is a component of human sweat.

Whatever clinicians might conclude, the fact is that Piedmontese white truffles are immensely appealing—and not just to male pigs, chauvinist or otherwise. And the Piedmontese know that they are not to be stinted. This is an important point. You'd think, given their preciousness, that you'd see only a few shavings on one or two dishes. But long experience has demonstrated to all who have lived with white truffles that you must be generous. In Piedmontese terms, generous really means profligate.

During truffle season, white truffles are showered over dishes with abandon. Connoisseurs prefer them over the simplest of foods. Piedmont has fantastic eggs—really, the most flavorful and freshest that I've eaten in Europe—and the Piedmontese know that nothing is better than a poached egg served with a mound of fresh white truffle shavings. The only other contender in the simplicity-is-next-to-godliness contest is truffles shaved over warm *fonduta*, the dish of melted Fontina cheese, similar to Swiss fondue.

The most common usage, and superb, is truffles shaved over *tajarìn,* tagliatelle. Or over agnolotti, the Piedmontese version of ravioli. Not least is risotto, which takes to truffles like few other foods.

Whatever you order, the ritual is the same. The restaurateur—it's always the owner or a family member—comes to your table with a bowl of truffles. These are oohed and aahed over like a prize baby. Only when your food is actually in front of you (unless you are at a large table) will the truffle-shaving ceremony commence. The owner places a truffle on a *mandolina*, on which the truffle is rubbed back and forth, passing over a razor-sharp blade that protrudes just barely above the rectangular plate of the *mandolina*. Truffle shavings settle on the plate like big pale-brown moths. The process continues almost shockingly long: You need at least a half-ounce of truffle for full impact. Not least there's the unforgettable sound of it all, the "phfft, phfft" of the truffle passing rapidly across the *mandolina*. It's the sort of thing you find yourself dreaming about months later.

The fact is (although you will hear outraged denials) many so-called Piedmontese white truffles—including ones sold in Alba—are from Umbria. Or somewhere else. There are a lot of (literally) shadowy goings-on in Piedmont's truly underground truffle economy. To see it, you have to prowl the streets of Asti at four or five in the morning. Asti is a good-size town, bejeweled with a really impressive cathedral and some pleasant shops. But in November and December, if you're up early—and know where to look—you can stumble across one of Piedmont's black markets in truffles.

The scene is out of a 1940s espionage movie, with the characteristic November fog swathing everything and everybody in a semi-opaque shroud. Questionable-looking characters—at that hour of morning, in dense fog, *everybody* looks suspicious—suddenly loom out of nowhere. Transactions are made quietly and entirely in dialect, to say nothing of cash. If you can't speak Piedmontese, you don't have any business being there.

Although no one can say for sure, a lot of (untaxed) money changes hands. After all, Piedmont's famous white truffles can sell for as much as a hundred dollars an ounce, depending on size, scarcity, and the quality of the year's harvest. (Generally, if it's a good vintage for wine, it's a poor one for truffles. Grapes suffer in autumn rain; truffles thrive on it.)

A more easily seen truffle exchange is available (at respectable hours) in Alba, which is Asti's rival city. Although smaller, Alba is wealthier and far more heavily touristed than Asti. In October (which, in fact, is not the best month for truffles; it's November), Alba sponsors an above-the-board truffle market where the truffle-hunters—in dialect, a *trifolau;* in Italian, a *tartufaio*—show their wares.

Of course, the problem with such a market is that the tax authorities can easily monitor the sales. Often the truffles at the Alba market are no bigger than golf balls; some are mere marbles. The really big ones always are sold outside the system, usually to restaurateurs. Everyone agrees that bigger is better. The price per gram increases exponentially in the larger sizes, especially when you see something the size of a softball.

Although truffles are genuinely rare, they are not especially localized. All sorts of truffles—black, white, gray, brown—grow in all sorts of places, including the United States. But it takes assiduous and knowledgeable looking, as they grow entirely underground, where tiny creatures, such as the mouselike vole, gorge on them. What's more, different species of truffles—at least twenty-two have been identified—offer different degrees of perfume and flavor. Some have almost no scent at all—the vegetable world's version of fool's gold.

Again, although others will deny it, the Piedmontese white truffle probably *is* the greatest version of its sort. Not only is it the most perfumey species—*Tuber magnatum*—but something about Piedmontese soil seems to magnify both its scent and size. But this applies only to the white truffles. Black Piedmontese truffles, which are reasonably plentiful, are curiously dull. Nobody knows why.

The difference between the black truffle and the white is, apart from color, easily distinguished: White truffles are best eaten raw, shaved in impossibly thin slices only when the dish is right in front of you and ready to be eaten. Black truffles, wherever they are grown, are best when cooked. Each has its virtues, but the scent of fresh white truffles is far more intense than that of even the best black truffles.

Although white truffles are shipped by air to wherever wealthy food lovers are found, the sorry fact is that what arrives is pale stuff indeed. The odds are overwhelming that you won't find the true Piedmontese white truffle—no matter how much the merchant or restaurateur insists that it's the real thing. Like as not, he or she was misled. Even in Piedmont, one must be cautious. There, however, the best restaurateurs know their truffles—and deal personally with a local *trifolau,* somebody like Aldo Drago.

You're not likely to find Aldo Drago at Alba's Fiera Nazionale del Tartufo or, for that matter, skulking the side streets of Asti. Drago is well known among truffle cognoscenti as a source of impeccable, authentic white truffles. He has private clients. He's the real thing—and he looks it. One of the features of most *trifolau* like Drago, who is in his late fifties, is that their faces show a life lived out-of-doors—gaunt and lined, the result of hard work and, likely, deprivation. Drago is an exception: round-faced and rosy-cheeked, the capillaries of his nose long ago having exploded in the fireworks of decades of grappa drinking.

Truffle hunting is an age-old affair, started not because of wage-earning urbanites like myself who are willing to pay boggling sums of money, but because of hunger. Much of Piedmont to this day is profoundly rural. Up to the 1950s its residents too often have been impoverished and hungry. They ate what they literally could find: mushrooms, wild fennel, herbs, and truffles. Their knowledge of the land was intimate, profound, and always superstitious. The moon, for example, figured prominently in their imaginations and the ordering of their days. No food is more mysterious, more susceptible to superstition, than truffles. Growing underground, they don't need light, they appear when all else has stopped growing, and they don't return with any evident regularity.

Drago lives in an exceedingly modest house that cannot be said to be decorated, let alone ever having been redecorated. Nevertheless, like all Piedmontese homes, it is almost fastidiously clean. Most of his income—probably nearly all of it—comes from the three or four months of the fall and early winter truffle season. His home is a place of polenta and homemade Barbera, both much appreciated. He himself rarely, if ever, savors a truffle. They are too precious.

As befits someone who spends twelve hours at a stretch alone with his dog, Drago is a man of exceedingly few words. As Daniela Signorini and Oriano Valli write in their book, *Il Tartufo,* "The *tartufaio* is a difficult person, solitary by definition, preoccupied by defending his territory and tending to his work." Simply put, they can be ornery men, made mean by equally mean circumstances. Drago is different: He is a surprisingly jovial fellow, with an essential kindness reflected in how he trains his dogs.

"I don't agree with the others about how to train truffle dogs," he told me as we followed his locally famous white truffle hound, Pulìn. The best truffle dogs are mutts, as Drago's is. And they usually are white. I ask Drago about that. He looks at me as if nobody could be that stupid. "So you can see them more easily at night," he replies tartly. Truffle hunters tend to work all through the night, so that no one can see where they find their truffles. Secondarily, the dogs can more easily pick up the truffle scent in the less distracting night air.

"Many of the men beat their dogs," he says. "To get them to pay attention." After a long pause he adds, "I don't think you should do that." Pulìn clearly loves his master. Back home, there are pups waiting to be trained, but at the moment, Pulìn is Drago's sole link to finding his truffles and keeping him and his wife financially solvent.

"The dog doesn't care about truffles," says Drago. "My job is to keep him interested. To make him *want* to find truffles." This is the key. Precisely because of a dog's profound lack of interest in truffles, it soon tires of the search. In fact, it won't even begin to search except to please its master—which is Drago's approach—or out of fear of its master's disapproval, which others use as incentive. Either way, the dog still must be directed to the general vicinity of truffles.

This is one of the truths of truffle-hunting: To find them, you already have to know where they are. Drago has a mental map of every spot in his territory where he has previously located truffles. These are many. But just as critical to the harvest is remembering when he last harvested truffles from the spot. Although truffles nearly always reappear in the same place, they don't necessarily do so within a year's time. So Drago has to get the dog to concentrate on those spots where the dog's chances of locating one are high.

Drago's truffle year begins in October. Much depends on the weather. If October is wet and cold, all the better for the truffles. If it is dry, his haul will be limited. Still, he has no choice but to look. "Truffles don't come to your door," he quips. Drago leaves his house at nightfall. It is bone-chilling work, flavored with the ever-present paranoia that some competing truffle hunter is tracking you to see where your truffle spots are found.

This paranoia is not entirely farfetched. Ask Manuela Corrado of the Vietti wine family in Castiglione Falletto. As a veterinarian, she responds all the time to cases of poisoned dogs. "It's simple," she says clinically, if disgustedly. "They try to poison the dogs so that there will be more truffles for themselves. At least that's what they imagine." Drago told me that one of his dogs was poisoned a few years ago.

Truffle season is not the most pleasant time to be mucking about in the woods. It's wet and densely foggy, and the damp cold seeps into your bones. Fiery grappa seems more than reasonable now—it's downright vital. But you can't drink too much. The walk occurs in darkness, a flashlight used only at the moment when the truffle is found, for it must be carefully and gently excavated. A flashlight will let others know you're out looking for truffles—and where you are.

Drago lets Pulìn trot ahead, content to let the dog enjoy himself until they reach a place where he believes there might be some truffles this year. Then he calls Pulìn back to him. Pulìn rushes to his side, glad for the company and attention. With a staff in hand, Drago leads Pulìn over to the spot. The dog knows what's expected and immediately starts sniffing. To keep Pulìn's attention from flagging, Drago makes clicking sounds with his tongue, a kind of man-dog metronome. Drago keeps tongue-clicking, pointing with his stick to where the dog might look. As long as he keeps clicking, Pulìn keeps searching.

Drago knows how to read Pulìn. If the dog doesn't find anything within a few minutes, Drago moves on. Unusually, he will reward Pulìn with a treat from time to time, even if the dog doesn't find anything. Like the best of business managers, Drago knows that it is far better for Pulìn to be interested in what Drago wants than for him simply to find a truffle. After all, Drago knows where the truffles are. He needs Pulìn, like a metal detector, to establish their exact locations.

Finally, Pulìn locates a truffle. He begins to dig with his paws. Drago is down on his knees next to the dog in a flash. Pulìn is genuinely excited. He's finally giving his master what he wants. Drago gives the dog a hug and, to distract him, feeds Pulìn another treat. He doesn't want Pulìn's paws to reach the tender truffle and rip it apart. So Drago uses his hands, gently pushing away what, all too often, is not dirt, but clayey mud.

However scientifically ignorant truffle hunters once were, they were vastly observant. Drago, for example, may or may not know about mycorrhizae, which are the microscopic filaments that are the actual fungi. The truffle is just the fruiting body, as mycologists call spore-creating mushrooms and truffles. But Drago knows, as generations of *trifolau* before him knew, that if you disturb the embedded truffle, if will cease to grow, even if covered over again. Once moved, the invisible strands of mycorrhizae connected to the truffle are severed: the truffle has lost its fungal umbilical cords. It will wither and die.

So when Pulìn locates a truffle, Drago must reach it first. Not only does he want to keep Pulìn's uncaring paws from shredding the fragile prize, but equally important, he wants to ascertain the size of the truffle. If it's too small, he wants to leave it undisturbed, still tethered to its mycorrhizae moorings. Then he can return in a few weeks—or sooner if the right combination of rain and warmth occur—to a much larger and more valuable specimen.

Drago announces this truffle is worth keeping. He motions me over. "Close your eyes," he says. "Smell this." The perfume of white truffle is overpowering. "My God," I exclaim, "this is a great truffle you've found." Then I hear Drago laughing. I open my eyes and under my nose is not a truffle, but just a great clot of mud. "Here's the truffle," says Drago, handing me a not especially large specimen. "That was just the mud around it." I close my eyes again, first smelling the mud, then the truffle. They smell equally scrumptious.

It is at this moment that I realize for the first time that, by doggy standards, finding a truffle is no great trick. Even we humans, whose sense of smell is nothing compared to that of dogs, could find truffles if we walked on all fours with our noses pressed against the ground. If, like Dr. Doolittle, we could talk to dogs and convince them of our cause, the truffle harvest probably would take no more than an hour or two. If only the dog cared.

Instead, Drago and Pulìn slog through the fog and mud all night, every night, for three or four months. And just because a truffle wasn't found a week or a month earlier in a particular spot doesn't mean that it won't be there soon. Truffles, like mushrooms, can grow startlingly fast. So Drago continues to lead the dog, keeping up its flagging attention by clicks and treats, leading it time and again to promising sites. Dozens of times through the night, Drago presses the search, urging on Pulìn, to find perhaps only a handful of truffles.

When we return to Drago's house, we sit in what might be called the parlor, on benches placed at the perimeter of the room, not actually at the table in the center of the room. This is old Piedmontese style. "Let's have some coffee," suggests Drago, which his wife has already prepared. Drago's taste in coffee doesn't surprise me. Not for him a tiny little espresso cup. Instead, out come large breakfast cups half-filled with coffee.

Alongside, Drago plunks down a clear, rustic-looking bottle without any label or identification. The liquid inside is water-white: grappa. It has blooming within it, so to speak, a branch of an unknown, but surely well-preserved, herb. Playing amateur ethnobotanist, I ask Drago what it is and have about as much luck getting an answer as if I were interviewing the medicine man of an Amazon tribe. Drago's response: "It's a local plant. You don't have it."

With that, he uncorks the bottle and tops up my coffee cup, creating a morning eye-opener that is literally half coffee and half grappa. Under normal circumstances, it should deliver a kick like a tax audit. But after a spell of truffle-hunting in the mud and fog, the combination of hot coffee and piercing grappa goes down the pipes like a drain opener. I've never felt better.

Polenta

In a slower world, ignorant of the frenzy, polenta keeps time like a clock. . . . It is unique, golden, a dish, a refuge.

Giovanni Arpino
L'Ombra delle Colline

The simpler and more cherished the food, the more imbued it is with emotion and endowed with ritual. Perhaps the most famous example is the fabled martini—a slug of gin with a mention of vermouth relieved by an olive. But in time, in the pursuit of an ever-more-mythical dryness, that mention of vermouth was reduced to a suggestion, then a whisper, and finally simply a rumor. The drink had to be shaken, not stirred—at least according to James Bond. Its devotees devised ever-more-complicated variations.

With this in mind, it's easy to understand why something as seemingly basic as polenta—cornmeal mush—is so emotionally and psychologically substantial to so many Northern Italians. To those not raised on polenta, the ritualism involved in making it, and the deep affection it evokes, can be hard to fathom at first. As a food of poverty it was, until recently, a daily staple in the majority of Northern Italian households.

Polenta requires involvement and anticipation. Ritual elevates it; unthinking convenience demotes it—to cornmeal mush. The various techniques for making polenta without participation (pressure-cooking, baking, using fast-cooking cornmeal) not only result in a poorer dish, but are deceitful, like using Liquid Smoke instead of barbecuing. Anybody who suggests that involvement cannot materially change the taste of a dish has been bewitched by microwaves. The appeal, and reward, of polenta lies in its (pleasurable) handcrafting. Like real oatmeal, the best polenta takes a bit of time.

In Northern Italy, the appeal of polenta begins to creep up on you, even if you weren't raised in a country farmhouse. I've been in such farmhouses and "atmospheric" doesn't begin to capture the sensation. You sit at a long oak table, worn concave by countless elbows and kitchen uses, and watch as a huge round-bottomed unlined copper cauldron (called a *paiolo*) is placed over an open fire in an equally capacious fireplace and filled with water along with a generous addition of salt. When the water reaches a boil, the cook—usually the grandmother in residence—begins strewing handfuls of golden cornmeal into the pot, stirring, stirring, all the time with a flat wooden paddle. The action looks like nothing so much as the sowing of seed.

Finally, all of the cornmeal has slowly been immersed into the boiling water. The reason for the measured strewing is to prevent the water from becoming tepid; otherwise, the cornmeal will lump. It then is left to cook, absorbing the water. But it must continue to be stirred. It takes little imagination to see how readily this simple matter of making cornmeal mush takes on ritualistic qualities.

Just exactly when the polenta finally is pronounced "done" is as much a matter of personal taste as determining the just-so dryness of a martini. Much depends upon the granularity of the cornmeal. More rustic polentas are made with a coarse grind of cornmeal. It takes longer to cook and often calls for an additional ladle or two of boiling water as you relentlessly stir. More finely ground cornmeal cooks more quickly and has a smoother texture.

This matter of timing is the topic of endless dining room discussion in Northern Italy. Some polenta connoisseurs insist that the usual thirty minutes' cooking typically prescribed is insufficient. They say that the best polenta is cooked for one hour, so as to remove the (imagined) bitterness of the cornmeal. For some particularly hard and coarse grinds of cornmeal, this is so.

The goodness of handcrafted polenta is demonstrable. But it is well to remember that the original appeal of polenta—which only arrived in Italy after the discovery of the New World—lay in its filling quality and cheapness. The exoticism of corn in Europe is revealed by its Italian name, *granoturco*—Turkish grain. Since no one has ever thought that corn originally came from Turkey, it strikes the outside observer as odd that the Italians should christen corn as such. The explanation is simple: Anything exotic to the Italians was seen as Turkish, in much the same way that mystical things in America invariably are Asian. So, linguistically, corn continues as *granoturco*.

Grinding corn into a meal and boiling it in water was obvious from the start, and indeed the recipe surely came from the New World. After all, the varieties of corn used then and now are so hard—especially after being dried in the sun for preservation—that little else could be done with it. But what the Indians of Mexico and Central America discovered (or stumbled upon) eluded the Europeans: that a diet largely confined to corn leads to trouble. This trouble acquired an Italian name, which in itself reveals just how widespread it was, first in Italy and later in France, Spain, Africa, and the American South.

The disease first came to attention only in the 1700s, when polenta consumption became widespread throughout Northern Italy. The name *pellagra,* literally "rough skin," was first used in 1771 in an Italian monograph on the mystifying disease. Skin lesions were only a symptom, accompanied by weakness and a gradual, noticeable mental deterioration. The cause was a vitamin deficiency, specifically of niacin. But this was discovered (in the United States) only in the late 1930s. Harold McGee, in *On Food and Cooking,* comments, "Often the symptoms would appear in the spring, after a long winter of living on corn, then gradually disappear during the summer as the diet improved, only to reappear intensified the following spring."

In Northern Italy, where corn grew abundantly, polenta became more than a staple. The widespread presence of pellagra demonstrated that it was virtually the *sole* source of nourishment. Stories still are told in Piedmont of how impoverished Piedmontese would eat polenta every day, the only addition to it being the flavor of a salt-dried anchovy. The anchovy would be rubbed across the hot polenta and then removed, to be used again until all of its meager flesh had finally been worn away.

A somewhat more rewarding picture is given us by Bolton King* and Thomas Okey in their book *Italy To-Day* (1909). They translate an anonymous Italian depiction of a "fairly well-to-do Italian peasant near Alba in Piedmont":

In the morning he works, except in winter, two or three hours before seven, when he has a little breakfast of bread and cheese, with capsicums [sweet peppers], celery or radishes in oil, and three quarters of a pint of thin wine. Breakfast lasts about half-an-hour. At eleven he has dinner from a great round dish of polenta, yellow as gold and smoking like a volcano, or else a *minestra* of maccaroni [sic] or rice and vegetables, cooked with lard, except on fast days, when oil takes the place of lard. The men sit in the kitchen round the table, the women serve and eat, the boys squat by the chimney or on the doorstep, eating greedily, porringer on knee.

If polenta is the dish, the women prepare a sauce, and what a sauce it is! Our peasant women all come from the same school of cookery, and all their sauces are made of oil and garlic and anchovies [*bagna caôda*]. Sometimes they eat with the polenta a kind of sheep's cheese, and on fast days salt-fish [*baccalà*] or rarely eggs. With a glass or two of the usual thin wine dinner finishes. The peasant rises, wipes his lips with his apron or hand, and goes

*Bolton King, an Englishman, married a Piedmontese woman and settled near Carmagnoa, a country town not far from Turin.

contented back to work and digest the two or three big slices of polenta he has inside him. He is never troubled with indigestion, and barely three hours later he is back again to eat his *merenda* [snack] of bread and cheese and salad. The *merenda* lasts, like breakfast, half-an-hour, and like it, it is taken under the shade of a tree. Finally, at dusk he leaves his work and comes home to find supper ready. If they eat polenta at dinner, they eat *minestra* now, and vice versa.

It should be noted that as widespread as polenta was and continues to be in Piedmont, it came there relatively late, compared to other parts of Northern Italy, especially that part of the Po Valley east of Milan. Historians suggest that polenta became common in Piedmont only in the latter half of the 1700s, which is centuries later than in some other parts of Northern Italy. (Corn first began to be grown in the 1500s in swampy land in the delta of the Po River between Padua and Ferrara.) Just why it took so long to reach Piedmont is unknown. But it soon became as fundamental to the Piedmontese diet as it was to virtually every other Northern Italian cuisine.

The ingenuity to which polenta has been put is admirable. Polenta is to cooking what a ball and a wall is to sport: out of such supremely basic materials is fashioned something of impressive complication. It can be cooked until stiff or intentionally be left runny. I once was served a fairly liquid polenta that had been combined with several soft cheeses. This was exalted with a mound of fresh white truffle shavings.

Less grand, but no less good, is the traditional combination of a stiff-cooked polenta serving as the base for a couple of good sausages. Served with a young, rustic red wine such as Barbera, it is food for the godly and ungodly alike. The best versions always have a bit of butter mixed in before serving, which makes them glisten. Alternatively, some polenta fans prefer olive oil.

Polenta takes to cheese almost as well as bread. One of the most memorable polenta dishes you can eat is nothing more than a steaming hot slab of stiff polenta—it always must be served hot—over which is placed a generous slice of creamy Gorgonzola. After the cheese, like a sunset, slowly sinks into the polenta, the resulting taste is something that lingers in the mind in a way that few fancy dinners are likely to equal.

Types of polenta There is no one true polenta. It can be coarse- or fine-ground, yellow or white. It needn't even be made entirely from corn, evidenced by *polenta taragna*, a blend of corn and buckwheat. *Polenta taragna* is a specialty of the Valtellina, a mountainous area at the foothills of the Alps north of Bergamo. (It's also the only place in Italy outside of Piedmont where the Nebbiolo grape is successfully grown.)

Piedmontese polenta is always yellow (white polenta is a specialty of the Veneto) and usually coarse-grained. Tastes in the granularity of polenta differ from region to region. Many polenta connoisseurs prefer to choose from different granularities, depending upon what is being added to the polenta. Hearty foods such as baccalà and sausages call for coarse-grained polenta; cheeses, mushrooms, fonduta, and the like are thought to be more appropriately paired to a finer-grained polenta. But this is only preference, and an arguable one at that.

Polenta brands Corn is divided into five groups, which are distinguished either by the shape of the kernel or a taste characteristic, such as sweet corn. Polenta is made from either of two groups: flint corn or dent corn. The names are suitably descriptive. Flint corn (*Zea mays* var. *indurata*) is very hard; dent corn (*Zea mays* var. *indentata*) is so called because of an indentation on top of each kernel. Most polenta is made from various varieties of flint corn; dent corn is commonly used for livestock feed. But either can be used for polenta. In Italy, two corn varieties are recognized by Italian polenta connoisseurs as offering the best old-fashioned flavors: *Otto File* and *Marano*. Occasionally, a package of imported polenta cites one of these varietal names on the package.

In Italy, some local polentas are made in the most traditional fashion, from flint corn that is left on the cob and allowed to dry in the sun. (The vast majority of corn for polenta is dried in ovens.) These dried cobs are then stored over the winter and husked and ground in the spring and summer. Whether such traditionalism really is needed I cannot say. But I will say this much: Such polenta offers a noticeable, even dramatic, difference in flavor. One such traditional polenta imported to this country is sold under the brand name Come Una Volta (Once upon a Time). It is a fine-grained yellow polenta distributed nationally.

An excellent, more conventional yellow coarse-grained polenta comes from California and is sold under the brand name Golden Pheasant. It is widely available and very good, as well as inexpensive.

If you go to Piedmont and visit the winegrowing Langhe area, you can find a superb local polenta made in the town of La Morra. Renzo Sobrino of Molino Artigiano Govine Sobrino in La Morra (Via Roma 110) makes old-fashioned polenta from locally grown stone-ground flint corn of exceptional taste.

Stirring the pot Much is made of how polenta needs to be stirred constantly. It is true that it's not a dish you put together and then walk away from. It *does* need to be stirred with some frequency. That said, many prospective polenta cooks have been spooked by admonitions that effectively have them standing over the pot and stirring frantically, like the sorcerer's apprentice in the movie *Fantasia*.

The fact is that polenta made in reasonable-size quantities and in a heavy-bottomed pot does not need stirring all that often. The reason why polenta is stirred—once all of the cornmeal is added to the water—is to expose the increasingly dense mass evenly to the heat. When polenta was made in massive quantities in a big *paiolo* over an open fire, the sheer mass of the polenta prevented the heat from penetrating much beyond the layer closest to the heat. Not least, the open fire provided uneven, and possibly scorching, heat. Constant stirring was essential. Making small quantities of polenta at home these days is less exacting. In a good, heavy pot, there is no need to stir the polenta any more often than every few minutes.

The beauty and utility of copper   Polenta, like risotto, is a dish where one is involved. A golden polenta in a gleaming copper pot is a sheer joy to gaze upon, a nourishing aesthetic. It evokes a sense of connection to antiquity. More practically, nothing transmits heat better or more evenly, including the sides of the pot (which for polenta is important, as well as the bottom), than copper. But if one is going to fork over for a copper pot—which these days will not be cheap—then it should be something heavy-gauge. A flimsy, thin-sided, lightweight copper pot is all show: Heft equals effectiveness.

One of the most price-competitive sources for copperware is Zabar's, 2245 Broadway, New York, New York 10024 (212-787-2000). Its French copperware (the Mauviel brand) is available either tin-lined or stainless steel–lined, which, unlike tin, never needs relining. Two gauges are available: The heavier gauge has traditional iron handles and very good prices. Zabar's will ship anywhere in the United States.

Cooking times   How long polenta should be cooked depends greatly upon the coarseness of the grind. Fine-ground polenta rarely needs more than 30 minutes, tops. Coarse-ground polenta is best cooked for 45 minutes. Polenta, unlike risotto, can be kept warm until needed, provided you keep stirring from time to time. Eventually it will become too dense. Just add a generous splash of boiling water and stir it in vigorously. But do not ever let it cool while it is waiting.

Water versus milk   The classic version of polenta has it cooked in water, but another has it cooked in hot milk. The milk rendition creates a gentler, milder-flavored polenta that can be ideal served with delicately flavored additions such as fish or mushrooms. It's worth trying.

Serving the polenta   When large quantities of polenta are made—or if the polenta is to be baked—the traditional technique of serving is to turn it out onto a large wooden board and mound it up into a golden, steaming hemisphere. It then is garroted into thick slices using a strong cotton string, which cuts through polenta better than any knife. The board is brought to the table. Alternatively, one can spoon polenta straight from the pot onto heated plates and serve it in individual golden mounds, with the appropriate sauce or added cheese and butter.

Cleaning the pot   There's no quick method I know of for removing the skin of cooked polenta from the bottom of the pot. Just fill the pot with cold water and let it soak overnight. The next morning, the polenta "skin" will come right off. Feed it to your pets.

Classic Polenta

The following quantity is sufficient for four to six people, depending upon whether you use the polenta as a side dish for meats or fish or as a first course with cheese unto itself. The ingredients can be multiplied as necessary. This makes a stiff polenta.

makes 4 to 6 servings

8 cups water

2 teaspoons salt

2 cups cornmeal

In a large heavy-bottomed saucepan, bring the water and salt to a boil. (If using fine-ground polenta, have the water only at a simmer. This will prevent clumping, which violently boiling water encourages with fine-ground cornmeal.) Strew the cornmeal into the boiling water a handful at a time, stirring constantly and taking care that the water continues boiling throughout. When all of the cornmeal is incorporated—about 5 minutes—continue stirring but lower the heat as the cornmeal mass thickens. It will soon become fairly dense and take on volcanic qualities as it erupts from time to time from the heat. Lower the heat again if necessary to keep these eruptions to a minimum, and give the polenta mass a good stir from time to time so as to expose all of the cornmeal to the heat.

As the polenta cooks, it will lighten in color and become slightly fluffy in texture. When the polenta is approaching the fully cooked stage, it will start to pull away from the sides of the pan as you stir. The texture will become airier, resembling that of mashed potatoes. At anytime after this stage—about 30 minutes' cooking—the polenta is ready to be served. If you prefer, continue cooking and stirring the polenta for another 10 minutes to enhance the texture, depending upon the grind. You can't overcook polenta, as long as you keep stirring it to prevent scorching. Serve very hot on warm plates.

Polenta with a Spicy Tomato Sauce
Polenta con Bagna d'Infern

⁂

Bagna d'infern is a classic Piedmontese sauce, the *infern,* or hellishy hot part, being provided by a hot red pepper. Depending upon whose grandmother is making the dish, the sauce is either spooned over individual portions of just-cooked polenta or layered between slices of cooked polenta and baked for thirty minutes. Partisans exist for both.

makes 4 to 6 servings

For the sauce:

1/4 cup olive oil, or more if needed

1 small head garlic (about 12 cloves), separated into cloves, peeled, and thinly sliced

6 whole salted anchovies, rinsed, filleted, soaked briefly in water, drained, and finely chopped

4 or 5 medium-size fresh tomatoes, peeled, seeded, and coarsely chopped, or canned tomatoes, seeded and coarsely chopped

Handful of fresh Italian parsley leaves, very finely chopped

1 jalapeño pepper, preferably red, seeded and finely chopped, or 1/4 teaspoon cayenne pepper

Cooked polenta made from 2 cups cornmeal (see page 193)

Put the olive oil in a small heavy-bottomed saucepan over very low heat. Add the garlic and anchovies. Add more olive oil if needed to barely cover the ingredients. Let cook for at least 30 minutes, taking care that the garlic does not color or burn.

Add the tomatoes, parsley, and jalapeño. Let cook over medium-low heat for another 30 minutes, stirring occasionally.

To serve, you could spoon the sauce generously over substantial portions of the just-cooked polenta. Or, preheat the oven to 375°F. Slice the cooked and cooled polenta into three thick slices. Make a "cake" of these slices, with sauce in between each slice and on top of the uppermost one. Put the "cake" in a shallow baking pan and bake for 30 minutes. Serve hot.

Polenta with Salt Cod and Parsley

Polenta con Merluzzo al Verde

Since polenta was the backbone of *la cucina povera*, it is not surprising that it should have been paired with that other standby of the "poor kitchen," salt cod. In this classic dish, the salt cod is sauced with onion, parsley, and garlic. For instructions on preparing salt cod, see page 257.

makes 4 to 6 servings

For the sauce:

6 tablespoons olive oil

2 medium-size onions, finely chopped

Large handful of fresh Italian parsley leaves, finely chopped

1 small head garlic (about 12 cloves), separated into cloves, peeled, and very finely chopped

2 tablespoons tomato paste

1 pound salt cod, soaked overnight in water to cover, drained, simmered in fresh water until tender, drained, and flaked into bite-size pieces

Just-cooked polenta made from 2 cups cornmeal (see page 193)

Add the oil to a large skillet over medium-low heat. When hot, add the onions and cook, stirring occasionally, until translucent, 5 to 10 minutes. Add the parsley, garlic, and tomato paste and whisk to combine thoroughly. Let cook, partially covered, over low heat for 30 minutes.

Add the flaked salt cod and let cook an additional 15 minutes.

To serve, spoon the salt cod mixture over the hot, just-cooked polenta. Serve immediately.

Baked Polenta with Leeks and Anchovies

Polenta ai Porri con Acciughe al Forno

✤✤✤

The taste of leeks is subtle and polenta shows it off better than any other backdrop. The addition of anchovies adds just the right contrasting note. This is one of those dishes that, simple as it is, packs a powerful, subtle flavor.

makes 4 to 6 servings

Several tablespoons water

2 pounds leeks, white part only, sliced into rounds and thoroughly washed

Cooked polenta made from 2 cups cornmeal (see page 193)

6 whole salted anchovies, rinsed, filleted, briefly soaked in cold water, and drained

1 large egg yolk, beaten with 1 teaspoon water for egg glaze (optional)

Put a few tablespoons of water in a large nonstick skillet over medium heat. When the water starts to boil, add the leek. Cover and let cook over medium-low heat until tender, 10 to 15 minutes. Add more water as needed. Drain and set aside.

To assemble the dish, preheat the oven to 375°F. Grease a baking dish with olive oil. Add a layer (or a thick slice) of the polenta. The number of layers or slices will depend on the size of the baking dish. Cover with an appropriate amount of the leeks. Arrange a layer of the anchovy fillets evenly over the leeks. Cover with another layer (or slice) of polenta. Repeat if necessary. Brush the top layer of polenta with the egg glaze, if you wish. Bake, uncovered, until the top is lightly glazed and a little golden, about 20 minutes. Serve hot.

Variation: In addition to the leeks and anchovies, add a layer of thinly sliced Fontina cheese.

Baked Polenta with Gorgonzola and Parmigiano

Polenta Mitonà con Gorgonzola e Parmigiano

✺

In Piedmontese dialect, anything cooked slowly, for a long time, can be called *mitonata* or *mitonà*. This recipe not only is a cheese lover's delight, it also employs an unusual twist for baked polenta: Milk is added to the baking dish to soften the polenta. It is an extremely unusual, and delicious, variation.

makes 4 to 6 servings

Cooked polenta made from 2 cups
  cornmeal (see page 193)
2 ounces Parmigiano-Reggiano cheese,
  grated (¹/₂ cup)

8 ounces Gorgonzola, either **dolce** or
  naturale, crumbled
4 cups milk

Preheat the oven to 325°F.

Put a layer (or a thick slice) of cooked polenta in an oiled deep baking dish. The number of layers or slices will depend upon the size of the dish. Sprinkle an appropriate amount of the Parmigiano on top. Add a layer of the Gorgonzola. Repeat if necessary. Pour in the milk and bake, uncovered, until the milk is absorbed and the dish is bubbling, about 1 hour. Serve hot.

✺

Polenta Conscia

⁂

Here creamy toma cheese sees another classic use, elevating polenta to another sphere of flavor. Texturally, this is a fairly liquid polenta, thanks to the addition of the creamy cheese. It is a traditional specialty of Biella, which lies astride the Oropa River, where the locals insist that their polenta tastes different (read "better") because of the distinctive quality of the the water of the alpine-fed Oropa River. Traditionalists do not stop there, though. They go on to say that the true *polenta conscia* is better not only because of the local water, but also because it is cooked slowly over rhododendron wood in, of course, a large copper cauldron. More convincingly, they note that the polenta itself must be stone-ground and come from an ancient corn variety.

makes 8 servings

12 cups boiling water

Salt

6 cups (2 pounds) cornmeal

1 pound toma, neither too fresh nor
    too aged, thinly sliced

¾ cup (1½ sticks) unsalted butter

2 large garlic cloves, very thinly sliced

Freshly ground black pepper

Freshly grated Parmigiano-Reggiano
    cheese

In a large, heavy-bottomed saucepan, bring the water and 2 tablespoons salt to a boil. (If using fine-ground polenta, have the water only at a simmer. This will prevent clumping, which violently boiling water encourages with fine-ground cornmeal.) Strew the cornmeal into the boiling water a handful at a time, stirring constantly and taking care that the water continues boiling throughout. When all of the cornmeal is incorporated—about 5 minutes—continue stirring but lower the heat as the cornmeal mass thickens. It will soon become fairly dense and take on volcanic qualities as it erupts from time to time from the heat. Lower the heat again if necessary to keep these eruptions to a minimum, and give the polenta mass a good stir from time to time so as to expose all of the cornmeal to the heat.

After about 10 minutes, add the toma slices, butter, and garlic. Continue cooking for another 15 to 20 minutes. As the polenta cooks, it will lighten in color and become slightly fluffy in texture. When the polenta is approaching the fully cooked stage, it will start to pull away from the sides of the pot as you stir. The texture will become airier, resembling that of mashed potatoes. At any time after this stage—about 30 minutes' cooking—the polenta is ready to be served. Just before serving, season with salt and pepper and add some Parmigiano to taste. Serve very hot on warm plates.

Polenta from Restaurant Tra Vigna

Polenta Tra Vigna

✵

This is an especially rich, tasty polenta from Michael Chiarello, the chef of Tra Vigna ("among the vines") restaurant in California's Napa Valley. Combining cornmeal with semolina creates a very smooth, refined polenta, especially when stock and cream are added too, as they are here. The result is, frankly, unlike any polenta I've eaten in Piedmont, but it's too good to pass up merely because of that.

Like all polenta variations, this is a terrific dish served with the Piedmontese tomato sauce called *Bagnet Ross* (see page 149), liberally sprinkled with Parmigiano cheese and run under the broiler, or simply sautéed in butter. Let the polenta rest in the refrigerator for several hours before being sliced, as this creates a better, firmer texture.

makes 6 servings

1 1/2 cups chicken stock

1 1/2 cups heavy cream

Pinch of freshly grated nutmeg

3/4 teaspoon salt

Pinch of freshly ground white pepper

1/2 cup cornmeal

1/2 cup semolina

1/4 cup freshly grated Fontina or Fontal cheese

1 ounce Parmigiano-Reggiano cheese, grated (1/4 cup)

Olive oil

Combine the chicken stock, cream, nutmeg, salt, and pepper in a large heavy-bottomed pot over high heat. Whisk to blend and bring to a boil. When the liquid is boiling, slowly add the cornmeal and semolina, whisking them in gradually so they don't clump.

Lower the heat to medium, so that the polenta is just barely burping in the pot. Continue whisking frequently and cook another 5 to 10 minutes; the polenta should be thick but still liquid.

Remove from the heat, add the cheeses, and let them rest on the surface until the Fontina begins to melt. Then gently stir the cheeses into the polenta.

Line a small baking pan with buttered waxed paper and spread the polenta evenly and smoothly in the pan to a thickness of approximately 1/2 inch. Let cool to room temperature, then cover with plastic wrap or waxed paper and refrigerate for at least 4 hours.

To serve, slice the polenta into squares or triangles. Place the polenta slices on a baking sheet, brush generously with olive oil, and run under a hot broiler until golden brown, 2 to 3 minutes. Serve warm as a snack or an accompaniment to fish or poultry.

Polenta with Melted Cheese Sauce and Porcini Mushrooms

Polenta con Fonduta e Funghi Porcini

❧❀❧

This dish is so simple—and so devastingly good—that it's not quite accurate to call it a recipe. The description alone suffices:

Broil, or briefly panfry, slices of polenta for a few minutes on each side. Set the slices in a single layer in a gratin pan or baking dish and top with hot *fonduta* (see *Fonduta Piemontese,* page 57). Run under a hot broiler for 1 minute. Serve with sautéed porcini mushroom slices (see *Funghi Trifolati,* page 27), sprinkled over the *fonduta* topping.

Chick-pea Flour Pancake

Farinata

❧❀❧

Farinata is a Ligurian and Niçoise specialty that you also find along the Piedmontese border in towns such as Acqui Terme. It is devastatingly good street food. You go up to a vendor who has big batches of *farinata* that he bakes in big, round pizza pans. Using a wide metal spatula, he scrapes up jagged shreds of it and puts them in a little sack, and you walk off, chewing happily on these scrapings.

There's no definitive thickness to *farinata*. The commercial vendors make theirs very thin, a quarter inch thick or so, as it cooks quickly that way. Many home cooks like the chewier quality of thicker *farinata*. As they do with their focaccia, Ligurians like to sprinkle thinly sliced raw onions over the *farinata* just before baking. Or, again like focaccia, mix chopped fresh rosemary into the batter, which is indeed delicious.

Chick-pea or garbanzo flour is readily available in health food stores and/or Italian or Indian groceries. Because of its distinctive flavor, no other flour will work.

An ancient Piedmontese version of *farinata*, called *paniccia*, employs chick-pea flour for a variation on polenta. The same quantities of flour and water specified below are cooked over the stove in the same fashion as polenta, with the cook strewing the flour into simmering water while stirring constantly. The resulting batter is poured onto a large plate and formed into a half-inch-thick circle. It's topped with a drizzle of olive oil, chopped onions, salt, and pepper and served in slices.

makes 6 servings

3¾ cups chick-pea (garbanzo) flour

6 cups water

½ teaspoon salt

⅓ cup olive oil

Freshly ground black pepper

In a large mixing bowl, whisk together the chick-pea flour, water, and salt. This will create a thin batter that runs easily from a spoon. Cover and refrigerate for 12 hours.

Preheat the oven to 475°F.

Before cooking, peel off the skin that has formed on the top of the batter and discard. Whisk the batter again to blend.

Pour the olive oil onto a large baking sheet with sides. Tilt the sheet so that the oil covers the entire surface. Pour the batter over the oil, tilting the pan to spread it evenly. Gently stir the mixture to blend the oil with the batter. The batter should be between ¼ and ½ inch thick.

Bake until the surface of the *farinata* turns a dark gold. The timing will vary, depending upon the thickness of the batter, from 15 to 25 minutes. Let cool slightly in the pan. Divide into rough bite-size pieces and serve sprinkled with a little pepper.

Classic Potato Gnocchi

Gnocchi di Patate

I have chosen to include a gnocchi (pronounced nyoh-kee) recipe in the section on polenta because I find the two dishes more similar than not. Gnocchi are, of course, a category unto themselves. Like polenta, gnocchi are filling, used as a vehicle for other flavors, especially cheese, and are usually served only in cold weather.

All sorts of gnocchi exist, made with potatoes, semolina flour, cornmeal, or even squash. The recipe below is a classic potato gnocchi, similar to ones I ate in Piedmont, except for the fact that these gnocchi are lighter (and better) because of the use of baking potatoes, which you don't see in Piedmont.

Gnocchi traditionally are served with melted butter or melted cheese. In Piedmont, the great specialty is gnocchi served with melted Castelmagno cheese, but that pleasure is unavailable to us here. *Fonduta* (see page 57) is perhaps the greatest topping of all. At least that's what I always go for.

makes 6 servings

6 Idaho-type (such as Russet Burbank) potatoes	About 4 cups unbleached all-purpose flour
2 large eggs, beaten with 1 teaspoon salt	Freshly grated Parmigiano-Reggiano cheese
Freshly ground white or black pepper	

Preheat the oven to 425°F.

Bake the potatoes until they are easily pierced with a fork, about 1 hour. When cool enough to handle, slice open the baked potatoes and scoop out the interiors, discarding the skins. Let the potato meat cool completely, then, push it through a potato ricer (or a large-holed colander).

Place the riced potatoes in a mound on a clean work surface. Punch a crater in the mound. Pour the beaten eggs into the crater, along with a few grindings of pepper. Work the potatoes and eggs together with your hands, adding the flour a little at a time and working as quickly as possible. The longer the dough is worked, the more flour is needed and the heavier the gnocchi become. When the dough is only just barely sticky, set aside briefly.

Lightly dust a clean work surface with flour. Knead the dough lightly, adding the minimum amount of flour necessary to keep it from sticking. Then divide the dough into 6 equal parts.

Roll each of the 6 portions into a $1/2$-inch-diameter rope. Cut the rope into $1/2$-inch-long pieces. The gnocchi can, at this point, be imprinted with a little finger depression or ribbed with fork tines, the better to allow sauce to adhere. Or they can be left as is.

Bring a large pot of salted water to a boil. Gently lower the gnocchi, a dozen or so at a time, into the boiling water. Stir the gnocchi gently until they rise to the surface, to keep them from sticking together. The total cooking time is 3 minutes. Remove the gnocchi from the water with a skimmer, drain briefly, and transfer to a hot serving platter or individual hot plates. Repeat until all the gnocchi are cooked. Serve with Parmigiano sprinkled on top.

Squash Gnocchi

Gnocchi di Zucce

It seems odd, at first glance, to make gnocchi from squash, especially when you're used to the classic potato gnocchi. But these winter squash gnocchi are a remarkable taste sensation—for gnocchi. All that's needed is a little melted butter and freshly grated Parmigiano to finish them.

The trick to making squash gnocchi is to have the cooked pulp as dry as possible.

makes 6 servings

2 pounds winter squash, such as
    butternut, acorn, or Hubbard
2 large eggs, beaten with
    1 teaspoon salt

1½ cups unbleached all-purpose flour
Melted unsalted butter
Freshly grated Parmigiano-Reggiano
    cheese

Preheat the oven to 350°F.

Slice the squash in half lengthwise. Wrap the halves loosely in aluminum foil. Place on a baking sheet and bake until tender, from 30 minutes to 1 hour, depending upon the squash. Remove from the oven and let cool.

When cool enough to handle, scoop out the seeds and discard. Scoop out the squash flesh and coarsely chop it. Discard the skin. Place the chopped squash in a fine-meshed colander set in a large mixing bowl. Refrigerate and let the squash drain excess moisture for several hours or, preferably, overnight.

Puree the drained squash in a food processor or blender. With the motor running, add the eggs and salt. Process to combine. Then add the flour, processing just long enough to blend. The dough will be soft and sticky. Transfer to a mixing bowl.

Bring a large pot of salted water to a boil. The gnocchi are crafted and cooked simply by scooping up teaspoonfuls of the dough and gently pushing them off the spoon into the boiling water. Let cook, in batches, for 2 to 3 minutes. Remove with a skimmer, drain briefly, and transfer to a hot platter or individual serving plates. Repeat until all the dough is used.

Serve with melted butter and freshly grated Parmigiano cheese.

Vegetables

The Piedmontese have a considerable vegetable repertoire, but unlike neighboring Liguria—which is largely vegetarian—in Piedmont, vegetables get swept up into other dishes, especially *antipasti*. For example, where other Italians serve red peppers in a straightforward fashion—grilled and anointed with olive oil—the Piedmontese instead make a flan of red pepper, or add it to braised rabbit, or use it to flavor a risotto, or employ it as an envelope for a puree of tuna. That said, vegetable dishes do appear—and deliciously so—as the following recipes demonstrate.

Piedmontese Scalloped Potatoes

Crema di Patate

Although food writers, like radio disc jockeys, are never supposed to say that they like one recipe (or record) more than another, I have to confess that *crema di patate* is one of my absolute favorites. After all, it's scalloped potatoes, and who doesn't love that? The twist here is the addition of a lavish quantity of finely chopped Italian parsley, as well as the old-fashioned method of letting the starch in the potatoes thicken the milk in which they are cooked. Interestingly, this same technique was one of the "tricks" used to create the much-admired *pommes gratin* at the famous old Paris restaurant Laperouse.

makes 4 to 6 servings

1 pound waxy-type potatoes, peeled and sliced about ⅛ inch thick

2 cups milk plus more if needed

Small handful of fresh Italian parsley leaves, very finely chopped

1 teaspoon salt

Freshly ground black pepper to taste

Freshly grated nutmeg to taste

Place the potato slices in a heavy-bottomed casserole or 2-quart saucepan. Add all the remaining ingredients, stirring to blend. Bring to a boil, then immediately reduce the heat to a low simmer. Let cook, uncovered, for about 20 minutes, until the potatoes are completely tender and create a dense, creamy mass when stirred. The potatoes will not keep their shape, but will instead break down a bit. Add additional milk if necessary. The dish should not be overly dry.

Potatoes and Capers

Patate ai Capperi

⁂

Capers and pancetta—unsmoked seasoned Italian-style bacon—add immense flavor to potatoes. The best capers, by far, are those dry-packed in salt, rather the the more commonly seen vinegar-packed type. It's worth going out of your way for salt-packed capers.

makes 6 servings

3 ounces pancetta, sliced into matchstick strips

1 large onion, coarsely chopped

Leaves from 1 large sprig fresh rosemary, finely chopped

2 pounds waxy-type potatoes, peeled and cut into $1/4$-inch-thick slices

6 tablespoons salt-packed capers, rinsed and finely chopped

Salt

Add the pancetta to a large sauté pan over medium-high heat. Sauté for several minutes. Lower the heat to medium-low, add the onion, and stir and toss vigorously to combine. Let cook, stirring frequently, until the onion is soft and translucent, do not allow it to color. Add the rosemary, stirring to combine. Add the potato slices, gently and repeatedly turning them to combine them with all of the ingredients in the pan. Continue to turn the potato slices frequently and cook until they are tender, about 15 minutes.

Shortly before they are cooked, add the capers and turn the potato slices to combine. Let cook for another 2 to 3 minutes. Taste for salt (little should be needed because of the capers) and serve hot.

⁂

Stuffed Potatoes

Patate Ripiene

✤❧✤

Instead of stuffing only zucchini, the Piedmontese like performing the same trick with potatoes. As I discovered upon returning home, this dish works even better with Idaho-type potatoes than with the waxy ones used in Piedmont. For a simple, easy-to-prepare-ahead-of-time lunch or dinner, these stuffed potatoes are the ticket.

makes 6 servings

6 Idaho-type potatoes, well scrubbed and
    pricked several times with a fork
$^1/_2$ pound ground veal or sausage meat
Small handful of fresh Italian parsley
    leaves, finely chopped
Small handful of fresh basil leaves,
    finely chopped

2 garlic cloves, finely chopped
1 large egg, beaten
Salt
Freshly ground black pepper
Extra virgin olive oil

Preheat the oven to 425°F.

Bake the potatoes until fork-tender, about 1 hour. Remove from the oven.

In the meantime, in a mixing bowl, combine the ground veal with the parsley, basil, garlic, and egg and season with salt and pepper. Mix together thoroughly. In a medium-size nonstick pan over medium heat, cook the meat mixture, stirring, until cooked through.

Split the baked potatoes open lengthwise. Scoop out most of the interiors. Let cool briefly. Combine the potatoes interiors with the meat mixture and stuff each potato half with this filling. The potatoes can be served lukewarm or reheated in the oven, as you prefer. Just before serving, drizzle a little extra virgin olive oil over each potato half.

Baked Beans, Hunter's Style

Fagiolini alla Cacciatora

✿✿✿

This is a simple baked bean dish that is utterly unlike anything we imagine when the phrase "baked beans" is invoked. This creation couldn't be easier. The choice of beans is entirely a matter of preference. In Piedmont, the most frequently used dried bean is the *borlotti*, which is known to us as the cranberry bean. It's a distinctive bean, red speckled with a nutty flavor, and if you want to be absolutely authentic, that would be the way to go. But pinto beans are sometimes easier to find, so I often use them instead.

makes 6 servings

2 tablespoons olive oil

1 medium-size onion, finely chopped

1 celery stalk, finely chopped

1 large carrot, finely chopped

2 ripe medium-size tomatoes, peeled, seeded, and coarsely chopped, or 1 cup chopped canned tomatoes

1 pound dried beans, such as cranberry, pinto, or Great Northern, picked over, soaked overnight in water to cover, and drained

$1/2$ teaspoon salt

$1/2$ cup water, stock of your choice, or dry white wine

Extra virgin olive oil

Preheat the oven to 350°F.

Heat the olive oil over medium heat in a casserole or sauté pan large enough to hold all of the ingredients. Add the onion, celery, and carrot and cook briefly, stirring, until the onion is translucent but not colored. Add the tomatoes and beans and stir to combine. Add the salt and water, cover, and let cook until the beans are tender, $1^1/2$ to 2 hours.

Serve with a drizzle of extra virgin olive oil on top, hot or at room temperature, depending on the season.

Bourgeois-Style Cauliflower

Cavolfiore alla Borghese

Combining cauliflower and anchovies is seemingly a favorite Piedmontese winter sport. This version makes an ideal accompaniment to all sorts of meat dishes, especially roasts. Although anchovies are a key flavoring, it's really the parsley that completes the flavor picture. Its green freshness counterpoints the anchovy, as well as, literally, brightens the dish.

makes 6 servings

1 large head cauliflower, separated into small florets

2 ounces Parmigiano-Reggiano cheese, grated ($^{1}/_{2}$ cup)

For the sauce:

2 tablespoons unsalted butter

2 whole salted anchovies, rinsed, filleted, soaked briefly in cold water, drained and very finely chopped

1 tablespoon finely chopped fresh Italian parsley leaves

Freshly ground black pepper

Preheat the oven to 350°F.

Steam the cauliflower florets until they are cooked through but still crisp, about 10 minutes. Place in a large mixing bowl, add the Parmigiano, and toss to combine.

To make the sauce, place the butter in a small nonstick skillet over medium-low heat. When melted, add the anchovies, parsley, and black pepper to taste. Let cook very gently for just 1 to 2 minutes.

Toss the cauliflower with the anchovy sauce, transfer to a lightly buttered baking dish, and bake until the cauliflower is hot, about 15 minutes.

Cauliflower and Winter Squash in Anchovy Sauce

Cavolfiori e Zucce in Salsa d'Acciughe

⚜

If a single vegetable dish could be said to fully capture Piedmontese tastes—at least the rustic, hearty sort—it's this purebred rendition of cauliflower and winter squash paired with that all-time Piedmontese favorite, anchovies. The combination is striking; the flavors meld like no others. This is one of those vegetable dishes that at first seems odd but then after a few bites, you wonder why nobody ever served it to you before.

makes 4 to 6 servings

1 pound butternut, acorn, or other winter squash
One 1-one pound head cauliflower, separated into bite-size florets
8 whole salted anchovies, rinsed, filleted, soaked briefly in cold water, and drained

1 large garlic clove, very finely chopped
Extra virgin olive oil

Cut the squash into halves or quarters, depending upon the size. Bake it in a preheated 350°F oven or steam it until fork-tender. When the squash is cooked, let cool. Scoop the flesh from the rind, discarding the rind. Cut the squash into bite-size pieces, the same size as the cauliflower florets. Set aside.

Meanwhile, steam the cauliflower until cooked through but still slightly crunchy, about 10 minutes. Set aside.

Very finely chop the anchovies until a fine paste is achieved. Combine with the garlic. Place a small pan over the lowest heat. Add a small quantity of extra virgin olive oil to the pan. Very gently cook the anchovy mixture in the oil for about 5 minutes, taking care not to let it burn.

Add a little olive oil to a large sauté pan over high heat. When hot, toss in the cooked squash pieces and cauliflower. Stirring and tossing continuously, reheat them thoroughly, then remove from the heat. Add the anchovy sauce and stir and toss to blend thoroughly. Serve on warm plates.

Ratatouille Piedmont Style

Ratatuia Piemontese

✻

Piedmont's proximity to Nice (which was considered part of the House of Savoy's Kingdom of Sardinia/Piedmont until 1860, when it was ceded to France) can be found in this distinctive version of what we know by its French name, ratatouille.

The two dishes are more alike than not, save for a few peculiarly Piedmontese touches, such as the incorporation of potatoes and an unusual last-minute addition of an anchovy/vinegar/herb mixture that gives the dish some zip. I like it very much and honestly think it better than the (good) French version. As always, this only improves if left overnight and reheated—or, better yet, served at room temperature.

makes 6 to 8 servings

¼ cup extra virgin olive oil

3 medium-size zucchini, sliced into
    ½-inch-thick rounds

2 medium-size eggplants, cut into
    1-inch cubes

2 medium-size onions, sliced

2 large carrots, sliced into ½-inch-thick
    rounds

2 red bell peppers, peeled with a
    vegetable peeler, cored, seeded,
    and cut into bite-size pieces

3 large ripe tomatoes, seeded, and cut
    into bite-size pieces

1 cup water

1 bay leaf

Salt

Freshly ground black pepper

3 medium-size waxy-type potatoes, peeled
    and quartered

To complete the dish:

6 whole salted anchovies, rinsed, filleted,
    soaked briefly in cold water, drained,
    and finely chopped

3 garlic cloves, very finely chopped

Small handful of fresh basil leaves,
    coarsely chopped

Small handful of fresh Italian parsley
    leaves, coarsely chopped

2 tablespoons salt-packed capers, rinsed
    and crushed

12 fresh sage leaves, finely chopped

¼ cup red wine vinegar

1 to 2 teaspoons sugar, to your taste

Add the olive oil to a large pot over medium heat. When hot, add the zucchini and eggplant slices, stir vigorously, and let cook for several minutes. Add the onions, carrots, bell peppers, tomatoes, water, and bay leaf and season with salt and pepper. Stir thoroughly to blend. Bring to a boil, then immediately reduce the heat to the barest simmer, letting the mixture just barely bubble. Let cook, partly covered, for about 1 hour.

Add the potatoes and continue cooking until the potatoes are tender. If the mixture is too dry, add more water to moisten. Remove from the heat. Let cool.

Just before serving, add the remaining ingredients. Stir vigorously to blend. Let sit briefly and serve at room temperature, lukewarm, or hot.

A "Salad" of Raw Winter Vegetables with Spicy Gorgonzola Dip
Insalata di Ortaggi Invernali con Gorgonzola Piccante

This could just as easily have been put in the *antipasti* section. But since it employs so many vegetables—enough for a light meal in itself—I decided that it was best included here. Like all raw vegetable presentations, putting this dish together takes almost no time. Just slice the vegetables into manageable pieces, place them attractively on a platter, and serve the spicy dip alongside. It's the dip, of course, that makes the dish—it's a knockout.

makes 6 servings

For the dip:

6 tablespoons extra virgin olive oil

2 tablespoons white wine vinegar

1 tablespoon fresh lemon juice

6 ounces Gorgonzola **naturale** *(very blue)*

1 tablespoon mild chili powder

To serve with the dip:

Celery hearts, cut into 3-inch lengths

Jerusalem artichokes, peeled and thickly sliced

Cauliflower, separated into florets blanched if desired

Broccoli, separated into small florets blanched if desired

Fennel bulb, thoroughly washed and thickly sliced

To make the dip, place all of the ingredients in a food processor or blender and process until smooth. Refrigerate and let the flavors marry for at least several hours. Bring to room temperature before serving with the vegetables.

Stuffed Zucchini

Zucchine Ripieni

Stuffed zucchini barquettes are typical of southern Piedmont. Indeed, the closer to the Ligurian border you get, the more frequently they appear. Every cook has his or her variation on the theme of scooping out the zucchini interior, combining it with some ground meat, returning it to the zucchini shell, and baking it briefly. What follows is classic, traditional, and stupendously good.

makes 6 servings

4 to 6 small zucchini

1 medium-size onion, finely chopped

2 garlic cloves, very finely chopped

Leaves from 1 large sprig rosemary, finely chopped

Small handful of fresh Italian parsley, leaves finely chopped

Small handful of fresh basil leaves, finely chopped

15 fresh sage leaves, finely chopped

½ pound ground veal or sausage meat

1 large egg

¼ cup dry bread crumbs, soaked in milk to cover

1 ounce Parmigiano-Reggiano cheese, grated (¼ cup)

Salt

Freshly ground black pepper

Extra virgin olive oil

Preheat the oven to 300°F.

Slice the zucchini in half lengthwise. Cut the halves into 3-inch lengths. Scoop out most of the interior of the zucchini and reserve it. Set aside the scooped-out zucchini.

Finely chop the zucchini interiors. In a mixing bowl, combine the chopped zucchini with the onion, garlic, rosemary, parsley, basil, and sage. Mix to blend thoroughly. Add the veal, egg, the bread crumbs, with any liquid, and the Parmigiano and season with salt and pepper. Mix thoroughly to combine.

Fill the scooped-out zucchini lengths with the meat filling. Drizzle a bit of olive oil over the filling. Place the stuffed zucchini in a large lightly oiled casserole. Cover tightly and bake until the filling is cooked through and the zucchini is tender, about 1 hour.

Grilled Fennel
Finocchio alla Griglia

Sweet fennel is the most flavorful of all wintertime vegetables. You find it nearly every-where in Italy. Although the most refined use for sweet fennel surely is in a risotto (see page 121), there's no disputing that its goodness comes shining through in this simple version of grilled fennel. In Piedmont, as elsewhere in Italy, many cooks still grill over wood coals, which adds a world of additional flavor. A little hibachi stove is ideal, if you've got a yen to do things *artigianale*. Add melted butter to the grilled fennel and top with Parmigiano just before serving.

makes 6 servings

3 small fennel bulbs (each about
    1 pound)
6 tablespoons unsalted butter or olive oil

2 ounces Parmigiano-Reggiano cheese,
    grated (¹/₂ cup)

Trim the stems from the fennel. Slice each bulb in half lengthwise, then slice ¹/₄ inch thick length-wise. Steam or boil the fennel slices until tender, about 15 minutes.

Preheat the broiler. Transfer the cooked fennel slices to a buttered baking dish or gratin pan. Distribute the butter or olive oil evenly over the slices. Sprinkle the Parmigiano evenly over the fennel. Place the pan under a broiler and broil until golden brown.

Sweet-and-Sour Onions
Cipolle Agrodolce nel Vino Rosso

Small onions cooked in vinegar and red wine is a favorite Piedmontese appetizer, condiment, side dish, what have you. There, they have a kind of small, squat onion called *cipollina* that is sweeter than our small, yellow "boiler onions." Since the onions must remain whole, our regular onions are simply too large. And our small white pearl onions are just too small. The best approach is to locate large shallots, which are ideally sweet-tasting, yet still possess a real onion taste. Also, they are an attractive size, although smaller than the onions employed in Piedmont. But they taste great, especially when served alongside a meat pâté.

makes 8 to 10 servings

2 pounds large shallots

1 cup dry red wine

½ cup red wine vinegar

1 cup water

2 bay leaves

10 fresh sage leaves

Grated zest of 1 lemon

1 tablespoon sugar

½ teaspoon salt

To peel the shallots, plunge them into boiling water for 1 minute. Drain and peel off the papery skin. Do not trim the root, as it will keep the shallot whole, but trim the root fibers if necessary, to create a more finished appearance.

Place the remaining ingredients in a large nonreactive sauté pan (do not use unlined cast iron). Bring to a boil. Add the peeled shallots and let boil, uncovered, until tender, about 20 minutes. Remove the shallots and let cool.

Once both the red wine mixture and the shallots have cooled, recombine them and refrigerate until needed.

To serve, strain the shallots from the liquid and serve cool, but not cold. The shallots will keep, refrigerated, for about 2 weeks.

Vinegar-Preserved Cherries
Ciliege Sottacete

A taste of sweet and sour works perfectly with many meat dishes. This version of preserved cherries is often seen accompanying various liver pâtés, as well as being one of the condiments used in Piedmont's mixed boiled meats feast, *bollito misto*. The trick to preserved cherries is time: They need at least a month to mature in the refrigerator before being served. But they're worth the wait. Any size preserving jars (or a porcelain tureen) can be used.

makes 1 quart

3 pounds Bing or Ranier cherries, stems
   removed
4 cups red wine vinegar
1⅓ cups sugar

1 teaspoon ground cinnamon
8 cloves
Pinch of salt

Pack the cherries loosely in preserving jars of any size you like. Set aside.

In a small nonreactive saucepan over high heat, combine the remaining ingredients. Whisk to blend. Bring to a boil, then lower the heat to medium-low and let simmer for 5 minutes. Remove from the heat.

While the vinegar mixture is still warm, pour it over the cherries, taking care that the cherries are fully covered by the vinegar. Let cool completely. Seal with screw caps and refrigerate. Leave in the refrigerator for at least 1 month before using, to allow the flavors to meld fully.

Pursuing Piedmont's Cheeses

Autunno, la mucca fa il formaggio.

(In autumn, the cows make cheese.)

Italian proverb

The gods were beneficent when we chose to spend our year in America dei Boschi, because in nearby Bra, just two and a half miles away, was Fiorenzo Giolito. As we subsequently discovered, the cheese shop he owns and presides over is renowned. Alba—which is a much bigger and more sophisticated town—has nothing, and nobody, like Fiorenzo Giolito.

Fiorenzo was born to cheese, as the Giolito family has owned a cheese shop for generations. The father made way for the son, who lives over the shop in a modernized apartment that is part of the Giolito family property. You can visit Fiorenzo's small shop six days a week. It's a modern, sparkling clean shop on a corner in downtown Bra. But the best place to banter with Fiorenzo is at Bra's big open-air Friday food market. There, Fiorenzo sets up his array of cheeses, standing behind them like a general reviewing his troops.

Now in his forties, Fiorenzo is divorced. This isn't to say that he is without opportunities. Fiorenzo is a trim, handsome man, trembling with energy like a springer spaniel. Like a lot of the men in Bra and the surrounding countryside, he only shaves every other day or so, which gives him a surprisingly attractive salt-and-pepper stubble. Coupled with his athletic appearance, he has an outdoorsy look, as if he's just come back from an alpine climb. His beloved Jeep Wagoneer—"*Ecco,* America!" he says proudly—only adds to the effect. Over time, we began to hear (from others) about Fiorenzo's various conquests. My wife says she believes them—there's something in the glint of his eyes, she says.

I don't know anything about this. All Fiorenzo and I ever talked about was cheese. The man knows his cheeses. I first realized just what Fiorenzo knew about cheese from, of all cheeses, his Parmigiano-Reggiano. This is odd on two counts. First, it's not a local cheese: Parmigiano-Reggiano is famously a product of Emilia-Romagna and, to a lesser extent, Lombardy. Both regions are east of Piedmont.

Second, as great cheeses go—and Parmigiano is one of the world's greatest—it is a somewhat industrial item. A lot of milk goes into making one of those huge, dense wheels. Typically, the farms are large and the cheese making is sophisticated and large scale. There's even a bank where the deposits are wheels of finished Paramigiano, left as collateral!

When I first met Fiorenzo, I naturally bought some Parmigiano, as it's a staple. But when I tasted what he offered, I found myself beaming with unexpected pleasure. This was immensely good Parmigiano. Really terrific. When I exclaimed to that effect, Fiorenzo grinned. No false modesty there. "It *is* good, isn't it?" he acknowledged. After establishing that its unusual goodness wasn't a matter of aging or some other unknown factor, I ran out of possible reasons.

Fiorenzo enjoyed watching me ponder the Parmigiano problem. Finally, he came across. "I get my Parmigiano from one small producer, whose herd grazes on hillsides as well as flat ground," he explained. "I know the fellow personally. His cheese gets made and stored the same way as everyone else's. So the only way I can figure why his Parmigiano is better is where his cows graze. Whatever the reason, his is the only Parmigiano I buy."

For what it's worth, I wasn't the only one captivated by Fiorenzo's Parmigiano. My friend Michel Bettane, who is France's best wine critic, came to visit us. We went to the Friday market and I introduced him to Fiorenzo. I suggested that he try the Parmigiano. Michel resisted. "You know, we get pretty good Parmigiano in Paris," he said reproachfully. Rightly, he wanted to sample something peculiar and local (which we later did). Even so, I said, give it a try.

I watched Michel's expressive face when he bit into the jagged chunk that Fiorenzo calved off from the mother wheel. "Uh, excuse me," said Michel. "Exactly how much is this Parmigiano?" Fiorenzo told him the price, which was cheaper than the going rate for Parmigiano in Paris. "I'll take three kilos," he said instantly.

On the way home I accused Michel of buying the cheese simply because, like all good Frenchmen, he was atavistically frugal. This was nonsense because Michel is an implacable connoisseur and spends a fortune on all kinds of expensive wines. He ignored the abuse. "That's the best Parmigiano I've ever eaten," he intoned, adding, *"Quel fromager!"* He's right. Fiorenzo is a great cheese merchant.

My cheese explorations with Fiorenzo quickly embraced various local items. Probably no region in Italy has more, or better, cheeses than Piedmont. Partly this is due to its size and the variety of terrain. A lot of mountains and valleys usually means plenty of cheese. Partly it has to do with the historical richness of Piedmontese cuisine. Proximity to France and Switzerland probably hasn't hurt, either. Whatever the reasons, Piedmontese cheeses are superb.

The most famous is Gorgonzola. Lombardy partisans will huffily point out that Gorgonzola is really a cheese from Lombardy because, after all, the town after which it was named is east of Milan, in Lombardy. This is a minor detail. The fact is that the vast majority of Gorgonzola is created in Piedmont's part of the Po Valley. And the clincher is that virtually every wheel of Gorgonzola is cured in one vast temperature-controlled facility in the Piedmontese city of Novara. I visited this facility and was shown around a warren of cold rooms, each belonging to a different Gorgonzola producer. Frankly, there was more to be learned from tasting than viewing.

Fiorenzo's Gorgonzola is exceptionally good. But even he admits that he could as easily choose from half a dozen others equally as good. "The real challenge with Gorgonzola," he says, "is not the heavily blue version, gorgonzola *naturale*, but the pale gorgonzola *dolce*. It has to be impeccably fresh and clean tasting."

Every Friday, I would buy a heavenly slab of Fiorenzo's freshly arrived gorgonzola *dolce*, take it home, and slather it liberally across a slice of thick-crusted bread. With this oh-so-simple pleasure I would break out a bottle of Barbera. It is, happily, an exportable pleasure, although the appearance of a really fresh Gorgonzola *dolce* is not as predictable, or expectable, as it was in Bra.

Probably Piedmont's greatest cheese—and the one Fiorenzo is most proud of—is also Piedmont's rarest: Castelmagno. It is also the most expensive cheese in Fiorenzo's shop, apart from a few specialty truffled cheeses. Castelmagno is probably Piedmont's oldest cheese as well, predating even the ancient Gorgonzola, which would put its origins at least as far back as one thousand years. It also has the odd distinction of having had a war fought over it, one that lasted thirty years. Actually, the cheese was a pretext for an ongoing aggravation between the cities of Cúneo and Saluzzo in the 1200s.

Castelmagno itself is made high up in the mountains, where it cures in naturally humid grottoes. It takes its name from the eponymous town. Visiting the town is quite an expedition. It lies at the end of a mountain road that takes you high up into the Alps very near the French border, just ten miles as the crow flies. The views are breathtaking and spectacular, with jagged, rocky peaks towering over you. The mountain meadows in the tiny Castelmagno cheese zone lie between three thousand and six thousand feet in elevation. Residents surely never came down from the mountains until early summer, so impassable and twisting were the roads.

Castelmagno cheese is a cylindrical item, about ten inches across and eight inches high. The interior usually is white, dense, and a bit dry in texture, with a faint hint of creaminess. The rind is tough-looking and crinkled. Typically, Castelmagno is aged for between two and five months in those humid mountain grottoes. Really aged versions, which are rare, are veined with mold. They are not to my taste.

What makes Castelmagno so distinctive, say the locals, is that the cows in the fairly small zone entitled to the designation graze on a flowering herb locally called in Piedmontese dialect *eves*. Just down the (mountain) road from the town of Castelmagno is another town called Pradlèves. It is an odd name that I couldn't quite figure out until Fiorenzo explained about the herb. Pradlèves actually comes from *prato dell'eves*—literally, "herb meadow."

Anyway, there's not much Castelmagno made and, according to Fiorenzo, what is made isn't consistently good. Castelmagno is a distinctly artisanal cheese and that explains its variability. It's estimated that only three thousand cows—of the ancient Piedmontese breed—supply the milk needed. And of that, some of the milk is diverted for butter production.

But when it's good, Castelmagno is like no other cheese anywhere: subtly flavorful, faintly herbal, and delicately dry and dense. It is a tremendous cooking cheese and if you get the chance to sample *gnocchi al Castelmagno*, you will see why it is so sought after. In the old days, Castelmagno used to be served with honey. I've tried this combination, but the appeal escapes me.

Where Castelmagno is the undoubted jewel of Fiorenzo's cheese selection, the mainstay is undeniably the array of soft, round cheeses that invariably are called by the dialect name, *toma* (pronounced too-ma). Toma is properly known in Italian as robiola, but I never heard anybody at Bra's Friday market voice that name. (Then again, I sometimes wouldn't hear any Italian spoken at all. Most of Fiorenzo's banter with his older customers was in dialect.)

Under the proper robiola heading, there are a variety of appellation-designated versions: robiola Piemontese, robiola d'Alba, robiola del bec (this must be a joke name, like Welsh rabbit, as *bec* is dialect for billy-goat), robiola di Bossolasco, robiola di Cocconato, and robiola delle Langhe. There are, it should be pointed out, yet other northern Italian cheeses called robiola that do not resemble anything the Piedmontese call toma.

All sorts of toma cheeses are made. Some are entirely cow's milk, others entirely sheep's milk. Yet others are a mixture of the two. Some are part goat's milk. Then there's the matter of aging, the *stagionatura*. Some toma cheeses are made to be eaten very fresh: white, young, and creamy. Often, these are made in small, inch-wide, inch-high cylinders. These are called, not surprisingly, *tomini*. They are my wife's favorite. (They were also favorites of Piedmont's royal family, the House of Savoy, in the 1800s.) Other toma cheeses can be aged as long as a year, which makes them pretty strong-tasting and dense.

Fiorenzo had competition in the toma department. There were two ladies, both farmers, who brought their homemade cheeses to the Friday market. We used to buy our toma cheeses from them. I always felt a little guilty about this, but then, Fiorenzo got quite a lot of business from us.

One of the cheese ladies was young and affable. Her specialty was a type of toma called *paglierina*, because it is aged on straw mats (*paglia*), an ancient and still much-used method of *stagionatura*. The other cheese lady was an old crone I couldn't understand at all. Her Italian was heavily laced with dialect; my Italian was equally laced with ignorance. The combination made for limited discussion. She wasn't local, either. She made the trip to the Bra market all the way from Murrazano, about fifteen miles away.

Murrazano is another world from Bra, as it's in what's called the Alta Langhe, the high-elevation towns in the Langhe hills. Because these towns were too high for successful grape cultivation, they have always been the poorest villages in the area, subsisting on sheepherding, chestnuts, and an unrelenting diet of polenta. This cheese lady made a type of toma called Murrazano, which is larger and classically made from sheep's milk. Murrazano cheese is one of the best versions of toma produced.

The most local of Fiorenzo's cheeses couldn't get any more so: its name is Bra. The cheese called Bra is a fairly bland affair, yellow gold in color and offered in either a young, soft *fresca* type like Jarlsberg or a more aged, hard *vecchio* version. We preferred the younger style, but I must admit that Bra cheese isn't a world-beater.

There was one local cheese that Fiorenzo himself wasn't wild over, although he stocked it. It's a truly local oddity called, in dialect, *brus* or *bros*. I actually like it, although I'd be less than honest to say that it was a staple around the house. Brus is a cheese, or mix of cheeses, lightened with a bit of cream or ricotta and left to ferment in a terra-cotta jar for the better part of a month. The fermentation is stopped by dousing the already pretty strong cheese with a generous quantity of grappa. It's then left to sit for another month or so.

This is the traditional brus. Fiorenzo's brus was much milder, quite creamy, and only slightly fermented. There wasn't enough grappa in it, to steal a line from A. J. Liebling, "to furnish a gnat with an alcohol rub."

Traditional brus is hard to find outside of private farmhouses inhabited by old peasants. I've eaten it—and enjoyed it—but it is the sort of cheese that can literally send people running from the room. It gets its name, by the way, from *bruciare*, to burn. That gives you an idea of its taste. The old cheese lady brought in some of her homemade brus during the winter months. I would buy it, later enjoying it at home by scooping it out with *grissini* (breadsticks). I had to do it alone, though. She made her brus with a mixture of her toma cheese and a ricotta that, in Piedmontese, is known as *seirass*—which word comes from *siero*, or whey. It had a kick, which made me conclude that it was the real thing.

Main Courses

*The consistently rich man is also unlikely to make the acquaintance of meat
dishes of robust taste . . . He will not meet the civets, or dark winy
stews of domestic rabbit and old turkey.*

A. J. Liebling
Between Meals: An Appetite for Paris (1962)

In the course of spending a year in Piedmont, winding through its hills and scurrying across its flat expanses of rice fields, I entertained a recurrent fantasy: I wished I were traveling with A. J. Liebling. (My wife knows about this and it's all right with her.) I had the luck to come across Liebling's writing years ago, when he was still shadowed in obscurity. Now, gratifyingly, he is recognized as one of the supreme stylists of modern American writing.

Piedmont is the only place in Europe where I think Liebling would be happy today. The great feeders of France celebrated in *Between Meals,* his last book, are all gone. France has become too fastidious—*déraciné,* as the French would say, uprooted. All the old, tough turkeys (both eaters and eaten) are gone. Piedmont still has them in abundance.

Liebling was a glutton—there's no other word for it. His grotesque girth would have been, if not endorsed, at least understood in Piedmont. He would have loved the Piedmontese and they him. He would have adored the restaurants, tucked away in improbably remote, tiny villages that serve the "dark, winy stews" that he so rightly praised. And they still serve the animal oddments that today are scorned: various innards that we can't even buy in America, let alone praise. Today, in Piedmont, these dishes still are part of heroic meals that might legitimately be described as Rabelaisian, but only if we envision a Piedmontese Rabelais: severe and serious rather than frivolous. Not as word-besotted, but his equal in unrepentant gluttony. The Piedmontese can *feast.*

The reason, as Liebling astutely notes, lies in not being consistently rich. Perhaps the Piedmontese were not as grindingly poor as other Italians, especially Southerners, but degrees of hunger soon become an academic distinction to its sufferer. The hundreds of thousands of Piedmontese who emigrated to Argentina and the United States are proof of the desperation. Now, thankfully, poverty in Piedmont is largely nonexistent. But the memory still remains, hence the feasting. And the love of meat.

All Piedmontese *secondi,* or second courses, are meat. It is not so much a gastronomic high point as an emotional one. A fine meat dish, like a good pair of shoes, is significant. It has resonance, a profound emotional satisfaction of well-being unavailable to those of us born in places where meat is ordinary, plentiful, and cheap. This is captured in the matter-of-fact definition of poverty by a worker who once lived in Australia and returned to Italy in the 1920s: "There was little poverty in Australia. We could have one kilogram of meat per day. Here you could not be certain of meat once a month."*

Unlike Tuscany, where the meat dishes are usually grilled, Piedmontese meats more often are braised, invariably in wine and stock. They are cooked slowly, luxuriating as much in time as in wine. Although game still appears in restaurants, a few meats preponderate: chicken, turkey, rabbit, and veal.

The traditional Piedmontese meat dishes that follow taste every bit as good here as they do in Piedmont. Quantities are intentionally small, as in Piedmont itself. In the Italian menu presentation, *secondi* are served alone, without accompaniments, as part of the sequence of a meal.

* Douglas R. Holmes, *Cultural Disenchantments: Worker Peasantries in Northeast Italy.*

Chicken Hunter's Style

Pollo alla Cacciatora

Everywhere in Northern Italy you will find one variation or another of *pollo alla cacciatora*. They more resemble each other than not, as they all incorporate onions, tomatoes, and herbs. To the extent that a Piedmontese *pollo alla cacciatora* differs from those elsewhere, it probably rests with a characteristic use of fresh rosemary, as well as fresh basil added at the last moment. It is most frequently served during the summer and early fall, when fresh tomatoes and basil are at their best.

makes 6 servings

5 tablespoons olive oil

4 medium-size onions, finely chopped

1 large roasting chicken (about
    4 pounds), cut into serving pieces
    and skin removed

1 cup dry white wine

Leaves from 2 large sprigs of fresh
    rosemary, finely chopped

2 bay leaves

2 large garlic cloves, finely chopped

1 pound ripe tomatoes (2 medium-size
    tomatoes) or canned equivalent
    (see Note on tomatoes, page 156),
    coarsely chopped

Salt

Freshly ground black pepper

Finely chopped fresh basil leaves

Place a large skillet over medium heat and add 2 tablespoons of the olive oil. When hot, add the onions and cook, stirring, until translucent but not colored, about 10 minutes. Transfer to a bowl and set aside.

Wipe out in the skillet and heat the remaining 3 tablespoons olive oil in it over medium heat. When hot, add the chicken pieces and brown on all sides. Pour in the wine, scraping up any browned bits from the bottom of the skillet. Add the remaining ingredients except the basil, cover, and let cook over medium-low heat until the chicken is tender, about 45 minutes. About 5 minutes before serving, stir in the basil.

Chicken Marengo Style

Pollo alla Marengo

❧

A few miles southeast of the city of Alessandria, Napoleon Bonaparte defeated the Austrians in what he considered the greatest battle of his career: the Battle of Marengo, on June 14, 1800. He probably thought so highly of this battle because, four years earlier, he had swept through Italy and felt he had pretty well conquered it. Austrians, Russians, and British thought otherwise. So when Napoleon went off to conquer Egypt in 1799, a combined Austrian-Russian army descended into Italy and took it back, helped by Lord Nelson and the British fleet. Napoleon was incensed and returned to Italy to retake what he thought was already his. The battle of Marengo was decisive. Shortly afterward, Napoleon crowned himself King of Italy at the great cathedral in Milan.

The origin of *pollo alla Marengo* is lost in time. Probably it was the invention of a favor-currying cook looking for a bit of *tangenti* (graft) from Napoleon's army. Folklore, however, offers two versions. One is that Napoleon himself showed up at an inn on the eve of the battle and the cook, upon learning that he disliked roasted chicken, concocted this braised version. The other story has it that the dish was prepared on the field of battle itself by the last surviving cook, who grubbed up what he could from what was at hand.

It's a tasty dish and certainly is Piedmontese in its flavors. The traditional use of Madeira, by the way, is typical of nineteenth-century Piedmontese cooking.

makes 4 servings

1/4 cup olive oil

1 roasting chicken (about 4 pounds), cut into serving pieces and skin removed

1 cup Madeira wine

Large pinch of freshly grated nutmeg

Salt

Freshly ground black pepper

1 ounce dried porcini mushrooms, soaked in 1 cup boiling water for 30 minutes

1 garlic clove, finely chopped

1 cup chicken stock (canned is fine)

Small handful of fresh Italian parsley, leaves finely chopped

Place a large skillet over medium heat with the olive oil. When hot, add the chicken pieces and brown on all sides. Pour off any excess oil. Reduce the heat to medium-low, pour in the Madeira, and season with the nutmeg, salt, and pepper. Let cook for 15 minutes.

Meanwhile, drain the mushrooms, straining the water of grit through a paper towel. If the mushrooms seem gritty, rinse them well. Add the mushrooms to the chicken, along with the soaking water. Stir in the garlic, then add the chicken stock. Cover and let cook until the chicken is tender, about 45 minutes.

To serve, place the chicken pieces on a warm platter or individual plates. Spoon some of the sauce over the chicken pieces and sprinkle on top a generous amount of parsley.

Chicken Stewed in Milk

Fricassea Bianca di Pollo

Braising meats in milk is common to several areas of Northern Italy, including Piedmont. Pork is a favorite meat for this purpose; chicken is another. This version sometimes goes by the name *pollo di primavera*, or spring chicken, perhaps because it uses green onions, which are more commonly available in spring than other times of the year.

makes 4 servings

2 tablespoons unsalted butter

1 tablespoon olive oil

1 large fryer chicken (about 3 pounds), cut into serving pieces and skin removed

2 large green onions (scallions), white and green parts, finely chopped

Small handful of fresh Italian parsley leaves, finely chopped

2 large garlic cloves, finely chopped

Leaves from 1 small sprig fresh rosemary, finely chopped

4 large fresh sage leaves, finely chopped

Large pinch of chopped fresh mint leaves (optional)

1 cup milk

Finely grated or chopped zest of ½ lemon

Salt

Freshly ground black pepper

Place a large skillet over medium heat and add the butter and olive oil. When the butter has melted, add the chicken pieces and brown lightly on all sides. Add the remaining ingredients and bring to a simmer. Immediately reduce the heat to medium-low, partially cover the skillet, and let cook until the chicken is tender, about 45 minutes.

Remove the chicken pieces to a plate and keep warm in a preheated 250°F oven and reduce the liquid remaining in the skillet over high heat until it thickens suitably for a sauce. Put the chicken pieces on a warm platter or individual plates and add a spoonful or two of the reduced sauce to each serving.

Herbed Rolled Chicken Breasts

Involtini di Petti di Pollo con Erbette

Involtini are anything rolled up. Here it's flattened chicken breasts slathered with herbs, rolled and tied, and briefly braised. It is compellingly good. Traditionally, this is made with turkey breasts. But turkey breasts, which have coarser fibers, do not flatten as thin as chicken. If you do use turkey breasts, have the butcher butterfly them first before flattening them, as they are fairly thick.

Some of the stuffing always leaks out during the braising. Make sure to keep the braising liquid, which is rich with herbs and cheese. What I often do the next day is bring the braising liquid to a boil, add some dried pasta, and, keeping it at a high boil, let the pasta absorb all of the liquid until just a thick sauce remains. If the braising liquid runs out before the pasta is completely cooked, I simply add a ladleful of water, letting it be absorbed before adding another if necessary. The idea is to have almost no liquid left when the pasta is cooked.

makes 6 servings

6 boneless, skinless chicken breasts

2 tablespoons olive oil

1 medium-size red onion or 10 shallots,
    finely chopped

A generous mixture (about 2 handfuls) of
    fresh basil, Italian parsley, rosemary,
    sage, thyme, and/or mint leaves,
    finely chopped

1 large egg plus 1 large egg yolk

2 ounces Parmigiano-Reggiano
    cheese, freshly grated ($^1\!/_2$ cup)

Freshly grated nutmeg

Salt

Freshly ground black pepper

2 cups dry white wine

2 cups chicken stock

Ask the butcher to flatten the chicken breasts as thin as possible. Or you can do it yourself by placing each one between two sheets of waxed paper or plastic wrap and slapping it with the side of the cleaver. Set aside.

Put the olive oil in a small sauté pan over medium heat. When hot, add the onion and cook, stirring, until tender but not browned. Set aside.

To create the filling, place the herbs in a large nonstick skillet. Moisten with just a little bit of water. Cook over medium heat just until the herbs have brightened in color. Drain if necessary and set aside to cool. You should have about $^1\!/_2$ cup.

When the herbs are cool, place in a large mixing bowl. Add the onion, the whole egg and egg yolk, and Parmigiano and season with nutmeg, salt, and pepper. Stir vigorously to combine.

Lay the flattened chicken breasts in a row on a work surface and spread one sixth of the herb mixture on each breast. Roll up the herbed breasts from a long side to create the *involtini*. Secure the rolls by tying each one with kitchen string. Or, alternatively, "staple" the open end with toothpicks (but tying with string creates a more finished look after cooking).

To cook, add the wine and stock to a saucepan large enough to hold the rolls in a single layer. Bring to a simmer. Gently place the rolls in the simmering liquid. Cover and let braise, turning the rolls once or twice, until they are firm to the touch, about 15 minutes.

To serve, remove the toothpicks or snip the strings and place on warm plates.

Capon with Honey-Hazelnut Sauce

Cappone con la Sausa d'Avije

A capon is an emasculated rooster. The procedure is done early in the bird's life so that it will grow unusually large yet tender. Capon is much prized in Piedmont and typically is reserved for the most important holiday feasts, especially Christmas. At that time, not so mysteriously, the price for capons soars and shoppers are heard grumbling—and not so quietly, either. Still, they buy.

What makes this dish so intriguing is not the capon but the sauce. It's entrancing, as well as ancient. The combination of hazelnuts, honey, and mustard is invigorating—and truly transforming. One added feature is that it is an ideal last-minute sauce, as it will keep indefinitely in the refrigerator. If the honey crystallizes (which it will), simply place the opened jar in barely simmering water and let the heat liquefy the honey.

You can substitute chicken or turkey breasts for the capon to fine effect.

makes 1 cup; 6 to 8 servings

For the sauce:

1/2 pound shelled hazelnuts

1 cup honey

2 tablespoons dry mustard, mixed with

  2 tablespoons hot chicken stock

For the bird:

1 capon, washed inside and out and

  patted dry

Olive oil

Preheat the oven to 350°F. Toast the shelled hazelnuts on a baking sheet until lightly browned, about 10 minutes. Rub off the papery skins, then let cool completely. Reduce the oven temperature to 325°F.

To roast the capon, rub it generously with olive oil and set on a rack in a roasting pan. Roast until an instant-read meat thermometer registers 170°F, about 2 1/2 hours (figure on about 20 minutes per pound). Baste occasionally with olive oil.

Let the bird sit in the turned-off oven, with the door slightly ajar, for 15 minutes to let the juices recede into the meat.

While the capon roasts, finish the sauce: Chop the hazelnuts very fine in a food processor or blender, taking care not to overprocess and turn them into hazelnut butter. Combine the honey with the mustard mixture, stirring vigorously to blend. Add the hazelnuts and set aside until needed. (This will keep for weeks in the refrigerator with no dimunition in flavor if kept tightly sealed.)

Piedmontese Stuffed Turkey

Tacchino Ripieno

The Piedmontese have a great liking for turkey. Their birds are much smaller than ours. In fact, finding a ten-pound turkey is perhaps the hardest part of this recipe. Like all stuffed poultry recipes, the twist here is in the stuffing, which works equally well with goose or with a capon, another Piedmontese favorite.

makes 12 servings

1 small turkey (about 10 pounds) or
    1 large capon, washed inside and out
    and patted dry
Olive oil

For the stuffing:
3 pounds fresh chestnuts
1 pound freshly ground pork, preferably
    pork loin
½ pound sausage meat

3 ounces Parmigiano-Reggiano cheese,
    grated (¾ cup)
2¼ cups dried bread crumbs, soaked in
    ½ cup milk
2 large eggs
2 tablespoons dry Marsala
Freshly grated nutmeg to taste
Salt to taste
Freshly ground black pepper to taste

Cut the chestnuts in half and boil them in water to cover until tender, 30 to 45 minutes. Drain. Remove the hard outer shells and the papery inner peels. Let cool. Over medium-high heat, sauté the pork and sausage in a large skillet until cooked through. Let cool.

Preheat the oven to 350°F. Crumble the chestnuts into small pieces into a large mixing bowl. Add the cooked pork and sausage and the remaining stuffing ingredients to the chestnuts and blend thoroughly.

Stuff the turkey and sew up the cavity opening, or skewer it closed. Place the bird on a rack in a roasting pan and roast, basting occasionally with olive oil, until an instant meat thermometer registers 170°F, about 3 hours (figuring 18 minutes per pound).

Remove from the oven, let sit for 10 minutes to settle the juices, and carve.

Bocconcini de Galletto alla Sabauda

✦❀✦

Whenever a dish is designated *alla Saubauda,* you're literally getting the royal treatment. Saubada was the name of the Piedmontese royal family, the richest family in Italy and, in 1865, the nation's royal family after Italy was united. This dish was a family favorite, served to them on casual, at-home evenings. When you see their numerous, ornate palaces in Turin, it's hard to believe that such occasions existed, but evidently they did.

Give them credit for taste: This is a terrific dish and surprisingly simple for royal fare. It's best served at room temperature and, because of its emphatic flavor, is an ideal warm-weather dish.

makes 6 servings

3 tablespoons olive oil

2 boneless turkey breasts, butterflied, flattened, and cut into strips 1 inch wide and 2 inches long, or 4 chicken breasts, flattened and cut into strips of the same size

2 garlic cloves, finely chopped

For the sauce:

12 whole salted anchovies, rinsed, filleted, soaked briefly in cold water, drained, and very finely chopped

10 fresh sage leaves, very finely chopped

1 garlic clove, very finely chopped

1 teaspoon freshly ground black pepper or cayenne pepper

Grated zest and juice of 2 lemons

Place the oil in a large sauté pan over medium heat. When hot, cook the strips of turkey, turning them, until just cooked through. Set aside.

Combine the sauce ingredients thoroughly in a large mixing bowl. Add the cooked turkey strips to the sauce and mix well with your hands to combine. Refrigerate. Let marry for several hours or, preferably, overnight. Serve at room temperature.

Turkey Breast Jewish Style

Petto di Tacchino all'Ebraica

✻❧✻

According to Piedmontese food writer Giovanni Goria, this dish is a specialty of the Jews of Moncalvo, a prosperous town north of Asti. As discussed in The Cult of *Bagna Caôda* (see page 131), Piedmont had a significant Jewish population, nearly all of which was located in the towns and cities where trade occurred. The large country towns of Moncalvo and Cherasco historically were centers of significant Jewish settlement.

However religiously separate Moncalvo's Jewish citizens may have been from their fellow Moncalvese, they shared identical Piedmontese tastes, as this is a quintessentially Piedmontese dish in its use of sweet red peppers, sage, and a sweet-sour, or *agrodolce,* sauce.

makes 6 servings

For the sauce:

*1 medium-size red bell pepper, peeled
      with a vegetable peeler, cored,
      seeded, and coarsely chopped*

1 small eggplant, cut into ¹/₂-inch cubes

2 celery stalks, coarsely chopped

¹/₂ cup water

¹/₂ cup red wine vinegar

1 tablespoon tomato paste

¹/₂ to 1 tablespoon sugar

2 tablespoons extra virgin olive oil

For the turkey:

1 cup dry white wine

2 cups chicken stock

20 fresh sage leaves, coarsely chopped

2 medium-size onions, coarsely chopped

*3 turkey breast fillets (about 1¹/₂
      pounds), butterflied and
      lightly flattened*

To make the sauce, place a large sauté pan over medium heat and add the red pepper, eggplant, celery, water, and vinegar. Bring to a simmer, stirring to combine. Let cook until the vegetables are tender. Add the tomato paste and stir to blend. At this point, taste and add sugar, a little at a time, until a pleasing *agrodolce*, or sweet-sour, balance is achieved. (Piedmontese tastes run toward the acidic side.) Add the olive oil, stirring to blend. Set aside until needed.

To cook the turkey, place a casserole with a tight-fitting cover large enough to hold the turkey over medium-high heat. Add the wine, stock, sage, and onions. Bring to a boil and immediately reduce to a simmer. Add the turkey breasts, cover, and let braise until the fillets are cooked through, 10 to 15 minutes. Remove from the heat and allow the turkey to cool in the braising liquid (if time permits).

To serve, slice the fillets in half crosswise, then slice into thin strips. Place the turkey breast strips on a warm plate and spoon the sauce on top or alongside. Serve hot or at room temperature.

Turkey Breast with Hazelnut Stuffing

Petto di Tacchino Ripieno alle Nocciole

✦

This is an elegant dish, which employs only the turkey breast, available everywhere these days. The stuffing is easily assembled, the turkey breast simply rolled and tied around it, then quickly roasted. The resulting slices are pretty and sure to impress. *Funghi Trifolati* (see page 27) is an ideal accompaniment.

makes 4 servings

For the stuffing:

¼ pound ground turkey

¼ pound ground pork

¼ cup heavy cream

1 large egg

Salt

Freshly ground black pepper

⅓ cup shelled hazelnuts

2 ounces pancetta or bacon, coarsely chopped

½ cup (2 ounces) white (Muscat or Thompson seedless) raisins, softened and plumped in white wine to cover

For the turkey:

1 boneless, skinless turkey breast, about 2 pounds

Salt

Freshly ground black pepper

3 tablespoons olive oil

6 fresh sage leaves, coarsely chopped, or ½ teaspoon dried

1 sprig fresh rosemary, or ½ teaspoon dried

1 large carrot, coarsely chopped

1 medium-size onion, coarsely chopped

1 cup dry white wine, or more if needed

2 tablespoons unsalted butter

To prepare the stuffing, put the ground turkey and pork in a food processor or blender. Add the cream and egg, season with salt and pepper, and puree the mixture. Transfer to a mixing bowl.

Toast the shelled hazelnuts on a baking sheet until lightly browned, about 10 minutes. Rub off the papery skins and let cool completely. Coarsely chop.

Add the hazelnuts, pancetta, and raisins to the mixing bowl and blend thoroughly.

To stuff and roll the turkey breast, place the turkey breast skin side down on a work surface. Salt and pepper the meat well. Spread the stuffing evenly across the length of the turkey breast, then, starting at a long side, roll up and tie it with kitchen string.

Preheat the oven to 350°F.

Place a pan large enough to hold the turkey breast over medium-high heat and add the oil. When hot, place the rolled turkey breast in the pan and brown on all sides, turning it frequently. Remove from the pan and set aside.

Add the sage, rosemary, carrot, onion, and wine to a deep baking pan. Bring to a boil on top of the stove. Then place the turkey breast in the pan and carefully transfer to the oven. Roast, uncovered, until firm to the touch and just cooked through, 50 to 60 minutes, adding more wine if necessary to keep the pan from drying out completely.

Put the turkey on a plate and cover to keep warm. Strain the liquid remaining in the baking pan into a small saucepan. Place over low heat and whisk in the butter.

Cut the turkey crosswise into $\frac{1}{2}$-inch-thick slices. Place the slices on very warm plates and spoon a little of the butter-enriched pan juice over each slice. Serve immediately.

The Marquis's Tart Sauce

Salsa Piccante della Marchese

It's never been clear to me exactly which Piedmontese nobleman liked this sauce. But there's no getting around the fact that it is a distinctively Piedmontese creation. One of Piedmont's signature tastes is for tart, especially a vinegary tartness. It lightens the region's sometimes rich foods. The Piedmontese use this sauce almost as an all-purpose "invigorator," employing it as a finishing touch on slices of flattened chicken and turkey breasts, cool veal, hard-cooked eggs, and all sorts of vegetables, especially greens.

makes 4 to 6 servings

2 tablespoons unsalted butter	*$\frac{1}{2}$ cup white wine vinegar*
2 tablespoons extra virgin olive oil	*$\frac{1}{4}$ cup dry white wine*
$\frac{1}{4}$ cup dried bread crumbs	*Salt*
1 large onion, very finely chopped	*Freshly ground black pepper*

Place the butter and oil in a small sauté pan over medium-low heat. When the butter is melted, add the bread crumbs and let brown lightly, stirring constantly. Add the onion, vinegar, and wine and season with salt and pepper. Stir to combine. Raise the heat to medium and let cook, uncovered, until the liquid is reduced by about half, about 15 minutes. Remove from the heat, let cool, and refrigerate until needed. The sauce will keep for at least a week if refrigerated and tightly covered.

Duck Braised in White Wine

Anatra al Vino Bianco

The Piedmontese love the taste of braised foods. Partly this is a reflection of their still-sedate sense of time: Time just moves more slowly in Piedmont and they have no intention of rushing it. The other, more practical, reason is that Piedmont overflows with wine. There's no lack of flavorful liquid in which to slowly cook almost anything.

Traditionally, duck braised in white wine would surely have been prepared with wild duck, rather than the fatter, more tender domesticated variety. Yet today, few Piedmontese have access to the tougher, gamier wild bird. They, like us, use domesticated duck almost exclusively. But that hasn't stopped them from continuing to braise the bird. And there's no reason why it should: It tastes great.

What is unusual (for them) is using a white wine, as Piedmontese instinct is always to reach for a red. (One winegrower told me that the only good use for white wine was for taking out red wine stains!) Piedmont does, in fact, produce a lot of white wine, the best known of these being Asti Spumante. But there are other, drier white wines from indigenous grape varieties such as Arneis and Favorita, as well as the Cortese variety that creates the wine called Gavi.

On restaurant menus you will see this dish called *Anatra alla Favorita* or *Anatra al Arneis*. But any good dry white wine will do, such as a Chardonnay, dry Riesling, or Sauvignon Blanc.

makes 6 servings

¹/₄ cup extra virgin olive oil

One 4- to 5-pound duck, cut into serving pieces

5 garlic cloves, finely chopped

10 oil-cured black olives, pits removed and coarsely chopped

2 bay leaves, crumbled

Leaves from 1 large sprig fresh rosemary, finely chopped

2 cups dry white wine, plus more if needed

Salt

Freshly ground black pepper

To brown the duck, put 1 tablespoon of the olive oil in a large sauté pan over medium-high heat. When hot, add the duck pieces. (This may best be done using two pans, or in batches, to prevent crowding the pieces; use an additional tablespoon of oil if necessary.) Brown them lightly on all sides. Remove the duck pieces to a large colander set in a mixing bowl to allow any excess fat to drain.

Put the remaining 3 tablespoons of olive oil in a casserole large enough to hold all of the duck pieces over medium-low heat. When the oil is hot, add the garlic, olives, bay leaves, and rosemary. Reduce the heat to low and stir vigorously to combine. Let cook for a minute or two; take care not to let the garlic color. Add 1 cup of the wine and stir to combine. Raise the heat to high and bring to a boil. Let the wine reduce by about one third.

Season the duck pieces with salt and pepper, then place them in the casserole. Add the remaining 1 cup wine. The wine should come roughly halfway up the meat; add a little more if necessary. Adjust the heat so that the wine is simmering lightly. Partially cover the casserole and let braise until the duck is tender, 20 to 30 minutes. Make sure that the wine does not evaporate too quickly; if that happens, lower the heat slightly, and add more wine as needed. The duck can be kept warm in its braising liquid, covered, for several hours.

To serve, place the duck pieces on very warm plates. Spoon a bit of the braising liquid over them and serve immediately.

Guinea Hen in an Envelope

Faraona in Cartoccio

Cooking *in cartoccio* is an old technique that works marvelously with meat, fish, or vegetables. In the past, the envelope was thick, greased paper, what we call today kitchen parchment. The cook artfully crimped and folded the parchment to create a near-airtight seal that kept in all the juices. For individual servings (especially with fish), each envelope was brought directly to the diner, the better for him or her to slice open the parchment and savor the aroma that burst free.

I don't bother with kitchen parchment myself, although it is pretty and gratifyingly old-fashioned. Aluminum foil works just as well and is far easier to seal. I do, however, suggest that you use heavy-duty aluminum foil, as it resists being poked through by a wing tip or leg bone better than regular-strength foil. The object, above all, is to keep the juices from leaking out.

makes 4 servings

3 ounces pancetta or bacon, blanched for
   1 minute in boiling water, drained,
   and finely chopped
Liver, heart, and gizzard of the guinea
   hen (if available), finely chopped
10 fresh sage leaves, finely chopped
1 garlic clove, finely chopped

$^1\!/_2$ dried hot red pepper, seeds removed
   and finely chopped
Salt
Freshly ground black pepper
1 guinea hen, washed inside and out
   and patted dry
2 tablespoons olive oil

Preheat the oven to 400°F.

To make the stuffing, combine the pancetta with the chopped guinea hen innards in a small mixing bowl. Add the sage, garlic, and red pepper and season with salt and black pepper. Blend thoroughly. In a small skillet over medium-high heat, sauté the stuffing briefly until about half-cooked. Remove from the heat and let cool completely. Stuff the guinea hen with the stuffing and tightly sew up or skewer the opening.

Place the bird breast up on a double thickness of aluminum foil twice as long as the bird, dull side down. Brush the bird generously with the olive oil. Pull both sides of the foil up over the bird, keeping it as close to the bird as possible. Bring the edges together and fold to seal, keeping the foil close as possible to the breastbone. Crimp or fold the two open ends as tightly as possible.

Place the wrapped bird in a roasting pan. Roast for 1 hour at 400°F, then lower the heat to 375°F and roast for 30 minutes more. Remove from the oven and let the bird rest at room temperature for 10 minutes. This will allow most of the juices to recede into the meat and the free juices to collect on the bottom of the foil.

Have ready a small bowl to collect the free juices. Unseal the foil, working from the top and taking care not to let the juices escape. Lift out the bird, and channel the juices at the bottom of the foil into the bowl. Carve the bird and serve on warm plates. Meanwhile, reheat the juices. Strain and spoon over the sliced meat.

Stuffed Pheasant

Fagiano Ripieno

Pheasant is one of those birds that is growing in popularity and availability here. Along with guinea hen, it's worth the premium it commands. Because of Piedmont's rural expanses, pheasant is commonly seen and much loved. This recipe is ideal for pheasant, because the bird can be a little dry and the juiciness of the pancetta stuffing provides an ideal compensation, basting it internally. An ideal accompaniment to this dish is *Crema di Patate* on page 206.

makes 4 servings

6 ounces pancetta, or bacon, blanched in
    boiling water for 1 minute, drained,
    and finely chopped

3 ounces sausage meat

Liver, heart, and gizzard of the pheasant,
    finely chopped

20 fresh sage leaves, finely chopped

Freshly ground black pepper

1 pheasant or 2 Cornish game hens,
    washed inside and out and
    patted dry

$1/4$ cup olive oil

$1/4$ cup grappa (optional)

Preheat the oven to 350°F.

To make the stuffing, using your hands, combine two thirds of the pancetta with the sausage meat and chopped innards in a mixing bowl. Add the sage and season with pepper, blending thoroughly.

In a small skillet over medium-high heat, sauté the stuffing briefly until about half-cooked. Remove from the heat and let cool.

Stuff the cavity of the pheasant with the stuffing and tightly sew up or skewer the opening.

Strew the remaining pancetta over the bottom of a deep roasting pan not much larger than the pheasant. Add the olive oil. Place the stuffed pheasant on a rack (optional) in the pan.

Roast, loosely covered with aluminum foil, dull side out, for 30 minutes. Then remove the foil, turn over the bird, and baste with some of the grappa, if using, and the pan juices. Continue roasting for about 50 minutes longer, basting with grappa and pan juices every 15 minutes, and turning the bird on the rack each time. The center of the stuffing should register 170°F on an instant-read thermometer.

Remove the pheasant from the pan, carve into serving pieces, and place on very warm plates. Spoon a small amount of the pan juices over each serving.

Quail in Sweet Peppers

Qualglie nel Peperoni

✿❧✿

I first tasted this elegant and easy quail dish at the restaurant Il Sole, which, it must be said, is in Lombardy, not Piedmont. Still, their food is more similar to Piedmont's than not. And besides, this is a great way to present quail. Because quail are small birds, this dish is best served following a fairly hearty dish, such as risotto. Or it could be served with some polenta and spinach alongside. The quail and peppers can be prepared well ahead of time and cooked shortly before serving.

makes 4 servings

1 strip pancetta or bacon, finely chopped	*Freshly ground black pepper*
¼ cup olive oil	*4 large red or yellow bell peppers*
4 quail	*½ cup water*
Salt	

Add the pancetta and olive oil to a large sauté pan over medium-high heat. When the oil is hot and the pancetta is crisping nicely, add the quail and brown them on all sides, turning frequently. While the birds are browning, sprinkle them with salt and pepper. When well browned, remove from the pan and set aside. Reserve the pan juices.

Preheat the oven to 350°F.

Slice off the top quarter of each pepper. This will create a cap. Clean the interior of each pepper of seeds and membranes. Stand the peppers upright in a baking pan just large enough to hold them. Add the water to the pan. Place a quail inside each upright pepper. Spoon one quarter of the pancetta bits and pan juices over each quail. Cover the quail with their pepper "caps."

Drape a sheet of aluminum foil, dull side out, loosely over the quail. Roast until the quail are tender, about 20 minutes. Serve the quail in their sweet pepper "nests," placing the caps alongside the open nests.

Rabbit with Sweet Red Peppers

Coniglio con Peperoni

This is a Piedmontese favorite, not surprisingly since it contains two of the region's favorite ingredients: rabbit and sweet red peppers. The Piedmontese love rabbit and seem to prefer it to chicken. Usually they purchase a whole rabbit and have the butcher cut it (rather crudely, it must be said) into eight or ten pieces. In America, objections to rabbit seem to be diminishing, albeit slowly, and rabbit is more widely available today than ever before. The meaty hindquarters are the most frequently seen part. This is the rabbit dish to make if you want to try your hand for the first time. As in all rabbit dishes, a cut-up skinned chicken substitutes easily. Traditionally, this dish is served with polenta.

makes 4 servings

¼ cup olive oil

4 individual rabbit hindquarters

2 medium-size onions, finely chopped

2 carrots, finely chopped

8 thin slices pancetta or bacon, blanched
    for 1 minute in boiling water, drained,
    and cut into matchstick strips

Leaves from 2 sprigs fresh rosemary,
    finely chopped

1 bottle dry red or white wine

3 large garlic cloves, finely chopped

4 red bell peppers, peeled with a
    vegetable peeler, cored, seeded,
    and sliced into thin strips

Small pinch of ground cinnamon

Salt

Freshly ground black pepper

2 tablespoons red wine vinegar

Small pinch of freshly grated nutmeg

Place a large, deep skillet over medium heat and add the olive oil. When hot, add the rabbit pieces and brown lightly on both sides. Remove the rabbit pieces and set aside.

Add the onions, carrots, pancetta, and rosemary to the oil in the skillet and cook briefly, stirring. Then add the remaining ingredients except the vinegar and nutmeg. Stir thoroughly to combine. Return the rabbit pieces to the skillet and bring to a simmer. Immediately reduce the heat to the barest simmer, cover, and let cook until the meat is extremely tender, about 1½ hours.

A few minutes before serving, remove the rabbit from the pan. Thoroughly stir in the vinegar and nutmeg. Return the rabbit to the pan and coat with the mixture. Serve hot.

Variation: This same dish can be made without the sweet peppers. Instead, only white wine is used (in Piedmont it would be Arneis, but that's too expensive), along with some moistening chicken, rabbit, or veal stock. Sage would be the herbal note instead of rosemary.

Rabbit with Sweet Fennel

Coniglio Arrosto al Finocchio

Traditionally, for this dish, a whole rabbit is stuffed with wild fennel and garlic and the cavity sewn up. Then it is browned and roasted. For myself, I substitute rabbit serving pieces or hindquarters for the whole rabbit. The mingled tastes of rabbit and fennel make this the sort of thing that can evoke memories of autumn with a single bite.

One of the best features of the dish is that I usually have leftover fennel and garlic after the meal. This gets scooped up, tossed into a food processor, and pureed until very smooth. I then use it some time in the coming week as a sauce for pasta. My wife says that she likes this dish for the sauce to come more than anything else.

makes 6 servings

1/4 cup extra virgin olive oil

1 rabbit, cut into serving pieces, or
*   4 individual rabbit hindquarters*

1 small fennel bulb, thinly sliced, including
*   stems and feathery fronds*

2 heads garlic, separated into cloves but
*   not peeled*

Leaves from 1 large sprig fresh rosemary,
*   finely chopped*

1/2 cup water

Salt

Freshly ground black pepper

Place a sauté pan large enough to hold all of the rabbit pieces over high heat. Add the olive oil. When hot, add the rabbit pieces and brown them well on both sides. Add the fennel, garlic cloves, rosemary, and water and stir to blend. Cover tightly and cook over medium-low heat (or in a preheated 300°F oven) until the meat is almost falling off the bone, for 1½ hours.

Before serving, season with salt and pepper. Stir to coat all of the pieces with the braising liquid, then serve together with the cooked garlic cloves, which you eat by squeezing out the garlic pulp with your hands.

Pork Braised in Milk

Arrosto di Maiale al Latte

The Piedmontese liking for braised meats is never better illustrated than in this simple classic of pork braised in milk. This dish is found all over Northern Italy. The Piedmontese make it theirs with a generous use of fresh rosemary. If you've never tried pork braised in milk, you're in for a pleasing revelation. The sauce is delicately sweet and laced with the scent and taste of rosemary.

Different cuts of pork can be used. Experiment reveals that the best is not pork loin, but rather the slightly fattier cut usually sold as boneless country-style pork ribs. Traditionally, this dish is served with boiled new potatoes.

makes 4 servings

1½ pounds boneless country-style pork ribs	*2 large garlic cloves, crushed*
1 cup milk, plus more if needed	*Salt*
1 sprig fresh rosemary	*Freshly ground black pepper*

Place all of the ingredients in a heavy skillet or casserole with a tight-fitting cover. Bring to a boil, then immediately reduce the heat to a simmer. Let cook, partially covered, until the pork is fork-tender, about 45 minutes. Remove the pork and keep warm in a 250°F oven.

Strain the remaining milk, return it to the pan (add a little extra fresh milk, if overreduced), and reduce it over high heat to the thickness of a sauce. It will be granular in texture, but delectable.

To serve, place the pork on warm plates and spoon the reduced sauce over it.

Rolled Stuffed Pork Loin

Quajetta

❦

A specialty of the mountainous Biella area, *quajetta* traditionally incorporates a generous amount of thinly sliced lard into the filling. This recipe omits the lard, which, although it does add a certain worthy flavor, hardly is essential to the robust quality of the dish.

Quajetta also makes for an appealing "salad" if left to cool, sliced crosswise and then into strips, and dressed with just a drizzle of extra virgin olive oil.

makes 6 servings

One 2-pound boneless pork loin roast, rolled and tied

2 large eggs, hard-cooked and finely chopped

Greens from 1 bunch beets, chopped and steamed for 2 minutes

Handful of fresh Italian parsley leaves, chopped

2 large carrots, sliced into matchsticks, cooked in boiling water until tender, and drained

2 large garlic cloves, finely chopped

Leaves from 1 large sprig fresh rosemary, finely chopped

Salt

Freshly ground black pepper

Freshly grated nutmeg

Olive oil

Place the eggs, beet greens, parsley, carrots, garlic, and rosemary in a large bowl, season with salt, pepper, and nutmeg, and mix to combine thoroughly.

A boned pork loin comes in two pieces, typically sold already tied. Snip the string and separate the two pieces. Lay one piece out flat and cover with the filling. Cover with the other half of the pork loin and tie up into a roll with kitchen string.

Preheat the oven to 325°F.

Heat a little olive oil in a roasting pan large enough to hold the rolled pork loin over medium heat. Brown all sides of the pork loin in the hot oil. Remove from the pan. Place a rack in the pan and return the browned pork loin in the rack to the roasting pan.

Roast until an instant-read meat thermometer inserted in the center registers 165°F, about 1 hour and 10 minutes (figure on about 35 minutes per pound). Remove from the oven and let the pork rest for 5 minutes to settle the juices. Snip the strings of the roast and cut crosswise into 1/4-inch-thick slices. Serve hot.

Lamb with Artichokes and Lemon

Agnello con Carciofi e Limone

🔹

Italian artichokes are different from the globe artichokes grown in California. They are conical, small, and tender enough that the leaves can be eaten. We are starting to see such artichokes here as well, but they are not yet widely available. If only globe artichokes are available, boil them as usual and use only the artichoke bottoms for this dish. It may even be better than the original, which employs the whole artichoke.

makes 4 servings

¼ cup olive oil

2 pounds boneless lamb (leg or shoulder of lamb), cut into 1-inch cubes

1 cup dry white wine

2 large garlic cloves, finely chopped

Large handful of fresh Italian parsley leaves, finely chopped

4 very young, conical artichokes, stems trimmed, cut into quarters

Salt

Freshly ground black pepper

Juice of 1 lemon

2 large egg yolks

Heat the olive oil in a nonreactive casserole over medium-high heat. Brown the lamb cubes on all sides in the hot oil (do this in batches if necessary). Pour off excess fat and oil. Pour in the wine and let it reduce by half over high heat.

Reduce the heat to medium-low and add garlic and parsley, stirring them in vigorously. Add the artichoke quarters and cook, stirring frequently, until fork-tender, 15 minutes. Season with salt and pepper.

Cover the casserole and cook over low heat (or in a preheated 300°F oven) until the lamb is fork-tender, about 1½ hours. Remove from heat.

Just before serving, whisk together the lemon juice and egg yolks. Pour this mixture over the warm lamb and stir it in thoroughly. Serve immediately on warm plates.

Oven-Roasted Lamb with Rosemary

Agnello al Forno con Rosmarino

※

In Piedmont, lamb is found mostly in the mountainous locales. That's where all the sheep grazing goes on. In the flat plains, veal reigns supreme. Lamb is available year-round, although not readily. For the most part, the Piedmontese, like the Tuscans, enoy it in its purest form, roasted simply with olive oil and fresh rosemary.

makes 8 servings

1 boneless leg of lamb, butterflied
   (about 6 pounds)
3 tablespoons olive oil
4 large garlic cloves, finely chopped
Leaves from 2 large sprigs fresh rosemary,
   finely chopped

Salt
Freshly ground black pepper
1 cup dry red or white wine, mixed with
   $^1/_4$ cup olive oil

Preheat the oven to 350°F.

If the leg of lamb is tied, remove the string. Place the lamb on a chopping board and open it out flat. Rub the olive oil into the meat on both sides. Distribute the chopped garlic and rosemary evenly across the interior of the butterflied leg and season with salt and pepper. Roll up the lamb and tie it tightly with kitchen string. (The easiest way is to make lateral bands of string across the leg, spaced 1-inch apart.)

Place the tied leg of lamb on a rack set in a roasting pan. Roast 25 to 30 minutes per pound, basting with the wine and olive oil mixture every 15 minutes or so. For medium-rare lamb, an instant-read meat thermometer inserted at the leg's thickest section should read 150°F. For well-done meat, cook until the reading is 160° to 165°F.

Remove from the oven and let sit for 10 minutes to let the juices settle. Snip off the strings, cut into $^1/_2$-inch-thick slices, and serve on warm plates.

Veal Patties Flavored with Apple

Polpette con le Mele

Here is yet another of those deceptively simple Piedmontese dishes that captivates on first taste. The use of apple is subtle yet invigorating—and utterly unsuspected. Although veal is traditional, and slightly juicer, I also make this with ground turkey. It, too, is delectable. The butter can be eliminated completely if you like, with the patties sautéed in a nonstick pan.

makes 4 servings

1 pound ground veal

2 tart apples, such as Granny Smith, cored, peeled, grated, and finely chopped

$^{1}/_{4}$ cup milk

2 large eggs

2 ounces Parmigiano-Reggiano cheese, grated ($^{1}/_{2}$ cup)

1 garlic clove, finely chopped

Salt

2 tablespoons unsalted butter

$^{1}/_{2}$ cup dry white wine

Freshly ground black pepper

In a large mixing bowl, combine the veal, apples, and milk. Blend well. Add the eggs, Parmigiano, and garlic and season with salt and pepper. Mix well. Form into eight small patties, about 2 inches in diameter and $^{1}/_{2}$ inch thick.

Add the butter to a large sauté pan over medium-high heat. When melted, place the patties in the pan and cook for 2 minutes on each side. Pour in the wine, raise the heat to high, and let cook, uncovered, until the wine is reduced to a glaze. Serve immediately, drizzling the glaze over the patties.

Veal Loin Chops with Sage
Nodi di Vitello con Salvia

Nothing about this exquisite dish is complicated. The trick, so-called, is cooking the veal over relatively low heat. This both ensures that the butter does not brown and helps preserve tenderness. An ideal accompaniment would be some spinach and small boiled potatoes.

makes 4 servings

3 tablespoons all-purpose flour, mixed
  with a large pinch of salt
4 veal loin chops, at least 1 inch thick,
  bone removed

¼ cup (½ stick) unsalted butter
4 large fresh sage leaves, finely chopped
⅓ cup dry white vermouth or white wine

Place the seasoned flour on a plate and lightly dredge both sides of each veal chop in it, knocking off any excess flour. Set aside.

Put the butter in a large nonstick sauté pan over medium-low heat. When the butter is melted, add the sage, stirring briefly. Cook the chops for about 3 minutes on each side, depending on their thickness. The chops should be pale pink inside. When pressed, they will give slightly. Add the vermouth, partially cover, and cook over low heat until the liquid has reduced to a glaze. Turn the chops once to coat both sides in the glaze and serve immediately on very warm plates.

Beef Braised in Red Wine

Brasato di Manzo al Vino Rosso

More popularly named *brasato al Barolo*, after the famous wine, this is one of Piedmont's signature dishes. The Piedmontese will braise almost anything in wine. Their beef, especially, needs it. Because the Piedmontese are much more devoted to veal, relatively few *vitelli* (calves) ever become *bue* (beef). Those that do are used largely for breeding stock and are at least four years old. The breed called *razza Piemontese* are enormous white-skinned creatures, one of the oldest cattle breeds in Italy, along with Tuscany's Chianina beef.

All sorts of *brasato* dishes exist, variations on a similar theme of braising a large piece of beef in a generous amount of red wine and herbs. Usually a cut from the thigh is used. This corresponds to our beef round. Sirloin tip would be another similar cut. Personally, I prefer an untraditional brisket of beef. Nearly all *brasato* dishes come out a bit too dry and densely chewy for my taste. (Good Piedmontese cooks will lard the roast with fine strips of pancetta, which offer some internal moistening.) That's the way it's supposed to be, but I like something a bit more moist. Brisket does the trick and besides, you can't overcook it.

As for the wine, yes, it does make a difference if you use something Piedmontese such as Nebbiolo or Barbera, the two traditional and best choices. But going to the expense of Barolo or Barbaresco is silly. That doesn't make a difference, especially given today's prices. A decent, inexpensive Cabernet Sauvignon works just fine.

Traditionally, the beef is marinated in the wine and herbs in the refrigerator for at least twenty-four hours, if not longer. Then it is braised for two to three hours. If you're using brisket, which takes longer to cook, the marinating is not necessary. It can cook at low heat in the oven overnight, absorbing the marinade flavors while it cooks.

makes 4 to 6 servings

3 tablespoons olive oil

2 to 3 pounds beef for braising, in one
    piece: sirloin tip, round, or, best of all,
    brisket (see Note)

2 bottles dry red wine, ideally Nebbiolo or
    Barbera

1 medium-size onion, sliced

1 large carrot, cut into chunks

Large pinch of ground cinnamon

2 bay leaves

2 sprigs fresh rosemary

Additional red wine or beef, veal, or
    chicken stock if needed

Heat the olive oil in a large skillet over medium-high heat. Brown the beef on all sides in the hot oil. Remove the beef from the skillet and set in a large glass or stainless steel mixing bowl. When cool, add the remaining ingredients to the bowl and stir to combine. Cover and refrigerate for at least 24 hours.

To cook, place the beef and its marinade in a nonreactive casserole with a tight-fitting cover. Bring to a simmer over high heat, then reduce the heat to the barest simmer and let braise for 3 hours. (The casserole can also be transferred to a preheated 300°F oven after the liquid is brought to a simmer.) Check occasionally to ensure that the beef is nearly entirely bathed in the marinade. Add more wine or stock as necessary.

When the beef is fork-tender, remove it from the casserole and keep it warm in a low oven. Strain the marinade into a saucepan. Place the saucepan over very high heat and reduce the marinade by boiling it, uncovered, until thick enough to constitute a sauce.

Cut the beef into ¼-inch-thick slices, place on a warm platter or individual plates, and spoon the reduced marinade over it.

Note: If using brisket of beef, omit the marinating period. Brown the brisket and add the other ingredients. Brisket takes a long time to cook. I like to start it in the evening, putting the tightly covered casserole in a 300°F oven and letting it braise overnight, for 8 to 12 hours. Then I remove the casserole from the oven and allow the beef to cool on top of the stove. When it's convenient, I reduce the braising liquid as described above and then serve.

Braised Beef with Capers

Bocconcini di Manzo con Capperi

✳

Whenever you see the word *bocconcini* on a menu, you know that whatever is being served will arrive in small pieces or mouthfuls (*bocca* means mouth). In Piedmont, *bocconcini* almost invariably refers to beef, veal, or pork that has been cubed and braised.

This particular version, employing salt-packed capers, is especially good. Here, the cubes are made smaller than usual, which I think works especially well for the lean, flavorful cut called sirloin tip. Top round is another good choice, as is brisket. This can also be made with a mixture of beef, veal, and pork.

Whatever is left over is ideal either as a filling for agnolotti or as a meat sauce for tagliatelle, fettuccine, or any of a number of other pasta shapes. All you need do is finely chop the meat.

Like all braised meats, *bocconcini* is even better when reheated the next day. The best, and most traditional, accompaniment is polenta, which perfectly sets off the savory sauce of the dish.

makes 4 to 6 servings

3 tablespoons extra virgin olive oil
1 pound beef, such as sirloin tip, cut into
    walnut-size pieces or smaller
2 medium-size onions, thinly sliced
6 garlic cloves, thinly sliced
1 pound ripe tomatoes, peeled, seeded,
    and coarsely chopped
1 cup dry red wine or beef, veal, or
    chicken stock

8 fresh sage leaves
1 bay leaf
Salt
Freshly ground black pepper
2 tablespoons salt-packed capers, rinsed
    and crushed

Place the oil in a large sauté pan over medium heat. When hot, add the beef cubes and quickly brown on all sides. Reduce the heat to medium-low, add the onions and garlic, and cook briefly, stirring, taking care not to let the garlic burn. Add the tomatoes, wine, sage, and bay leaf, and season with salt and pepper. Bring to a simmer and let cook, covered, at the barest simmer (or in a preheated 300°F oven) for about 1 hour.

After an hour, add the capers. Let cook for an additional hour, covered. The dish can be served immediately or refrigerated and rewarmed, as it improves on keeping over at least 3 days.

Braised Beef Val d'Aosta Style
Carbonade Val d'Aosta

✿❧✿

In France and Belgium, a *carbonnade* traditionally is made with beer. But in Val d'Aosta, an autonomous province once part of Piedmont where French is as native as Italian, their version of *carbonade* uses the local red wines.

Like all braised beef dishes, this version is best when cooked slowly and gently. How long depends on the cut of beef used. The best beef for this purpose is not the most expensive. Rather, it's a relatively tough cut such as chuck or shoulder, which take longer to cook, but eventually become meltingly tender. Any beef that you would use (or is designated) as a pot roast works perfectly with this dish. *Carbonade Val d'Aosta* is always served accompanied by polenta, which is ubiquitous in the area. But a side dish of plain pasta such as wide pappardelle noodles, fettuccine, or any number of short, stubby shapes works equally well in absorbing the braising sauce.

makes 4 servings

2 pounds beef in one piece (chuck, shoulder, or bottom round cuts)

¼ cup (½ stick) unsalted butter

2 tablespoons olive oil

2 pounds onions, thinly sliced

¾ bottle inexpensive dry red wine

Salt

Freshly ground black pepper

½ teaspoon freshly grated nutmeg

Cut the beef across the grain into slices about ⅓ inch thick.

Add the butter and oil to a large sauté pan or casserole over medium-high heat. When the fat is hot, brown both sides of each slice, one or two at a time, setting aside each slice after it is browned.

After the beef is browned, reduce the heat to medium-low. Add the onions and cook, stirring frequently, until softened. Pour in 2½ cups of the wine, reserving the balance to replenish the pot if necessary during cooking. Season with salt and pepper, stirring to blend.

Raise the heat, bring to a boil, and add the beef. Immediately reduce the heat to very low, cover tightly, and let cook until the meat forks apart, 1 to 2 hours, depending upon the cut of beef. Check occasionally that the beef is well moistened with wine and add more as needed.

When the meat is tender, add the nutmeg and check for seasonings. Let cook for another 15 minutes. Serve on warm plates with a few spoonfuls of the braising liquid, accompanied by polenta.

Calf's Liver with Lemon and Sage

Fegato di Vitello con Limone e Salvia

This is, I must say, one of the finest calf's liver dishes I've ever eaten. Everyone who has sampled it has raved over it. Like all the best Piedmontese dishes, it is memorable, simple, and slightly rich. Don't miss it. Polenta is an ideal accompaniment.

makes 4 servings

1 pound fresh calf's liver

2 tablespoons unsalted butter

1 tablespoon olive oil

10 large fresh sage leaves, finely chopped

Finely grated or chopped zest and juice
  of 1 lemon

¼ cup milk, whisked together with
  2 large egg yolks

¼ cup chicken or beef stock (canned is fine)

Freshly grated nutmeg to taste

Salt to taste

Freshly ground black pepper to taste

Cut the liver into bite-size strips about the size and thickness of a finger or a stick of chalk: approximately 2 inches long and ½ inch thick.

Place a large skillet over medium-high heat and add the butter and olive oil. When the butter is melted, add the calf's liver and stir-fry the pieces so they are browned on all sides. When the first pearls of red appear on the surface of the liver, reduce the heat to low and add the remaining ingredients. Raise the heat to the barest simmer, and cook, stirring frequently, until the sauce thickens, 2 to 3 minutes. Test the liver for doneness; ideally, it should be slightly rosy in the interior. Serve on very warm plates.

Calf's Liver with Pancetta, Bread Crumbs, and Parsley

Fegato di Vitello con Pancetta, Pangrattati, e Prezzemolo

The original version of this flavorful dish incorporates small pieces of lard cut to the same size as those of the calf's liver. The following recipe omits the lard and substitutes pancetta, the seasoned but not smoked Italian bacon that is now widely available.

The Piedmontese are great lard lovers, by the way. I remember eating more than my fill once at a party hosted by what many Piedmontese consider the best source of lard, a butcher's shop called Macelleria Brarda in the town of Cavour. Silvio Brarda is famous for his lard, which is packaged and shipped throughout Piedmont. His lard is very lightly seasoned with salt, pepper, and rosemary. He served it sliced as thin as lingerie, in supple, cream-colored strips. Once you acquire a taste for it—which takes no effort at all—the only challenge is to forget that it is, well, lard.

makes 4 to 6 servings

¾ cup finely ground dried bread crumbs

Small handful of fresh Italian parsley leaves, finely chopped

1 pound fresh calf's liver, thinly sliced

½ pound pancetta, sliced into strips similar in size to the calf's liver

Salt

Freshly ground black pepper

Combine the bread crumbs and parsley on a flat plate and mix well. Dredge both sides of the calf's liver slices in tapping off any excess. Set aside, preferably on a large wire rack, to allow the crumbs to dry slightly. Otherwise, arrange on a large platter, so that the slices are in a single layer.

Place a large sauté pan over medium-high heat. When the pan is hot, add the pancetta strips and sauté until crisp. Remove the pancetta and keep warm. Drain off most, but not all, of the fat.

Return the pan to medium-high heat. Add all of the crumbed liver strips. Sauté quickly, for only a minute on each side. Transfer immediately to warm serving plates. Season with salt and pepper. Distribute the pancetta strips equally over each serving. Serve hot.

Calf's Liver with Anchovies and Lemon

Fegato all'Acciughe e Limone

Seemingly, there's nothing that the Piedmontese will not treat to anchovies or lemons. This buttery exaltation of calf's liver is yet another variation on this beloved theme. Any number of other strongly flavored meats can be similarly treated, such as kidneys (an excellent choice) or lamb's hearts (rarely seen, but delicious). This is a dish that waits for no one, as sautéed liver is best when served sizzling, on very warm plates accompanied by mashed potatoes.

makes 4 servings

1/4 cup (1/2 stick) unsalted butter

2 whole salted anchovies, rinsed, filleted, soaked briefly in cold water, and drained

1 tablespoon all-purpose flour

3 tablespoons olive oil

1 garlic clove, very finely chopped

1 pound fresh calf's liver, thinly sliced

1 tablespoon finely chopped fresh Italian parsley leaves

2 tablespoons fresh lemon juice

Put the butter, anchovies, and flour in a food processor or blender and process until thoroughly mixed. Set aside.

Place the olive oil and garlic in a large sauté pan over medium heat. Cook for 1 minute, taking care that the garlic does not burn. Add the liver slices and cook briefly on each side. After turning the slices, watch for a little pearl of blood to appear on the surface. This signals that the liver is at the medium-rare point. Reduce the heat to very low and add the anchovy mixture in pieces, stirring constantly. When the butter has melted completely, add the parsley and lemon juice, stir to blend, and serve immediately on very warm plates.

The Beauty of Baccalà

Being landlocked, the Piedmontese do not have much of a repertoire of fresh fish, except for carp and trout. They do love trout, which are prepared in characteristically simple fashions. But the great Piedmontese fish passion is *baccalà*, or salt cod. Salt cod is an old-fashioned taste, as all salted fish are these days. The Piedmontese are great connoisseurs of salt cod and buy varying grades and qualities of *baccalà* with as practiced and knowing an eye as the Portuguese (who probably are the greatest of all salt cod connoisseurs).

Salt cod is available in America, although its distribution is uneven. Areas boasting large numbers of Italians, Spaniards, or Portuguese offer salt cod at its best: a whole fish split open, splayed flat, and immortalized in a thick layer of salt. It looks like a road kill on the Great Salt Lake. No matter. When revived—rehydrated, really—its taste is like no other. The more plank-hard the fish, the heavier the salt cure. A more flexible fish usually has seen less salt. They can be equally good, although soaking time will vary.

Alternatively, the other sort of salt cod available comes in little coffinlike wood boxes. You slide open the top and interred inside is a square-cut, salt-encrusted section of cod. This version is a Canadian specialty and it's very good, although a bit less flavorful than the whole dried cod.

The height of Piedmont's *baccalà* craving comes during the late fall and early winter. That's when the best salt cod from Spain and Portugal appears on the market. Then, the *baccalà* is less heavily salted, more tender, with a higher moisture content. Where a regular-cure salt cod might have from fifteen to thirty-five pounds of salt applied to every one hundred pounds of cod, this more seasonal (and perishable) version sees as little as five pounds of salt per one hundred pounds of cod.

A linguistic note: In Piedmont you often see the terms *merluzzo, baccalà*, and *stoccafisso* used interchangeably. This reflects a certain casualness, rather than the three items actually being identical. Technically, *merluzzo* is the fresh version, a type of cod from a large family of about sixty species of white-fleshed, firm-textured fish found only in the Atlantic Ocean and Arctic Sea.

Baccalà, in comparison, is *merluzzo* that has been dehydrated by salt-curing. And *stoccafisso* (stockfish) differs from *baccalà* by being just air-dried rather than salt-cured. As a result, *stoccafisso* takes twice as long to soak and has a stronger taste, as well as typically being sold as a whole fish, rather than being split as for *baccalà*.

Soaking It's almost impossible to oversoak the typical salt cod available in American markets. The more changes of water, the better. I usually soak the salt cod I get (the kind in little wood boxes) in a large bowl of water overnight in the refrigerator.

Cooking salt cod All salt cod needs to be cooked after soaking, to further soften and rehydrate it. This couldn't be simpler: Just simmer it in liquid until tender. Depending upon how hard the salt cod, and how prolonged its presoak, this will take anywhere from 15 to 45 minutes. It's hard to overcook it, so not to worry. Some cooks like to simmer salt cod in milk rather than water, to reduce the salt taste and further whiten the flesh. This does not seem to be a Piedmontese habit, in my experience.

Salt Cod with Potatoes and Olive Oil

Baccalà con Patate e Olio

✱❀✱

This partnership of cooked salt cod with slices of waxy potatoes, anointed with extra virgin olive oil, couldn't be simpler. Lidia Alciati, of Ristorante Guido, makes the most sublime version of this dish possible, adding to it a benediction of thinly shaved fresh white truffles just before serving. A few drops of white truffle oil, although not quite the same, work awfully well instead.

makes 4 to 6 servings

1 pound dried salt cod, soaked overnight in cold water to cover and drained	*Freshly ground black pepper*
	Extra virgin olive oil
1 pound waxy potatoes, peeled	*White truffle oil (optional)*

In a large saucepan, simmer the salt cod in fresh water to cover until bright white and tender, 15 to 45 minutes. Drain. Separate the cod into flakes by breaking it apart with your hands. Place them in a large mixing bowl and set aside.

Steam or boil the potatoes until tender but still firm; a fork should easily penetrate the potatoes. While they are still warm, slice the potatoes into 1/4-inch-thick slices. Using your hands, mix the potato slices with the salt cod flakes.

Place the mixture on warm individual plates. Add a sprinkling of black pepper, drizzle a generous swirl of olive oil and just a few drops of white truffle oil, if using, over the top, and serve warm.

✱❀✱

Salt Cod with Spinach and Parsley

Baccalà al Verde

⚜

Carlo Petrini, the director of Arcigola (see Arcigola Slow Food, page 285), has a characteristic Piedmontese passion for *baccalà*. Arcigola's headquarters restaurant, Boccondivino, obliges him on Fridays. This dish always gets billed, confusingly, as *Merluzzo al Verde*, even though the fish is the dried *baccalà*, rather than fresh *merluzzo*. This dish is best served with polenta alongside, as the tastes are complementary. Mashed potatoes are also wonderful.

makes 4 servings

1 pound dried salt cod, soaked overnight in cold water to cover and drained

Flour for dusting

Olive oil for frying

3 tablespoons unsalted butter

1 pound fresh spinach, thoroughly washed, tough stems removed, and leaves very finely chopped

Large handful of fresh Italian parsley leaves, very finely chopped

¼ cup chicken stock

Salt

Slice the salt cod into finger-thick sticks. In a large saucepan, let simmer very gently in fresh water to cover until the fish is bright white and tender, about 15 minutes. Drain and dry thoroughly with paper towels. Lightly dust all sides of each stick with flour, knocking off any excess.

Add ½ inch olive oil to a large skillet over medium-high heat. When the oil is hot, add the floured fish sticks and fry until they are golden on all sides. Remove from the pan and drain on paper towels. Keep warm in a low oven until needed.

Add the butter to a nonstick skillet over medium heat. When melted, add the spinach and parsley, stirring well to combine. Cook for 5 minutes, then add the chicken stock and cook until most of the moisture has evaporated, about 5 minutes. Season with salt.

Add the fried salt cod to the spinach mixture and gently toss to combine. When well mixed and warmed through, serve on hot plates.

Desserts

By the time the Piedmontese finish one of their heroic meals, they really do not have much room for dessert. Nearly all of the really fancy desserts that one might see in Turin are imports from France and not seen, even by the Piedmontese, as indigenous.

The giveaway to authentic Piedmontese desserts is their simplicity. The scale of their meals leaves so little room for anything else. Like many other Italian regions, the Piedmontese like desserts that employ the fresh fruits of the season. This also means the nuts of the season, which in Piedmont means an emphasis on hazelnuts and chestnuts.

Piedmont grows a particularly tasty type of hazelnut, which is called *tonda gentile*. It is an unusually sweet, rich-tasting hazelnut. But Oregon, which grows ninety-nine percent of all the hazelnuts produced in America, has hazelnuts every bit as good.

A word also should be said about chocolate. The residents of Turin like to point out that it was they who, centuries ago, taught the Swiss how to make chocolate. There's a good chance that they're right about this, but it's really not an argument worth getting tangled up in. Suffice it to say that Turin is home to superb confectioners. (They also like chocolate in their coffee, presented in the form of the exclusively Torinese drink called *bicerin*.)

Local hazelnuts figure prominently in many of these chocolate confections, none more so than Turin's greatest chocolate-hazelnut creation, *gianduiotti* or *giandujotti*. It was invented by the still-thriving confectioners called Caffarel in honor of a *Carnivale* celebration in 1865 and given its name two years later. The name is that of a then-famous puppet show figure (and carnival mask), a character called Gianduiotto.

Gianduiotti are stubby, finger-thick lengths of soft chocolate mixed with ultra finely ground hazelnuts. And although others make gianduiotti, Caffarel's still are the best. When I asked around if there was a recipe for making them at home, the locals looked at me as if I had arrived from outer space. Nobody makes them at home; everybody buys them commercially. I could not figure out a way to get the hazelnuts as finely ground as the confectioners can. Gianduiotti can, however, be purchased in specialty shops in America, so keep a lookout for them.

Turin's Traditional Chocolate and Coffee Drink

Bicerin

Like all Italians, the Torinese are devoted to coffee, in all the many forms that make ordering coffee in Italy such a bewildering experience for outsiders. But *bicerin* (pronounced beech-eh-REEN) is exclusively Torinese, a legacy of the 1700s and 1800s still cherished today.

Bicerin is a blend of chocolate, coffee, and hot milk. What makes *bicerin* interesting is not only that it tastes good, but also that it has such an interesting history. A Piedmontese word, *bicerin* means *piccolo bicchiere* or little glass, which is how it's served, in a clear glass cup inserted into a metal holder, so that the drinker's fingers aren't burned by the heat. This same drink used to be known as a *bavarese*, a word we know better in French as *bavarois*. Today, a *bavarois* (usually translated as Bavarian cream) signifies a rich, cold dessert made from a custard sauce mixed with gelatin, beaten egg whites, lightly whipped cream, and some sort of flavoring. These are gently combined, put into a decorative mold, chilled until firm, and served unmolded on a platter.

But what is largely unknown (except to the Piedmontese) is that this name came not from Germany's Bavaria region, but from the original version of the *bicerin* drink, which was called *bevareisa*, "drinkable." It is thought to have been invented in 1678. By the early 1800s, the word *bicerin* had come into more common usage. (I am indebted to Sandro Doglio's invaluable *Gran Dizionario della Gastronomia del Piemonte* for this information.)

Today, you can get a *bicerin* only in Turin, usually at one of its imposingly elegant old cafés that tenaciously hold to tradition. Then you will have the privilege of agreeing with the great French writer Alexander Dumas *père* who, after visiting Turin in August 1852 wrote, "I will never forget the *bicerin,* a sort of excellent drink composed of coffee, milk and chocolate, which is served in all the cafés at a relatively low price." Like cappuccino, it is one of those coffee drinks deemed appropriate only for morning or early-afternoon drinking. Barring a trip to Turin, I suggest you make some at home, which is easy enough.

makes 4 to 6 servings

2 cups milk

3 ounces bittersweet chocolate, finely grated

2 cups strong black coffee

2 tablespoons sugar

In a small heavy-bottomed saucepan, heat the milk very hot, but do not let it boil. Slowly add the grated chocolate to the coffee, whisking constantly to ensure that it is fully blended. Whisk in the sugar. Finally, add the hot milk. Check for sweetness and modify as desired. Serve hot.

One traditional touch, not usually seen today, is the addition of a small amount of orange blossom water to the drink. It does add an unexpected, and pleasing, flavor note. You can find orange blossom water most easily at shops that cater to a Middle Eastern clientele.

Hazelnut Cake

Torta di Nocciole

This is one of the most straightforward of Piedmont's many hazelnut cakes. Here, a hazelnut-infused batter is created, poured into a baking dish, and briefly baked. I find that a little sweetened whipped cream alongside is just the ticket.

makes 6 to 8 servings

²/₃ pound shelled hazelnuts

³/₄ cup sugar

2 cups all-purpose flour

3 large eggs, lightly beaten

¹/₄ cup (¹/₂ stick) unsalted butter, melted

¹/₄ cup strong black coffee

¹/₄ cup milk

2 teaspoons dry yeast

2 tablespoons dark or light rum

1 teaspoon pure vanilla extract

Preheat the oven to 350°F. Butter an 8-inch baking pan. Set aside.

Toast the shelled hazelnuts on a baking sheet until lightly browned, about 10 minutes. Rub off the papery skins and let cool completely. Increase the oven temperature to 400°F.

Chop the hazelnuts very fine in a food processor, taking care not to overprocess, which would turn them into hazelnut butter. In a mixing bowl, combine the hazelnuts, sugar, and flour. When well mixed, add the remaining ingredients, one at a time, stirring until the batter is well blended.

Pour the batter into the prepared baking pan, shaking the dish gently to even it out. Bake until golden brown, about 30 minutes. Let cool in the pan, then invert and serve in slices.

Hazelnut Cake with Chocolate

Torta di Nocciole con Cioccolato

✣

It couldn't have taken more than a few minutes, centuries ago, when the first hazelnut cake had been created, before some Piedmontese cook said, "You know, adding chocolate to this would be swell." So they did. This cake delivers an intense taste of hazelnuts, with the backdrop of chocolate heightening their flavor.

makes 6 servings

10 ounces shelled hazelnuts

1½ cups sugar

3 ounces bittersweet chocolate, grated

2 tablespoons all-purpose flour

1 teaspoon dry yeast

½ cup (1 stick) unsalted butter, melted and slightly cooled

6 large eggs, separated

Preheat the oven to 350°F. Butter and lightly flour an 8-inch baking pan, knocking out the excess flour.

Toast the shelled hazelnuts on a baking sheet until lightly browned, about 10 minutes. Rub off the papery skins and let cool completely. Leave the oven on.

Chop the hazelnuts fine in a food processor, taking care not to overprocess and turn them into hazelnut butter. Set aside.

Combine the sugar, chocolate, flour, yeast, and melted butter in a mixing bowl. Stir vigorously to combine. Add the hazelnuts and stir to blend thoroughly. Add the egg yolks and stir to combine.

In a large bowl beat the egg whites with an electric mixer until stiff peaks form. Fold the beaten egg whites into the hazelnut mixture until evenly distributed. Turn the batter into the prepared baking pan. Bake until golden brown, about 30 minutes. Let cool in the pan, then invert and serve in slices.

Hazelnut and Cornmeal Cake
Schiacciata di Nocciole

✦✶✦

Cesare Giaccone, chef/owner of Dei Cacciatori in Albaretto della Torre, high in the Langhe hills, revived this ancient recipe. It is the only cake I have ever come across that combines ground hazelnuts with cornmeal. The resulting taste is certainly that of another time, but good. It's worth trying.

makes 6 to 8 servings

3 ounces shelled hazelnuts

$^1/_2$ cup (1 stick) unsalted butter, at room temperature

$^1/_3$ cup sugar

Grated zest of 1 lemon

2 large egg yolks

Scant $^1/_2$ cup fine-ground cornmeal

$^1/_2$ cup all-purpose flour

$1^1/_2$ tablespoons honey

1 teaspoon pure vanilla extract

Preheat the oven to 350°F. Butter and flour an 8-inch round cake pan. Set aside.

Toast the shelled hazelnuts on a baking sheet until lightly browned, about 10 minutes. Rub off the papery skins, then let cool completely. Reduce the oven temperature to 300°F.

Chop the hazelnuts very fine in a food processor, taking care not to overprocess and turn them into hazelnut butter. Set aside.

In a food processor, combine the butter, sugar, and lemon zest and process to blend. Add the egg yolks, cornmeal, flour, hazelnuts, honey, and vanilla and process briefly to blend thoroughly.

Turn the batter into the prepared cake pan. Bake until pale gold, 20 to 25 minutes. Serve warm in slices or let cool, inverted onto a cake rack, before slicing.

Sweet Cornmeal Cake

Torta di Farina Gialla

❧❦❧

When you taste this cake for the first time, your initial reaction is, "Cornmeal, how interesting." But what surprises is how readily you return for a second and third bite, as the flavor is insinuating. The addition of lightly sweetened whipped cream, by the way, is a necessity. It adds richness and a contrasting velvety texture to the reserved dryness of the cake. It also looks good atop the sunny yellow crust.

WORTH NOTING

It is essential that the cornmeal is very finely ground. Most cornmeals are coarsely ground. This can be effectively modified by placing coarsely ground cornmeal in a food processor and processing until a very fine, sandlike consistency is achieved.

makes 6 servings

¾ cup milk

2 tablespoons dry yeast

1 cup fine-ground cornmeal

1 ½ cups all-purpose flour

1 cup sugar, plus extra for sprinkling

2 large eggs, beaten

Grated zest of 1 lemon

Generously butter an 8-inch round cake pan. Set aside.

In a large mixing bowl, whisk together the milk and yeast. Gradually whisk in the cornmeal, flour, sugar, eggs, and lemon zest. Whisk until the ingredients are well blended.

Turn the batter into the prepared pan. Let rest for 30 minutes.

Preheat the oven to 350°F.

Sprinkle the top of the batter generously with sugar. Bake for 40 minutes until browned. Let the cake cool completely, then turn it out of the pan. Serve with lightly sweetened whipped cream.

Apple Cake

Torta di Mele

✦

A simple country dessert, this apple cake needs nothing more than lightly sweetened whipped cream—if that. The best sort of apples for this are slightly tart, such as Granny Smiths.

makes 6 servings

3 pounds apples

6 tablespoons sugar

6 tablespoons all-purpose flour

Grated zest of 1 lemon

1 large egg

2 teaspoons dry yeast

1/4 cup (1/2 stick) unsalted butter, melted

Preheat the oven to 350°F. Butter a 10-inch round cake pan or baking dish. Lightly flour the pan and knock out the excess flour. (Alternatively, you could line the buttered pan with very finely ground amaretti crumbs.) Set aside. Core, peel, and finely chop the apples. Set aside covered in cold water to prevent discoloration until needed.

In a large mixing bowl, whisk together the sugar, flour, lemon zest, and egg. Add the yeast.

Drain the apples thoroughly. Add to the mixing bowl and gently fold in to blend thoroughly. Fold in the melted butter. Gently transfer the batter to the prepared cake pan. Shake the filled pan gently to even out the batter. Bake, uncovered, until golden brown on top, about 45 minutes. Let cool and serve in slices.

✦

Apple and Bread Crumb Cake

Torta di Mele e Pangrattati

✥

This is a lovely old-fashioned apple cake popular in Piedmont's mountainous areas, where every farmer has an abundance of apple trees. Nothing about the cake is complicated. Indeed, its generous use of butter, sugar, jam, and bread crumbs bespeaks a farmhouse quality. But the flavor is superb: honest, direct, and transparent. A dollop of sweetened whipped cream served on top or alongside completes this memorable dessert.

makes 6 to 8 servings

³/₄ cup (1¹/₂ sticks) unsalted butter

3 pounds Granny Smith or McIntosh
*   apples, cored, peeled, and thinly sliced*

2¹/₂ cups fresh bread crumbs

¹/₂ cup sugar

¹/₄ teaspoon ground cinnamon

6 tablespoons apricot jam

Juice of 1 lemon

Slightly sweetened whipped cream
*   for serving*

Preheat the oven to 325°F. Butter an 8- by 4-inch loaf pan. Line the bottom with a sheet of waxed paper cut to fit. Butter the waxed paper.

Place a large nonstick sauté pan over medium-low heat and add ¼ cup of the butter. When melted, add the apple slices, tossing or stirring gently to coat them evenly. Cook over low heat, uncovered, until the apples are slightly soft, about 15 minutes. Set aside.

Meanwhile, combine the bread crumbs, sugar, and cinnamon in a mixing bowl and mix thoroughly to combine.

Place another large sauté pan over medium heat and add the remaining ¹/₂ cup butter. When melted, add the bread-crumb mixture and cook, stirring, until the crumbs are golden brown. Remove from the heat.

Sprinkle one third of the bread crumbs over the bottom of the prepared pan. Spoon 3 tablespoons of the jam as evenly as possible over the bread crumbs. Place half the apple slices on the jam. Sprinkle with half the lemon juice. Repeat with another layer of bread crumbs, jam, apples, and lemon juice, and cover the top with the remaining bread crumbs.

Bake until golden brown, 45 to 50 minutes. Remove from the oven and let the cake cool in the pan. When cool, invert onto a serving platter and peel off the waxed paper. Serve with the whipped cream.

Apple Mousse with Orange-Flavored Liqueur

Mousse di Mele con Grand Marnier

Italians like liqueurs and, it seems to me, the Piedmontese particularly like Grand Marnier. Its orange flavor adds a note of sunshine to Piedmont's bone-chilling autumn and winter fogs.

In this dessert, a puree of apples is uplifted by beaten egg whites and flavored with a dash of Grand Marnier. Traditionally, the cake pan is caramelized on the bottom, which I have forgone.

makes 6 servings

2 pounds baking apples, such as Rome or Granny Smith, cored, peeled, and thickly sliced

1/2 cup water

3 tablespoons delicately flavored honey

1/2 cup Grand Marnier or other orange liqueur

6 large egg whites

Simmering water for the hot-water bath

Preheat the oven to 400°F.

Place the apples in a large baking dish and moisten with the water. Bake until the apples slices are tender, about 20 minutes. Drain.

Puree the baked apples in a food processor. With the processor running, pour in the honey. Process briefly to blend.

Transfer the mixture to a large nonstick skillet over high heat and cook the puree, stirring frequently, to evaporate the excess moisture, 5 to 10 minutes. Let cool, then transfer the apple puree to a medium-size bowl and refrigerate until cold.

Preheat the oven to 350°F. Grease a 9- or 10-inch round cake pan. Have ready a large pan in which the cake pan can fit.

Whisk the Grand Marnier into the chilled apple puree.

In a large bowl with an electric mixer, beat the egg whites until stiff peaks form. Gently fold the beaten egg whites into the chilled apple puree until well distributed. Gently transfer the mixture to the cake pan and set it inside the larger pan. Carefully pour simmering water into the larger pan to come about halfway up the side of the cake pan.

Bake until the mousse is firm and pale gold, 30 to 40 minutes. Serve hot or cold.

Fresh Chestnut Mousse
Spuma di Castagne

Chestnuts appear everywhere in Northern Italy, as they grow abundantly there. Piedmont has great stretches of chestnut forests. Indeed, they lined the road near our house and during the fall, local farmers hopped off their tractors and collected them greedily.

Although chestnuts are most frequently oven-roasted and eaten out of hand, they also are a favorite medium for stuffing poultry, especially turkey. Not least, they are seen in a variety of desserts, such as this elegant, subtle *spuma* (literally, "foam"). This recipe works best with fresh chestnuts, as their flavor is more subtle than the dried.

makes 6 servings

1 pound fresh chestnuts	*1 cup milk*
One 2-inch piece vanilla bean, split	*3 large egg yolks*
* lengthwise*	*¼ cup brandy, whiskey, or light or*
½ teaspoon ground cinnamon	* dark rum*
1 cup sugar	*⅔ cup heavy cream*

Using a paring knife, cut a small cross in the rounded side of each chestnut (the nut is more securely held with the flat side on the cutting board), penetrating the thick outer covering. This not only aids in peeling, but also prevents the chestnuts from bursting when heated.

Place the chestnuts in a large pot and cover generously with water. Bring to a boil and simmer for 15 to 25 minutes, depending upon the size and freshness of the nuts. They are cooked when you can squeeze them easily. Drain and peel, removing both the hard outer shell and the papery inner lining.

Coarsely chop the peeled chestnuts. Put the nuts in a large saucepan along with the vanilla bean, cinnamon, ½ cup of the sugar, and the milk. Stir to blend well and bring to a near-boil over high heat. Just before the milk starts to boil, reduce the heat and let simmer over medium-low heat until the chestnuts have absorbed nearly all the milk, about 30 minutes. Remove the vanilla bean and discard.

Place the chestnut mixture in a food processor or blender and puree, letting the machine run for several minutes. Set aside.

In a large mixing bowl, combine the egg yolks and the remaining ½ cup sugar and whisk until the mixture is thick and pale lemon yellow in color. Fold in the chestnut puree, along with the brandy.

continued

In another large mixing bowl, whip the cream with an electric mixer until it forms firm peaks. Fold the chestnut puree mixture into the whipped cream, taking care that the two are well mixed.

Spoon the mousse into individual serving dishes, such as petits pots de crème or coffee cups, or spoon into a bowl. Cover tightly with plastic wrap and refrigerate at least 2 hours before serving.

Puree of Chestnuts with Whipped Cream
Monte Bianco

This may well be Piedmont's most famous dessert—except that the world knows it better under its French name, *Mont Blanc*. It is a matter of endless dispute as to who first devised this delectable concoction. No one really knows, although it's generally agreed that it was born somewhere in the Alps, never mind which side of the border.

In Piedmont, *Monte Bianco* is a signature dessert for New Year's Eve celebrations. It's really one of the easiest desserts to put together—the whipped cream must be added only at the last minute—and is always carried into the room on a platter to the applause of the already pretty well stuffed guests. Asti Spumante, or its less bubbly twin, Moscato d'Asti, is always served alongside.

makes 6 to 8 servings

1 pound fresh chestnuts or 8 ounces dried	*¼ cup superfine sugar*
6 cups milk	*1 cup heavy cream, or as needed*
2 ounces unsweetened chocolate	*1 teaspoon pure vanilla extract*
2 tablespoons unsalted butter	*1 tablespoon confectioners' sugar*

If using fresh chestnuts, using a paring knife, cut a small cross on the rounded side of each chestnut (the nut is more securely held with the flat side on the cutting board), penetrating the thick outer covering. This aids in peeling, and prevents the chestnuts from bursting when heated.

Place the chestnuts in a large pot and cover generously with water. Bring to a boil and simmer for 15 to 25 minutes, depending upon the size and freshness of the nuts. They are cooked when you can squeeze them easily. Drain and peel, removing both the outer shell and the inner lining.

If using dried chestnuts, bring the milk to a near-boil in a large saucepan and add the chestnuts. Let simmer for 5 minutes. Remove from the heat and let the dried chestnuts soak in the milk for several hours, until soft.

Either way, puree the chestnuts and milk together in a food processor or blender until smooth. Set aside.

In a medium-size saucepan over very low heat, combine the chocolate and butter. Stirring constantly, melt the chocolate and butter. Then add the superfine sugar and stir until smooth. Add the chestnut puree and stir to blend thoroughly. If the mixture is too dense, add a little cream.

To create the "mountain," put the puree through a potato ricer held above a platter. Let the strings fall onto the platter, creating a small, loose mound. Using your fingers, gently rearrange the chestnuts strings to make a more conical shape.

In a medium-size mixing bowl, combine the cream, vanilla, and confectioners' sugar. Beat with a whisk or electric mixer until firm peaks form. Using a spatula, coat the upper third of the chestnut mountain with the whipped cream to simulate a "snowcap," creating a peak of whipped cream at the top. Serve immediately.

Cooked Cream

Panna Cotta

Of all of Piedmont's desserts, the one everyone swoons over is *panna cotta*, **literally, "cooked cream." Here we have to use a bit of gelatin, as our cream is nowhere near as dense as Piedmont's. Their cream is so thick it actually gets squeezed out of the cardboard container in which it's packaged. Sometimes the** *panna cotta* **is served with caramel, like the French** *crème caramel*, **sometimes not.**

makes 8 servings

1 envelope unflavored gelatin	*1 quart heavy cream*
¼ cup cold water	*1¼ cups sugar*

In a small cup, sprinkle the gelatin over the water. Let soften for 5 minutes.

Place the heavy cream in a large heavy-bottomed saucepan over medium-low heat. Bring the cream to a near-simmer. Gently whisk in the softened gelatin, then gently whisk in the sugar and whisk constantly until the sugar is fully dissolved, about 5 minutes. Remove from the heat and let cool completely.

Pour the cooled panna cotta into eight 4-ounce ramekins or other small molds. Refrigerate for several hours, until firm. Unmold before serving.

Ricotta Cheese Dessert
Coppa di Seirass

✦❀✦

This is a most unusual, and pleasing, dessert that dates back centuries. *Seirass* is the Piedmontese name for what we know as ricotta cheese. Here it is sweetened, combined with raisins, rum, heavy cream, and lemon zest, and chilled. Then it is served with shavings of grated chocolate on top.

makes 6 servings

1 tablespoon golden raisins, soaked in 2 tablespoons Marsala for 30 minutes	¼ cup sugar
½ pound ricotta cheese	2 tablespoons light or dark rum
½ cup heavy cream	Grated zest of 1 small lemon

Combine all of the ingredients in a large mixing bowl. Stir gently to blend thoroughly. Transfer to individual serving cups and refrigerate, covered, for at least 2 hours.

Serve decorated with candied fruits or shavings of dark chocolate.

Wine-Infused Egg Mousse
Zabaione

✦❀✦

Sometimes you see this world-famous dessert spelled *zabaione* and sometimes it's *zabaglione*. There's no definitive spelling. The former reflects this dessert's dialect origins, for in Piedmontese it is *sanbajon*, as there's no *z* in Piedmontese.

Although it's not certain that *zabaione* is a Piedmontese creation, no other region in Italy has claimed it so vociferously. Piedmontese cookbooks dating to the 1700s offer recipes, although the earliest recorded recipe does come from a book published in Mantua (in Lombardy) in 1662.

Today, *zabaione* is seen more in Piedmont than anywhere else. In addition to its plain form, the now-classic variations incorporate Piedmont's famous red wine Barolo and its equally famous sweet Moscato wine. Both variations are memorably good.

Unusually, *zabaione* can be served two ways: either refrigerator-cold (in summer) or barely warm when just made (in the winter). Connoisseurs of the dessert prefer the barely warm style for its delicacy. A warm *zabaione*, like a soufflé, waits for no one, as its appeal lies in its texture and gentle warmth. It needs no accompaniment, except, perhaps, a few plain sugar cookies alongside.

makes 6 servings

4 large egg yolks

½ cup superfine sugar

½ cup Moscato d'Asti or Asti Spumante

⅔ cup heavy cream

In the top of a double boiler set over simmering (not boiling, or you'll set the eggs) water—or in a heavy-bottomed, nonreactive copper-lined saucepan set over very low heat—whisk together the egg yolks with the sugar. Add the wine and cook, whisking constantly, until the mixture is thick and pale yellow and has doubled in volume. Remove from the heat.

In a medium-size bowl with an electric mixer, whip the heavy cream until soft peaks form. Fold the still-warm egg yolk mixture into the cream. Serve warm, accompanied by Moscato d'Asti or Asti Spumante. Alternatively, the mixture can be chilled and served cold. Traditional accompaniments are fresh fruits and plain ladyfinger-type cookies.

Red Wine–Infused Egg Mousse
Zabaione al Barolo

This variation employs Piedmont's famous Barolo or Barbaresco wine. For once, it really pays to use the real thing, as the flavor of the wine does shine through. This recipe is less sweet than the preceding one, the better to let the flavor of the wine dominate.

makes 6 to 8 servings

6 large egg yolks

¾ cup Barolo or Barbaresco wine

6 tablespoons superfine sugar

Place the egg yolks, wine, and sugar in the top of a double boiler set over barely simmering water (not boiling, or you'll set the eggs) or in a heavy-bottomed, nonreactive copper-lined saucepan set over very low heat. Whisk constantly until the zabaione is fluffy, 3 to 4 minutes. Serve immediately in glasses or shallow bowls, accompanied by plain cookies.

Frozen Custard

Semifreddo

✿

Why this dessert is called "half-cold" I have never figured out. It's fully frozen. The Piedmontese dote on it, incorporating all sorts of additions to the *semifreddo* base. This version employs two of Piedmont's favorite tastes, hazelnuts and chocolate, embedded in the creamy, frozen richness of the *semifreddo* mixture.

makes 6 to 8 servings

½ cup whole hazelnuts

4 ounces bittersweet chocolate, grated

6 amaretto cookies, crumbled

2 tablespoons light rum

5 large eggs, separated

1 cup superfine sugar

2 cups heavy cream

Preheat the oven to 350°F. Toast the hazelnut on a baking sheet until lightly browned, about 10 minutes. Rub off the papery skins and let cool completely. Chop the nuts fine in a food processor, taking care not to overprocess and turn them into hazelnut butter.

Combine the hazelnuts, chocolate, amaretto cookies, and rum in a small bowl. Set aside.

Line a 9 × 5-inch loaf pan with plastic wrap, taking care to fit it into the corners of the pan as closely as possible. Set aside.

Whisk the egg yolks in a medium-size bowl with ½ cup of the sugar until thick and lemon yellow in color. Set aside.

Beat the egg whites with an electric mixer in a large, very clean stainless steel or copper bowl until soft peaks form. Add the remaining ½ cup sugar and continue to whisk until stiff peaks form.

Beat the heavy cream in another large bowl with an electric mixer until stiff peaks form.

Gently fold the egg yolk mixture into the beaten egg whites until amalgamated. Then fold the mixture into the beaten whipped cream.

Transfer one third of this mixture to the prepared pan. Shake the pan to create an even layer. Distribute half of the hazelnut mixture over the layer as evenly as possible. Repeat with another third of the whipped cream mixture. Add the remaining hazelnut mixture. Cover with the remaining whipped cream mixture. Smooth the surface with a spatula. Cover with plastic wrap and freeze overnight.

To serve, invert the pan onto a serving platter and rap the pan smartly with the back of a knife to loosen the *semifreddo*. Peel off the plastic wrap. Serve in thick slices.

Baked Pears in White Wine

Pere Martin Sec al Vino Bianco

✿✿✿

One of the classic country desserts in Piedmont is the little pear called a Martin Sec, which is baked and served lukewarm or at room temperature. In America, the closest pear to the Martin Sec is our Seckel, which works beautifully.

makes 6 servings

½ cup sugar

2 cups dry white wine

3 cloves

1 cinnamon stick

2 pounds Seckel pears, washed

Combine the sugar, wine, cloves, and cinnamon in a covered nonreactive casserole in which all the pears can be arranged standing upright. Stir over low heat until the sugar is dissolved. Add the pears, standing them up. Cook, covered, over low heat until the pears are tender, about 40 minutes. The liquid should have reduced considerably and started to caramelize.

Remove the pears from the pot and reduce the liquid to a syrup over high heat. Pour the syrup over the pears and serve lukewarm or at room temperature.

✿✿✿

Pears with Chocolate Sauce

Pere con Salsa di Cioccolato

Italians love pears and the Piedmontese, in particular, love chocolate. A dish that combines the two, with an added sprinkling of chopped hazelnuts, was surely inevitable. This dessert can be prepared well in advance, as it keeps beautifully. The pears should be served at room temperature or slightly cool, rather than refrigerator-cold. The chocolate sauce can be reheated if necessary just before serving. A dessert such as this is frequently served with ice cream alongside. Experience reveals that the two best flavors are vanilla and, especially, pistachio.

makes 4 servings

6 shelled hazelnuts

2½ cups sugar

4 cups water

Juice of 2 lemons

Pinch of ground cinnamon

2 large, ripe Bartlett or Bosc pears,
    washed and peeled

½ cup black espresso-type coffee

5 tablespoons heavy cream

3½ ounces bittersweet chocolate, coarsely
    chopped

1 tablespoon unsalted butter

Toast the shelled hazelnuts on a baking sheet until lightly browned, about 10 minutes. Rub off the papery skins and let cool completely. Coarsely chop and set aside.

In a large heavy-bottomed saucepan over high heat, bring the sugar and water to a boil. Add the lemon juice and cinnamon and let boil, uncovered, for 5 minutes.

Carefully lower the pears into the sugar syrup, reduce the heat to medium, and poach until tender, about 10 minutes. Remove the pears and let cool completely. (If desired, save the syrup for another dessert.)

To make the chocolate sauce, combine the coffee and cream in a small saucepan over medium heat. Bring to a simmer and cook, stirring frequently, for 5 minutes. Reduce the heat to medium-low and add the chocolate and butter, stirring continuously. When the chocolate sauce is completely melted and smooth, set aside until needed. The sauce should be served hot, so either keep warm or reheat over low heat just before serving, stirring until smooth.

To serve, slice the pears in half lengthwise. Scoop out the cores. Slice each pear half into four lengthwise slices and fan out the slices on individual serving plates. Spoon one quarter of the hot chocolate sauce around each serving, with a little of the sauce covering part of the pear slices. Sprinkle with the chopped hazelnuts and serve immediately, while the sauce is still warm.

Stuffed Peaches

Pesche Ripiene

✣❦✣

This is one of the best summer desserts I know. If you're in Piedmont in the summertime, you're guaranteed to come across it. Some like serving it warm from the oven, others prefer room temperature. The filling is based on crushed amaretti, the kind that you (and Italians) buy in stores. Here, the crushed cookies are combined with cocoa, to create a chocolate filling.

makes 6 servings

6 ripe but not overly soft fresh peaches

For the filling:

2 large egg yolks

2 tablespoons sugar, or more to taste

3 tablespoons unsweetened cocoa powder

3 tablespoons dark or light rum

2 tablespoons brandy

6 amaretto cookies, finely crushed

¼ cup (½ stick) unsalted butter

Preheat the oven to 400°F. Lightly butter a baking sheet. Set aside.

Peel the peaches by immersing them in boiling water for 1 minute. Drain, cool under cold running water, and gently remove the skins. Slice the peaches in half. Remove the pits and discard.

Enlarge the cavity of each peach half by scooping out approximately 1 tablespoon of flesh (more, if the peaches are large). Set the peach halves aside. Finely chop the scooped-out flesh.

To make the filling, place the chopped peach flesh in a mixing bowl and whisk in the filling ingredients. The mixture should have the consistency of a moist paste. Taste for sweetness and add more sugar, if desired.

Place the peach halves on the prepared baking sheet. Fill each cavity with a portion of the filling. Top each half with a small nugget of unsalted butter. Bake until the peaches are tender, about 1 hour. Serve lukewarm or cool, but not refrigerator-cold.

Sweet Winter Squash

Dolce di Zucca Rossa

Piedmontese cooks are among Italy's most inventive when it comes to using winter squash. This is surely one of the most creative, and surprisingly good, uses for winter squash that I've come across. The inherent sweetness of a winter squash (butternut is my favorite) is amplified by the addition of honey. It is then leavened with the addition of beaten egg whites.

makes 6 servings

2 pounds winter squash, such as butternut or Hubbard, seeded and cut into chunks

1/4 cup honey, mixed with 1/2 cup very hot water

1 cup all-purpose flour

1/4 cup (1/2 stick) unsalted butter

2 large eggs, separated

Steam the chunks of squash in a large pot with a steamer gizmo until tender, about 20 minutes. When cool enough to handle, scoop out the squash flesh and discard the skin.

Puree the squash until very smooth in a food processor. With the processor running, pour in the honey mixture. Add the flour and process to blend thoroughly. The mixture should be fairly thick. Transfer to a large mixing bowl and let cool completely.

Preheat the oven to 325°F.

Mix the egg yolks into the cooled squash mixture. In a very clean stainless steel or copper mixing bowl, whisk the egg whites until stiff peaks form. Gently fold the beaten egg whites into the squash mixture until well incorporated. Turn the mixture into a baking dish. Bake until lightly golden, about 30 minutes. Serve lukewarm.

Venetian Lemon Cookies

Bisse

⚜

This is a hybrid recipe, combining Piedmont's love of cornmeal with Venice's liking of lemon. *Bisse* means water snake, a reference to the S-shape of these cookies. Variations on this theme abound. The Venetians themselves have their own cornmeal cookies called *zaleti*, which incorporate raisins in the dough. This version uses a mix of flour and cornmeal, which makes for a finer-textured dough that still has the flavor of cornmeal. The cookies keep well if tightly wrapped.

makes about 40 cookies

3 large eggs

¾ cup sugar

⅔ cup vegetable oil

Grated zest of 1 lemon

3 cups all-purpose flour

2 cups fine-ground cornmeal

Pinch of salt

Place the eggs and sugar in a large mixing bowl and, using an electric mixer or a whisk, beat until the mixture is pale yellow. Whisk in the oil and lemon zest. Using a rubber spatula, fold in the flour, cornmeal, and salt. Turn the dough out onto a floured board and knead it thoroughly. Wrap it tightly in plastic wrap and refrigerate for at least 1 hour to let the dough rest.

Preheat the oven to 425°F. Butter and flour two baking sheets, knocking off any excess flour. Set aside.

Pull off balls of dough about the size of a Ping-Pong ball. Roll each ball into a cylinder about 4 inches long. Shape into an S and set about 1 inch apart on the prepared baking sheets.

Bake the cookies for 5 minutes at 425°F. Reduce the heat to 350°F and bake until golden on top and lightly browned in the bottom, about 10 minutes longer. Remove from the oven and let cool.

Barolo-Flavored Cookies

Albesi al Barolo

The classic cookie of the Langhe zone takes its name from the most prominent town of the area, Alba, hence *albesi*—little Albas. The addition of the famous wine of the area to the cookie was probably inevitable and is certainly worthwhile. Still, I usually just add whatever red wine I happen to have open, as the flavor of the cookie doesn't justify the expense of Barolo.

makes about 25 cookie sandwiches

1/2 pound shelled hazelnuts	5 large egg whites
2 1/2 cups sugar	1 cup Barolo or Barbaresco wine
1/2 cup unsweetened cocoa powder	3 ounces bittersweet chocolate, chopped
1 teaspoon baking powder	1 tablespoon unsalted butter

Preheat the oven to 350°F.

Toast the hazelnuts on a baking sheet until lightly browned, about 10 minutes. Rub off the papery skins, then let cool completely. Reduce the oven temperature to 325°F.

Chop hazelnuts very fine in a food processor, taking care not to overprocess and turn them into hazelnut butter. With the processor running, add the sugar, cocoa, baking powder, egg whites, and wine. Process briefly to combine.

Line four baking sheets with nonstick cooking parchment or waxed paper and brush with melted butter. Transfer the batter to a pastry bag fitted with a 1/2-inch plain round tip. Pipe thin 1-inch-diameter rounds of batter onto the baking sheets, with 2 inches space between each one. Alternatively, drop the batter from a half teaspoon.

Bake the cookies until light brown, about 10 minutes. Remove from the oven and let cool slightly, then transfer with a spatula to wire racks to cool completely.

Melt the chocolate and butter together in the top of a double boiler set over barely simmering water or in a heavy-bottomed saucepan over the lowest heat. When the chocolate mixture is melted, spread a thin layer of it over the bottom of half of the cookies. Cover with the remaining cookies to create cookie sandwiches with chocolate filling. Let sit for at least 1 hour before serving. These will keep well for several days, if kept refrigerated and tightly sealed. Before serving, bring to room temperature.

Soft Almond Cookies

Amaretti Morbidi

⁂

The Italian almond cookies that nearly all of us know are the hard ones that come in those colorful (and expensive) cans. But there's another sort of amaretto, one that's *morbido*, or soft. It is a different cookie altogether and quite wonderful. They do not keep especially well, however, compared to their harder cousins.

makes about 30 cookies

½ pound almonds	10 large egg whites
1½ cups sugar	Melted butter, if needed
½ teaspoon pure almond extract	

Bring a small pot of water to a boil. Drop in the almonds for 1 minute. Drain and rinse with cold water. This will loosen the skins of the almonds, which will slip off when pinched between two fingers. Dry the skinned almonds thoroughly in a towel.

Preheat the oven to 375°F. Line one or two baking sheets with cooking parchment or waxed paper and brush with melted butter.

In a food processor, grind the almonds as fine as possible, taking care not to overprocess and turn them into almond butter. Slowly process in the sugar and extract. Transfer to a large mixing bowl and set aside.

In a very large, very clean stainless steel or copper bowl, beat the egg whites with an electric mixer until stiff peaks form. Fold the egg whites into the hazelnut mixture until well distributed.

Drop the batter from a teaspoon onto the prepared baking sheet(s), leaving 2 inches of space between each cookie. Bake for 15 to 20 minutes; they will still be soft, but offer resistance when pressed. Remove from the oven and let cool slightly, then transfer with a spatula to a wire rack to cool completely.

Cornmeal Butter Cookies

Krumiri

※⚜️※

One of Piedmont's most commonly seen cookies, *krumiri* (also spelled *crumiri*) are thought to have originally come from the town of Casala Monferrato, near Alessandria. They are shaped like horseshoes to honor the crown of King Vittorio Emanuele II, who ruled during the mid-1800s. In fact, this cookie easily predates that period, as there are similar cornmeal-based cookies found elsewhere in Piedmont under yet other names.

Buttery, slightly granular, and flavorful, *krumiri* are ideal accompaniments to *zabaione*. They're also a snap to make, especially if you use an electric mixer. If you don't have a pastry bag, just roll the dough into walnut-size balls, flatten slightly, and bake as directed.

makes about 36 cookies

¾ cup (1½ sticks) unsalted butter, softened

¾ cup sugar

Grated zest of 1 lemon

1 large egg plus 1 large egg yolk

¾ cup all-purpose flour

⅔ cup coarse-ground cornmeal

Preheat the oven to 350°F. Lightly butter two baking sheets.

In a large bowl with an electric mixer, cream the butter, sugar, and lemon zest at medium speed until the mixture is light and fluffy. Beat in the egg and egg yolk. Add the flour and cornmeal and mix until all of the ingredients are well blended. Do not overmix, as that will produce gluten and toughen the cookies.

Fit a pastry bag with a ½-inch star tip. Fill the pastry bag with the dough and pipe onto the baking sheets in small horseshoe shapes about 2 inches in diameter. Bake until the cookies are golden, about 12 minutes. Cool on wire racks.

Arcigola Slow Food—The World's Most Extraordinary Food Club

❧

The town of Bra, near where we lived, is always good for a smile among English speakers. The name seems a bit odd. Those Braidese—there are twenty-seven thousand—who speak English happily share in the amusement. The origin of the name is straightforward, if still controversial: Bra is thought to derive from the de Brayda family, which ruled the area nine hundred years ago. Some say, however, that the name antedates the de Braydas.

Its name aside, the most significant feature of Bra (at least to the outside world) is that it is the headquarters of Arcigola Slow Food, the world's most ambitious food club. Arcigola is a not-for-profit association of twenty thousand Italian members who have—even by Italian standards—a vigorous interest in food and wine.

In exchange for dues of sixty-five thousand *lire,* or about forty dollars, annually, its members receive a thick monthly newsletter running to forty pages or more, as well as discounts on various food and wine books published by Arcigola and others. They are offered wines or olive oils by mail, which are "discovered" by the organization. Its members snap them up.

More unusual yet is that Arcigola (pronounced archee-go-lah) is, effectively, a one-man band, although one of orchestral proportions. Its conductor is Carlo Petrini (born in Bra in 1949), who founded Arcigola in 1987. As might be expected in an organization devoted to eating well, Petrini is all affability. His smile flashes with the same neon readiness as Pavarotti's. Both share a similar full beard and some girth, although as to the latter, Pavarotti truly is operatic while Petrini is, in comparison, a mere (asparagus) spear carrier.

I would drop in from time to time to chat with Carlo—and also to eat at the organization's superb restaurant, Boccondivino ("the divine mouth"). Both are housed in an ancient, somewhat off-tilt building in the heart of Bra.

Carlo Petrini is an impresario of the first rank, as well as outspokenly socialistic in his political leanings. This, despite the fact that Bra is a conservative country town—politically, socially, and gastronomically. On the last point, by the way, the locals are one with Petrini. They flock to Boccondivino, where "New Wave" is presumed to be a California surfing term.

But beneath Carlo's veneer of genuine friendliness is a bedrock political talent. He knows how to make things happen, which is no small feat in a country notorious for things not happening easily, if at all. Italian food and wine would be noticeably the lesser for his absence. Arcigola's existence alone is an accomplishment.

His instincts for organization and affiliation can be seen in Arcigola's involvement in the publishing house called Gambero Rosso. The story involves—only in Italy—leftist politics allied to good eating. Gambero Rosso is well known in Italy for its restaurant guide and food publications. Petrini was present at Gambero Rosso's beginnings in 1987. I once asked Carlo if the Gambero Rosso ("red crawfish") name was chosen because of the founding group's leftist orientation. He laughed and replied, "No, it had nothing to do with reds or anything. This was a bunch of intellectuals, remember? It was the name of the inn where Pinocchio ate a meal, the Osteria del Gambero Rosso."

They decided that what Italy lacked was a newspaper with a leftist orientation. So they started one, called *Il Manifesto*. It turned out to be a great success, with a daily circulation of about fifty thousand copies. Because of the success of the newspaper, Gambero Rosso branched into other publishing ventures. Carlo's newly founded Arcigola helped put together the first *Guide to Italian Wines*, which is still being published today.

All this history is important for one reason: Arcigola owned a forty percent share in the profit-making Gambero Rosso. But by 1990, the two organizations had diverged. By then, Arcigola's membership had ballooned to twelve thousand dues-paying members, helped in large part by the publicity offered through the *Il Manifesto* newspaper. The divorce was occasioned by, of all things, Gambero Rosso's insistence upon publishing a restaurant guide. This always puzzled me, as Petrini was all for publishing food and wine guides of every sort.

When I asked Carlo about this he explained, "We disagreed about the publication of this guide. Italy already had at least five restaurant guides. There really wasn't a need for another one. What I thought there was a need for was a guide to the *osterie*, the small, humble restaurants that are ignored by the typical restaurant guides. *Osterie* are the great patrimony of Italy. This is what I thought should be published."

Upon the breakup—which was profitable for Arcigola—the organization immediately set out to publish, under its own imprint, just the sort of restaurant guide that Petrini insisted was needed all along. Titled *Osterie d'Italia*, the first edition appeared in 1992 and is now issued annually, with sales of seventy-five thousand copies a year.

Osterie d'Italia may well be the most significant book about Italian food published in our time. Only an organization such as Arcigola could have attempted the daunting challenge of identifying—and celebrating—the best of Italy's thousands (but nevertheless still dwindling) heart-and-soul restaurants: the modest, frequently out-of-the-way local restaurants. They are found in cities as well as deep in the countryside. The guide, which is selective and highly reliable, locates these *osterie* in every region of Italy. Its recommendations come from local chapters of Arcigola, in effect, real insider knowledge. No better guide to Italian restaurants exists. (Gambero Rosso, by the way, did bring out an upscale annual restaurant guide, which touts restaurants offering the latest Italian food fashions.)

But the most ambitious—and ambiguous—project of all is Petrini's revision of Arcigola itself into something more international. Like King Canute commanding the waves to go back,

Petrini is spearheading a quixotic movement he has baptized "Slow Food." As the name suggests, it is an attempt to counter the mentality, and reality, of fast food.

At first, the idea of Slow Food was something of an intellectual joke. Petrini crafted a tongue-in-cheek manifesto after learning, in 1986, of a proposed McDonald's at the base of the famous Spanish Steps in Rome. (It's there today.) Aided by the Gambero Rosso contingent, Petrini and friends issued a "Slow Food Manifesto," as well as formed what they called the International Movement for the Defense of and Right to Pleasure.

Petrini happily admits that it was all a lark. But, this lighthearted lark suddenly took wing. Food fans in France, Italy, and elsewhere found, in a two-word slogan, a rallying cry. In 1989, what came to be called the Slow Food Movement was formally founded at a conference in Paris. Effectively, Slow Food *is* Arcigola, although Petrini takes pains to point out that Slow Food now has ten thousand members and chapters in fifteen countries, including the United States.

The Slow Food theme has become Petrini's new hobbyhorse, so much so that he has modified the Arcigola name. Today, it is formally called Arcigola Slow Food. Yet despite the clever phrase—and an equally clever insignia of a snail—Slow Food so far appears to be an updated twist on the old theme of like-minded food enthusiasts marching together toward long lunches or dinners. Absent so far is the publishing muscularity that propelled Petrini and Arcigola into a force to be reckoned with among Italian food and wine producers.

Meanwhile, back at the ranch, Petrini's ambition keeps Arcigola surging forward. In addition to a superb guide to restaurants and food sources in Petrini's home district of the Langhe (*Guida Turistica Enogastronomica delle Langhe e del Roero*) and the annual *Guide to Italian Wines*, Arcigola's own publishing imprint (Slow Food Editore) has issued yet another wine book, *The Guide to Everyday Wines*. It annually recommends Italian wines selling for less than sixty-five hundred lire, or about four dollars a bottle. Yet another wine book, *Guide to the Wines of the World*, was recently published in Italian, English, and German.

More ambitious yet—and more politically risky—is Petrini's personal project: creating detailed maps of Italy's two most famous wine districts, Barolo and Barbaresco. Both districts are near Bra, so it's home territory. It is an ambitious undertaking because the vineyards of Barolo and Barbaresco have never previously been delineated, let alone with the exactitude that Petrini pursues. In fact, no legal vineyard boundaries actually exist.

Since a new Italian wine law stipulates that a vineyard name cannot be cited on a label unless, and until, that vineyard's boundaries have been legally delimited, laying down the lines is sure to invite controversy, even rancor. Petrini's maps will be the starting (and possibly the end) point for drawing the boundaries of Barolo's and Barbaresco's hundreds of informally named vineyards. Vineyard owners could make or lose fortunes based upon whether their parcels are included as part of a famous vineyard.

The first set of maps—the Barolo district—has already been created and is beautifully printed and magnificently detailed. Yet it has not sold well, with more than half of the first printing still available. Undeterred, Petrini now is embarking on creating a companion set of maps for the Barbaresco area. He hopes that the two sets together will prove more commercially attractive. And that the ruffled feathers will smooth down in time.

But if a disgruntled grower did want to find Petrini, that would be no problem. At lunchtime, you can find him presiding over the large communal dining table at Boccondivino, the lunchtime lair of Arcigola employees. Petrini never seems to eat his meal uninterrupted. Characteristically, he works the room, seemingly knowing everyone who dines there, making a point of coming over for a chat, recommending a new wine, or just chewing the Piedmontese fat, which is especially delicious in dialect. Slow Food, it turns out, requires fast footwork.

Piedmont's Wines

The red wine of Nebiule . . . is very singular. It is about as sweet as the silky

Madeira, as astringent on the palate as Bordeaux, and as brisk as

Champagne. It is a pleasing wine.

Thomas Jefferson (1787)
The Papers of Thomas Jefferson, **Volume II**

Conventionally, wine is an afterthought in cookbooks, if it's mentioned at all. Understandably, many cookbooks are content to brief their readers by suggesting a suitable wine at the end of each recipe. There's nothing wrong with this, but it does inadvertently leave the impression that only that one wine, or category of wine, goes with the dish in question.

Although many have tried—present company included—the fact is that it is nearly impossible to write persuasively about both food and wine at the same time. They are separate and only vaguely related disciplines, like music and mathematics.

Each appeals to the other, but no more than that. The intent of this chapter is to signal, in the most practical way, some of the best Piedmontese wines.

This is not merely to underscore the importance of wine, but more so, to emphasize the fact that wine in Piedmont is as much a fundamental ingredient in their cooking as fresh rosemary or anchovies. This is not to say that the average Piedmontese (or any other Italian) actually knows much about wine. He doesn't. The only difference between an Italian and an American on the subject of wine is that nearly all Italians are comfortable with wine. Their comfort derives not just from everyday consumption, but also from a cultural sense that wine is simply part of their identity as Italians, in the same way that baseball is part of being American.

The Piedmontese wine intimacy is, inevitably, with the local item. Partly it's chauvinism, but mostly it's price. Local wines invariably are the cheapest, the more so when you grow them yourself. It's only the wine fanciers who seek the next level of knowledge beyond the supermarket offerings.

What Makes a Wine Good?

The most important question about wine is: How do you know when a wine is good? The answer isn't anywhere near as simple as the question. The pat response is: If it tastes good to you, it's good. That's a safe, populist answer. But it begs the question. After all, just because something appeals doesn't make it good. Look at junk food. Even its admirers don't object to the name.

What makes a wine good is a distinctiveness. After tasting a few different Cabernets or Chardonnays or Pinot Noirs, you get a sense of what these wines generally taste like. In the same way that cocker spaniels are supposed to look like what they are, rather than some other breed, a good Chardonnay should be easily identifiable. Once past that, you get into the fine points. At dog shows, the issue is not whether the dog is a cocker spaniel—that's no trick to anyone who's seen one—but rather, how fine a representative of the breed it is. It's no different with wine. There's plenty of room for debate, but, as in dog shows, the discussion proceeds from an already substantial foundation of agreement. With wine it's simply this: A wine of "breed" should exhibit a distinction that sets it apart from others of its class.

If distinction is what makes a wine good, then what makes a wine distinctive? Here the answer is simple, if ambiguous: A distinctive wine is one that tastes as if it comes from somewhere. It is what allows certain wines to remain compelling and intriguing over a span of generations. Winemakers can, and do, attempt to imbue wines with cosmetic distinctions by various wine-making techniques, such as using small new oak barrels to make the wine feel smoother and more supple. Or emphasizing the fruitiness of the wine and saturating its color by leaving the juice with the skins of the grapes for days or even weeks before starting the fermentation. With today's technology, the bag of tricks bulges.

But once the flashiness fades—which it always does—only those wines that deliver a sensation of "somewhereness" deliver honest, substantive character. They are transparent to place. It is what makes them profound, or at least perpetually intriguing. This is why generations of wine drinkers return to them. A characterful wine cannot come from just anywhere.

This explains why Piedmont is one of the world's greatest wine regions. In Italy it is acknowledged as supreme; it has no rival. No other Italian region has such an abundance of distinction.

Piedmont's soulmate is Burgundy. Both share an intense, almost maniacal devotion to tending tiny plots of vines planted to quarrelsome grapes (Nebbiolo in Piedmont, Pinot Noir in Burgundy). The cultures of both remain, to this day, profoundly agrarian, even as riches and fame have become entwined in their daily lives. In both cultures, vineyard ownership is emotional, as well as highly fractionalized. For example, the landholdings in the Langhe area—home to the famous Nebbiolo wines called Barolo and Barbaresco—are as fragmented as those in Burgundy's famous Côte d'Or. The average Langhe vineyard holding is four acres; in the Côte d'Or, it's five acres. And in both places, these small holdings are not even one contiguous piece, but rather are a patchwork of plots in several vineyards.

Moreover, both see wine as the received message of the land, which explains the absence of any significant history of blending multiple grape varieties to create one marketable wine, as is done in Bordeaux. Nebbiolo, like Pinot Noir, is most articulate when left to speak for itself. When blended, its expressiveness is stifled. To blend Nebbiolo is like putting Pavarotti in the chorus. This explains why Barolo and Barbaresco must, by law, be one hundred percent Nebbiolo.

Deciphering Piedmont's Wines

Wines at their best are an expression of place. This is why in Europe the name of the wine is that of the place where it is grown, unlike in the New World, where it's the grape that counts. That said, the grape variety is critical. In every European wine region, several grape varieties are usually found, each recognized as having a certain relative stature. A signature variety, such as Nebbiolo in Piedmont or Pinot Noir in Burgundy, is considered so not because of flavor, but because of its ability to convey the nuances of place. Other varieties can do so too, but they are deemed lesser because of a more limited expressiveness. They're just not as articulate.

This explains the seeming arbitrariness of pronouncing one grape variety or wine superior to another. It is not as arbitrary as it appears. In Piedmont you can find the same vineyard planted to several different grape varieties, each vinified (made) into separate wines. In a vineyard in a district where the earth speaks, such as Barolo, it is possible to try a Dolcetto, a Barbera, and a Nebbiolo all grown in one vineyard. When tasting the wines side by side, looking past the different flavors each grape variety brings with it, you discover that the expressiveness of place amplifies as you go from the Dolcetto (rich, pleasing, but somehow vague) to Barbera (rougher, harsher, but more detailed), and finally to Nebbiolo (exquisitely refined, dramatically detailed, and possessed of a dimension of flavor absent or distant in the others). There's a commonality among the three: clarion in the Nebbiolo and muted in the Dolcetto.

Nebbiolo is the most profound; it has the most to say. But it requires attention, like a symphony. This is one reason why Nebbiolo, although the most acclaimed and respected wine in Piedmont, is not the most frequently drunk, any more than symphonies are everyday listening. A nice concerto (or pop tune) in the form of a Dolcetto or Barbera is more often soothing and comforting.

Not to be ignored is that Nebbiolo's very transparency to place makes it less conducive to being grown in just any old spot. It is so transparent, in fact, that it can be grown successfully in a surprisingly few spots—at least with a result that anyone would find appealing. Dolcetto and Barbera are more accommodating, sometimes too much so. Unlike Nebbiolo, they will grow almost anywhere. But what results can be boring, or worse. That's why there's so much more Dolcetto and, especially, Barbera of indifferent quality. The best examples, though, can speak of place, if in a more general, less site-specific fashion than Nebbiolo.

Dolcetto

The most common observation about Dolcetto is that it is "the Beaujolais of Piedmont." (Here we again find, unwittingly, the Piedmont/Burgundy linkage. Beaujolais is a district in southern Burgundy, which grows the Gamay grape variety.) Dolcetto is a seductive wine: It goes down like praise. The most basic version is very much a wine to be drunk as young, cool, and fresh as possible, just like Beaujolais. Although this sort of Dolcetto can age for a year or two without deteriorating in quality, it does not improve for being cellared. A fresh, grapey fruitiness is its appeal. The Piedmontese drink it habitually and unthinkingly.

Once past that level, Dolcetto has greater prospects. Unlike Nebbiolo or even some Barberas, even a great Dolcetto does not improve with age. But the more profound Dolcettos, like *grand cru* Beaujolais, do take a year or two simply to open up fully. The really good ones (listed below) are at their best two or three years after the vintage, although rarely more than that.

As for expression of place, Dolcetto from the district of Dogliani is always more supple than others grown elsewhere. In contrast, Dolcetto grown in the Alba zone can be richer tasting but firmer in texture and less insinuating than that from Dogliani. Each has its appeal; both areas can create exceptionally good Dolcettos.

Piedmont has seven zones with a Dolcetto-related appellation: Dolcetto d'Acqui, Dolcetto d'Alba, Dolcetto d'Asti, Dolcetto Diano d'Alba, Dolcetto di Dogliani, Dolcetto delle Langhe Monregalesi, and Dolcetto di Ovada. Of these, three stand out: Alba, Diano d'Alba, and Dogliani.

Producers to look for

Azienda Azelia (Dolcetto d'Alba). Single-vineyard Dolcetto from the Bricco dell'Oriolo vineyard located in the high-elevation town of Montelupo Albese. Very refined and pure.

Chionetti (Dolcetto di Dogliani). Quinto Chionetti is perhaps the best producer of Dolcetto di Dogliani. Three single-vineyard Dolcettos: Le Coste, San Luigi, and Briccolero. Le Coste is the lightest, San Luigi has an intense scent, Briccolero is the richest and fullest. All are Dogliani-supple.

Aldo Conterno (Dolcetto d'Alba). Grown in the Barolo zone in the vineyard area called Bussia Soprana (literally, "the upper slope of the Bussia vineyard"). Compare with Conterno's Barolo Bussia Soprana. Superb, concentrated.

Poderi Einaudi (Dolcetto di Dogliani). Famous estate originally owned by the late Luigi Einaudi, an economist and president of Italy after World War II, now owned by his niece. Three single-vineyard Dolcettos: Vigneto Tecc, San Luigi, and San Giacomo. All are classic Dogliani issue in intensity and suppleness.

Giovanni Gillardi (Dolcetto di Dogliani). Two single-vineyard Dolcettos: Vigneto Maestro and Vigna Cursalet. The former is fuller and more perfumey, the latter richer and more complete.

Elio Grasso (Dolcetto d'Alba). Single-vineyard Dolcetto from a subplot in the Gavarini vineyard in the Barolo zone called Vigna dei Grassi. Strong, intense.

Marcarini (Dolcetto d'Alba). Two single-vineyard Dolcettos: Fontanazza and Boschi di Berri. Both are very rich, round, full wines from the La Morra area of the Barolo zone. Compare with Marcarini's Barolo Brunate or La Serra (q.v.). Boschi di Berri comes from century-old vines.

Bartolo Mascarello (Dolcetto d'Alba). A famous Barolo producer's equally fine Dolcetto. Austere, detailed, very pure.

Giuseppe Mascarello (Dolcetto d'Alba). Single-vineyard Dolcetto called Vigna Bricco (literally, "crest of the hill") located in a famous Barolo-zone vineyard called Monprivato, of which Mascarello owns nearly all. Firm, austere, convincing.

Pecchenino (Dolcetto di Dogliani). One of the best producers of Dolcetto di Dogliani. Striking, colorful labels. Two single-vineyard Dolcettos: Pizzabò and Sirl d'Yermu. The former is lighter and raspberry-fresh, the latter fuller and richer. Both are pure Dogliani in their silky texture.

Francesco Rinaldi (Dolcetto d'Alba). Single-vineyard Dolcetto called Vigneto Roussot. Severe, austere, compelling.

Paolo Scavino (Dolcetto d'Alba). Single-vineyard Dolcetto called Vigneto del Fiasc from the Barolo-zone vineyard of the same name. Compare with Scavino's Barolo Bric del Fiasc (q.v.). Rich, very intense, yet austere.

Pira (Dolcetto di Dogliani and Dolcetto d'Alba). A Dolcetto specialist with two single-vineyard Dolcettos from Dogliani: Vigna Bricco dei Botti and Vigna Landes. Also, a single-vineyard Dolcetto d'Alba: Vigna Fornaci. Comparing either of the Dogliani wines with that from the Barolo-zone Dolcetto d'Alba shows perfectly how even Dolcetto can offer a sensation of (generalized) somewhere-ness.

Vajra (Dolcetto d'Alba). Two opposite-facing vineyards in the Barolo zone blended into one Dolcetto called Coste e Fossati. Austere, concentrated, very pure and fine.

Vietti (Dolcetto d'Alba). Two single-vineyard Dolcettos: Disa and Sant' Anna. Both are fragrant, concentrated wines. Very pure and fine.

Other good producers of Dolcetto d'Alba: Elio Altare; Gianfranco Bovio; Brovia; Giuseppe Cortese; Giacomo Conterno; Angelo Gaja; Bruno Giacosa; Marchesi di Gresy; Poggio Petorchino di Elvio Cogno; Parusso; Prunotto; Renato Ratti; Bruno Rocca; Luciano Sandrone, La Spinetta; Gianni Voerzio; Roberto Voerzio.

Good producers of Dolcetto di Diano: Apart from Alba and Dogliani, Piedmont's other noteworthy, although much smaller, zone for fine Dolcetto is the hilltop town called Diano or Diano d'Alba. The Diano d'Alba district is an island almost smack in the middle of the vast sea of the Dolcetto d'Alba zone. But Dolcetto is its specialty (indeed, the wine can legally be called simply Diano, which the growers prefer) and its quality is second to none. There is only one sixth as much Dolcetto di Diano as Dolcetto d'Alba: eighty-four thousand cases compared with Dolcetto d'Alba's half-million. The distinction of its Dolcetto is that it can be as firmly structured as a good Dolcetto d'Alba, but with more finesse and refinement. Look for: Coluè (Vigna Tampa), Fontanafredda (Vigna La Lepre), Gigi Rosso (Vigna Moncolombetto), Mario Savigliano (Sorl del Sot), and Giovanni Veglio (Sorl Ubart and Puncia del Bric).

Barbera

Of all Piedmont's wines, the one I love the most is Barbera. Piedmont's greatest red wines are incontestable: Barolo, Barbaresco, and Gattinara, all made from the Nebbiolo grape. But it's Barbera that I reach for more often than any other. This amuses my Piedmontese friends. It's not that they disagree. Rather, it's just that Barbera has for so long had such a bad reputation in Italy that the idea of an American in their midst insisting that Barbera is the wine of his daily dreams strikes them as implausible.

In fairness, I am not alone in this. Some of Piedmont's greatest winegrowers, such as Alfredo Currado, Giuseppe Colla, Aldo Conterno, Giovanni Conterno, Enrico Scavino, Angelo Gaja, Elio Grasso, Renato Trinchero, and a few dozen others, have long, and expensively, nursed their ancient Barbera vines simply because they, too, believe in Barbera. It has been an expensive undertaking because even the best Barbera fetched a derisory price until very recently. Often these producers could have grown Nebbiolo in the same plot and produced, if they were in the right zone, a more lucrative wine such as Barolo or Barbaresco.

The problem with Barbera—the reason it got such a bad name and such a low price—is that it grows like a weed. Unlike Nebbiolo, it will seemingly grow anywhere. Again, unlike Nebbiolo, it will give its grower almost embarrassingly high yields—except that the impoverished peasant growers of Piedmont weren't embarrassed. They were grateful. The great authority on Italian wines Burton Anderson once pointed out that where all wines in Piedmont, and elsewhere, take the masculine article (*il* Nebbiolo, *il* Dolcetto, *il* Freisa), only Barbera is accorded the feminine: *la* Barbera. It is a linguistic sign of affection.

But this affection did not extend to quality. Barbera was thought of as the peasant's grape. Its appeal was its high yields and undemanding ability to grow anywhere. After the infestation of the root louse called phylloxera, which wiped out all the vineyards of Europe in the late 1800s, including Piedmont's, the wine-starved peasant growers turned to Barbera. In the early 1900s it was planted everywhere. Never before had Barbera been seen in so many Piedmontese vineyards. What resulted was a tidal wave of crude, industrial Barberas, which persist to this day. In Piedmont, if it was cheap and of no account, it was Barbera.

Knowing this, it is the more impressive to learn that some growers still make Barbera—if only for themselves and their friends—in vineyards with soils and exposures usually reserved only for Nebbiolo. And that these same growers prune their Barbera vines severely to limit the yield, thereby concentrating the flavor and amplifying its intensity.

Then came the renaissance. The growers who believed saw their devotion to Barbera rewarded. Prices increased dramatically and deservedly. Barbera saw its first-ever respect. Fanciers of Italian wines recognized that a truly great Barbera—from old vines on a superb site with low yields—if one was so inclined, could age as long, and transform almost as well, as a Barolo.

Some of these renaissance Barberas gained attention and respect by having been treated differently in the winery. Traditionally, all Barberas used to be aged in big wood casks. In the '80s, Piedmont was swept by the worldwide vogue for aging red and white wines in small French oak barrels called *barriques*. Where the old casks held one or two thousand gallons of wine, these small *barriques* hold just sixty gallons, or about twenty-five cases, of wine. The vastly greater ratio of wood surface to wine meant that the wine inside is infused with a vanilla-scented oak flavor, especially if the barrel is brand-new or has only been used for two or three vintages. The oak tannins they impart also can make a wine taste smoother, as well as help it keep a deeper, richer color, which is yet another attraction. Oaks from French forests are thought to offer the most interesting, subtle flavors. The barrels cost between four and five hundred dollars each, and lose their all-important flavor after four or five years.

The idea of lavishing such expensive barrels and sophisticated winemaking techniques on the lowly Barbera struck Piedmontese old-timers as preposterous, as well as heretical. Indeed, the taste that resulted was like nothing anybody had ever associated with Barbera before. But outsiders—and Italians craving modernity—loved the new-style Barbera. After all, the oak veneer in the wine reminded them of every other great red wine they also admired: Bordeaux, Burgundy, expensive California wines. Barbera became a wine of respect.

Producers to look for

Elio Altare (Barbera d'Alba). Exemplar *barrique*-aged Barbera, with a single-vineyard bottling: Vigna Larigi.

Ceretto (Barbera d'Alba). Single-vineyard called Piana. Fresh, fruity-style Barbera but no oak. Old vines.

Domenico Clerico (Barbera d'Alba). New-style Barbera that sees some time in small oak barrels. High quality.

Aldo Conterno (Barbera d'Alba). Single-vineyard called Conca Tre Pile, Barolo zone. Sees time in small oak barrels. One of the most successful of all the new-style Barberas.

Giacomo Conterno (Barbera d'Alba). Classically made Barbera from old vines in the Barolo district in the Serralunga d'Alba area. Superb traditionalism.

Giuseppe Cortese (Barbera d'Alba). Excellent traditional Barbera from Trifolera vineyard in the Barbaresco district.

Angelo Gaja (Barbera d'Alba). Single-vineyard wine called Vignarey. One of the best of the *barrique*-aged new Barberas. From old vines (planted in the early '50s) just outside the Barbaresco zone. Very expensive, but excellent.

Bruno Giacosa (Barbera d'Alba). Single-vineyard called Altavilla. Traditional and excellent.

Elio Grasso (Barbera d'Alba). Single-vineyard called Vigna Martina, which is a subplot of the famous Barolo-zone vineyard called Gavarini. Sees time in small oak barrels but with great deftness. One of the best new-style Barberas.

Marcarini (Barbera d'Alba). Single-vineyard called Ciabot Camerano, in the La Morra district of the Barolo zone. Traditional. Very concentrated, soft, and rich. (*Ciabot* is Piedmontese dialect for a small worker's hut in the middle of a vineyard, used as a refuge and to store tools.)

Marengo-Marenda (Barbera d'Alba). Single-vineyard Barbera called Cerequio, in the Barolo zone. Famous Barolo vineyard in the La Morra district. Traditional and fine.

Giuseppe Mascarello (Barbera d'Alba). Two single-vineyard Barberas: Fasana and Ginestra. Both traditional, both superb. Fasana is the lighter of the two; Ginestra (a famous Barolo-zone vineyard near Monforte d'Alba) is fuller, richer, more complete.

Moccagatta (Barbera d'Alba). Single-vineyard called Vigneto Basarin, in the Barbaresco zone. New-style, aged in small oak barrels. Excellent vineyard; exemplar of new-style Barbera.

Prunotto (Barbera d'Alba). Single-vineyard called Pian Romualdo, in the Barolo zone. Traditional, superb. Pian Romualdo is one of the Barolo zone's greatest Barbera sites. Rich, intense, round. (See also Vietti.)

Paolo Scavino (Barbera d'Alba). One of the finest of small oak barrel–aged Barberas. From two vineyards in the Barolo zone near Castiglione Falletto: Fiasco and Codana. Very rich and concentrated. Expensive.

Vajra (Barbera d'Alba). Single-vineyard called Bricco delle Viole in the Barolo zone. Traditional but very fresh and pure. Excellent.

Vietti (Barbera d'Alba). Two single-vineyard Barberas from the Barolo zone: Scarrone and Pian Romualdo. The two best traditional Barberas available. Scarrone is near the famous Rocche vineyard (same rare blue tufa subsoil). Austere, profound, very long lived. Pian Romualdo (see also Prunotto) is soft, rich, voluptuous, superb.

Roberto Voerzio (Barbera d'Alba). Single-vineyard called Vignasse, in the Barolo zone near La Morra. New-style. Oaky, soft, juicy.

Good producers of Barbera d'Asti: Because Barbera does best in great vineyard sites, it is no brain-banger to realize that the finest Barberas are from the Barolo and Barbaresco zones around Alba. That said, a vast quantity of Barbera is produced in the Asti area, which is farther north. The reputation of Barbera d'Asti couldn't be lower, thanks in large part to the domination of big winegrowers' cooperatives that issue floods of industrial, junk Barbera. Yet a really good Barbera d'Asti can rival all but the very greatest bottlings of Barbera d'Alba. Offerings at that level are, so far, too few. Typically, most Barbara d'Asti of decent quality are lighter and more rustic than good Barbera d'Alba wines. But Barbera d'Asti is worth keeping an eye on.

Braida di Giacomo Bologna (Barbera d'Asti). Three single-vineyard Barberas: Ai Suma, Bricco della Bigotta, and Bricco dell'Uccellone. Also a Barbera called La Monella, which is lightly fizzy, or *frizzante*, a once-common style that is fading. The late Giacomo Bologna ignited the fashion for small oak barrel–aged Barberas. He singlehandedly brought respect to Barbera d'Asti, as well as unprecedented prices. The Ai Suma bottling is fresh and perfumey; Bricco della Bigotta is more austere and finer. The signature wine is Bricco dell'Uccellone, which is rich, intense, and very oaky, as well as the most expensive of the three.

Scarpa (Barbera d'Asti). Three single-vineyard Barbera d'Asti bottlings: Il Piazzaro, La Bogliona, and Bricchi di Castelrocchero. All three are extremely traditional in style and superb examples of old-fashioned Barbera d'Asti at its best. Scarpa is a producer of numerous wines, all old-fashioned in style and substantive.

Renato Trinchero (Barbera d'Asti). Two single-vineyards: Vigna del Noce and La Barslina. Vigna del Noce is perhaps the greatest traditionally made Barbera d'Asti. Very old vines dating to 1929. La Barslina is another old vineyard (1936), but the wine sees time in small oak barrels. Both rival, in their fashion, the best Barbera d'Alba bottlings.

Other good Barbera d'Asti producers: Bricco Mondalino (Vigna Il Bergantino); Carnevale (Il Crotino); Cascina Castlet (Vigna Malabaila); Coppo (Camp du Rouss); La Fagianella (Vigneto Garavagna); Achille Ferraris (Vigneto Nobbio); Renato Rabezzana (Il Bricco); La Spinetta (Ca' di Pian); Enrico Vaudano; Viarengo (Vigna Morra).

Piedmont's Great Nebbiolo Wines

One of the many confusions about Piedmontese wines is that sometimes they use grape names (Barbera d'Alba, Barbera d'Asti, Moscato d'Asti, various Dolcettos) and sometimes they use place names. It is no coincidence that Nebbiolo (Jefferson's "Nebiule"), alone among Piedmont's best grape varieties, almost always is identified by geographic place names: Barolo, Barbaresco, Gattinara, Carema, Ghemme, Sizzano, Fara, Boca, and Lessona.

Nebbiolo has alway been widely planted. And over the centuries growers learned that a Nebbiolo wine from, say, Gattinara, tasted consistently different from one from nearby Ghemme. Precisely because of this transparency to place, it was inevitable that place names, rather than a grape name, would become the most efficient descriptive vehicle.

(Nebbiolo does get named in two lesser-quality wine categories: the catch-all designations of Nebbiolo d'Alba and Nebbiolo delle Langhe. And in northern Piedmont, around Novara, one sees the dialect name Spanna used as a synonym for Nebbiolo on inexpensive bottlings.)

Given the centuries-old tradition of growing Nebbiolo, and the evident awareness of its place-sensitivity, it is surprising that Piedmont did not develop a tradition of wines labeled with vineyard names. Although Piedmont has long had a folkloric tradition of named vineyards, the practice of citing a vineyard name on a label was unknown until relatively recently.

Astonishingly, in fact, such anonymity persisted until the 1970s. With the sole exception of the Cannubi vineyard in the Barolo zone (which name was put on labels as far back as the mid-1700s), no Langhe vineyard name was seen on a label until the early 1960s, when Angelo Gaja, the late Renato Ratti, Giuseppe Colla of Prunotto, and Alfredo Currado of Vietti tentatively inaugurated the practice. Despite their examples, they were not joined by other producers for nearly another decade. Effectively, single-vineyard labeling was not practiced until the 1980s. Today, virtually all of the best Piedmont wines are vineyard-named.

Because the tradition did not pursue named-vineyard wines, Piedmont—like everywhere else in Italy—never developed either legally delimited vineyard designations or quality rankings of the vineyards, like Burgundy's *grands* or *premiers crus*. Vineyard names currently are outside the law, although local usage and peer pressure keep producers from being too egregious in their declarations. However, new Italian wine regulations require that any vineyard named on a label now be from a legally delimited site. As for official quality rankings of the vineyards, as exists in France, don't hold your breath. That is still decades away.

Any country as mountainous, and as densely populated, as Italy is bound to develop a complex, ever-finer delineation for residents to use in describing where they are from. Piedmont is no exception. Residents of every hilly area—there are thousands of them—long ago assigned themselves local place names, a kind of not-so-secret handshake of self-recognition and public identity. Language, in the form of dialects and highly localized pronunciations, reflects this insularity.

In Piedmont, such a place is a set of hills locally called the Langhe. Technically, the Langhe has no legal boundaries. Locally, everyone knows its precise limits in the same way that we all carry around a mental map of our own neighborhoods.

The Langhe name most likely derives, rather poetically, from "tongues" (*le lingue*), a reference to the shape of the hills. No one really knows the origin. It is an unusual, perhaps unique, collection of plunging, freestanding hills that look less like tongues and really more like a vast, repeating terrestrial bosom. Many of the hills offer exposures on all sides, so deep are the cleavages. In the distance are the (surprisingly close) Alps, which on a rare clear day in winter are tooth-achingly white with still-unmelted winter snow.

The Langhe is famous because these isolated hills—on the way to nowhere and bounded by rivers and by flat plains—are home to Nebbiolo's finest, most articulate expressions. They are summed up in two place names: Barolo and Barbaresco. The prosperous town of Alba lies between them, which explains why the Barbera and Dolcetto grown in the Langhe are given a designation "d'Alba." Really, they should have been called "delle Langhe," but the Langaroli seem to feel that this vaunted designation should be reserved only for Nebbiolo.

Barolo

The most profound expression of Nebbiolo, as well as the greatest variety of these expressions, comes from the Barolo zone. As mentioned previously, many grape varieties are grown in the Barolo zone, such as Dolcetto and Barbera, but only a 100 percent Nebbiolo wine grown there is entitled to be called Barolo. That's the law. Moreover, not every Nebbiolo vineyard in the zone automatically becomes Barolo. Only the more appropriate sites are authorized. A great Barolo is a wine experience like no other. The distinctive flavors of Nebbiolo are more resonant and dimensional in Barolo than in any other wine, including its rival Barbaresco.

Yet despite this seeming rigor, the fact is that Barolo for too long rested on its laurels as Italy's most famous, and grandest, red wine. Too many Barolos were of mediocre quality. Too many were poorly, even incompetently, made. It was the intractable problem of tradition, nowhere more tenacious than in Italy's many mountainous, tucked-away wine districts.

Partly the difficulty lies in Nebbiolo itself. For centuries it has been the pride of the Langhe. It is a beast of a grape, highly acidic and ferociously tannic. Its flavors, though, are original and somehow magical. Classically described as having intermingled tastes of tar and roses, only in the Langhe, specifically in its Barolo and Barbaresco districts, is Nebbiolo fully resonant. The Langhe is to Nebbiolo as Burgundy's famed Côte d'Or is to Pinot Noir.

The locals long ago learned to live with the beast, even to love its beastly qualities. They tried to tame it, sometimes harshly so. "I remember when my father, and other winemakers of his generation, used to put their Barolos on the roof to soften them up," recalls Aldo Conterno, who at sixty-two is one of the Langhe's most deft, and modern, winemakers.

"In the old days the Barolos were so tannic, because of how they were fermented," explains Conterno. "They used to leave the juice and then the brand-new wine in the vat with the tannin-rich grape skins for two months or more. Today, the whole maceration process rarely goes for much more than thirty days. After the wines were drawn off from the skins, the Barolo would remain in casks for five, six, seven years, sometimes even more. And then it would be transferred from the cask into glass demijohns. Even then, the wine could still be pretty tannic. So sometimes, to soften it up, they would put the demijohns outside, on the roof, for the summer and part of the winter. Of course it was oxidized all to hell by then, but anyway, they liked that taste."

That's all gone now. In the past decade—it's as recent as that—the once ferociously traditional Langhe has seen a stunning amount of revisionist thinking in how best to handle Nebbiolo. The so-called traditional style (it really only dates to the 1930s) employed forty-five- to sixty-day fermentation and maceration of the wines on the skins and cask aging that extended for as long as six years or more. What resulted was, too often, wines with excessive tannin, high volatile acidity, and pronounced oxidation.

"The taste of my father's customers was in the direction of this kind of oxidation," recalls Angelo Gaja, who is easily Piedmont's most famous wine producer and now produces Barolo as well as Barbaresco. "I remember some older customers coming here in the 1960s. My father would open old bottles of Barbaresco. And they were enthusiastic, exclaiming, 'This is like Marsala! It's fantastic.'"

Gaja still can't get the taste of the memory out of his mind. Or forget the indignity of an aesthetic that valued Barbaresco or Barolo looking like Sicily's famous amber-hued sweet wine. "My God, Marsala!" he groans, his lips contorting into a pained grimace. "I remember this happening many times. I decided that if they wanted Marsala, then they could go to Sicily."

Today, the drift is steadily toward a greater freshness. Not least has been a near stampede to using the small French oak barrels, or *barriques*. In this, the jury still is out. "It's not a Barolo if it is in *barriques*," declares Aldo Conterno. "It may be a great wine. But it's not Barolo." As it happens, Aldo Conterno issues several wines using *barriques*, including a Nebbiolo as well as his superb Barbera d'Alba "Conca Tre Pile Vyd." But his Barolos are stored in large oval casks—and emerge with stunning freshness.

No one, at present, can say what the "new traditionalism" will be. As for great wines everywhere in the world, it surely will be toward capturing a greater freshness of fruit, pursuing a greater expressiveness and particularity of vineyard site, and increased concentration. Whether the taste of oak and the suppleness that comes from using small oak barrels will be a permanent part of the picture remains to be seen. The producers that follow represent some of the best of Barolo today, traditional as well as New Wave. Many make a regular Barolo as well as single-vineyard bottlings. Almost always, single-vineyard bottlings are superior.

Producers to look for

Elio Altare. Two single-vineyard Barolos: Cascina Nuova and Arborina dell'Annunziata. New Wave winemaking. Lovely fruit intensity with a glossy veneer of new French oak.

Azienda Azelia. Two named-vineyard Barolos: Bricco Fiasco and a subplot of Bricco Fiasco called Bricco Punta. Pure, delicate, traditional but modern winemaking resulting in firm, detailed wines. Winemaker Luigi Scavino shares the Bricco Fiasco hillside with his cousin Enrico at the Paolo Scavino winery.

Cappellano. Small, revitalized estate in the Serralunga d'Alba district. Some oak used, but deftly so. Very fine Barolo of intensity and depth.

Ceretto. Two single-vineyard Barolos: Rocche and Prapo. Large, forward-thinking winery specializing in relatively early maturing style, although without any new oak. Be aware that Ceretto's Barolos are released under the brand-name label of Bricco Rocche. It is the name of one of their several wineries, despite its being the name of a vineyard. Several identified vineyards are sold under the Bricco Rocche label, including that of the Rocche vineyard itself.

Domenico Clerico. A single-vineyard Barolo called Ciabot Mentin Ginestra. Another New Wave winery entranced by the possibilities of French oak barrels. Good quality; much obvious style.

Aldo Conterno. Two single-vineyard Barolos: Vigna Cicala and Vigna Colonello. One of Barolo's supreme producers. The foremost practitioner of modern traditionalism: winemaking with virtually digital definition. Vigna Cicala and Vigna Colonello are subplots of the much larger Bussia vineyard. A regular Barolo called Bussia Soprana, as well as a superb Bussia wine brand-named Granbussia, issued only in the best vintages.

Giacomo Conterno. Owner/winemaker Giovanni Conterno is Aldo Conterno's brother. (Giacomo was their father.) Entirely separate winery and different styles. Great, traditional winemaking from Conterno's sole ownership of the Cascina Francia vineyard. The brand-named wine called Monfortino is from the Cascina Francia vineyard in the Serralunga d'Alba commune, but it is vinified at a higher temperature and aged longer than the regular Barolo. Both are stunning.

Fontanafredda. Eight single-vineyard Barolos: Lazzarito, Gattinara, La Rosa, San Pietro, Gallaretto, La Villa, Bianca, and La Delizia. One of Langhe's largest wineries. Old-fashioned winemaking results in wines of depth, but with occasional coarseness, even rusticity. A taste of the past.

Angelo Gaja. A single-vineyard Barolo called Sperss. Previously known only for unique Barbarescos, Gaja purchased a sixty-nine-acre vineyard in the Serralunga d'Alba commune of the Barolo zone. First vintage was 1988. Modern style with noticeable use of small new French oak barrels. Quality is superb.

Bruno Giacosa. One single-vineyard Barolo: Rocche. One of the Langhe's most talented producers. Strong, long-lived wines of great depth and precision. The Rocche vineyard is magnificent. (See also Vietti.)

Elio Grasso. Four named Barolos made from subplots in two vineyards. Gavarini vineyard: subplots Chiniera, Grassi, and Runcot. Ginestra vineyard: subplot Casa Matè. Modern traditionalism strongly influenced by Aldo Conterno. Beautifully made, detailed wines.

Marcarini. Two single-vineyard Barolos: Brunate and La Serra. The reference standard for the Brunate and La Serra vineyards, both in the La Morra commune. For decades, winemaker Elvio Cogno was in charge. Recent family disputes gave him the push. But the vines remain and, one hopes, Cogno's implacable standards. Traditional yet modern.

Bartolo Mascarello. Bartolo Mascarello issues a wine simply labeled Barolo. In fact, it comes mostly from the great Cannubi vineyard. Traditional, superb, beautifully supple.

Giuseppe Mascarello. Two single-vineyard Barolos: Monprivato and Villero. The label reads Giuseppe; the winemaker is the son, Mauro. Traditional winemaking. Voluptuous, concentrated wines. The Monprivato vineyard is this producer's signature wine. Villero is another terrific vineyard.

Parusso. Two single-vineyard Barolos: Bussia and Mariondino. Fresh, modern style of Barolo with some oak. Very fine.

E. Pira. Only one Barolo is made at this tiny winery: a rich, intense, slightly rustic wine ninety percent from the great Cannubi vineyard. Very traditional. (This is a different Pira from that making Dolcetto di Dogliani.)

Prunotto. Two single-vineyard Barolos: Cannubi and Bussia di Monforte. One of the best wine shippers of the Langhe. Cannubi is Barolo's most famous vineyard. Prunotto makes a reference-standard Cannubi. Bussia vineyard also is excellent. Many other fine wines. Prunotto was purchased in 1989 by the Antinori family, of Chianti fame. Stylistically, the wines changed beginning with the 1985 vintage, thanks to the use of large casks (as opposed to small barrels) crafted from French oak. The result is greater polish and finesse than in the past.

Renato Ratti. Three named Barolos from one vineyard: Marcenasco vineyard and two subplots, Marcenasco-Conca and Marcenasco-Rocche. The late Renato Ratti was a viticultural and political leader in the Langhe. Ratti wines were, and still are, designed for early consumption, although without using any small oak barrels. Fine quality. Soft, ripe, intense.

Francesco Rinaldi. Two single-vineyard Barolos: Brunate and Cannubi. An old-fashioned producer issuing supple, traditionally made wines. The Brunate and Cannubi (labeled Cannubio) vineyards are impressive and insinuating.

Luciano Sandrone. One single-vineyard Barolo: Cannubi, from a subplot called Boschis. A fashionable New Wave producer issuing oaky but intense wines aged in small French oak *barriques*.

Scarpa. Two single-vineyard Barolos: Coste di Monforte and Tettimorra. Old-fashioned producer located outside of the Langhe that nevertheless has long issued excellent Barolo. Strong wines of depth and breed in a very traditional style that is rewarding only when tasted with food.

Paolo Scavino. Two single-vineyard Barolos: Bric' del Fiasc' and Cannubi. A tiny winery of extra-ordinary accomplishment. Unlike many other young winemakers using small French oak barrels, Enrico Scavino (the son) is by far the most deft. Everything he makes is stunning. Bric' del Fiasc' (from the Piedmontese dialect for the Bricco Fiasco vineyard) and Cannubi are magnificent. The Cannubi may well be the single best rendition made.

Vajra. Two single-vineyard Barolos: Bricco Viole and Fossati. Modern style with freshness and depth. No oak. Round, intense wines of considerable interest and depth.

Vietti. Three single-vineyard Barolos: Rocche, Villero, and Lazzarito. Winemaker (and husband of Luciana Vietti) Alfredo Currado's style is for clean-tasting wines of almost monumental scale. Little oak here, but enormous depth and definition. Vietti's is the supreme rendition of the Rocche vineyard; Villero is also superb, as is Lazzarito. Everything produced is reference-standard.

Roberto Voerzio. Two single-vineyard Barolos: Cerequio and La Serra. New Wave winery empha-sizing an intense, perfumey grapiness. The quality of the wine is very fine; the vision is avant-garde.

A word about Barolo *Chinato* One of the Barolo zone's distinctive creations is a Barolo steeped in *china*, or quinine. The name comes from the cinchona tree, the bark of which creates quinine. Like vermouth (q.v.), the idea of using a wine as a base to which herbal extracts are added, for medicinal as well as gustatory reasons, is ancient. Barolo *chinato* is used as a *digestivo* after dinner, sipped from small glasses.

Although a number of old-time growers make a *chinato* for their private use, only a few com-mercial bottlings are available. This is because Italian wine law requires a producer to have an entirely separate winery facility just to make *chinato,* as sugar is added to the wine to increase alco-hol during fermentation. Known as chaptalization, it is illegal in regular winemaking in Italy. So although the authorities allow it for making Barolo *chinato,* whoever does so must therefore go to the expense of creating an entirely separate winery to do it. Few bother.

Happily, two producers do take the trouble and their versions of Barolo *chinato* are superb: Ceretto and Cappellano. .

Barbaresco

Until the 1970s, Barbaresco was unknown to the world outside of Northern Italy. Unlike nearby Barolo, which has been famous for centuries, Barbaresco didn't even exist as a separate wine until 1894, when a liberal-minded local aristocrat, Domizio Cavazza, formed a growers' cooperative. Previously, all the Nebbiolo grown in the Barbaresco area was sold as Barolo.

Barbaresco is an *arriviste* compared to Barolo, and a conspicuously successful one at that.

Inevitably, claims of Barbaresco having a more prestigious, and ancient, heritage are now submitted with assiduity, reminding one of Giuseppe di Lampedusa's immortal line in *The Leopard*, when the Prince, of impossibly ancient lineage, remarks about a newly rich and eager arrival to the upper classes, "His family, I am told, is an old one or soon will be."

Today, however, Barbaresco is perhaps the Langhe's most sought-after wine. It is a much smaller district than Barolo (twelve hundred acres of vines compared to Barolo's twenty-nine hundred vineyard acres) with less variability in its vineyard sites, as well as fewer producers. The result is that Barbaresco is a more consistent wine, both in quality and range of tastes. From a marketing perspective, this is a boon.

Barbaresco has become world famous in the last twenty years thanks to the efforts of just one producer, Angelo Gaja. He singlehandedly stole the limelight—and the high prices—from Barolo, with his own wines capturing some of the highest prices (and greatest publicity) ever achieved by an Italian wine. He also revolutionized Piedmontese winemaking, pioneering the use of small French oak barrels and high-tech equipment. The rest of Barbaresco rode—and continues to ride—his coattails.

Gaja is a kind of Piedmontese Joan of Arc, who led a reluctant, resistant winemaking populace to rise up against their own oppressive traditionalism. During a long lunch, he once reminisced about one of the turning points in his struggle to free himself from the sticky grip of the Langhe's insularity. "I was very lucky," he began. "I had many sleepers." At first, I thought I had misunderstood. Sleepers? "Yes, sleepers," he replied. "In 1973, Robert Mondavi came here to visit the winery."

Mondavi, who started his own winery in Napa Valley in 1966, when he was fifty-three years old, was singularly instrumental in launching California wine to new levels of prestige, price, and accomplishment. He is a hero to Gaja, who is a full generation younger than the eighty-four-year-old Mondavi.

"It was the first time I met him," Gaja continued. "He spent the day. He asked me to accompany him to look at the other vineyards of the area. The day was very nice. We went and had lunch at Ristorante Belvedere in La Morra, which as you know has a good view of the Langhe. We spoke at the table about wine and so on. He offered a lot of compliments. I was so proud of the area. When we walked back to the car, he stopped me and said, 'Don't you hear a noise in the air?' I tried to listen. I didn't hear any noise. I said, 'No, I don't hear any noise.' So he said, 'OK, probably I am wrong.'

"Then we went to Ristorante Felicìn to say hello to Giorgio, the chef. And we went out on the balcony of the restaurant to look at the view. And again he mentioned the noise. And again I said, 'I can't hear any noise.' After that, we went to look at more vineyards. And again, he mentioned the noise. 'What noise?' Finally, we returned to Barbaresco and on the way back I said, 'Now look, what is this joke about the noise?' He told me, 'Don't you hear it? The people in the Langhe are snoring. Not just at night, but during the day.'

"This was a very important lesson!" exclaimed Gaja. "So I told this story to some of my colleagues. They were not happy at all. In fact, they were offended. This surprised me. Only Aldo

Conterno was capable of understanding. It was such a good lesson. Can you imagine what a man like Mondavi could be capable of doing in an area like the Langhe?"

Gaja could. Mondavi's challenge was convincing Americans of the goodness of their own wines, a task nowhere better expressed than by H. G. Wells's memorable observation, "You Americans have the loveliest wines in the world, you know. But you don't realize it. You call them 'domestic,' and that's enough to start trouble anywhere."

Unlike Americans, Italians were already convinced of the goodness of their own wines. But they were unwilling to pay anything more than a pittance. Wine in Italy has long been regarded as a cheap staple, like bread or salt. Until the '70s, the ceiling price for Barolo was just the thousand *lire,* which even then was a nominal sum. Barbaresco got no more than seven hundred and fifty *lire.* (Barbera never topped a few hundred *lire.*) Today, Barbaresco fetches at least as much as Barolo. Some Barbarescos easily exceed all but the most expensive Barolos.

Now that Barbaresco and Barolo are seen as equals, one question remains: Are they different? The answer is that they are, but not dramatically so. Barolo is the more muscular of the two, with greater depth and resonance. It tends to reward longer aging. But both are 100 percent Nebbiolo. Both work with similar chalky-clay soils. Both extract virtually everything Nebbiolo can offer. Because of its greater variety of vineyard sites, with consequent variety of exposures and soil variations, Barolo offers a greater range of Nebbiolo expression.

As in Barolo, many Barbaresco producers make a regular Barbaresco as well as single-vineyard bottlings. The single-vineyard bottlings are almost always superior.

Producers to look for

Castello di Neive. One single-vineyard Barbaresco: Santo Stefano. A large vineyard owner, Castello di Neive issues two versions from its exclusively owned Santo Stefano vineyard: a regular and a reserve. Predictably, the reserve is better. The style is slightly coarse, but still impressive. (See also Bruno Giacosa.)

Ceretto. Two single-vineyard Barbarescos: Bricco Asili and Bricco Faset. (A *bricco* is the sun-catching crest of a hill.) Ceretto's two Barbarescos are their best wines. Polished, early-drinking style. Asili is the better vineyard, creating more complete and finer wine; Faset is more early-maturing, but with an intriguing herbal quality.

Giuseppe Cortese. A single-vineyard Barbaresco: Rabaja. Tiny producer offering an authentic, slightly rustic style of wine from the fine Rabaja vineyard.

Angelo Gaja. Three single-vineyard Barbarescos: Sori Tildin, Sori San Lorenzo, and Costa Russi. (*Sori* is Piedmontese dialect for a south-facing slope.) The epitome of modern Piedmont wine, using small, new French oak barrels. Great depth and freshness. A regular Barbaresco also is produced. The single vineyards are dramatically finer—and much more expensive. The wines are oaky but profound.

Bruno Giacosa. Two single-vineyard Barbarescos: Santo Stefano and Gallina. Bruno Giacosa's greatest fame derives from his Santo Stefano wine, the grapes of which are purchased from Castello di Neive. Yet the Giacosa version always is superior. Usually, the Santo Stefano is massive. Traditional, intense, beautifully detailed.

Le Colline. Although better known for its Gattinara wine called Monsecco (q.v.), Le Colline also issues a first-rate Barbaresco. Traditional, very long-lived.

Marchesi di Gresy. Three named-vineyard Barbarescos: Martinenga and two subplots, Camp Gros and Gaiun. Elegant, supple wines made using small French oak barrels. Many consider the thirty-acre Martinenga vineyard the single best vineyard site in Barbaresco. It is owned entirely by the di Gresy family. The two subplots, Camp Gros (5.2 acres) and Gaiun (5.1 acres), are best; the wine labeled La Martinenga is from the rest of the vineyard and, in lesser vintages, incorporates the two subplots as well.

Moccagatta. Two single-vineyard Barbarescos: Basarin and Moccagatta. Up-and-coming winery using small, new oak barrels. Early efforts were over-oaky; recent vintages (e.g., 1990) are more convincing.

Produttori del Barbaresco. Seven single-vineyard Barbarescos: Asili, Ovello, Montefico, Moccagatta, Montestefano, Rabaja, and Pora. Also a regular Barbaresco. Barbaresco's famous wine-growers' cooperative. Collectively, the Produttori del Barbaresco own at least 40 percent of all the best vineyards in the area. In every good vintage it carefully issues various named-vineyard wines. The winemaking is traditional but modern, clean, and detailed. The single-vineyard bottlings are some of the best Barbarescos made today, as well as the best value of any Langhe wines.

Prunotto. Two single-vineyard Barbarescos: Montestefano and Rabaja. As with their Barolos, the style since the 1985 vintage has steered toward greater polish. Both single-vineyard wines are profound, traditional yet modern.

The Novara Hills—Gattinara and Company

Because Nebbiolo's standard-bearers, Barolo and Barbaresco, both hail from the Langhe, the casual observer could easily be forgiven for concluding that the Langhe is the sole source of superb Nebbiolo. It surely is the richest and finest source. But Piedmont is a huge region.

Another trove of fine Nebbiolo is found much farther north, in what might be described as the true, literal *piemonte*—the actual foothills of the Alps. These are the hills northwest of Novara, just where the alpine foothills and the flat, rice-growing plain begin. The region is different from the Langhe in two immensely significant ways: soil and temperature. As a result, the Nebbiolo-based wines grown in these true foothills taste noticeably different from Nebbiolo grown in the Langhe.

One of the fascinations of wine is that it can transmit, through the right grape variety, differences in soil types. Just what it is about a soil—structure, trace elements, etc.—that influences the wine is the source of endless argument. What is important is that it can be sensed.

Where the soil of the Langhe is an alkaline chalky clay left behind when a great inland sea receded eons ago, in the Novara hills the soil is an acidic, glacial limestone created by ancient receding alpine glaciers. Nebbiolo grown in this kind of soil results in a hard-tasting wine of greater delicacy, as well as longevity, than that grown in the richer soils of the Langhe.

The Novara hills are cooler, being farther north and at the actual foot of the Alps, than the Langhe farther south. Every grape variety, especially highly sensitive sorts such as Nebbiolo, has its ideal temperature sites. Over centuries, patient, curious winegrowers have learned, like cunning parents, to maneuver each variety to just the right zone and vineyard site to bring forth its full potential. The ideal is when a sensitive variety is stretched to where it will ripen, but only after really extending itself, like pushing a talented kid from inspired noodling on the piano to something more rigorous, such as Bach.

Farther north, the temperature is just a little too cool for Nebbiolo. Though wonderfully perfumey, it too often emerges a bit too thin and acidic, and needs a bit of blending help. This explains why the Langhe never developed a tradition of blending Nebbiolo with other grape varieties, whereas in the Novara hills, Nebbiolo was always blended.

The finest Nebbiolo wine of the Novara hills is indisputably from the Gattinara zone. All of the seven appellations of the area are allowed to blend other grape varieties with Nebbiolo. Gattinara is too—but less so than any of the others. A Gattinara is allowed by law a maximum of just 10 percent of something other than Nebbiolo. This says a lot about Gattinara's superiority in an area unconducive to growing a pure Nebbiolo wine.

The problem with Gattinara is that it is not only a tiny zone (some two hundred and twenty-five acres of vines), but its growers, sad to say, are notoriously unambitious. The name is famous; most of the wines are lackluster. This is near criminal, because when you taste a truly fine Gattinara, you know in an instant what is being lost. A fine Gattinara is as great a wine as the best Barolo. Interestingly, it also is the longest-lived Nebbiolo wine. Where even the best Barolos fade after twenty years or so, a great Gattinara can be superb for as long as thirty years.

Producers to look for

Le Colline. This is the benchmark producer for Gattinara. For decades, the Gattinara from this producer was the personal pride of a local count, the Conte Ugo Ravizza. His pride was so personal, in fact, that he labeled the wine "Monsecco," literally, "my dry (red wine)." The label never even mentioned Gattinara. It was aged for years in large, ancient casks, then it would age for years more in bottle. Eventually, he got around to selling it. He also got around to dying, and the estate was sold in 1979.

The new owners, reverent of the Count's traditional high standards, are striving to restore its original quality, which was slipping as the Count aged and fewer resources were put into the vineyards and winery. The new owners called their operation Le Colline (the hills) and appended Gattinara to the Monsecco label. They also chose to make only a 100-percent-Nebbiolo Gattinara, never mind the law's indulgence of 10 percent of something else.

Gattinara is a wine best bought only in the finest vintages, where the growing season allowed the Nebbiolo to ripen fully. In such years (1982, 1985, 1989), Le Colline's Monsecco Gattinara is to be sought out, and, as the locals like to say, "then forgotten about"—a tribute to Gattinara's capacity for aging.

Travaglini. One of the larger owners of Gattinara vineyards, Travaglini bottles his wines in an odd, almost surrealistic bottle shape with squared sides. Two Gattinaras are offered: A regular version is light, pleasant, and generally undistinguished. The better version—a genuinely fine Gattinara—is identified as Selezione Numerata (numbered bottling) and put in a special matte-finish, opaque-looking bottle. This is Gattinara's other great wine, fresher and more modern-tasting than Le Colline's Monsecco, but as good.

Other Gattinara producers worth noting: Antoniolo (especially the three single-vineyard bottlings: Osso San Grato, San Francesco, and Castelle); Dessilani; Nervi (especially two single-vineyard bottlings: Molsino and Valferana).

Gattinara's company are the six other appellations in the Novara hills: Boca, Bramaterra, Fara, Ghemme, Lessona, and Sizzano. All are Nebbiolo wines blended with two local red wine grapes: Vespolina and Bonarda Novarese. Typically, these other grapes account for one third to one half of the blend, the balance being Nebbiolo (locally known in dialect as Spanna). Collectively, all of these wines are light in weight and with some flavor interest. But they are not usually worth going out of one's way for.

Ghemme is the best, and fullest, of the bunch. This district also has some of the best growers, notably Le Colline of Gattinara fame and the charmingly named Antichi Vigneti di Cantalupo, which issues two excellent single-vineyard Ghemme wines: Collis Breclemae and Colli Carellae.

As for the others, the Sella family makes intriguing Lessona, as well as a Bramaterra.

Carema

Even farther removed from the main Nebbiolo action of the Langhe is the district of Carema. Located at the very edge of the Piedmont border, almost due north of Turin, near the town of Ivrea, the Carema district grows only Nebbiolo. (Proving just how geographically isolated the Carema district is, their local dialect term for Nebbiolo is Picutener.) Carema grows its Nebbiolo in a fashion unseen anywhere else in Piedmont. Where most other Nebbiolo vines are trained on the usual wires strung between slender posts, in Carema the vines are trained on a support system so imposing and massive that it is better described as architectural rather than agricultural. Imagine a steep, stone-terraced slope where each narrow terrace supports a row of massive stone columns of the sort that might have been found in front of an old-fashioned bank—only much cruder. On top of these pillars rests a crisscross of heavy wood beams, upon which the grapevines are trained.

This uniquely massive trellising system tells us something about the climatic harshness and ferocious winds that afflict this true alpine foothill wine district, located near the banks of the Dora Baltea River (a main water supply for the rice-growers in the Po Valley). The alpine winds howl through the Dora Baltea valley. Growing Nebbiolo in the Langhe—itself a temperamental spot subject to vicious hail storms—it's a wonder that anyone thought to try their luck with the likes of Nebbiolo.

Few people do. There are only fifty acres of Nebbiolo vines (one hundred acres are authorized, but remain unplanted). Most of the grapes are made into Carema wine by the local winegrowers' cooperative, the Produttori Nebbiolo di Carema, which makes sense considering that the typical vineyard ownership is little more than one acre. The Produttori make a good wine. The one to look for—if you can find it—is their best bottling, called Carema dei Carema.

The best Carema comes from the one significant private producer in the district, Luigi Ferrando. This producer owns some of the best vineyard plots in Carema's tiny vineyard. Two bottlings are issued: a regular (good) white-label Carema and a (much better) black-label Carema bottling that appears only in the best vintages.

A fine Carema is a Nebbiolo of unusual delicacy allied with impressive longevity. Only a good Gattinara can equal it.

Other Piedmontese Red Wines

Piedmont is a large region and its wine districts are far-flung. Its parallel universe, Burgundy, also used to have dozens of highly localized wines. But where Burgundy lost many of its (uneconomic) local wine districts after the phylloxera blight of the late 1800s, Piedmont retained nearly all of its wine localism even though it, too, was devastated by phylloxera. As a result, the region abounds in wine districts whose wines remain largely unfamiliar outside of their areas of production, let alone in export markets. There's a reason for this: Most wines remain local simply because they are not compelling. This is so for Piedmont's many other red wines. Like butterfly collecting, the search for them is a delight. But rarely does one come across something exceptional that hasn't already been discovered, noted, and celebrated.

That said, these are a few of Piedmont's lesser-known red wines. They are worth trying if you're in the area.

Bonarda. A pleasant red wine grape with some berryish scents. You can still find a few 100-percent-Bonarda bottlings, but nowadays it's used almost exclusively for blending. Bonarda is a specialty in the Novara hills where, along with Vespolina, it is the main blending grape for wines such as Far, Boca, Sizzano, and the rest.

Brachetto. One hundred years ago Brachetto was the rage of fashionable Piedmont, when it was synonymous with a sweet, bubbling red wine made either half-bubbling (*frizzante*) or fully foaming like champagne (*spumante*). Brachetto is enjoying a modest comeback, mostly for nostalgia's sake.

Freisa. Like Brachetto, this red wine grape also was *molto alla moda* a century ago. Various versions used to be made: sweet, dry, half-sparkling, and fully foaming. Possessed of a strong black raspberry scent, Freisa is one of the most attractive of the "antique" Piedmontese grapes. Two Freisas are worth seeking out, each very different in style. Aldo Conterno makes a light, fizzy Freisa brand-named La Bussianella. It's perfect for cool summer sipping. A more serious, even stern Freisa—also from the Langhe—is produced by Vajra. Its dry, dense Freisa probably is the finest made today of its long-aging type.

Grignolino. A very pale red wine of high acidity, once much in fashion. Some growers still enjoy it and continue to grow the grape, such as Aldo Conterno. It is best drunk very young.

Pelaverga. The appeal of this red wine variety escapes me, although maybe it's the name that enchants the advocates of this ancient "born again" grape: Pelaverga means, literally, "bared rod." It is a specialty of the Langhe hill town of Verduno.

Roero. To classify this as "other" is a bit harsh, as Roero (a district name) really is Nebbiolo. But the law allows the Roero growers to blend a little of the white wine grape Arneis into their Nebbiolo, which tells you something right there. The district of Roero lies directly across the dividing Tanaro River from the Langhe. Its soil, however, is dramatically different: very sandy with some clay, compared to the Langhe's enviable chalky clay and marl. Anyone who doubts the informing influence of soil on wine need only compare a Roero vineyard of good exposure planted with Nebbiolo to a Langhe vineyard of comparable exposure and elevation. The Roero wine invariably is lighter, thinner, and much shorter-lived. Roero is a pleasant Nebbiolo for early drinking, but rarely more than that.

Rouchet or Ruché. A rare red wine grape enjoying a comeback. Wonderfully scented, yet simultaneously austere, Rouchet is in vogue among fanciers of Piedmontese wines. Rouchet is a specialty of the town of Castagnole Monferrato, which is about forty-five miles east of Turin.

I have pointed memories of Rouchet, if only because of a dinner with friends in a famous Turin restaurant called San Giors, which is located near Turin's vast and fabulous food market. San Giors (Piedmontese dialect for Saint George) is an ancient establishment, with hotel rooms upstairs, that looks like my imaginings of an early 1800s Italian brothel.

No sooner had we sat down than one of our Piedmontese gang announced, in a voice the envy of any Swiss yodeler, that they had with them a true wine *esperto*. And not only that, he went on to say, this fellow was an *American esperto* of, particularly, Piedmontese wines. The waiter goggled at me as if I were an albino rhinoceros. I smiled weakly.

As it happens, I had quickly looked around the restaurant when we had entered, spying out their cache of wines. The only way you can discover which wines are available in an Italian restaurant is to peruse the shelf where the wines are stored. Sometimes it is in an easily seen, obvious location. Sometimes, it is near the chef's ankle next to the oven. Here, it was helpfully in full view.

The restaurant's limited selection of wines happened to include a Rouchet. So when the time came to pronounce—an *esperto* does not merely order wine in Italy—I played the Rouchet card. If Mister Ed, the talking horse, had done the ordering the waiter could not have been more astonished. He immediately commenced upon a discussion of the many fine points of Rouchet. As an *esperto*, I had no choice but to hold up my side, undeterred by the fact that, until then, I previously had tasted only one other Rouchet in my life.

There really isn't much about Rouchet that distinguishes it from several hundred other red Italian wines. I have a pretty extensive vocabulary of wine-tasting terms, even in Italian, so I was able to hold forth on this with, if not eloquence, then at least the usual obscure wine babble. But no sooner had two bottles of the Rouchet arrived and been tasted than somebody at the other end of the long table pronounced it unsuitable. I was not in a position to call the man a *cretino*, which he was. Granted, I had only tasted one other Rouchet in my life, but we *esperti* know a good Rouchet when we taste one. This one was fine, which is to say that it was clean-tasting, well-made, and, I thought, appropriately young. (Italians can't drink a wine young enough.)

But it wasn't young enough. The fellow summoned the waiter and asked—I swear this is true—if the restaurant didn't have something younger. I was boggled. This Rouchet was something of a palate scraper as it was. The waiter assured him that not only did the restaurant have such a wine, but in fact, Signor, it just so happened to be a Barbera of their own making.

Naturally, I was urged to inquire more about the wine. So I asked the waiter if it came from a single vineyard, as opposed to being sluiced from one of Piedmont's many god-awful winegrowers' cooperatives. He beamed and declared that it was. I then inquired where the vineyard was located and was told of a site equivalent to growing grapes in a landfill. What's more, he said proudly, the wine was a 1992. With this, I felt genuine fear.

Nineteen ninety-two was a great vintage for frogs, tadpoles, and anything aquatic. The autumn rains just before and during the harvest were nearly biblical in their vengeance. Piedmont experienced flash floods and power outages. The vineyards looked like rice paddies, at least those on flat ground. The roads were clogged with soil runoff from the hillsides. The average 1992 wine is fairly described as "watery."

So out comes this restaurant's homemade 1992 Barbera. It was mean enough to have been the house wine of Italy's terrorist Red Brigade. Whether out of solidarity or simple fear, the folks at my end of the table pronounced themselves much more satisfied with the 1990 Rouchet and rather ostentatiously called for another bottle.

However, the fellow at the other end of the table tasted the wine, loudly smacked his lips, and declared that *this* was more like it. The Piedmontese at his end of the table assented quietly, but without the usual Italian fanfare that accompanies even the flimsiest proclamation. I noticed that several of them, almost in unison, asked for more bottled mineral water.

Since then I have tasted a number of Rouchets. The leading producer, and the best in my experience, is Scarpa.

Piedmont's White Wines

Piedmont is not a notable white wine area, with the great exception of the famous Asti Spumante. This is not lost on the Piedmontese, who are strenuously trying to find white varieties to grow in order to take advantage of the strong world demand for white wine. The Langhe, for example, has seen an outbreak of Chardonnay. A few of them are good; most of them are boring. Ditto for Sauvignon Blanc.

There's some dry white Malvasia of interest (Trinchero of Barbera d'Asti fame making one of the best). Also, an indigenous white wine grape called Favorita has been revived. It, too, is only a curiosity. The grape variety called Cortese makes the dry white wine called Gavi, which has become very fashionable in the last decade or so. It is dry, fresh-tasting, and insipid.

Piedmont's only noteworthy dry white wine—and one of the few indigenous white grape varieties—is Arneis. The name is a dialect term that, politely put, means rascal, thanks to its unpredictability as a plant. A more vivid (and accurate) translation is earthier than that. Arneis is found almost exclusively in the Roero district, as it likes Roero's sandy soil. Formerly made as a sweet wine, Arneis almost winked out of existence until it was revived in the early 1970s. Alfredo Currado of Vietti was the first, I believe, to issue a dry Arneis bottling. He was soon followed by Bruno Giacosa, whose version remains the reference standard, with Vietti's close behind.

Today, Arneis has become very chic and plantings have increased dramatically. Consequently, there's a fair amount on the market today. Ceretto is the single biggest producer. Arneis is a dry white wine with an almond scent that is best drunk as young as possible. It does not improve with age. Indeed, two or three years after the vintage date, the average Arneis is bland and flat-tasting. Youth gives it life and flavor. It is the only wine I know of that its growers say goes well with asparagus—which is so. (The Roero district also grows large quantities of asparagus, which thrives in sandy soil.)

Piedmont's Extraordinary White Muscat Wines: Asti Spumante, Moscato d'Asti, and Loazzolo

Asti Spumante

Perhaps the most memorable line I ever heard about Asti Spumante came from an American who had lived in Tuscany for a number of years, spoke Italian well, and was superbly informed about Tuscan food. Somehow, the subject of Asti Spumante came up. "Is that still around?" she asked incredulously. "*Nobody* drinks Asti Spumante." The latest figures show Asti Spumante sales at around six million bottles a year.

Despite its undeniable market success, Asti Spumante does have an image problem. Really, it's the Muscat grape that has the problem. The name alone reminds Americans, at least, of Muscatel, something to be drunk straight from the bottle without even the nicety of removing it from its brown paper bag. Apart from similar-sounding names, Muscat and Muscatel have absolutely nothing to do with each other.

Muscat is one of the world's great wine grapes. At its best—which is where Piedmont comes in—Muscat is the world's most persuasive grape. Almost no one can resist the seductive scent of a well-made Muscat. Its history dates to ancient Persia; it grows almost anywhere the sun shines generously. Numerous subvarieties exist; in Piedmont, it is *moscato bianco*, or white Muscat, also called Moscato di Canelli, which is a town in the Asti zone.

Precisely because Muscat can grow in so many places, its image has suffered. Too many are sickly sweet, with no compensatory and redemptive acidity. This is what makes the white Muscat grown in Piedmont so extraordinary. It simply is the source of the most delicate, beautifully balanced, refined Muscat in the world. The proof of Piedmont's distinction with white Muscat is discovered by pairing a good Asti Spumante or Moscato d'Asti with chocolate. A chocolate truffle is ideal. With it, one discovers the backbone of high acidity present in Asti Spumante and Moscato d'Asti. That crisp acidity, allied with ripe Muscat flavors, is what sets Muscat from Piedmont apart from all others. Not least, it is delightfully low in alcohol, at just 7 to 9 percent alcohol—almost half of that of a Chardonnay.

Regrettably, this isn't revealed by some of what is sold under the name of Asti Spumante. Indeed, it remains questionable to this day whether everything sold as Asti Spumante (technically a delimited geographical area) actually comes from Piedmont. The area has seen a series of scandals involving the importation of Muscat wines grown elsewhere in Italy to create Asti Spumante. These seem to have abated recently, but given Muscat's ubiquity and industrial quality and the price-is-everything mentality of some Asti Spumante producers, only the naive could think that some fraud will not persist. Beware of unusually low priced Asti Spumantes from unknown producers.

That said, some superb, reference-standard Asti Spumantes are widely available. Look for Asti Spumante from Fontanafredda, Bera, and Felice Bonardi, as well as from the biggest houses, such as Gancia, Contratto, Martini & Rossi, and Cinzano.

Moscato d'Asti

Much less well known, but far more revered, is the lightly fizzy, or *frizzante,* version of Piedmont's white Muscat, called Moscato d'Asti. Unlike Asti Spumante, which is bottled and looks like champagne, a Moscato d'Asti is put in a regular wine bottle. It froths a bit when poured, but the bubbles are intentionally faint.

Among fanciers of Piedmontese wines, Moscato d'Asti is counted among Piedmont's finest wines. Nowhere in the world is a finer, more delicate, more profound Muscat created than in Piedmont. And no wine reveals it more fully than a young, fresh, beautifully made Moscato d'Asti. It is a revelation at first sip, partnered with nothing more than a few simple butter cookies.

Unlike Asti Spumante, which is the creation of large wine companies, Moscato d'Asti is the province of small producers. Like the best Piedmontese reds, production is limited and sometimes hard to locate. Among the best producers are Rivetti, Saracco, Bera, Gatti, and I Vignaioli di Santo Stefano (which is partly owned by Ceretto). Moscato d'Asti is a wine best drunk as young and fresh as possible. The alcohol is even lower than that of Asti Spumante, at 5 to 6 percent. It is so low, in fact, that technically Moscato d'Asti is not a wine according to European regulations.

Loazzolo

Piedmont's rarest version of Muscat is an unusually made dessert wine from the hills around the town of Loazzolo in the Asti zone. Before Asti Spumante, the Muscat grapes from Loazzolo historically were made into a concentrated, rich wine by drying the grapes on straw mats, a process called *passito*. This was a common practice in many areas of Italy, as well as France, in centuries past.

In the 1980s one producer, Giancarlo Scaglione of Forteto della Luja, decided to return to the past, but using a different technique. This time the grapes were left to shrivel on the vine, the better to pick up the same type of delectable rot that makes French Sauternes taste so distinctive. The resulting wine tastes like no other Muscat made anywhere: touched with the flavor of the "noble rot," slightly sweet, and more alcoholic than Moscato d'Asti—but no more than a Chardonnay, about 13 percent alcohol.

Inspired by Scaglione's example—and the praise heaped upon him—other growers in the town of Loazzolo decided to follow his example. Also, they applied for a special Loazzolo appellation. Loazzolo is a Muscat like no other. Only a few producers issue the wine, all of them admirable: Forteto della Luja, Borgo Maragliano, Borgo Sambui, and Bricchi Mej.

A Word About Vermouth

One of the sources of Piedmont's wine wealth, literally, is its creation of vermouth. Although vermouth is not associated with Piedmont in the same way as, say, Barolo or Barbaresco, it is a uniquely Piedmontese creation.

Vermouth began in the late 1700s in Turin, originally concocted by the still-extant company called Carpano. Their brand, Punt e Mes, is Piedmontese dialect for "point and a half," which supposedly derives from the confused exclamation of an agitated broker at a café near the Turin stock market who, in the middle of a business deal, called out *"punt e mes!"* in trying to order a glass of Signor Carpano's vermouth.

The idea of vermouth—a red or white wine blended with extracts of aromatic herbs and spices—is anything but new. The ancient Romans delighted in such mixtures. The name itself isn't even Italian. *Vermouth* comes from the German *wermut,* or wormwood, which is the stuff of absinthe. It was also one of the original ingredients of vermouth, long since banned.

The original base wine for vermouth was Muscat from the Asti zone, and the herbs came from the nearby Alps, which explains why, when the French took up making their own vermouth, their makers located just over the Italian border from Piedmont in Chambéry, as well as down the coast in Marseilles.

Today, Turin's vermouth is based upon wines from Sicily and other cheap-wine places in Italy. But the blending still occurs in Turin and its environs, in huge industrial wineries. It is no coincidence that the same enormous vermouth manufacturers, such as Gancia, Cinzano, and Martini & Rossi, also are the leading producers of Asti Spumante. One wonders what a traditional Muscat-based vermouth would taste like. Maybe some small, *artigianale* producer will create one, as is done for Barolo *chinato*.

A Word About Grappa

Grappa differs from brandy and Cognac in that those are made from a proper, if thin, wine. Grappa is made from the skins of grapes that have already been crushed. Ideally, the grapes aren't pressed too diligently, leaving some juice or newly fermented wine clinging to the skins. The grappa maker adds water to these skins, along with some sugar to create a fermentation, and makes an anemic little wine from the mixture. It is this wine that he distills into grappa. Although many wine regions everywhere in Europe produce such local distillate (in France it is known as *marc*), two regions in Italy are famous for their grappa. Piedmont is one; the other is Friuli.

As might be expected, the great Piedmontese grappa is crafted from Nebbiolo. Grappas, like wines, taste of the grapes from which they are made. So one finds grappas from Nebbiolo, Dolcetto, Barbera, Freisa, Rouchet, Arneis, and seemingly every other Piedmontese grape variety grown. Usually the grappas are aged in stainless-steel tanks and then bottled. Sometimes they are aged in wood casks and take on a yellowish hue as a result.

Until the mid-'80s, grappa was an inexpensive, even cheap, wine by-product that had no cachet. It was drunk by old-time farmers. (In the old days, Piedmontese children used to be sent to school with a shot of grappa inside, the better to ward off Piedmont's bone-chilling winter cold, or so it was thought.) All over Italy, grappa is used as the "correction" in *caffè corretto,* which is an espresso with a shot of booze.

Today, grappa has become unaccountably chic and expensive. This can only be traced to the vogue for bottling grappas in stunning, collectible bottles. Some of these bottles are as fanciful, and imaginative, as art glass. But even those grappas still bottled conventionally have risen correspondingly in price.

Piedmont's best grappas are, not surprisingly, crafted by small, artisan producers who work with grape skins supplied to them by some of the finest growers. Two of the best are Fratelli Marolo and Fratelli Rovero. Many producers have their own grappas bottled specially for them by local distillers, sometimes specifying the crop of a single vineyard. The most famous, and expensive, of all Piedmontese grappa producers is Romano Levi in Neive. His hand-drawn, childlike labels colored on torn pieces of paper have become so renowned that an elegant book of reproductions has recently been published.

Bibliography

Brooke, Christopher. *Europe in the Central Middle Ages, 962–1154.* New York: Holt, Rinehart and Winston, 1963.

————. *The Monastic World, 1000–1300.* New York: Random House, 1974.

Cantor, Leonard M. *A World Geography of Irrigation.* London: Oliver and Boyd, 1967.

de Giacomi, Luciano, and Giuseppe A. Lodi. *Nonna Genia.* Alba: Ordine dei Cavaliere del Tartufo e dei Vini di Alba and Famija Albeisa, 1982.

Doglio, Sandro. *Piemonte.* Milan: Edizioni Sipiel, 1991.

————. *Gran Dizionario della Gastronomia del Piemonte.* San Giorgio di Montiglio (Asti): Daumerie Editrice, 1990.

Gambera, Armando, ed. *Ricette delle Osterie di Langa.* Bra: Arcigola Slow Food Editore, 1992.

Goria, Giovanni. *La Cucina del Piemonte.* Padua: Franco Muzzio & Company, 1990.

Grégoire, Réginald, Léo Moulin, and Raymond Oursel. *The Monastic Realm.* New York: Rizzoli, 1985.

Guide Italia. *Piemonte 1.* Milan: Fabbri Editori, 1986.

————. *Piemonte 2 e Valle d'Aosta.* Milan: Fabbri Editori, 1986.

Holmes, Douglas R. *Cultural Disenchantments: Worker Peasantries in Northeast Italy.* Princeton: Princeton University Press, 1989.

Jefferson, Thomas. *The Papers of Thomas Jefferson,* ed. Julian P. Boyd et al. 25 vols. to date. Princeton: Princeton University Press, 1950–.

King, Bolton, and Thomas Okey. *Italy To-Day.* Rev. ed. London: James Nisbet & Company, 1909.

McGee, Harold. *On Food and Cooking: The Science and Lore of the Kitchen.* New York: Charles Scribner's Sons, 1984.

Malone, Dumas. *Jefferson and the Rights of Man.* Vol. 2. Boston: Little, Brown & Company, 1951.

Peterson, Merrill D. *Thomas Jefferson and the New Nation.* New York: Oxford University Press, 1970.

Robertson, C. J. "Italian Rice Production in Its Regional Setting." *Geography: Journal of the Geographical Association* (Sheffield, England): 20 (1935): 12–27.

Schena, Elma, and Adriano Ravera. *La Cucina di Madonna Lesina.* Cúneo: L'Arciere, 1988.

————. *Galuperie del Vecchio Piemonte.* Cúneo: L'Arciere, 1991.

Signorini, Daniela, and Oriano Vialli. *Il Tartufo: Habitat, Ricerca, Zone di Reperimento, Addestramento del Cane, Techniche di Coltivazione del Bianco e del Nero.* Sommacompagna: Ottaviano-Mistral, 1990.

Young, Arthur. *Travels in France and Italy During the Years 1787, 1788 and 1789.* London: J. M. Dent & Sons, 1915.

Index

Barbaresco area, 288

Barbarossa, Frederick, 97

Barbaroux, Count Giuseppe, 176

Barbera, 93, 133, 292, 294–298,
      299, 315
   beef braised in, 250–251
   in Count Barbaroux's lavish
         stuffed pasta, 176–178
   red wine risotto, 116–117

Barbera d'Alba, 296, 297, 298

Barbera d'Asti, 297–298, 312

Barolo, 9, 95, 179, 287, 292, 298,
      299–303, 304, 307
   in Count Barbaroux's lavish
         stuffed pasta, 176–178
   -flavored cookies, 282
   -infused egg mousse, 274
   red wine risotto, 116–117

Barolo Bric del Fiasc, 293

Barolo Brunate, 293

Barolo Chinato, 303

Barolo district, 288, 296

barriques, 295, 296, 300, 302

Barslina, La, 297

Bartlett pears with chocolate
      sauce, 278

Basarin, 306

basil:
   in chicken hunter's style, 225
   in pesto, 162–163, 164–165

basilico fino verde compatto, 162

basilico Genova, 162

Basso Monferrato, 90, 93, 94

bavarese, 262–263

beans, baked, hunter's style, 209

Beaujolais, 291

Béchameil, Marquis Louis de, 47

béchamel, for Count Barbaroux's
      lavish stuffed pasta,
      176–178

beef:
   braised in red wine, 250–251
   braised Val d'Aosta style, 253
   braised with capers, 252

beef marrow, in red wine risotto,
      116–117

beef stock:
   in braised beef with capers,
      252

in little "marbles" in broth,
      80
in pasta and lentil soup, 79

beet greens, in rolled stuffed pork
      loin, 245

bell peppers, see red bell pepper;
      yellow bell peppers

Belvedere, 5

Benedictine abbeys, 98–99

Bera, 313, 314

Beretta, 106

Bernard, Saint, 99

Bettane, Michel, 219

Between Meals (Liebling), 223–224

Bianca (Barolo), 301

bicerin, 95, 262–263

Biella, 96, 115, 198

Bing cherries, vinegar-preserved,
      217

bisse, 281

bittersweet chocolate:
   in Barolo-flavored cookies, 282
   in frozen custard, 276
   sauce, pears with, 278

black olive paste:
   chicken pâté with, 30–31
   homemade, 31

black Piedmontese truffles,
      180–181

blender, mortar vs., in making
      pesto, 163–164

blue cheese:
   focaccia with, 45
   risotto with, 114

Boca, 298, 309

bocconcini di manzo con capperi, 252

bocconcino de galletto alla Sabauda,
      232

Boccondivino, 20, 144, 288
   Jerusalem artichokes with
         creamy anchovy sauce,
         138

Bogliona, La, 297

boletus mushroom, see porcini
      mushroom

bollito misto, 3

Bonaparte, Napoleon, 96, 226

Bonarda, 309

Bonardi, Felice, 313

Borgo Maragliano, 314

Borgo Sambui, 314

Bormida River, 91

Boschi di Berri, 293

Boschis, 302

Bosc pears with chocolate sauce,
      278

bourgeois-style:
   cauliflower, 210
   oven-baked fish, 65

Bovio, Gianfranco, 6–8

Bovio, Maria Vittoria, 6–8

Bra, 20, 89, 91, 132, 218, 222,
      285

Bra cheese, 162, 222

Brachetto, 309–310

brandy:
   in fresh chestnut mousse,
      271–272
   in stuffed peaches, 279

Brarda, Silvio, 255

brasato di manzo al vino rosso,
      250–251

bread:
   focaccia, 44–45
   Piedmontese garlic, 43
   potato and broccoli rabe soup,
      78–79

bread crumbs:
   and apple cake, 269
   calf's liver with pancetta,
         parsley and, 255

breadsticks, 6, 46–47, 132

Bricchi di Castelrocchero, 297

Bricchi Mej, 314

Bricco Asili, 305

Bricco della Bigotta, 297

Bricco delle Viole, 297

Bricco dell'Oriolo, 292

Bricco dell'Uccellone, 297

Bricco Faset, 305

Bricco Fiasco, 301

Briccolero, 293

Bricco Punto, 301

Bricco Rocche, 301

Bricco Viole, 303

Bric' del Fiasc', 303

Broadbent, Daphne, 141

Broadbent, Michael, 141

broccoli, in "salad" of raw winter vegetables with spicy Gorgonzola dip, 213

broccoli rabe, potato and bread soup, 78–79

brodo, 108

Brooke, Christopher, 99, 99*n*

broth, little "marbles" in, 80

Brunate (Marcarini), 302

Brunate (Rinaldi), 302

brus (bros), 222

bruschetta, 43

Buoni Indirizzi per Mangiare e Bere, I (Doglio), 90

Burbank potatoes:
    in classic potato gnocchi, 202–203
    flan, 52–53

Burgundy, 292, 298, 299

Bussaniella, La, 310

Bussia (Parusso), 302

Bussia di Monforte, 302

Bussia Soprana (Dolcetto), 293

Bussia Soprano (Barolo), 301

butter:
    cookies, cornmeal, 284
    risotto and, 110–111
    and sage sauce, 148

butternut squash:
    and cauliflower in anchovy sauce, 211
    gnocchi, 204
    risotto with, 118–119
    sweet, 280

cabbage:
    flan, 54
    green, with anchovy sauce, 20–21
    leaves, stuffed, 66–67

Cafarel, 262

caffè corretto, 315

cake:
    apple, 268
    apple and bread crumb, 269
    cornmeal, 267
    hazelnut, 264

hazelnut, with chocolate, 265

hazelnut and cornmeal, 266

potato, with smoked salmon, 62–63

calf's liver:
    with anchovies and lemon, 256
    with lemon and sage, 254
    with pancetta, bread crumbs, and parsley, 255
    pâté, 32

California wines, 304

Calliano, 167

Camera, 298

Camp Gros, 306

Caniglie, 140

cannelloni, 176

cannelloni alla Conte Barbaroux, 176–178

Cannubi (Sandrone), 302

Cannubi (Scavino), 303

Cannubi (vineyard), 298

capers:
    braised beef with, 252
    and potatoes, 207

capon, with honey-hazelnut sauce, 230

caponèt, 26–27

caponèt di cavolo, 66–67

Cappellano, 301, 303

cappone con la sausa d'avije, 230

carbonado Val d'Aosta, 253

cardoons, 6

Carema, 308–309

Carmagnoia, 189*n*

Carnaroli rice, 104, 106
    in lemon risotto, 120
    in mushroom risotto, 122–123
    in red wine risotto, 116–117
    in risotto with blue cheese, 114
    in risotto with hops, 124–125
    in risotto with melted cheese, 115
    in risotto with Parmesan, 112–113
    in risotto with sausage and rum, 128
    in risotto with squash, 118–119

in risotto with sweet fennel, 121–122

in sweet pepper and prosciutto risotto, 126–127

carne cruda, 6

Carpano, 314

carpione di uova e zucchine, 40–41

carrot(s):
    in chicken pâté with black olive paste, 30–31
    in ratatouille Piedmont style, 212–213
    in rolled stuffed pork loin, 245
    salad with tongue, Tornavento Restaurant's, 22–23
    soup, 83
    in "tuna" of rabbit, 38–39
    in veal with tuna sauce, 36–38

Carru, 90

Casala Monferrato, 284

Cascina Francia, 301

Cascina Nuova, 301

Castagnole Monferrato, 310

Castegnate, Livio Cerini di, 97

Castello di Costiglio d'Asti, 141

Castello di Neive, 305

Castelmagno cheese, 202, 220–221

Castiglione Falletto, 179, 183, 297

cauliflower:
    bourgeois-style, 210
    in mixed salad of vegetables in mayonnaise, 24
    in "salad" of raw winter vegetables with spicy Gorgonzola dip, 213
    soup, traditional, 82–83
    and winter squash in anchovy sauce, 211

Cavazza, Domizio, 303

cavolfiori:
    alla borghese, 210
    e zucce in salsa d'acciughe, 211
    see also cauliflower

cavolo con salsa acciughe, 20–21

Cavour, Camillo Benso di, 2

Celebrating Italy (Field), 103

Fara, 298

faraona in cartoccio, 238–239

farinata, 200

Fasana, 296

fava bean(s):

fettuccine and zucchini soup, fresh, 86

gnocchette and potatoes with pesto, 165–166

fegato:

all'acciughe e limone, 256

di vitello con limone e salvia, 254

di vitello con pancetta, pangrattati, e prezzemolo, 255

fennel:

grilled, 215

rabbit with sweet, 243

risotto with sweet, 121–122

in salad of chicken breasts and prosciutto, 25

in "salad" of raw winter vegetables with spicy Gorgonzola dip, 213

Feria d'Agosto (August Holiday) (Pavese), 5

Ferrando, Luigi, 309

fettuccine, fava bean and zucchini soup, fresh, 86

fettunta, 43

Fiasco, 297

Field, Carol, 103

Fiera Nazionale del Tartufo, 182

Figoni, Vince, 145

Figoni Hardware Company, 145

filling:

for Count Barbaroux's lavish stuffed pasta, 176–178

spinach and potato, ravioli with, 172–173

fillings, agnolotti, 170–174

cheese, 171

herb-, with marjoram sauce, 174–175

Lidia Alciati's three-meat, 170–171

fino, 105

finocchio alla griglia, 215

fish:

baccalà, 257

oven-baked bourgeois-style, 65

penne pasta with roe, 160–161

polenta with salt cod and parsley, 195

salt cod with potatoes and olive oil, 258

salt cod with spinach and parsley, 259

trout seasoned with mountain herbs, 64

flan:

cabbage, 54

Parmesan cheese, 50

potato, 52–53

red pepper, 48–49

spinach, 51–52

see also sformato

flat omelette:

with mint, sage, and parsley, 59

with onions, 60–61

with salami, 63

flint corn (*Zea mays* var. *indurata*), 191

flour, chick-pea, pancake, 200–201

focaccia, 44–45

fondue Piedmont style, 57–58

fonduta, 93

piemontese, 57–58

Fontanafredda, 301, 313

Fontanazza, 293

Fontina, Fontal:

agnolotti filling, 171

in fonduta Piedmont style, 57–58

Gruyère vs., 57

in old-fashioned rice and leek soup, 84

in oven-baked penne with mushrooms, 159

in polenta from Restaurant Tra Vigna, 199

fornelletto, 132

Forteto della Luja, 314

Fossati, 303

France, 95, 96, 99, 224

cuisine of, Italian cooking vs., 102

cuisine of, Piedmontese cuisine and, 2–3

Fratelli Marolo, 316

Fratelli Rovero, 316

Freisa, 310

Freisa grape, 315

fricassea bianca di pollo, 227

frittata:

di cipolle, 60–61

di erbe aromatiche, 59

rognosa, 63

fritto misto, 3

Friuli, 315

frozen custard, 276

funghi trifolati, 27

Gaiun, 306

Gaja, Angelo, 88, 141, 294, 296, 298, 300, 301, 304–305

Gallaretto, 301

Gallina, 306

Gamay, 292

Gambero Rosso, 285–286

Gancia, 313, 315

garlic, 132, 189

bread, Piedmontese, 43

mushrooms in parsley and, 27

soup, 81

and walnut sauce, tagliatelle with, 158

garnish, for risotto with squash, 118–119

Gastronomy of Italy (Conte), 48

Gatti, 314

Gattinara, 106, 298, 301, 306–308

Gavarini, 293, 296

Gavarini vineyard, 302

Gavi, 312

gelatin, in cooked cream, 273

Germanetti, Lina, 87

Germanetti family, 12

Ghemme, 298

Giaccone, Cesare, 22, 150, 266